ALL of the *GHAZALS*
from the
*DIVAN* of SADI

I never felt envious of any rank or wealth, but only of that one
who is attaining Union with his Sweetheart… his only One!
Do you know what kind of truth it is that cannot be described?
It's of the eye that each moment on that One's beauty is open.
Happy is that one through whose door the Beloved does enter:
like fortune given to a beggar without begging for even a token.
The lover and Beloved are like two almond kernels in one shell,
being together in close intimacy… each weary of the other one.
Are you aware who the ignorant boor is, laughing at our state?
It's one who can't experience ecstasy for as long as life goes on.
After Beloved left I saw nothing but the image of the Beloved…
and, it left nothing of this poor, shattered body but a phantom.
You might say… a year of being with that One was like a day:
while now during this waiting, a day seems like a year has run!
Time has a new moon once a month, while that heart-ravishing
moon of mine wears a crescent every night… every single one!
The Sufi can only be absorbed in the company of such a friend,
and… Sadi can only sing his ghazals in honour of such a One!

# ALL of the *GHAZALS* from the *DIVAN* of SADI

Translation & Introduction
Paul Smith

NEW HUMANITY BOOKS
BOOK HEAVEN
Booksellers & Publishers

NEW HUMANITY BOOKS
BOOK HEAVEN
(Publishers & Booksellers for over 50 years)
47 Main Road Campbells Creek
Victoria 3451 Australia

For our over 1200 publications go to
amazon.com/author/smithpa

ISBN: 9798833180983

Poetry/Mysticism/Sufism/Middle Eastern Studies/
Persian History/Sufi Poetry/Persian Poetry

# CONTENTS

*You, whose body is so agile that is clothed with beauty!*
*None but the pure of eye Your perfect loveliness can see!*
*If I am really fortunate I'll die upon the dust of Your door,*
*it could be some day You'll pass over that dust, over me.*
*I know that one day my head shall be falling at Your feet,*
*let me flee now to You, hold to Your saddle-strap, tightly!*
*O You, by whose fair face the eyes of Reason are dazzled!*
*You, whom power of our vision's too limited to see clearly!*
*I thought I'd avoid grappling with serpents of Your curls;*
*but, I remained so helpless before Your lips smiling at me!*
*If the lustre of Your face should fall upon dome of the sky,*
*moon would veil her face, and the sun ashamed would be!*
*If You pardoned us it'd be as a favour to Your friends and*
*if You burn us You've control over possessions, obviously!*
*If You shed blood of all, You can do it without retribution:*
*if You pardon faults of all, there's none to fear… You see?*
*Practice as much cruelty as You may happen to wish to do*
*for pleasant memories will send grief from heart… of Sadi.*

# LIFE & TIMES & POETRY OF SADI

Musharrif-ud-din bin Muslih-ud-din 'Abdu'llah, is better known under his poetical pen-name or *takhallus* of 'Sadi' (meaning 'fortunate'), which was acquired either from his first patron, the ruler of Fars, Atabeg Sa'd b. Zangi, whose ascension to the throne took place in 1195 and who died in 1226... or his son, also named Sa'd: Abu Bakr ibn Sa'd ibn Zangi (ruled 1226-60) to whom Sadi dedicated his *Bustan* or *Orchard* in 1257 and his most famous work the *Gulistan* or *Rose Garden* a year later. Sadi was born at Fars' capital... the beautiful, fabled city of Shiraz, in south-west Persia, around 1208.

Terror, plunder, rape and murder on a vast scale engulfed Persia during the thirteenth century at the hands of the Mongols... but, fortunately Shiraz, in the mountains of the south-west, was almost unaffected. It was a cultured and famously beautiful city with wise and enlightened rulers, that passed on to future generations its great traditions of culture and civilized life from past ages.

'The Mongols, surpassing in cruelty the most barbarous people, murdered in cold blood, in the conquered countries, men, women and children; burned towns and villages; transformed flourishing lands into deserts; and yet were animated by neither hate nor vengeance, for indeed they hardly knew the names of the peoples whom they exterminated. One would suppose that history had exaggerated their atrocities, were not the annals of all countries in agreement on this point. After the conquest, one sees the Mongols treat as slaves under a frightful tyranny those whom the sword had spared. Their government was the triumph of depravity; all that was noble and honorable was abased, while the most corrupt men, attaching themselves to the service of these ferocious masters, obtained, as the price of their vile devotion, riches, honors, and the power to oppress their fellow-countrymen. The history of the Mongols, therefore, stamped with their barbarity, offers only hideous pictures, though, being closely connected with that of several empires, it is necessary for a proper understanding of the great events of the thirteenth and fourteenth centuries.' Baron d'Ohsson. *Histoire des Mongols. Paris 1834-5.* Sadi's father, 'Abdu'llah, was a descendant of Ali, the cousin and son-in-law of the Prophet, and was for some time in difficult circumstances, but having obtained a petty government appointment through an influential patron, his zeal, ability and integrity raised him in the estimation of his superiors and gained for him a promotion and opened up a prospect of future advancement. Unfortunately, he died while Sadi was a child of ten or eleven, leaving him and his mother a small amount of money which soon disappeared through the intrigues of false friends and Sadi and his mother were obliged to live for a time either on the bounty of the Atabeg, or some say a relative who was probably his uncle on his mother's side, the celebrated Mulla Kutb, the learned disciple of Khwaja Nasiruddin of Tus. This story is remarkably similar to that of Shiraz's next great poet and master of the poetic form of the *ghazal*, Hafiz, who also lost his father at a similar age and he and his mother were forced to live with his uncle… a second-rate poet who used the pen-name *Sadi!* Nizami, the other great Persian Master of the *ghazal* form of poetry was also orphaned and went to live with an uncle! In this poem from his *Bustan* Sadi laments the fate of not having a father…

*You should protect the orphan… whose father is dead,*
*brush mud from his clothes, stop pain hitting his head.*
*You don't know how hard for him living happens to be:*
*when the root is cut away… does life exist in the tree?*
*Do not hug and do not kiss that child that is your own*
*where an orphan can see it… so neglected and so alone!*
*If the orphan cries tears, who will comfort his suffering?*
*If he loses his temper… who his rage will be believing?*
*You make sure he doesn't cry, for surely God's throne*
*begins to shake violently from the orphan's sad moan.*
*With pity that is infinite… and with most tender care,*
*wipe tears from his eyes… and brush dust from his hair.*
*There's not a shield of parental protection over his head*
*sheltering him: you, be that protector he needs, instead.*
*When the arms of a father around my neck could fold…*
*way back then I was crowned like a monarch, with gold.*
*Back then, if even a fly should come and alight upon me:*
*not one heart… many, were scared by what they'd see!*
*But now, if I'm taken captive and they do what they will,*
*I call out loud, but no friend comes, no matter how shrill!*
*Sorrows of orphans I can always understand… and share,*
*way back in my childhood… I tasted the orphan's despair.*
Sadi mentions his mother in his *Gulistan* (chapter 6, story 6)…

'One day, due to the ignorance and folly of youth, I shouted at my mother. She was cut to the heart and she sat in a corner and began to cry, saying: "Perhaps you've forgotten being an infant, that you would speak to me so harshly." '

Sadi completed his early years of education in Shiraz and during this time Sa'd b. Zangi (the First) fought a drawn-out eight-year war with his cousin to keep the throne but this long struggle had devastating consequences. The young Sadi was passionately fond of learning, and, in pursuit of knowledge, determined to travel to Baghdad at that time famed for its learned men and schools. He states in his preface to his *Gulistan*...

*Do you know why, as an outcast and exile...*

*in lands of a stranger I sought refuge for awhile?*

*World was unravelling like an Ethiopian's hair,*

*when I fled the Turks and their reign... terror!*

On arrival at Baghdad his prospects were not so good, as he was without money and was a stranger. He was fortunate in relating his tale to a wealthy and benevolent inhabitant of the city, who sympathized with him, and provided for to go to a private school. He worked hard and when he twenty-one years of age composed some verses of poetry which he dedicated to a professor of literature in the famous Nizameh College. The professor was so pleased with the poem that he gave Sadi an allowance and promised to assist him in his literary pursuits. Soon Sadi gained admission to the Nizameh College and by his intelligence and effort, aided by able instructors, obtained a scholarship which enabled him to pursue his studies comfortably.

There his teachers included the great Sufi Master and teacher Shaikh Abdul Kader Gilani from whom he leaned the nature of Divinity and Sufi doctrine. It is said that he also met the Sufi Perfect Master *(Qutub)* Shihab al-Din al-Suhrawardi (d.1234) the founder of a famous order of dervishes. Under the Caliph, Mutasim-Billah, the youngest son of the much celebrated Harun-ar-Rashid, the court of Baghdad had become corrupt and the government weak. The Mongol chief, Hulagu Khan had overrun the province and hearing of the state of anarchy existing in Baghdad he besieged the city and eventually he captured it. His soldiers sacked the city and pillaged and murdered and raped. The Caliph and his family was cruelly put to death. Sadi laments this in a *qasida*...

*It is proper for tears of blood from the heavens upon the earth to flow,*

*for ruler of the Faithful, Caliph al-Mutasim has been felled, so low!*

*If, Mohammed, at the Judgement from the dust your head you raise...*

*raise it now and witness the Judgement fallen upon your people below!*

*Great waves of blood overwhelm the low thresholds of the palace beauties*

*as out from my heart blood of my life dyes these sleeves, colour of woe!*

*Fear how Fortune changes quickly and the fast turning of the Sphere...*

*who could ever dream that such splendour such a fate could overthrow?*

*Raise your eyes, all of you who once upon that Holy House did look,*

*watching Khans and Caesars that cringing, under its portals did go.*

*Now, on that same threshold where many kings their foreheads laid, from children of the Uncle of the Prophet streams of blood now flow!*

Sadi fled with his Master Shaikh Gilani… to Mecca, the first of fifteen pilgrimages he would make to that place.

After leaving the college at the age of twenty-seven he then spent thirty years wandering and travelling as a poor dervish throughout many lands and had many adventures and the people he met and the spiritual and worldly knowledge he acquired on these extensive travels (he has been called 'The Marco Polo of the East') he recorded when he finally came home to Shiraz in 1256. He wrote them down in his *Bustan* and *Gulistan* in moral and even ribald stories and sayings and philosophy in poetry *(Bustan)* and in poetry and prose *(Gulistan)* that would bring him both fame and fortune at home and in many lands. Both would be dedicated to the son of Atabeg Sa'd b. Zangi, Abu Bakr ibn Sa'd ibn Zangi… who took over ruler-ship of Shiraz after his father died in 1226 and Sadi earlier praised him in this *ghazal*…

*Lord of Eternal Faith, in that one's auspicious fortune be rejoicing*
*and in that one's well-established throne, happiness be abounding:*
*the Protector of the Age and the Defender of the faithful ones…*
*the Chosen of God, the religion of Mohammed who is upholding!*
*You, who are ruler of the Empire of Solomon and the sovereign…*
*Muhammad the Atabeg, who always justice is evenly dispensing!*
*Down from Abu Bakr and up to Sa'd Zangi, all of your ancestors*
*every generation after every generation great fame were knowing.*
*Every renowned and every exalted human being has been bound*
*by the obligations of your favours that in the past you we giving!*

*Every person that was famous on the sea... and at all the frontiers*
*upon the ground at the dust of your feet bow their heads, praising!*
*O you king of much wisdom, O you asylum of all of your subjects,*
*may you always be distinguished by God, Who... you is aiding!*
*Please listen closely to an old saying that's coming from Sadi*
*"May your fortune stay young and dignity in glory be remaining!"*
*And the revolution of Time, for as long as it has ever lasted...*
*hasn't been accustomed to preserving mankind, as one is knowing.*
*Kingdom of the world is never everlasting and so it is therefore*
*not fitting to place reliance on it or any authority of it be trusting.*
*Be ruling with justice your empire and do the same with your life:*
*so, eternally in the world your good name and fame be remaining.*

'The *Bustan,* which like all poems of proverbial wisdom defies adequate translation, had brought its author immediate fame which the passing centuries have only served to increase. In later years calligraphers and artists delighted to copy and illustrate it for wealthy patrons of art and letters, who have never been wanting in Persia, and so produced some of the great manuscripts of the world. The *Gulistan* scored an equal success, and emperors have been proud to see it adorn their libraries. Not only so, but both books, being written in simple yet correct and most elegant Persian, have served many generations as models of how to write, and both books, being replete with the kind of pithy sentiments schoolmasters love to inculcate, have been compulsory reading in every seminary of Persia for nearly seven hundred years. It would be no exaggeration to say that they, after the *Koran,* have done most to shape the Persian outlook.' A.J. Arberry.

From Sadi's *Bustan* or 'Orchard'. He gives the reason why he composed the book…

*I travelled much throughout the world's distant places,*
*and I've passed much time with those of different races.*
*From each corner where I ventured I discovered pleasure,*
*and I did obtain from many a harvest, many a corn's ear.*
*Like those pure folk of Shiraz who are as humble as dust*
*I have never seen another: mercy be on that place's dust.*
*Cultivating of friendship of the men of this sacred land,*
*from Syria and Turkey turned away my heart and hand.*
*From all of those fragrant gardens of the world I wanted*
*to bring to my friends something, not be empty-handed.*
*I said to myself… "From Egypt, one often brings sugar,*
*it's done so, brought home to friends, a present to offer!"*
*And, even though these hands of mine carry no sugar…*
*in my possession I've words that than sugar are sweeter:*
*and not that kind of sugar that men may happen to eat;*
*but, the kind that is kept on paper, a more lasting treat!*
*When this palace of great wealth I had finally designed*
*I did build into it ten doors of instructions for the mind.*
*The first is a chapter on Justice and Good Judgement…*
*how to care for the people and to fear God's Judgement.*
*The second chapter: I laid the foundation of Generosity;*
*for one in being generous, is praising God's Generosity.*
*The third is about Love and Madness and Intoxication;*
*but, not that worldly love, that men… usually dwell upon.*

Emerson, appreciating the *Gulistan* on reading Gladwin's translation, wrote this at Concord in 1864. 'Sadi, though he has not the lyric flights of Hafiz, has wit, practical sense, and just moral sentiments. He has the instinct to teach, and from every occurrence must draw the moral, like Franklin. He is the poet of friendship, love, self-devotion, and serenity. There is a uniform force in his page, and conspicuously, a tone of cheerfulness, which has almost made his name a synonym for this grace. The word *Sadi* means *fortunate*. In him the trait is no result of levity, much less of convivial habit, but first of a happy nature, to which victory is habitual, easily shedding mishaps, with sensibility to pleasure, and with resources against pain. But it also results from the habitual perception of the beneficent laws that control the world. He inspires in the reader a good hope. What a contrast between the cynical tone of Byron and the benevolent wisdom of Sadi! By turns, a student, a water-carrier, a traveler, a soldier fighting against the Christians in the Crusades, a prisoner employed to dig trenches before Tripoli, and an honored poet in his protracted old age at home: his varied and severe experience took away all provincial tone and gave him a facility of speaking to all conditions. But the commanding reason of his wider popularity is his deeper sense, which, in his treatment, expands the local forms and tints to a cosmopolitan breadth. Through his Persian dialect he speaks to all nations, and, like Homer, Shakespeare, Cervantes, and Montaigne, is perpetually modern.'

His thirty years of travels on foot and every other way took him through many countries in Mesopotamia, Asia Minor, North Africa, Arabia and to Syria and probably into India (though recent studies dispute that he went there). He said, 'I have wandered to various regions of the world and everywhere I've mixed freely with the inhabitants, gathering something in each corner, gleaning an ear from every harvest.'

Some of his travels brought him into very difficult circumstances. On one occasion in the Holy Land he was taken prisoner by the Franks and was finally ransomed but had to pay the ransom back by marrying a wife who made his life a misery, as he states in the *Gulistan...* 'Weary of the society of my friends at Damascus I fled to the barren wastes of Jerusalem, and associated with brutes, until I was made captive by the Franks, and forced to dig clay, along with Jews, in the fortifications of Tripoli. One of the nobles of Aleppo, an old friend, happened to pass that way and remembered me, saying, "What a state you're in... how are you?" I answered, "Seeing that I could place confidence in God alone, I retired to the mountains and wilds to avoid the society of man; but judge what is now my situation, that I am confined in a trench in company with wretches who deserve not the name of men. To be chained by the feet, with friends, is better than to be free to walk in a garden with strangers." He took compassion on my forlorn condition, ransomed me from the Franks for ten *dinars* and took me with him to Aleppo. My friend had a daughter to whom he married me and presented me with one hundred *dinars* as her dowry. After some time my wife unveiled her disposition that was bad-tempered, quarrelsome, obstinate and abusive, so that the happiness of my life vanished. It has been well said, "A bad woman in the house of a virtuous man is his hell, even in this world. Take care not to connect yourself with a bad woman.

Save us, O Lord, from this fiery trial!" Once she reproached me with the following taunt: "Aren't you the creature whom my father ransomed from captivity amongst the Franks for ten *dinars?*" "Yes," I answered, "he redeemed me for ten *dinars* and enslaved me to you for a hundred." I heard that a great man once rescued a sheep from the mouth of a wolf, but at night drew his knife across his throat. The expiring sheep then complained, "You delivered me certainly from the jaws of a wolf, but in the end I perceive that you have yourself become a wolf to me." '

Sadi had more luck in his second marriage and was said to have had a son and a daughter. The son whom he loved very much died in childhood and his untimely end was a source of great grief to him.

Sadi's amazing travels and stories, morality and philosophy and poetry can be discovered though his two books the *Gulistan* and the *Bustan* and as stated these two works have been a great influence on the whole world ever since.

On returning to Shiraz he penned his two most-famous works and with the vast proceeds built a hostel near the 'God is Great' Gate to Shiraz where travelers could stay, get refreshments and wash their clothes. This location later became that of his tomb.

Two years after Sadi finished his *Gulistan* and dedicated it to his patron Abu Bakr ibn Sa'd as he did a year earlier with his *Bustan,* on May 18, 1260 Shiraz's ruler died and his son who had waited long for his chance at ruler-ship died within two weeks. His baby son Muhammad succeeded him, but his life ended in two years in 1262.

His cousin Muhammad Shah ruled for a couple of months but was murdered and the throne came to his brother Seljuk Shah who Sadi praised in these couplets...

*Obliterate the volume of the poetry that you have written:*

*nothing but prayer for welfare of Seljuk Shah be composer.*

*God, grant him eternal life, so he may punish his enemies*

*in his wrath... by his bounty his well-wishes be rewarder.*

*May his tent-pitchers make ropes of his royal pavilion's*

*door... like iron spits in throats of his enemies everywhere.*

But, within eighteen months the Mongols had invaded Shiraz and put him to death. After that, many different governors ruled over the city.

Sadi is credited with having worked some miracles, especially that of restoring to life a young lover who had thrown himself from a tower one hundred feet high to the ground.

According to 'Shaikh' Sadi, he was modest in manner and could not tolerate vanity in others. He dressed modestly, was short in stature, thin and like Hafiz was not handsome and was soon bald; but a face beaming with intelligence and a long-flowing beard that gave him an engaging and venerable appearance.

His written works consists not only of his two most famous books (in the West) the *Bustan* and the *Gulistan*. In fact his *Kulliyat* or 'Collected Works' consists of twenty-four separate volumes including a volume of *Khabissat* or 'Indecencies' that he claimed in the Introduction he was forced to compose by 'one of the descendants of the king' who threatened him with death if he did not do so! He then asks God to forgive him... but adds that such stories and poetry are like 'salt in food'. An example of an 'indecent' poem of his is as follows, a *ruba'i*...

*Some idiot's wife from him got a divorce...*

*found another husband as a matter of course.*

*One had hands on head from wife's betrayal*

*the others cock was left to its own resource.*

Sadi is also said to have composed the *Pandnameh* or 'Book of Counsels' although early manuscripts do not contain this work and most likely it is written by another hand over a hundred years later.

Among his collected works are four volumes of his *ghazals* written from his teenage years up until the day he died on the 9th of December 1292... his *Divan*... that are more loved by his countrymen than all other works (including the *Gulistan* and the *Bustan*). In fact most Persians see and cherish Sadi as the forerunner to the greatest Master of the *ghazal*... Hafiz of Shiraz, who took many of Sadi's *ghazals* and perfected them. And before Sadi's appearance most Shirazis looked to the spiritually inspired *ghazals* of Nizami, Sana'i and Farid-ad-din Attar. To Iranians the *ghazals* of Sadi are still the creations of his that they love the most. This form of poetry which Sadi throughout his long life used and which he loved more than any other was the *ghazal* (pronounced 'guz'el'). There is really no equivalent to the *ghazal* in English poetry, although as Masud Farzaad, the great Iranian authority says, the sonnet is probably the closest. As a matter of fact, the *ghazal* is a unique form and its origin has been argued about for many centuries. Some say that the *ghazal* originated in songs that were composed in Persia to be sung at court before Persia was converted to Islam, but not one song has survived to prove this. It is also possible that originally the *ghazals* were songs of love that were sung by minstrels in the early days of Persian history and that this form passed into poetry down the ages. I find this explanation plausible for the following reasons: firstly, the word *ghazal* means 'a conversation between lovers.' Secondly, the *ghazals* of Nizami, Sadi, Hafiz and others were often put to music and became songs, which have been popular in Persia from ancient times until now. Whatever the origin, by the thirteenth century the *ghazal* had become a mature form of poetry. Among the great *ghazal* writers of the past were Sana'i, Farid ud-Din Attar and Nizami. 'The *ghazal* is certainly one of the most successful genres in world literature. Due to extensive migrations it is spread over a vast geographical space of multiple literary languages: from Arabic it migrated via Persia into Turki and the languages of India, in Spain into Hebrew via Arabic and, finally, transmitted by Persian models, it even emerged in the poetic canon of German literature.' *Ghazal as World Literature*. Thomas Bauer and Angelika Neuwirth. Orient-Institut Beirut (page 9).

The form of the *ghazal* at first glance seems simple, but on a deeper inspection it will be found that there is more to it than one at first sees. It is usually between five and fifteen couplets *(beyts* or 'houses'), but sometimes more (as is often in Sadi's case). A *beyt* is 'a line of verse split into two equal parts scanning exactly alike.' Each couplet has a fixed rhyme which appears at the end of the second line. In the first couplet which is called the *matla* meaning 'orient' or 'rising,' the rhyme appears at the end of *both* lines. This first couplet has the function of 'setting the stage' or stating the subject matter and feeling of the poem. The other couplets or *beyts* have other names depending on their positions. One could say that the opening couplet is the subject, the following couplets the actions: changing, viewed from different angles, progressing from one point to another, larger and deeper, until the objective of the poem is reached in the last couplet. The final or second-last couplet is known as the *maqta* or 'point of section.' This couplet or the second last often contains the *takhallus* or pen-name of the poet, signifying that it was written by him and also allowing him the chance to detach himself from himself and comment on what effect the actions of the subject matter in the preceding couplets had on him. Often the poet uses a play on words when he uses his own pen-name.

In the *ghazal*, Sadi found the ideal instrument to express the great tension between the opposites that exist in this world. Having the strict rhyming structure of the same rhyme at the end of the second line of each couplet (after the first couplet) the mind must continually come back to the world and the poem and the rhyme. But by being allowed to use any word at the end of the first line of each couplet, one can be as spontaneous as possible and give the heart its full rein. This of course happens also in the first line of the first couplet, for whatever word (or rhyme sound) that comes out in the first line sets the rhyme for the rest of the *ghazal*. So the 'feeling' created by the rhyme is one that comes spontaneously from the heart, and this spontaneity is allowed to be expanded from then on in the not rhyming lines, and to contract in those lines that rhyme, when the mind must function as an 'orderer' of the poem. This expansion and contraction, feeling and thinking, heart and mind, combine to produce great tension and power that spirals inward and outward and creates an atmosphere that I would define as 'deep nostalgia.' This deep nostalgia is a primal moving force that flows through all life, art and song, and produces within whoever comes into contact with it when it is consciously expressed, an irresistible yearning to unite the opposites that it contains. So, the subject matter of Sadi's *ghazals* is the movement of the opposites towards unity: grief and bliss, lover and Beloved, fear and bravery, desire and patience, separation and union, madness and sanity, youth and old age, drunkenness and sobriety, life and death, slave and king, the outcast true lover of God and tile hypocritical laws of the Church, friendship and loneliness, rose and nightingale, the church and the wine-house, the world that is passing and God Who never dies, the Perfect Master of Knowledge and the ignorant disciple, and so on in every *ghazal*. Sadi, however, not only points out and explains these opposites, but also shows the invisible connection between the two; and this connection is there in all of his poetry, in every line and couplet; and this connection is connected to a point of Unity which flows through all the opposites and makes one yearn even more to be united with that Unity.

This optimism in Sadi's poetry can only be the result of one who has loved, and it is this love which is the unifying thread running through all his poems (even the ones criticising the hypocrites, who Sadi feels for because they are the furthest from this Unity). This takes us along with him, for we ourselves recognise in his feelings, feelings that we have also experienced; and the same 'deep nostalgia' which he expresses is an expression of an area existing in everyone's soul, for it is the soul itself which is longing to be United with Itself, and the humour of this predicament has an irony which is not missed by Sadi, and which is there in his poems all the time.

Jan Rypka states in his *History of Iranian Literature* (see bibliography) 'Sadi's *ghazals* are held in especially high esteem, nowadays perhaps more than ever before, although it should be emphasized that from the very first the innovations introduced in them were afforded due appreciation. The great Amir Khusrau Dihlavi (d.725/1325) describes himself as Sadi's successor in the *ghazal,* and even Hafiz makes use of Sadi's wording in certain passages, though without stating his source. It is natural that Sadi should also borrow to a large extent from his precursors, especially since he was thoroughly familiar with their works; but thanks to his ingenuity and his special fondness for the *ghazal* his work surpasses all previous achievements. While for a long time the poets had expressed their amorous and other emotions mainly in the introduction to the *qasida* and had devoted but little attention to the independent *ghazal,* the Mongol period was to witness a change caused by the altered social conditions. With the rise of the towns the *ghazal* acquired more prominence and the cultivation of the panegyric *qasida* gradually waned. The *ghazal* even obtained primacy, thanks to the genius of Sadi. 'According to Altaf-Husayn Hali, the special features that characterize Sa'di's *ghazals* are the following: (1) the melodious form, that so harmonizes with the subject as to cause the 'lovers', listening to these *ghazals* in the *sama,* to lose consciousness; (2) love predominant among the motifs, without affectation; (3) a plastic form arising from the genuine inward experiencing of real impressions and emotions; (4) effect enhanced by the use of metaphor; (5) graceful simplicity; (6) mystic love in the guise of earthly love; (7) contempt of the hypocritical priesthood and those in authority. Is there not something rather old-fashioned in these lines of Hali's? We can detect nothing that was not present in one *ghazal* or another before Sadi's time, but such synthesis accompanied by such a total harmony has certainly never been met with before. With Hafiz the composition is set to quite another key. Another formulation of the revolution brought about in the *ghazal* by Sadi is given by M. F. Koprulu: a mixture of love and Bacchic themes with *'irfan,* 'theosophy', and *hikmat,* 'wisdom'. A more accurate view is that of M. Bahär, who points out that in the work of Sadi, as in that of Hafiz, in point of fact many *ghazals* almost, as it were, proclaim political opinions under cover of Wine and the Beloved. It is indeed not advisable to look for Sufism always and everywhere… either in Sadi or in other poets. Sadi adheres to the opening theme throughout the whole *ghazal* until he has exhausted it.'

'Before the time of Sadi not much attention was given by poets to composing *ghazals* and it could be stated that this form became important in the time of the master and through his genius came to the height of advancement and esteem.' Garakani.

It is said that on his travels when he reached India he met the great poet Amir Khusrau who composed in Persian and that many of the *ghazals* of Khusrau were greatly influenced by Sadi and Khusrau was often called 'the Sadi of India' and the *ghazals* and other works of Sadi have always been popular there.

In fact Sadi has always been a popular throughout the world being translated into Latin first in 1686.

'... the learned have not pointed out any books more distinguished for their advantages to the present and future state of mankind, in prose or in verse, than the *Gulistan* and the *Bustan*; nor is it concealed from the decorator of the tree of poesy that the *ghazal* was first planted in the soil of captivating language by this eminent bard.' John H. Harrington. (See bibliography).

In the West the works of Sadi in translation were admired by and influenced Hugo, Balzac, De Musset, Renan, Heine, Goethe and many others. Across from Europe in America Emerson and Thoreau amongst others came under his spell. Emerson stated: '... though he has not the lyrical flights of Hafiz, (he) has wit, practical sense and just moral sentiments... Sadi is the poet of friendship, of love, of heroism, self-devotion, bounty, serenity, and divine Providence.' (Journals. 1865)

In *his* 'Journal' Thoreau states his fellowship with the poet '... I can find no difference between Sadi and myself... He is not Persian, he is not ancient, he is not strange to me... If Sadi were to come back to claim a personal identity with the historical Sadi, he would find there were too many of us...'. Herman Melville also came under his spell and that of Hafiz and Khayyam.

The importance and influence of Sadi's many writings on the Islamic and Western world is vast and I recommend the reader to the following bibliography to follow it up and to discover one of the world's great Master Poets, who was also a unique and wonderful storyteller, moralist, philosopher and traveller.

In the Persian language there is no 'she' or 'he'… only *'oo'* or the person or object referred to… i.e. 'you' or 'that one'. Most translators wrongly either use 'he' or she' depending on their interpretations. I have not done this. Usually Sadi is addressing the Divine Beloved (or Spiritual Master or *'Qutub'* in Sufi terminology) and sometimes an earthly beloved, so I make the judgment as to which and either capitalize or not, as in 'You' and 'you', 'that one' and 'that One'.

# THE *GHAZAL*

There is really no equivalent to the *ghazal* (pronounced *guz'el*) in English poetry... although as Masud Farzaad, the greatest Iranian authority on Hafiz and his *ghazals* said, the sonnet is probably the closest. As a matter of fact, the *ghazal* is a unique form and its origin has been argued about for many centuries.

Some say that the *ghazal* originated in songs that were composed in Persia to be sung at court before Persia was converted to Islam, but not one song has survived to prove this. It is also possible that originally the *ghazals* were songs of love that were sung by minstrels in the early days of Persian history and that this form passed into poetry down the ages. I find this explanation plausible for the following reasons: firstly, the word *ghazal* means 'a conversation between lovers'. Secondly, the *ghazals* of Hafiz, Sadi and others were often put to music and became songs, which have been popular in Persia from ancient times until now.

Other scholars see the *ghazal* as coming from Arabic poetry, especially the prelude to longer poems, i.e. the *qasida:* they say that this prelude was isolated and changed, to eventually become the *ghazal.* The Arabic root of the word *ghazal* is *gazl* which means: spinning, spun, thread, twist... the form of the *ghazal* is a spiral.

Whatever the origin, by the fourteenth century the *ghazal* had become a mature form of poetry. Among the great *ghazal* writers in Persian of the past were Nizami, 'Attar, Rumi, and Sadi; but with the *ghazals* of Hafiz this form reached its summit.

The form of the *ghazal* at first glance seems simple, but on a deeper inspection it will be found that there is more to it than one at first sees.

It is usually between five and fifteen couplets *(beyts* or 'houses'), but sometimes more. A *beyt* is 'a line of verse split into two equal parts scanning exactly alike.' Each couplet has a fixed rhyme which appears at the end of the second line. In the first couplet which is called the *matla* meaning 'orient' or 'rising,' the rhyme appears at the end of both lines. This first couplet has the function of 'setting the stage' or stating the subject matter and feeling of the poem. The other couplets or *beyts* have other names depending on their positions. One could say that the opening couplet is the subject, the following couplets the actions: changing, viewed from different angles, progressing from one point to another, larger and deeper, until the objective of the poem is reached in the last couplet. The final couplet is known as the *maqta* or 'point of section.' This couplet or the one before it, almost always contains the *takhallus* or pen-name of the poet, signifying that it was written by him and also allowing him the chance to detach himself from himself and comment on what effect the actions of the subject matter in the preceding couplets had on him. Often the poet uses a play on words when he uses his own pen-name... ('Hafiz' for example, means: a preserver, a guardian, rememberer, watchman, one who knows the *Koran* by heart. "Attar' means: seller of perfumes and drugs).

In the *ghazal* the Persian, Turkish and Urdu Master Sufi Poets found the ideal instrument to express the great tension between the opposites that exist in this world. Having the strict rhyming structure of the same rhyme at the end of the second line of each couplet (after the first couplet) the mind must continually come back to the world and the poem and the rhyme. But by being allowed to use any word at the end of the first line of each couplet, one can be as spontaneous as possible and give the heart its full rein. This of course happens also in the first line of the first couplet, for whatever word or rhyme-sound that comes out in the first line sets the rhyme for the rest of the *ghazal.* So the 'feeling' created by the rhyme is one that comes spontaneously from the heart, and this spontaneity is allowed to be expanded from then on in the non-rhyming lines, and to contract in those lines that rhyme, when the mind must function as an 'orderer' of the poem. This expansion and contraction, feeling and thinking, heart and mind, combine to produce great tension and power that spirals inward and outward and creates an atmosphere that I would define as 'deep nostalgia.' This deep nostalgia is a primal moving force that flows through all life, art and song, and produces within whoever comes into contact with it when it is consciously expressed, an irresistible yearning to unite the opposites that it contains. In the *ghazal* any metre can be employed except the *ruba'i* metre.

The true meaning of Sufism, apart from the recognition of God in human form as the *Qutub* or the *Rasool* or the Christ is *tassawuf...* which means to get to the essence of everything. Adam was the first poet and it is said that he named everything and invented the first alphabet from which all others come. But Adam was not only the creator of conscious language as we know it, he was also the creator of song and the perfect form through which he created songs in praise of Eve his true Beloved, her beauty was displayed in the spiral form of the *ghazal*. So, the *ghazals* he composed and sung to her before their eventual Spiritual Union were of longing and separation and those after… of the bliss of Union. He used the same form of song about other events including the great sorrow and deep nostalgia about the loss of his favourite son Abel.

Two of Arabia's most careful and serious historians Tabari (d.923) and Masudi (d.957) state that the first poem ever composed in known history was one by Adam (the original Sufi *Qutub* or First Perfect Master… God-man) on the death of Abel and the form was the *ghazal*.

It is said that thousands of years after Adam, the Perfect Spiritual Master Noah, settled Shiraz after his ark landed in the Turkish lands on the mountains of Ararat and was a vintner who brought the first vines that he carried with him was also a poet who composed in this form as did the *Qutub* of some three thousand years later who also settled his people he had led from their homeland in Bactria (northern Afghanistan) to Fars (Persia)… Zoroaster.

His *gathas* or hymns are in rhyme-structure the first two couplets of the *ghazal* which would later be known as the *ruba'i*. And so the *ghazals* of the Zoroastrians were sung in their winehouses and fire temples throughout our land until the Muslim Arabs invaded and converted most to Islam, but poets and minstrels would not give up their much loved eternal God-given *ghazal* or the wine of Noah as well, which had its distant progeny in the *mesqali* grape.

The clandestine winehouses run by the Zoroastrians and Christians became the venues for many hundreds of years of the *ghazal.* In these winehouses Persians could criticize their Arab and Turkish rulers and their police chiefs and false Sufi masters and hypocritical clergy who censored and forbade them to practice the drinking of wine and the appreciation of beautiful faces and forms of unveiled women and handsome young men.

In the winehouses the truth could be told and this truth was quickly spread by the minstrels in the market places and even at court through what was becoming a popular form of expression amongst the masses. And although in fact the actual drinking of wine finally became less because of the religious restrictions, it as a symbol of truth, love and freedom became more widespread.

Of course there always existed another 'Winehouse' where the Wine of Divine Love and Grace was poured out by the Winebringer or *Qutub,* the Perfect Master or the Old Magian. Here the wine and truth that flowed freely from heart to heart was of the spiritual nature and made the lover or drunkard so intoxicated with the Divine Beloved that he became *mast*-like... mad with longing to be united with the Eternal One, Whose beauty he saw and appreciated in the face and form and personality of his earthly beloved whom he praised, wooed, begged, cajoled, described, desired and desperately longed for through his *ghazals* and by his actions and with each breath of his whole life he came closer to the Eternal Beloved. Human love became transmuted into Divine Love. Hafiz's love for Shakh-e Nabat and Ibn 'Arabi's for Nizam are examples of this.

Although the poets of the *ghazal* may appear to many as open-minded, drunken, outcast lovers, it does not necessarily mean that they all drank the juice of the grape... for it is an inner state that they

31

often were expressing. The *ghazal* is a conversation between the lover and the beloved and as in all intimate conversation… the talk flows both ways. The subject may not necessary be about love, but it is always from the point of view of one who loves truth, love and beauty. For more on this form and those who used it see my *The Ghazal: A World Anthology* and *The Sufi and Dervish Ghazal: An Anthology,* both published by New Humanity Books 2012.

# GLOSSARY

NOTE: Please read this Glossary carefully before reading Sadi's poems so that the spiritual meaning of his poetry may be understood. As there are many shades and levels of meaning in Sadi's poems it is necessary to understand the symbols in the context of each poem. Sometimes Sadi uses the symbol in a spiritual sense, sometimes in a physical sense and sometimes both. For Sadi, as a true Sufi, everything in Creation is a symbol of a higher Reality. In this Glossary I have explained only those symbols which appear most frequently. I have not arranged this Glossary alphabetically as is usual, but in a manner which I hope the reader will find less boring and more enjoyable and enlightening. Other explanations are given in the Notes.

THE SKY: The sky symbolises fate: unpredictable, untrustworthy, always changing.

THE SUN: The Beloved, God. The bright face of the Beloved. The Power of God's Light revealing the Truth.

THE MOON: The Beauty of the true Beloved also (in context) the false beauty of the Creation, physical beauty. The Moon cannot be seen unless the light of the Sun is upon it (i.e. the Light of God). The sickle-shaped Moon represents the bent shape of the poor suffering lover and when waning, old age and death. The half (split) Moon symbolises the opposites existing in the psyche, and throughout Creation. The full Moon usually means the Beloved, showing fully the Beauty of God.

VENUS: Music, dance and song. The sky's minstrel. Good fortune.

PLEIADES: Sometimes used as a symbol for the tears of the lover and sometimes as a necklace of jewels to place around the Beloved's neck. Other meanings in context.

THE WIND: The bringer of bad news, misfortune. Sometimes it symbolises one who brings news of death.

THE BREEZE: The bringer of messages from and to the Beloved. Often the messenger who brings good news. Divine inspiration.

THE SEA: The ocean of love to be crossed by the lover. The immensity of Divine Love, of which human love is but a mere drop. The turbulent sea represents the difficulties the lover must endure on the voyage to God.

THE BOAT: The form, energy and mind of the lover of God of whom the Perfect Master is the Captain. Sometimes the boat represents the Perfect Master who sails us to the Divine Shore.

THE PEARL DIVER: The lover of God, the seeker of the Truth.

THE PEARL: God, Divine Knowledge, Truth, a lover's true Self. THE SHELL: The outer form, the physical illusion, the false, the ego. THE DESERT: The long period that the lover of God must pass through when the lover's thirst for God's Grace remains unquenched.

THE HILLS AND VALLEYS: The ups and downs experienced by the lover on the Path of Love.

THE FIELD: The world, whereupon the Game of Love is played.

POLO: Polo is a symbol for the Game of Love. The horseman represents the Beloved and the ball symbolises the lover's mind and sometimes the lover's heart. The Beloved's long curling hair symbolises the polo-mallet that strikes the ball (the lover's heart).

THE GARDEN: The special place in the world (and in the inner realms) where the lovers see, meet and converse with the Beloved. The Presence of the Beloved.

THE ROSE: The true Beloved, i.e. God. The Perfect Master whose heart has expanded like the rose. Sometimes the rose signifies a beautiful woman. The rosebud sometimes signifies the lover, whose heart has yet to become expanded by Divine Love, i.e. love that is still young.

THE TULIP: The humble, faithful, tragic lover of God. The tulip, blood-streaked, cup-shaped, often symbolises the heart of the grief-stricken lover.

THE VIOLET: The patient obedient servant or disciple of the Perfect Master (the rose). In Persian gardens violets are often planted in rows leading up to the rosebushes, i.e. like attendants, or lovers waiting to serve the Beloved.

THE HYACINTH: The Beloved's hair is often compared to the hyacinth because of its beautiful perfume.

THE LILY: The lily often symbolises a gossip, its long yellow stamen representing a tongue.

THE ARGHAVAN: The arghavan or Judas tree has crimson flowers. This represents the mature, long-suffering lover.

THE NARCISSUS: A proud beautiful one, jealous of the Beloved's (the rose's) beauty. Sometimes Hafiz refers to the Beloved as the narcissus, telling the Beloved not to be so proud and to call on the lover. Often the eyes of the Beloved are symbolised by the narcissus.

THE CYPRESS: The cypress symbolises the form of the Beloved because of the tall, upright stature of the cypress and because like God Who never changes, the cypress remains green all throughout the year.

THE NIGHTINGALE: The lover of the Beloved (the rose). It also symbolises the poet who sings of the beauty of the Beloved.

THE PARROT: The poet who talks to the Beloved in the hope that the Beloved will reward him with sugar (Love, Grace).

THE FALCON: God. The Perfect Master or the Beloved, who preys upon the lover who is a mere fly by comparison.

THE KITE AND THE CROW: Ignorance, false poets, false masters.

THE PARTRIDGE: False pride, pomposity. Often the partridge symbolises an earthly king, or person in power, who prides himself on his position.

THE HOOPOE OR LAPWING: The messenger of the Perfect Master. A faithful servant.

THE MOTH: The lover, who wishes to extinguish himself in the flame (Love) of the candle (God).

THE PATH, STREET, HIGHWAY: The Path of the love of God in human form i.e. the Perfect Master. The Spiritual way. The path that leads to the Winehouse, wherein is found the Perfect Master. The journey through the inner realms of consciousness to the true Self (God).

THE WINEHOUSE: The place where the lover goes to be with the Beloved, the Perfect Master. The dwelling of the Perfect Master. Sometimes the Winehouse symbolises the inner Self of the lover.

THE WINE: Truth, Love, Grace, Knowledge. As ordinary wine changes a person's personality, so Divine Wine changes the inner consciousness and brings the lover closer to God and intoxicates the lover with God's Love and Truth. The more the lover drinks of this wine, the more he becomes addicted to it and the more he loses his reasoning. Wine (in the ordinary sense) was forbidden to Muslims.

THE CUP: The heart of the lover of God and sometimes the Beloved, from whom flows the wine of Divine Love.

THE FLAGON AND WINECASK: The Perfect Master, God.

THE WINEBRINGER: The Beloved, the Perfect Master, the God-man, or anyone who brings to the lover (the drunkard) God's Love, Truth and Beauty. Sometimes Sadi means Destiny, which brings the cup from which we must drink.

THE FRIEND: God, the Perfect Master.

THE BELOVED: God, the Perfect Master. God perceived in beautiful human form as in the female 'Muse'.

THE BELOVED'S HAIR: The attraction of God's Grace. The Mystery that conceals the Divine Essence. The hair sometimes symbolises the world with its problems (tangles) and mysteries, in which sometimes we get trapped.

THE BELOVED'S CURLS: The beauties of God's Manifestation. The charms of the Beloved. The twists of Fate.

THE BELOVED'S EYE: The Power of God. One glance and we can become annihilated in His Love.

THE BELOVED'S EYEBROW: The eyebrow of the Beloved is often compared with the arch towards which one prays (in the direction of Mecca) in a Mosque.

THE BELOVED'S DOWN (ON CHEEK OR LIP): This is a symbol of the attractions of Divine Love. It also symbolises the sprouting forth of Life.

THE BELOVED'S LIP: The lip of the Beloved will heal the lover because from it the lover can taste the Water of Everlasting Life and the Wine of Divine Love.

THE BELOVED'S MOLE: An attraction of the Beloved, full of Mystery. The Perfect imperfection?

THE WINEMAKER: The Messiah, Prophet, Rasool, Avatar e.g. Adam, Jesus, Mohammed, Noah.

THE WINESELLER: The Perfect Master.

MONARCH'S CROWN: God's Glory.

THE SLAVE: The lover of God (the King), who is bound by God's Beauty, which is sometimes represented by the long flowing (chainlike) hair of the Beloved.

THE PAINTER, THE ARCHITECT: God the Creator.

THE RUIN: This world, wherein one can find the Treasure (the Perfect Master, the Truth). It also symbolises the lover's body which though ruined through searching and longing for God, still contains the jewel of the Soul.

THE INN, HOTEL: The world, where we must stay awhile before passing on.

THE SUFI: The Muslim mystic.

THE DERVISH: The true lover of God, the real mystic.

THE KALANDAR: Like the dervish, a true lover of God.

# SELECTED BIBLIOGRAPHY

*DIVAN* OF SADI: His Mystical Love Poems, Translation & Introduction by Paul Smith, New Humanity Books, Campbells Creek, 2008.

*TAYYIBAT.* The Odes of Sheikh Muslihu'd-Din Sa'di Shirazi. Translated by Sir Lucas White King. Luzac & Co. London, 1926.

*BADAYI.* The Odes of Sheikh Muslihu'd-Din Sa'di Shirazi. Translated by Sir Lucas White King. Kaviani Press 1925.

RUBA'IYAT OF SADI. Translation and Introduction by Paul Smith. New Humanity Books, Campbells Creek, 2005.

SADI: SELECTED POEMS, Translation & Introduction by Paul Smith, New Humanity Books, Campbells Creek, 2012.

SADI'S PAND-NAMA OR BOOK OF WISDOM Translation & Introduction by Paul Smith, New Humanity Books, Campbells Creek, 2016.

A SELECTION OF SAADI'S GHAZALS. English Translation by Simindokht Seyedfatah. Mirdashti Farangsara Publishers, Tehran. 2000.

IMMORTAL ROSE, An Anthology of Persian Lyrics. Arthur J. Arberry. London 1948. (pp. 73-92 , selection of *ghazals* in verse forms).

THE PERSIAN AND ARABICK WORKS OF SADEE. John H. Harrington editor. (Introduction in English) Calcutta 2 vols, 1791-5. Reprint of vol 2, 2009 Kessinger Press.

THE BUSTAN by Shaikh Muslihu-D-Din Sa'di Shirazi. Translated by H. Wilberforce Clarke, R.E. 1879. Reprint Darf Publishers Limited. 1985.

THE GARDEN OF FRAGRANCE: Being A Complete Translation of The Bostan of Saadi... From the Original Persian into English Verse By G.S. Davie, M.D. Keegan, Paul, Trench and Co. London. 1882.

MORALS POINTED AND TALES ADORNED. THE BUSTAN OF SAADI. Trans. by G. M. Wickens. University of Toronto Press. 1974.

THE GULISTAN or Rose Garden of Sa'di. Translated by Edward Rehatsek. Kama Sutra Society. 1888. New Humanity Books 1988.

SADI: GULISTAN OR FLOWER GARDEN. Translated with an Essay by James Ross. Walter Scott. London. No date.

THE ROSE-GARDEN OF SHEKH SADI OF SHIRAZ: Translated by Edward B. Eastwick. Reprint 1979. Octagon Press.

THE GULISTAN Being the Rose-Garden of Shaikh Saadi. Trans. in Prose and Verse by Sir Edwin Arnold. Harper & Brothers Publishers. N.Y. 1899.

SADI'S SCROLL OF WISDOM With an Introduction By Arthur N. Wollaston. John Murray. London 1906.

THE POET SA'DI: A PERSIAN HUMANIST By John D. Yohannan. Rowman & Littlefield Publishers Inc. 1987. (A mine of information of the life, poetry and influence on the west of Sadi.)

SA'DI: The Poet of Loving and Living. Homa Katouzian. Oneworld Publications. 2006.

DIVAN OF HAFIZ. Translation & Introduction by Paul Smith. 2 vols. New Humanity Books. 1986. Revised one vol. edition 2012.

HAFIZ OF SHIRAZ: by Paul Smith, New Humanity Books, Campbells Creek. 2000-12. (Throughout this long 'living biography' written from the oldest Persian and other sources using Creative Imagination or *himma'* the verse and influence of Sadi on later poets and the Shirazis is evident).

SHIRAZ IN THE AGE OF HAFEZ. The Glory of a Medieval City. John Limbert. University of Washington Press. 2004. (See in particular chapters 1 & 2.)

SHIRAZ. Persian City of Saints and Poets. Arthur J. Arberry. University of Oaklahoma Press. 1960. (See chapters 2 & 5).

THE IRANIAN CITY OF SHIRAZ. John I. Clark. University of Durham. 1963.

A LITERARY HISTORY OF PERSIA. By Edward G. Browne. 4 vols. Cambridge University Press. 1920. (See in particular vol. 2.)

CLASSICAL PERSIAN LITERATURE. A.J. Arberry. George Allen & Unwin Ltd. 1958. (See chapter 8.)

ASPECTS OF ISLAMIC CIVILIZATION As Depicted in the Original Texts by A.J. Arberry. George Allen and Unwin Ltd. 1964.

HISTORY OF IRANIAN LITERATURE. Jan Rypka and others. D. Reidel Publishing Company. 1968.

A GOLDEN TREASURY OF PERSIAN POETRY by Hadi Hasan. Indian Council for Cultural Relations. 1966. (Pages 168-198).

THE SHAHNAMA OF FIRDAUSI. 8 vols. Translated by Arthur George Warner and Edmond Warner. Kegan Paul, Trench, Trubner & Co. Ltd. 1923.

BORROWED WARE. Medieval Persian Epigrams. Trans. by Dick Davis. Mage Publishers. 1997. (Pages 143-151).

A THOUSAND YEARS OF PERSIAN RUBA'IYA'T by Reza Saberi. University Press of America. 2000.

TRAVELS IN PERSIA. Sir John Chardin. 1671. AMS Press. 1972.

THE LANDS OF THE EASTERN CALIPHATE. Guy Le Strange. Cambridge University Press 1905.

MEDIEVAL PERSIAN COURT POETRY. Julie Scott Meisami. Princeton University Press. 1987.

WIT, HUMOUR AND FANCY OF PERSIA by M. N. Kuka. Bombay 1937.

PERSIAN PROVERBS by L.P. Elwell-Sutton. John Murray. 1954.

PERSIAN-ENGLISH DICTONARY (Comprehensive) by F. Steingass. Oriental Books Reprint Corporation. 1973.

THE COMPLETE BOOK OF MUSLIM & PARSI NAMES. Maneka Gandhi & Ozair Husain. Indus. 1994.

THE ART OF PERSIAN MUSIC. Jean During, Zia Mirabdolbaghi and Dariush Safvat. Mage Publishers. 1991.

THE OCEAN OF THE SOUL. Men, the World and God in the stories of Farid al-Din 'Attar by Hellmut Ritter, Translated by John O'Kane with Editorial Assistance of Bernd Radtke. Brill. 2003.

THE CONFERENCE OF THE BIRDS. Farid ud-din Attar. Translated with an Introduction by Afkham Daranbi and Dick Davis. Penguin. 1984.

THE ILAHI-NAMA or Book of God of Farid al-Din 'Attar. Translated from the Persian by John Andrew Boyle. Manchester University Press. 1976.

THE QURAN. 2 vols. Translated by E.H. Palmer. Sacred Books of the East Series. Clarendon Press. 1880.

THE KASHF AL-MAHJUB. The Oldest Persian Treatise on Sufiism, by Al-Hujwiri. R. A. Nicholson. Luzac. 1911.

SUPPRESSED PERSIAN. An Anthology of Forbidden Literature. Translated with Notes and an Introduction by Paul Sprachman. Mazda Publications. 1995. (Some of Sadi's 'obscene poetry'. See pages 33-44).

LAYLA & MAJNUN by Nizami. Translation and Introduction by Paul Smith. New Humanity Books 2005, 12.

GHAZAL AS WORLD LITERATURE 1. Thomas Bauer, Angelika Neuwirth editors. Orient-Institut Beirut 2005.

TRANSLATIONS OF EASTERN POETRY AND PROSE. Reynold A. Nicholson. Cambridge 1922 p.p. 145-8 are from the *Tayyibat.*

# GHAZALS...

# Tayyibat...

Introduction of this volume is in Name of God, the Omniscient:
the Creator and the Provider... the Eternal and the Omnipotent.
The Greatest and Most Mighty, Who had created Adam with
a fine physical form and mental qualities, so noble and intelligent.
By reason of His bounty and gracious favour, the birds of the air
and fishes of sea gain their subsistence... for them to be content.
Both the rich and the poor are enjoying what is allotted to them;
gnat and griffin due to that One, of their livelihood are confident.
That One's understanding, through of having Divine Knowledge,
of ant's need, whether at well's bottom or under rock... is evident.
He creates animals from a clot and from cane is extracting sugar:
from dry stick... a fresh leaf, a spring of water from the rock's vent.
He creates sweet mead from the bees... and He creates a strong
date tree from seed of the date fruit, a tall tree that's magnificent!
He is independent of everyone and yet He is gracious to everyone.
He is invisible to the world, but... still He remains, Omnipotent.
Who ever does not recognise the thanks due to His bounty in this
life, will be grieved at his Fate when on arriving that Final Event!
O God, O Almighty Lord, O You... our Protector and our Ruler!
You, the only One Who is totally free from every blandishment!
We do not have the ability to sing Your true worth in sacred praise
with all of the Pure Angels that in Your Heaven are so prevalent!
Sadi has uttered these words, as much as he can understand; or...
how could his highest flight of imagination reach the Omnipotent?

The moon is in a state of bewilderment by Mohammed's beauty:
  because of his graceful stature... the cypress will not grow free!
The glory of sky is possessing neither dignity nor perfection when
  to consummate grandeur of Mohammed it compares unfavourably.
Promise of each one of Vision will be fulfilled at the Resurrection:
  the night of Mohammed's journey was the night of... his Unity!
Adam and Noah and also Abraham and Moses... and also Jesus,
  under shadow of Mohammed's protection are, and will always be!
For scope of Mohammed's magnanimity the world is too confined:
  no, it's the Day of Resurrection that will give him the opportunity.
The Garden of Paradise is adorned with all of those lovely things
  in the hope that Mohammed's Bilal* accepting them... will be!
There will be neither sun or moon in the Plain of the Resurrection,
  no light will be there except Mohammed's breathtaking beauty!
The sky is desiring to fall down just like the earth is laying down,
  in order that it also to be kissing the shoes of Mohammed may be!
It is not right for the sun or the moon to be shining... before those
  two eyebrows of Mohammed... which as crescent one could see!
Ever since my eyes did see the beauty of Mohammed in a dream,
  sleep is failing to keep them from the perfect image of his beauty!
O Sadi, if you wish to make love and to follow youthful ways...
  totally sufficient for you is to love Mohammed, and his family.

* Note: Bilal was originally a black slave whom Prophet Mohammed,
who this ghazal is in praise of, had ransomed and freed and appointed as
his first muezzin, or the one who calls the faithful to prayer.

46

See that face obscuring moon and trap of that One's hair,
also look at  grain of that One's black mole, just… there!
I have never heard of a cypress ever putting on a tunic…
nor have I ever seen a cap on the head of the sun… never!
If such a fair face was produced on the Day of Judgement,
lovers would give so many excuses for sins, here and there.
I have heard that Joseph* was imprisoned down in a pit…
but this is a Joseph in whose chin is a pit beyond compare!
That One is seeing all of that One's lovers with the same
arrogance of a king when viewing soldiers standing there.
It'd be a pity if people did not sweep with their eyes that
stately cypress' path: every step it of that One does bear!
I cannot be any more patient, away from that One's face:
for how long the weight of a mountain can the straw bear?
You sunk in sleep… don't you hear sighs of an insomniac?
Find no fault with him, heartache makes him sigh louder!
O Sadi, tell no more the tale of intoxication, of profligacy
and lovemaking, for on the Sufi monastery it is a slander!
Obliterate the volume of the poetry that you have written:
nothing but prayer for welfare of Seljuk Shah* be composer.
God, grant him eternal life, so he may punish his enemies
in his wrath, by his bounty to well-wishes he'll be rewarder.
May his tent-pitchers make ropes of his royal pavilion's
door… like iron spits in throats of his enemies, everywhere.

* Notes: Joseph was not only a Qutub or Perfect Master but was known
for great physical beauty. Seljuk Shah, Shiraz's ruler 1263-4. This ghazal
was written in the year 1263.

47

Tonight the untimely drum they have beaten too early
or the bird of dawn… time of rising, crows mistakenly!
Was it a moment or a whole night that went from our
life while we with lips on lips desired unsuccessfully?
I'm joyful… at the same time I'm ashamed: ashamed
but I'm also sorry, for I cannot pay back such beauty!

If You place foot on my head You do me no favours…
welcoming Your footsteps I lay head, in all humility.
Because our auspicious fortune is perfectly reconciled,
let a malignant slanderer perish in his own jealousy!
Sadi's a world-celebrity… let Sufis and the herd know
he worships an idol… but an Idol, deserving idolatry!


O pleasant breath of the breeze you've come from quarter
of the Beloved*… my welcome to you, I now kindly offer!
O caravan of night… what have you heard of the dawn?
Bird of Solomon, what news from Saba* do you deliver?
Is that dear Companion of mine still angry with me… or
is it a falsehood that about that One I did recently hear?
Have you come with a message of peace, or… of hostility?
And shall we now walk with steps full of hope… or fear?
O courier of breeze blowing from the Eastern direction…
if again you are passing along Beloved's street remember
to tell that One this weak lover has almost passed on…
is gasping his last… he can survive for how much longer?
But if the occasion of Union with that One should arise,
the past will be forgotten… when we are again together.

Until the hand of death reaches our collar let it be known
that we shall never be letting go of Beloved's skirt, never!
That one could never be referred to as being a friend who
is one who forgets a friend when any calamity does occur!
To be exhausted from seeking Beloved is to be at ease…
because it is suffering pain in the hope of receiving a cure!
Like the harp I am unable to lift my head… even though
blows on my neck like on a drum should off my skin tear!
If I should speak any morning about this love of mine…
next day, throughout the streets, of it I constantly hear!
Story of my heartache has spread throughout the world,
but… on You there is no effect from words of Your lover.
If Sadi's lamentations should ever reach the mountains;
even it, would resound with Echo's tongue, this I swear!

*Note: The Eastern breeze or zephyr is a medium for communication
between the lover and Beloved as was the hoopoe bird who carried the
message of Solomon who understood the language of the birds to his
beloved, Bilquis, the queen of Sheba (Saba), the beloved's homeland.*

Beloved, if You are indifferent to condition of Your lover
I cannot obtain peace of my mind without You… never!
A sight of Your beautiful face in the mirror will explain
what to Your impatient lover may ever happen to occur.
Come… because it is the season of spring… so let us be
leaving the garden and the pleasure-grounds to another.
Why aren't you looking at the graceful Beloved, instead
of at a cypress, that over bank of the stream does tower?

That One is a young shoot… and describing such beauty
in any eloquent tongue's speech… there exists no power.
Who is it who says it is a sin to look at a lovely face, say:
it'd be wrong if a man on a beautiful face is never a gazer?
By our love… even if poison was to offered by Your hand,
with as much relish as if it was sweetmeat I'd be an eater!

My dear friend, anyone who never saw the face of Azra,*
only out of ignorance, would of Wamik* be a reproacher!

I suppose that You are not aware of the secret fire in me:

is it possible You can't see my tears that are everywhere?
Sadi, did not I tell you that your heart would be ravished,
when to the beauties of Yagma* you are the surrenderer?

*Notes: Azra and Wamik were two famous lovers whose story was most
notably told by the poet Usuri (d. 1039). Yagma: a city in Turkistan noted
for its beautiful women… it also means 'plunder'.

It is not our practice to violate the promise of faithfulness:
God's sake, don't of our friendship, practice forgetfulness.
One slack in fulfilment of a promise, not enduring cruelty,
doesn't tread truth's path, seeing Love as only worthless.
If I was asked what I wanted on Judgement Day I'd say…
"Give us Beloved, have Paradise… we couldn't care less!"
If You don't believe what we say then look in the mirror so
You'll know what ails all in this calamity… this sickness!
If soft breeze's hand should be reaching to Your long hair,
it'd instantly petals of garden's flowers no longer caress.

Wisdom is completely bewildered and bites fingers in awe
viewing such beauty that on no other eyes can suppress!
In my helplessness I'm longing to be burnt like the candle,
completely consumed in the presence of You: this, I stress!
Short-sighted eyes only see features on page of Your face,
but a true seeker sees in it God's pen of high Art-fulness!
Eyes of everyone see Your face, but those worshipping self
cannot distinguish worldly lust from Divine Truthfulness!
Learn Love from me… and if I happen to be passing away
from here, seek Love's plant on Sadi's grave, nevertheless!
None of sober nature will find fault with our intoxication:
tell it to that sober One who left all drunk… on Loveliness.


Get up, so we can throw aside this dervish's blue cloak quickly,
and give to the winds of revelry this duality that is called piety!
Each hour a new point of worship presents itself to the worshipper,
so that I may become an idol-breaker declare to me God's Unity.
My mind keeps desiring to be drinking wine with the young ones,
so that children may see and follow this old drunkard, with glee!
It was from helplessness that the dog Katmir* became a man…
while mania for greatness, turned Balaam* into a dog, eventually!
From constraint of this seclusion my mind draws me to the desert,
for morning breeze brings a happy message from Beloved to me.
If you are wise, then be alert, and if you have any spiritual insight
seize opportunity: that you will not have the chance again, may be.
Let's be leading into the dance that cypress with the silver body at
place where garden's cypress sways with wooden feet, gracefully.

That is Beloved: promise-breaker, eyes-attractor, heart-comforter:
ah, not… 'heart-comforter': that peace-depriver of the heart in me!
World, religious duties, patience and sense I have forsaken, loving
that One… where king pitched tent, it… of mob's clamour is free!
Rain of my tears pours down, lightning flashes from the clouds…
tell only to initiated, such ardour isn't felt by the novice, obviously.
Sadi will not listen to reproaches even if losing his life in this love!
Mystic, have no heavy heart! Winebringer… bring that cup to me!

*Note: See the story in the Koran of the Seven Sleepers… (xv.3). Katmir
was the dog of a shepherd boy of Ephesus (Turkey) who is said to have
hidden himself in a cave with six friends so as to escape the persecution of
the Roman Emperor Decius. They slept there for 187 years until the reign
of Theodocius the Younger. According to the Sunni tradition the dog
followed them into the cave and went to Paradise instead of Balaam (who
cursed Moses and the Israelites at request of the Canaanites) while
Balaam went to Hell in the dog's place.

It would never, never compromise a king's dignity if he
should regard even the most humble beggar, favourably.
I swear by Beloved's soul that even an enemy wouldn't
allow door in face of a friend, to be shut… permanently!
No… it isn't lawful that the servants of kings should
send away beggar from the royal household, so cruelly!
All the rest of mankind want the safety of their souls,
while on the contrary I barter my life for the calamity!
One who in his whole life has not knocked his head on
door of Beloved's house… does not know Love's story.
My imagination roamed throughout the world… then

returned, as it saw nothing but You, acceptable to me!
For the sake of the friendship of Your helpless lovers…
lower head, so that they kiss dust at Your feet humbly.
Is it possible for a body to be clothed in a richer tunic?
More beautiful than Yours clothed in tunic is no body!
If You do not veil face that has such beauty and grace,
a self-controlled person in Persia You will no longer see!
I beg You by Your soul, not to place load of separation
on my hurt heart: gnat can't carry millstone, obviously!
You will never again find like me such a faithful lover…
one who'll not break promise given to One of infidelity.
If You listen to the prayer of Sadi it won't do You harm
because it may be that prayers are answered eventually.

What can the slave do but his master be obeying?
What is the ball to do, but to the bat be yielding?
He is a true lover who places on eye arrow's point
shot from thumb-pinch of Beloved… so charming!
Help, because beyond all limit's my helplessness:
love me, and at Your feet my life I will be spilling.
Ah, that the veil would fall from my eyes so that
the whole of mankind a picture-gallery is seeing!
Eyes of all have been dazzled by Your attributes:
let them not fault me who them find bewildering.
It is true that not all have eyes to see the picture
which in the face of You, Beloved, I'm beholding.

I told a physician condition of my weeping eyes,
he replied, "One kiss, on that smile, be placing!"
I said, "O no, from such suffering I'll pine away,
it is impossible such a remedy I'll be obtaining!"
It wasn't wise to fight against such a silver arm:
it was folly's limit, fist upon anvil to be striking!
Sadi doesn't dread the criticism of people, O no!
One drowning in the sea, fear of storm is having?
You intend to list in this game? Lay down head!
It's necessary ball for playground one's providing.


I enjoy these heart-breaking lamentations, as they
somehow or other allow me to get through the day.
Night passes in expectation for that dawn-bright
face whose beauty exceeds the sun's brightest ray.
If only I'd again see Beloved's face inspiring love,
I'd thank my lucky star… until the Judgment Day!
If I turn face from criticism I am a woman: for men,
against heart-piercing arrow… lives as a shield play.
All left for those seeking desire is disappointment:
patiently endure winter, to get to New Year's Day.
The wise, mere gleaners, know not Layla's* secret…
this honour upon harvest-burning Majnun* does lay.
Bring others in Your trap, Your slaves we freely are:
bird trained on hand needs not feet tied, in any way.
The fair flirtatious One stole heart... grief increased,
patience's exhausted, heart's pain that One lets stay!

Lovers giving up this world's joy, hope of next... have
depth not in pious folk who seek gold, position, today.
O Sadi, yesterday's gone, tomorrow is still to come,
today you've a chance between this and that anyway.

*Note: Layla and Majnun are of course the famous, tragic, mystical,
young lovers whose story has been told many times but truly
immortalised by the master poet Nizami (d. 1209). See my translation:
Layla & Majnun by Nizami (See Bibliography) and my 'Poems of
Majnun' New Humanity Books, 2012.*

If You're tired of our company we're ready to be departing:
any service You tell our hands to do we'll try to be doing.
We've got up and left but Your image is such in our mind,
that wherever it wanders Your company it's never leaving.
If You want to fight, fight with an equal: we are helplessly
weak, so of what use would our loss be to You? Be telling!
We've committed no crime that Beloved should punish us,
but Beloved doesn't kill in ways religious law is allowing.
Thank God that my Idol was not faithful… because now
my idol-worshipping heart may at long last be repenting.
O Sadi, didn't I tell you… you could not easily reach that
One's high tree… with this small stature, you are having?

Your face is well reflected in our heart's mirror…
for Your face is lovely and mirror clear, my Dear.
Your noble nature's shown by Your face's beauty,
exactly like wine in a goblet, that is crystal clear!

One in Your company for a moment… only once,
cannot be patient without You, in any place or year!
The game of the desert is to be avoiding the snare,
but we twist voluntarily into Your noose… no fear!
The poor bird that set its aim on a particular place,
won't go elsewhere even if killed… it does adhere!
Jealousy prevents me complaining of You to others:
I don't tell lover's heartache to doctors, I persevere!
May I be the ransom for Your soul, for the lamp of
the Pleiades* by sun is extinguished, there and here!
If You, sweetly smiling, are not driving them away,
a sugar-eating parrot is every fly that does appear!
If that sweet Darling is not showing any boredom,
false lovers to get that One's delights, act sincere.
Sadi is eager for a stroll in garden of Your beauty;
but, the rabble want to plunder it… like a buccaneer!

*Note: The Pleiades are a loose cluster of many hundreds of stars in the
constellation of Taurus of which six can be seen by ordinary sight… often
mentioned in Persian Poetry. In Greek mythology the seven daughters of
Atlas. Sadi here means of course that even the Pleiades is extinguished
by the sun of the Beloved's great beauty.

I'm thirsty beyond limit! Winebringer, bring us that wine!
First satisfy me, then give it to those companions of mine.

In the past I also enjoyed a sweet sleep… I said farewell to
sleep upon the day myself away from Beloved I did confine.

Each devotee before whose mind's eye that Idol is passing
has a look at those eyebrows… rejects prayer niche's shrine.
I am no wild animal of the chase that is anxious for its life:
that One strings bow against me, I stand as target's sign!
No one knows the value of a close friend as well as I do…
fish on the land knows well the worth of the ocean's brine.
There was a time when I struggled in water waist-deep…
now… I have discovered it is a sea without any shoreline!
Today I am drowning, let me see if I can reach the shore…
then tale of a drowning man's anguish, I will tell every line.
If I was unfaithful I would complain to the king that while
infidel kills enemies this One kills friends, me… and mine!
That One's guardian complains about us lovers… and the
palace minstrel's voice annoys doorkeeper with its whine.
"Sadi, being object of Beloved's cruelty, don't come back!"
"Fool! I'd go, but like a fish, I'm hooked on Beloved's line!"


I do not need a bed-quilt of brocade on night of separation,
in a lonely bedroom it'd feel like thorns: no exaggeration!
From the helplessness of the wretched one mad with love
the wise can't know that one's impatience is at limitation!

If you saw that One and could distinguish hands from an
orange, it'd be fine if you reproached Zuleikha* and cut on.
A young girl like You should lower the veil… or else heart
of this steady old man could so easily be lost to oblivion!
You are the rose bush, the symmetry of whose figure has
caused the value of the tall cypress to suffer depreciation.

I shall never again contradict what You're saying because
without You pleasure for me is far off, beyond my station.
With both eyes open I've been sitting up all night through:
like the Farkadans*... watching the Pleiades constellation.
When night, candle, company combine, it's nice watching
Your face until dawn... to enemies envied consternation.
To whom can I complain against You? Under Love's Law
Beloved is forgiven, even in a wilfully murderous situation.
You're robbing the hearts of a whole city with one glance:
like servants on Banu S'ad plunder table... of any nation.
Because of Your graceful walk You can practice cruelty on
thousands like Sadi! Darling, stop causing consternation!

* *Notes: Zuleikha, the wife of Potiphar, was madly in love with the
heart-ravishingly handsome Joseph, the Perfect Master. In order to justify
her love for him she invited her female friends to a feast where oranges
were handed to her guests and as they were about to cut them Joseph was
announced. He entered and they were all so astonished by his beauty that
they all cut their hands instead of the oranges. Farkadans are two bright
stars in the constellation of the Lesser Bear, sometimes called the 'twins'.
The Pleiades... see previous note.*

Once upon a time my mad soul in garden was wandering.
I was sent crazy by scent of rose and sweet basil blowing,
suddenly nightingale poured out its song, rose burst into
bloom: I remembered You, each of them I was forgetting.
You whose love is in our hearts, seal on our lips... whose
tumult disturbs our minds, whose secret our soul's filling!
Since I promised You, I have broken promises to others...

to break promises is possible, after You one is promising.
So long as the thorn of Your Love's pain clings to my shirt
it would be stupid to in a garden go, and be promenading.
That one who is ruined because of such agony as this, has
to live a life of such despair that a cure he'll not be finding.
If seeking You we've to suffer, it doesn't matter; for when
one desires Mecca, across deserts is easy to be travelling.
Let every arrow in Your quiver strike my wounded heart:
we'll be one of many who for You, life has been sacrificing.
Whoever looks on the Beloved with the bow-like eyebrows
has to become a shield against all arrows that are coming!
They say… "Sadi, don't talk so much of that One's love!"
I'll talk of it as others will too: for ages, it'll be happening!

It was season of rapturous joy I met that flirtatious Sweetheart:
Winebringer, a wine-bowl! Musician, on your instrument start!
Tonight when festivities of seekers is lit by Your face's candle,
move quietly… so the sensual-minded profligates play no part!
Dear One, last night You drank wine, Your eyes told me that…
at least be looking for companion who Your secret won't impart!
A lovely face and beautiful voice, both have a distinctive charm:
think how delightful is a sweet voiced and beautiful Sweetheart!
Your listless eyes and Your eyebrows shoot darts into the soul:
O God, who to such a lovely archer has given a bow and a dart?
It would be a shame to repress such a passion for that One…
whisper of it into lute's ear, so a mention of it lute may impart.
Shiraz has become full of turmoil from mischief from Your eyes:
I fear that this sweet uproar through all of Shiraz will now start!

I'm like a small bird with wings that are tied, and so I'm sitting
in the cage… if the cage were broken away I would then depart.
"O Sadi, you bird of such a quick wit, I have subtly caught you:
difficult to capture a royal falcon like you… by any hunter's art."

O Muslims, I complain against those enchanting eyes,
  snatching patience, peace, submission, that in me lies.
With a Greek-like face, Abyssinian black curls, moles;
  see eyebrows bow puckered with frowns, causing sighs.
Until I'd seen my Beloved's form that elates the soul…
  I'd not lost my senses, my patience, stirrup of one wise.
I clearly see uniting in unveiled face of that Sweetheart,
  thirty-two attributes from the world's wonders to prize:
Moon, the Pleiades, Mercury, Venus, Sun, Sagittarius;
  cypress, ivory, myrtle, narcissus, ruby, rose of each size:
verdure, wine, coyness, coquetry, myrobalan, a candle…
  marshmallows, sandalwood, milk, pitch, light and fires;
and honey and sugar and musk and ambergris… pearls,
  and jewels and pomegranates, and apples of every size.
Miracles of five Prophets, namely Mohammed, David,
  Jesus, Khizer,* Moses can be seen in Your face's eyes.
Beloved, if I die before tasting your lips, God will make
  You give justice to me upon Judgement Day, I surmise.
O Sadi, haven't you heard it stated as a fact, that every
  up will have its down… every down, must always rise?

*Note: Who or what Khizer (Khidr) was and still is, has almost been
totally misunderstood by authors and commentators of Sufism and

*Persian literature and religious history. The first Qutub or Perfect Master, Adam, established an 'Office of Khizer' that goes with the subsequent roles of the Head of the Spiritual Hierarchy filled by the Qutub-e-Irshad or Chargeman Perfect Master of the Five Perfect Masters always on Earth. Of course with the coming of the Rasool or Messiah or Avatar (the incarnation of the first Perfect Master) this 'Office' becomes His responsibility. So, the Perfect Master (some say an 'old man', some say a 'youth') who had accompanied Alexander on his journey into the Land of Darkness (India) had gained immortality or God-consciousness (The Fountain or Water of Life) while Alexander the Great failed to reach this stage of consciousness due to his lust for power and physical immortality. See my 'Khidr in Sufi Poetry: A Selection' New Humanity Books, 2012.*

You have departed: hundred thousand hearts follow in Your train.

O Soul of Lovers, who can be patient when You are gone, explain!
Are You saying that he who cannot stand reproaches for a moment

is able to endure a long time of separation from You, it's inhumane!
Until You come again like the sun all of our eyes are on the path,

while all of our fingers are counting… again and again… and again!
I will fall at feet of courier by whose hands Your letter comes here,

and I will be placing it onto my head… and I will cease to complain.
You never leave my heart as with others, although You may pass

from my eyes… You are in my soul, though away You may remain.
The hope of the Day of Union encourages people, or else separation

from You would clot one's blood from the horror of it… the strain!
In Your palace's garden how could one find bloom of pomegranate,

quince's fresh beauty, apple's rosy blush… where don't You reign?
This *Id* Festival of breaking fast, people won't all be participating

as some adorn themselves... expecting You be approaching again!
Endowed as You are with an auspicious face do not be downcast,
for fortune will be Your friend in all misfortunes, that m ay remain!
All Sadi's thoughts are with You because Your friendly disposition
like his poetry is charming to the heart... so, need this one explain?

Those who are drunk with sleep of life are unconscious:
real life is intoxication produced by Wine, nothing less!
Don't think that by what I've said to you I meant wine
intoxicating the body: that, destroys all reasonableness.
Become intoxicated with Wine of love for the Beloved...
wine destroying reason is harmful, only a liquid I stress!
If you wish to be near Beloved do not give up obedience:
if you look for mastership... from service do not digress.
You are lying asleep in the desert, caravan has departed:
I fear you won't destination, except in a dream, access.
Until scattering devotion's seed joy's harvest isn't had,
for a treasure is only found by work and so much stress!
The Fountain of Life is in the darkness and pearls are to
be discovered in the sea, treasure in a ruin... it's obvious!
That one who is constantly knocking upon the door will
on one day in the future unexpectedly be gaining access.
You must travel in order to obtain your heart's desire...
you've to stay up all the night for the sunrise to impress.
O Sadi, if you desire wages without doing work, that a
caravan in a mirage sleeps the thirsty, should be obvious!

We did not manage to get one wink of sleep last night.
O you wasting your lives in sleep, beware your plight!
The thirsty travellers in that wilderness all perished...
though water flows from Halla to Kufah* day and night.
O You who are such a hard-hearted and faithless One,
is this the way to keep faith with Your Lover, is it right?
Even a couch that is made out of ermine, without Your
face to see... feels like thorns in the side of an anchorite.
O You towards whose face eyes of lovers are directed,
as is face of the worshippers to the prayer niche's light...
I have submitted myself to all of the mandates of love,
and I have entered into this school, my old age despite.
Poison that has been given by the hands of the Beloved
slips down the throat easily... like pure rosewater might.
The cruelty of the doorkeeper can't be driving away that
one who in street of the beauties is discoverer of delight.
There is not one thing in this world that can kill Sadi...
except for separation from face of Beloved, by eyesight.

*Note: The reference is to Halla and Kufah which in ancient time were
two locations on opposite banks of the Euphrates about four days march
from Baghdad which during the wanderings of the ancient Israelites were
missed by them as was the river and so they died of thirst even though
they were all nearby.

O my beautiful One, do not turn Your face from me...
You think it is right to slay one without fault, so easily?

Last night while I was sleeping I was embracing You…
I experience such a delight only in a dream… obviously.
From my heart burning away and my eyes being fringed
with tears I am between fire and water… no escape I see!
Souls of dervishes are the targets of that One's arrows…
helpless lovers' blood colours that One's nails dark ruby.
That One speaks… by doing so robs all listeners' hearts:
that One torments… all souls are consumed immediately.
If anyone enters by the door I think it has to be that One:
a thirsty wretch always thinks the mirage water must be!
It would be a pity to clothe such a body with a garment…
to cover such a face with a veil, amounts to much cruelty!
From the ear-lobe of that One mop sweat with your shirt
so garment you wear smells of rose-water… so fragrantly.
A sweetheart, with a candle in hand and eyes heavy with
slumber and drunken with wine, often acts mischievously!
Do not be veiling Your face from morning until night falls
so that You may be obscuring the sun's splendour, totally.
Sadi, if you wish lie like a harp upon that One's breast,
have your ear twisted while tuned like a *setar,* constantly.


Those are not curls, but night: this is not an earlobe, it is day:
that One's symmetry is not the fir's… more date-tree's I say.
This mouth of Yours cannot be imagined, even by the poet…
it is only when You speak, he knows You have lips, anyway.
As the fire of Your face has consumed mankind like this…
one is not surprised they are burnt but that raw they'll stay.

In the season of spring one who is not a lover, is not a man:
tree without moving sap is mere fuel upon New Year's Day.
Do not think sway of the cypress is due to eastern breeze:
no, it is dancing for joy at cries of birds in the garden, today!
I wish that my life may reach its end in my quest for You...
although distance is out of proportion to power to find a way.
Everyone has not the same devotion for You that I have, for
You are like sun: the short-sighted like bats in the night stay.
Every event has a cause and I'm plunged in grief by Beloved.
Fate drags me to my doom, separation is why I am this way.
I can't tell to any strangers this story because to complain to
enemy of the Friend I would from etiquette of lovers... stray.
It's impossible for this condition of mine to remain concealed;
You rip coats of armour while my curtain is of muslin crochet.


You smiling One, who has ever bitten Your lips of ruby...
who has plucked roses of Your face from garden of beauty?
That one who kissed them has attained his heart's desire
and that one who failed to do so is enduring anguish daily.
Who has eaten any better fruit than this in his whole life?
Who has ever sliced a more sweet water-melon... tell me?
O Khizer, I will not be permitting you the Fountain of Life:
you know trouble Alexander had with it, on land and sea?
You associate with everyone else, while fleeing from us...
the fault is not Yours, it is unfavourable Fate that is faulty!
The fruit on a tree that is laden will never be lasting long
when all the rabble know that it is sweet... ripe and ready!

I am giving many thanks that the wall's completely fallen,
so that it'll never again be said… this garden none can see.
The rose also during that short time didn't open its petals
but today morning breeze its envelope tears… completely!
The time has gone when we could enjoy You once again…
we have had enough of a jar that strangers sucked on freely.
O Sadi, knock at the garden's gate of some other passion,
and abandon this field… where the herd grazes, constantly.

You, sight of whom gives comfort, smile causes calamities,
in grace You have completely surpassed all other beauties.
You who are in way of beauty a lovely picture from Khata*
and are as pure as a raindrop that in spring-time one sees.
Reason, did not I tell you, you and Love are irreconcilable?
In Emperor's domain another cannot reign, even if he tries!
They say, "Leave that One so heart is weaned from Love!"
I fear that the distance would only make this passion rise!
In comparison with Your form the cypress is not graceful,
in contrast to Your face moon is not so lovely… I surmise.
One seeking desired thing sets hundred tables for enemies
in hope that friend comes, to feast on what upon table lies.
Sword of sweet affection is swung by Sweetheart's hand;
the spiritual seeker should not be annoyed, even if he dies!
O Sadi, since you have been trapped, submit to your Fate:
sea has pearls and corals,  terror and dread there, also lies.

*Note: Khata was a province in China at that time noted
for its painters of pictures.

That which You have isn't a body but a nine days wonder,
and that's no smile but a miracle and a marvel, as it were!
One who has seen Your moon-like face made of his breast
a shield against arrows of criticism… this, one may infer.
Every moment in all days and nights of my life passing in
Your absence is filled with a thousand regrets that I incur.
The period of my time spent in indifference to You cannot
be seen as life: the rest of it to be making amends, I prefer.
Swaying cypress doesn't resemble Your symmetrical form
and all eulogy lavished upon its stature, does not matter.
When eyes of the traveller saw Your beauty, his intention
to keep going was changed to determination to stay here.
The people of both classes will be astounded at You…if of
the tribunal of Judgement Day You should be an attender.
All of this distress and disappointment Sadi endures… are
happiness and patience to him, if of them You are approver.


The mad lover is once again today in a state of ecstasy:
surrender is Layla's religion, every other creed is heresy.
Why should Farhad* care if Shirin is harsh towards him,
for he knows she can't bear him of her to become weary.
Azra,* one who can read love's story that is not written,
knows the message, Wamiq's* tears, was told faithfully.
Minstrel, be careful to sing this *ghazal* in the same way
for the tune that it follows shows the direction perfectly.
O you pretender to Love passing along the Sea's shore,
you can't understand how we are, drowning in that Sea!

How can we leave that door, we're assigned to its dust!
All our blood is entrusted to that One to shed as booty!
If I don't place my head at that One's feet I'd not be able
to raise it among seekers... it'd become the shame of me.
Whatever you do, except thinking of Beloved is a waste:
whatever you say, except for Love's mysteries, is vanity!
From each cruel act of that One, Love's scent is exhaled:
in each fault-finding, thousand attempts to conciliate be!
We have no more dealings with anyone else: the sale that
we conclude in Your absence... is a bargain of no validity!
Sadi, wash from heart's tablet image of all but Beloved,
knowledge not pointing out way to the Truth is stupidity!

*Note: All are all famous lovers in Persian Literature.*

Is that a moon that is two weeks old, under a veil hiding:
or a virgin of Paradise, with hands that henna is dyeing?
Is it indigo tincture on that One's heart-alluring eyebrows
or could it possibly be a rainbow, that sun is over-curving?
O You who are the talk of the city, playing mischief upon
all the people: night and day in Your face they are seeing!
Any person who is not enamoured of Your fair face could
rightly be called a beast, that a human form is inhabiting!
Even though You're the Monarch and we all Your slaves,
even though You are great and we... we're worth nothing;
even though You are fabulously rich and we're all so poor:
it is still the right thing... hearts of lovers to be soothing.

O my Beloved, I have become overwhelmed by a torrent!
Such cruelty that goes beyond all limits, do not be doing!
Ah... please, return to us, because through love for You,
a thousand fountains of tears from our eyes keep gushing!
O You who are the most agreeable medicine for our pain,
as You know... that to serve You, I have been promising.
You know that I shall never be turning away from You...
whatever wrong You've done is right: this, I am believing.
You... You whose face I see as the gateway to Paradise,
this heart is on fire from thinking Your lips I'll be tasting!
I'd thought that I would extinguish my fire with water...
but water is useless for the fire of heart to be quenching.
O You cypress, so graceful... O You rose-bush, so fresh!
O You possessor of moon-like face... like the sun shining!
Be taking... but be giving: be speaking, but be listening,
such nights as these, are never the time for any sleeping.
O please, O my lucky star... help, my favourable fortune!
Tonight is a night of intimate communion, until morning.
Light a candle where we are, or do not set up any candle,
for tonight there is a lovely light off the moon... glowing.
Listen... there is a hungry, merciless wolf that has never
eaten enough even if all mankind's blood it is devouring!
One could say the people of this world resemble wheat,
while this present cycle of Time is a mill that is grinding.
O Winebringer, give a goblet of wine to my companions!
Let the mad be, our intoxication from wine is not arising!
All of this pride about being alive is really a lot of wind...

and that glitter of youth is nothing but a flash of lightning!
Be using this present hour well, while you are still able:
hurry up... because your life towards its end, is speeding.
O Sadi, you are not really fit for Union with that One...
you keep bragging yet that One's favour you keep seeking?
You... so thirsty, how long will you wander, bewildered?
The road you are taking, leads only to a mirage appearing.

Of all things to happen Beloved's words are most sweet...
they're a friendly, soul-refreshing message, never obsolete!
Have you ever heard of a being present... yet still absent?
I'm in assembly's midst, yet heart's elsewhere! Some feat?
If the Sweetheart is not with us let lamp be extinguished:
if here, there's plenty of warmth even without lamp's heat!
Worldly folk wend their way to pleasure grounds, gardens:
pleasure ground and seekers' garden, are Beloved's street.
God grant that the Beloved, who left angrily, comes back
in a spirit of friendship: eyes of lover turn to door to greet.
Darling, You've consumed my heart like aloes on fire and
my breath's like smoke from censer, my love gives off heat!
Nights I spend in Your absence resemble the 'night of the
grave': if I pass dawn without You, the Final Day I meet.
Hair, so fragrant with ambergris;* neck, aloes compacted:
what need for such a lovely One of ornament, my sweet?
Sadi, you entertain vain hopes of Union, separation from
that One killed you and Union with that One is a conceit.
Regrets for this long-cherished hope, still fills your heart?
Ah no, this impracticable idea your mind does still greet!

70

\* Note: Ambergris was found in pieces floating in the sea near the coasts of India, Africa and Brazil. It is formed in the stomach of the sperm whale, as a result most probably of a disease. It has a wonderful aroma and was highly prized in Persia and by its poets.
Aloes is fragrant when dried and burnt and is of the lily family.

You, whose body is so agile that is clothed with beauty!
None but the pure of eye Your perfect loveliness can see!
If I am really fortunate I'll die upon the dust of Your door,
it could be some day You'll pass over that dust, over me.
I know that one day my head shall be falling at Your feet,
let me flee now to You, hold to Your saddle-strap, tightly!
O You, by whose fair face the eyes of Reason are dazzled!
You, whom power of our vision's too limited to see clearly!
I thought I'd avoid grappling with serpents of Your curls;
but, I remained so helpless before Your lips smiling at me!
If the lustre of Your face should fall upon dome of the sky,
moon would veil her face, and the sun ashamed would be!
If You pardoned us it'd be as a favour to Your friends and
if You burn us You've control over possessions, obviously!
If You shed blood of all, You can do it without retribution:
if You pardon faults of all, there's none to fear… You see?
Practice as much cruelty as You may happen to wish to do
for pleasant memories will send grief from heart… of Sadi.

I have happened to fall in love in Beloved's street,
in which many a victim like me… such a Fate meet!

Send some news of us to the birds of the garden...
tell them their song-mate's entrapment's complete.
Breath of morning breeze tell the Sweetheart that
like the dawn we've nothing but our sighs, replete.
What can a sweet face with black mole be called?
It is honey, into which the fly has fallen... in defeat!
No one will resolve to make love like us unless it is
one who has fallen into trap of such desire, I repeat.
Sadi, that one only knows the ball's mad state who
all through his life under another's bat is off his feet!


Is it You, or a garden's cypress that has been walking?
Or is it an angel in human form, that has been talking?
I see that this beautiful angel who was concealed from
mankind for a long time again in the world is appearing.
Friends, is it aloes burning or rose's scent in the garden,
or a musk-laden caravan, that from Tartary... is coming?
Camel driver, if a glance at face of that One was given
in  exchange for a life... here is one, who it is purchasing!
Since I became familiar with features of that One's face
others I see seem to be a mere picture on wall I am seeing.
I'll no longer stay inside my house a prisoner, heart-sick,
especially now when you say rose into market is coming.
If you do decline to take a look at such divine handiwork
I'd answer that the eyes for this purpose He was creating.
If only I might at least once more see the face of Beloved:
you would then a dead man coming to life be witnessing.

O You solace of my soul, I'll tell whatever I experience at
Your hands, to who into my kind of trap has been falling.
Why is the flute wailing in the group of the free of spirit?
If you look closely at it many a wound you will be seeing!
Don't ever imagine that since You have left me deprived
of Your sleepy eyes, sleep to my wakeful eyes is visiting.
Sadi, if you've spirit don't complain of Beloved's cruelty:
since the world began... 'trouble from friends is coming'.

From fingers of that One comes the honoured letter...
from mouth is sweet-meat of speech... nothing better.
This fragrant perfume of friendship is proceeding from
that Court of the Beloved... affectionate like no other.
I pulled away that seal from the envelope... one could
say that it was the stopper in top of flask of rosewater.
Perhaps the courier was some musk-deer from Khutan,
who had of course a musk-pod inside its waist... or near.
How so very exquisite is the style of it... and also what
beautiful harmony and eloquence it does graciously offer.
It has become quite apparent that these honeyed words
have come from mouth of that One, the sugar-scatterer!
This letter should never be thrown away, on the ground,
because from the moon of heaven it's coming, as it were.
Some day in the future the soul of Sadi will be leaving,
because it is the truth that this life is not eternal, either.
But most happy is that one whose poetry is appreciated
when the time arrives for his soul to leave body, forever.

Is it the breeze of spring from garden coming
or fragrance of Union with Beloved blowing?
This embellished writing attracts the heart:
like down on a heart-alluring face, growing.
O you bird trapped in the snare of the rose:
come back here for it is time for the nesting.
During the night both the candle and I melt:
difference is… mine is a flame that is hiding.
My ears are always listening to the road and
eyes always upon the threshold… expecting.
And when cry of the caller to prayer is heard
I think it must be the caravan's bell sounding.
In spite of this hostility which You've shown,
come back… for my love for You is remaining.
Grip of the hand of patience is now powerless
against strength of Your arms: overwhelming.
Misunderstanding between intimate friends is
like splitting soul from body, a great parting!
The lamentation of Sadi that breaks heart is
a testimony to all who love can be claiming.
The reed of his pen did catch fire… and the ink
flowing is smoke of his sighs that keeps rising.


What is this face… that is in front of the caravan?
It is a candle… in hands of the camel driving man?
You could say that it was Solomon in his litter…
carried along on the eastern breeze, upon his divan.

Beauty of the moon-faced Beloved who is on high
is resembling the moon way up in the azure span.
The heavenly faced Beloved inside the camel litter
is like the sun under a canopy… imagine if you can.
Angel-faced Beloved is behind a veil of China silk,
like a lotus in water… or moon, behind a cloud ran.
That One who is hidden behind veil has suddenly
unveiled all of my secrets… I am now an open man!
Camel outstripped me when it comes to running…
for I keep carrying a heavier load than he ever can!
O such unfaithfulness, and such a perfidious One
is One who is so hard hearted and unkind, O man!
Even though Your love for me is such a little thing,
our faith and loyalty are the best that to do I can.
We were faithful while You were treacherous to us!
"Go, O Sadi, this is payment for what you began!
Did not you know in advanced old age it is totally
inopportune to see, if you a youth are stronger than?"

Alas… for the eyes that Your face have not seen,
or seeing it, looking upon another face has been.
If love pretenders saw Your angelic form they'd
know why to the mad to rip garments is routine.
Who is it who has drawn around sun of Beloved's
beauty a circle of black musk… to set the scene?
Sage, if your feet stumble against a stone, you'd
understand why Farhad a stone-cutter had been.

75

One who never heard Shirin speaking has no pity
for Farhad's heart, madly in love with that queen.
There is not a heart in the city that aflutter like a
pigeon from Your eyebrows crossbow hasn't been.
It can't be imagined how desirable a tree You are:
and it's obvious that from it none a fruit did glean.
Mystery of pen of matchless power of God, is as
clearly visible on Your face as on a mirror screen.
We desire nothing from You, except for Yourself:
give sweets to one who not tasting love has been.
No wonder with calamity's rain on Sadi's head,
that his eyes house should be leaking, in between.


In all truth… tonight, this night of ours, is as bright as the day:
it is the festival of Union with Friend, despite enemy in the way.
Is it the breeze of Paradise blowing or breeze from the garden or
is it the fragrance of Your mouth, or perfume that does stay?
These eyes that are in my head and the soul that is in my body
can never be more dear to me than Your body or soul: this, I say!
I'll bend my neck to serve You and lend my ears to Your words,
for as long as mind on Your ears and upon Your neck does play.
O my Sovereign, do not take Your protection from us beggars,
out of necessity there has to be a gleaner, upon the harvest day.
I have no scope for movement away from You in this wide world:
the world's like a needle's eye, heartsick lovers want it that way.
It's impossible for the lover to ever be escaping because the hand
of Love, whatever way he happens to go… on his coat does lay.

That Sweetheart's never leaving the house without a guardian:
sugar knows that it is the fan that is keeping all the flies away.
Cruelty of the guardian and reproaches of my contemporaries
are to me like the story of the bullock and the drummer's display.
O such a prey as this makes the royal hawks all become nervous
because… that nest of that falcon, is this heart of Sadi… today.
For how long can a tender heart be concealing the story of love?
Whatever you may cover with a glass can be seen by all anyway!

Is this soul-displaying fragrance from the Beloved's street:
is this Water of Life from Kauther* in Paradise, so sweet?
O breeze of the garden, is a musk-pod in Your waist-belt?
O friendly bird, there's a letter under your wings that beat?
Is it Paradise's breath blowing or Beloved's sweet breath;
or dawn's caravan as the illumination of world is complete.
From what musk-scented land has this courier arrived, and
what is in letter, that envelope such perfume does excrete?
Has aloes been burnt in breeze's path, or could it be that in
the land where You dwell… the dust, ambergris does meet?
Come… strike door-knocker of Your love-entrapped ones,
for both eyes of Your lovers are on door like a nail: I repeat!
Do You know how we pass our time? Each day that goes
by without You is like Judgement Day, that all must meet.
Come back, for during separation from You our expectant
eyes like faster's ears yearn for the cry of, "God… is great!"
I spoke of curing love with patience, but my love increases
each day, while my patience is much smaller, less concrete!

77

Your physical form is out of sight… Your qualities, present
in our memory: body veiled, but spiritual reality, complete!
How much of love's story can ever be contained in a letter?
I'll have to shorten it, our tale would make books obsolete!
Sadi's consumed by the lightening of Love like a tree in the
desert… but the fruit of his poetry still remains fresh to eat.
Really, time spent with friends is fragrant from the aloes…
but, they're indifferent to the censer's burning, bitter-sweet.

*Note: Kauther is a lake in Paradise which Mohammed is said to have seen on his night journey there. He described it as a month's journey in circumference with water whiter than milk, smell sweeter than musk. He who drinks of its waters shall never thirst.*

You who said the worst is… from Beloved experiencing separation;
it is not so hard to stand, if there is still hope left… for Unification!
People should realise they cannot escape the great flood of my tears,
but the wonder is… I am weeping when all sleep without inhibition.
Tips of my eyelashes tell my love's tale in red on white of my face
and so there is no need to of it be making any kind of an exhibition.
I faulted heart-sick lovers… then as a matter of course I too became
mad with love: for such a sin this punishment isn't much contrition.
Morning breeze, if a chance again should offer itself to you, please
convey our homage to that Presence… where we have no admission.
Often in this misery of mine I am turning my face towards the wall;
if I tell heart's grief to one, than wall none better to give a rendition.
We have held back our tongue from talking to men… also our face

should be with Beloved, not strangers, if there's to be conversation.

You have the power to do anything You desire, except to hurt me, for if You lay sword on my head it would not hurt or cause volition.

One must put up with the sting to be getting the honey... to support the pillar-less mountain wasn't hard, for Shirin * was his inspiration.

You have appearance of a cypress but the cypress is unable to walk: You are likened to the moon, but the moon has not power of oration.

If my heart is mad from being in love with You, do not blame it for a full moon wanes, gold has impurities, a rose has thorn's penetration.

How beautiful is the figure and symmetry of that straight cypress, because there is nothing to compare to it under this dome's rotation.

My friends say, "O Sadi, go and pitch your tent in a rose-garden": but, that rose that I am in love with, is not in any garden's location!

* Note: The tragic love story of Farhad and Shirin has been told in verse by many master poets of Persia, Nizami's being a masterpiece and the most popular (this work has yet to be completely translated into English, unfortunately). Shirin was married to King Khosrau and Farhad, a famous sculptor, had fallen in love with her. The king said he could have her if he cut a passage through a mountain (thinking it to be an impossible task).
Farhad worked for many years inspired by his love and eventually succeeded. The king on hearing this sent a messenger to tell him a lie... that Shirin had killed herself. On hearing this he threw himself off the mountain. On finding out this Shirin too committed suicide. See my English translations of Nizami's 'Treasury of the Mysteries' and 'Layla and Majnun' chapters 3, Khosrau and Shirin, that are about his telling of this famous tale.

That one, to whom patience and resignation are an impossibility, should not gird himself with the waistband of service of a devotee!

When you have the Friend, why worry about the blood-thirsty foe?
Let him beat the drum of reproach and kettledrum of abuse loudly!
Though that One practices all kinds of oppression don't complain:
torture by Beloved is preferable, to using any kind of intermediary.
I shall endure with resignation whatever You may have to say…
patience, contentment without You for me is… an impossibility!
And if an exact picture of Your face was brought into the  market,
all the painters would close the doors of their studios immediately!
Make the most of a moment's company with the Beloved, because
once gone that moment and that hour will not ever… returning be!
It is not just that I who am wounded and sick in the heart, should
be that One's moth, while that One is the candle of our assembly.
But… what is there to do, seeing that Destiny cannot be resisted,
even with strength of the arm of courage, and total implacability?
His heart bleeds from passion for You, soul burns seeking You…
but in spite of all this Sadi's ashamed of his capital's inadequacy!


O You, like ball in curve of whose bat are the souls of the wise:
a ball that is thrown in Your polo-ground a way out can't devise!
Dawn of the day of all others has appeared above the mountain,
but the sun of our night will only from Your collar for me, rise.
The souls in the bodies of ardent lovers are dancing with delight
when wind is shaking a branch that in Your garden does arise!
Although Your stony heart does not sympathise with this one,
one might say my heart is a stone that in well of Your chin lies.
It is an easy thing to forfeit one's life in Your presence… but,
I do not regard this emaciated body as a sacrifice You'd prize!

No painter is required for the wall of Your house because You
are ornament of Your palace and not its paintings to idealise!
Anguish due to Your brand is better than being far from You:
slavery is better to death that being far from You would arise!
Desert of separation, as long as is love for Mecca's precincts,
lovers will have no fear from the mimosa's thorns, that surprise.
It is a fact that I was no longer able to avoid temptation, ever
since I had fallen under the sorcery… of Your fascinating eyes!
It may be that Sadi, who loves You like his life… no more dear
than life itself… will never in this world experience his demise.
This thirsty one dying at Your fountain of life has wandered far
and wide in the world, as did Alexander the great and the wise!


You have not given up life and for the Beloved you're still longing;
you have not cut thread of infidelity, yet the true faith are desiring.
At Palace's gate where kettledrums of inaccessibility are beaten
you are not an ant, yet for Solomon's Kingdom are still yearning.
You are not even a man, nor have you rendered manly service, but,
still after the row of benches of Perfect Men you keep hankering!
Like Pharaoh you keep on boasting that you, you're the Almighty!
But, still you the favour of Moses, the son of Imran,* are desiring.
Like the child who makes horse out of its skirt, at riding you play
upon horseback… and still ambitions for the field, you are having!
You have, in all sincerity, done justice to your own way at least…
but, you haven't yet felt the pain and remedy for it you're wanting!
You are calling it 'abstinence from all carnal desires' and… yet…
for a hundred varieties of food upon the table… you are hungering.

At the table of the spider whose roasted meat is merely a fly...
you, pinion of Angel Gabriel's wings as a fly-whisk are coveting!
And... every single day you are requiring one cup of soup and two
loaves of bread... for Abu Said's* 'dog... that keeps on lusting'.
Sadi, be like an atom in this world in which you are a sojourner,
if your heart, closeness to the Divine Majesty, keeps on desiring.

* Notes: According to the Koran, Imran was the father of Moses and
Aaron. Abu Said was the celebrated Perfect Master (Qutub) of Mahna
who spent 14 years in the wilderness and composed many spiritual
ruba'is... quatrains. His 'dog of lust' is craving for food and the good
things of the world. For his life story see... R.A. Nicholson's 'Studies in
Islamic Mysticism'. Cambridge University Press 1921.
See also my 'Ruba'iyat of Abu Said', New Humanity Books, 2012.

It is totally wrong without You, to remain in retirement,
to shut the door a such a face is completely unintelligent.
If you let go the skirt of Good Luck, when in your grasp...
it may not... never, into your hands again... itself present.
Whoever falls because of Your arrow will never rise again,
and one caught in Your noose can't escape imprisonment.
We have become totally captivated by You all of a sudden,
that this bird has been trapped and a fish hooked is evident.
What kind of glances were those which shed my blood...
what salt was it that made my wound even more virulent?
Patience was rebuffed... and it decided it would be fleeing,
and wisdom which suffered discomfit, went for retirement.
I have the power left to be bearing the burden of contempt:

I still cannot to violating my lover's promise give a consent.
And even this last breath of my life which still remains…
it can't be said to exist in presence where You are existent!
An idol worshipper, would never adore a physical form even
if it had realised the meaning of spiritual enlightenment.
A one who like Sadi happens to be intoxicated with love…
will not desire intoxication caused when wine does ferment.

Let the lover perish in his passion for the Beloved,
for such a one… life consists in self becoming dead.
In my eyes Your cruelty and fidelity are the same:
what Beloved wants for lovers is right to go ahead.
What is eaten by the spiritual beings is appropriate
especially when from One of high station it is fed.
Fate birthed me and my love for You in one womb
like two souls in body: two kernels in a shell's bed!
A cypress-statured beauty stole my heart contrary
to habit of those cypress trees growing by riverbed.
Last night I dreamt I took hold of that One's curls:
hands still with musk and ambergris… are scented.
I went on head like a ball in the universe from love
for One, but One's polo-stick chases ball: my head!
Everyone you see wishes to gain his own desires…
in Sadi's mind is for that One to get what's desired.
There are some people who only see these tears and
don't know a fire inside my skin has for long burned.

I'm happy in this world because through Him it's joyful:
I'm in love with creation for He is its author, Masterful!
O friend, regard as gain Jesus' refreshing morning breath
reviving a dead heart… coming  from Him, of life it's full.
That which was in the secret of heart's core of mankind
was not entrusted to the Heavens… nor angels powerful.
I'll drink poison with relish for Beloved's my Winebringer:
I'll bear pain willingly… through Him I'll be cured in full.
It'd be alright if my bleeding wound weren't made better:
wound is pleasant when He applies salves… so bountiful.
What difference to a  Mystic is grief or joy? Winebringer,
give wine to drink to Him… Who makes me of grief full.
Sovereignty and poverty are the same to us… for at this
door the backs of mankind to Him are bent… devotional.
O Sadi, if destruction's torrent demolishes house of your
life be brave: from Him is existence's core, most powerful!


Fragrance of rose wafts, warbling of birds one does hear,
the time for delight and day for pleasure-grounds is here.
Autumn, the carpet-spreader, has strewn leaves and the
painter, the breeze, has adorned the garden far and near.
But, we do not have any desire for the orchard or garden…
wherever You are is the place and we want to play there.
It is said that to look at the beautiful ones is forbidden…
but, not to look at them the way we do… without a care!
The mystery of the art of the Perfect One is as obvious in
the face of Yours… as water in the glass lying over there.

I shall be plucking out my left eye, so that I may not see
Your face except in the right way in which one may stare.
Every human being, on whom the seal of Your love hasn't
been stamped is like hard flint for You to strike, whenever.
Some day my whole existence will be consumed by the fire
which under pot of my mad passion... is hotter and higher!
People say… that all of this excessive lamentation of Sadi
to opinion of those who are wise is quite contrary however;
but that one who is still remaining at ease on the seashore,
knows nothing of the whirlpool in which one like we… are.


To me who's drunk morning's winecup, patched cloak's forbidden:
O companions of mine, tell me where is the Winehouse's location?
Each in the world have chosen for himself some form of happiness
for us, love of that fair-faced moon, is all-sufficient now and then.
Get up, so that we may sit under the shadow of a cypress because
wherever You sit, cypress' posture is to stand, wherever and when.
The curl of Your long hair is a snare for the hearts of the mystics,
and that mole and that earlobe of Yours are grain and trap again.
If I drank wine with a companion like You in this place and time
it'd be lawful, as drinking wine of Paradise is… no matter when.
Say this to this city's religious censors, "Take care, and throw no
stones at this gathering of ours for it is a cup of glass, unbroken."
A spirit of chivalry does not allow me to say who has killed me…
or it would be possible for people to hear Beloved's name spoken.
O no, we've been consumed by this secret pain, while the novice is
knowing not one thing about the fire that is burning us… again.

O Sadi, don't be afraid: even if you are in crocodile's jaws within sight of Beloved you have fulfilled your desire, there… and then.

The foot of the cypress of the garden in the earth
is:
the foot of our spiritual cypress in heart's hearth
is!
That one whose glance has fallen upon such a face
has a lucky star… that omen of auspicious worth
is.
Those wishing me well still keep on criticising me:
but, to keep on making bricks in sea of no worth
is!
O brother… we are engulfed inside the whirlpool,
while one criticising us upon shore's safe earth
is.
Power of Love is always prevailing over patience:
wisdom's pretension above Love… full of mirth
is.
People say that the lover is lacking in discretion…
he with no Beloved  giving discretion wide berth
is!
You may've seen a thirsty man impatient for water:
my soul for the Beloved in same way full of thirst
is.

To sacrifice wealth, position, to give up reputation,
the first stage on the Path of Love of any worth
is.
If a seeker should die in the chains of the Beloved it
is an easy thing: difficult, living upon this earth
is.
While his blood kept flowing a lover was saying:
"Soul is in peace, for Beloved a killer of worth
is!"
O Sadi, in the opinion of lovers it is all the people
who are insane, while Majnun sane from birth,
is!


That One is wise, beautiful, also pure and good-natured…
I've never seen a form where reality has been so contained.
If one thinks of a sweetheart, let it be a Beloved like You:
if they think of a friend, let a Friend like You be imagined.
I will kiss dust of those feet… let that One dishonour me,
for honour of lovers is water in a stream in eyes of Beloved.
Your form and speech are lovely, brows and eyes confuse…
Your ways and walk are wonderful and make all attracted.
Soon as I come to my senses I'll describe face of that One.
Why ask me when in this playground like a ball's my head!
My friends all criticise me because I'm tearing at my shirt:
I'm a faithless lover: I've torn my shirt but skin not ripped!
The earth is green, wind scatters roses, stream is pleasant,
clouds are dropping pearls… and air with musk is scented.

But arrows rain on seeker's head absorbed in contemplation
and pretender talks on, while a true one seeks the Beloved.
Keep back your hand from one adopting a life of seclusion,
for foot of such a heart-lost creature in a treasure is located.
If eyes are fixed upon the Friend do not lend ears to enemy.
Sadi... love, reputation are stone and pot to be shattered!


Come, as it is the occasion for reconciliation, a time for kindness,
on the condition I do not complain of what happened, this I stress.
I had formed in my mind a resolution that I'd not indulge in love:
doom of Love supervened, the eyes of intellect closed, under duress.
One not understanding how boundless is my love... how limitless
Your beauty... can to a poor wretch like me be full of reproaches?
The destruction of my precious life at Your hands is a thousand
times more pleasant than to go to another for protection... no less.
What could my efforts accomplish? Grant me access to You...

eye of endeavour's weak without lamp of Your guidance, I confess.
If You want to know the truth, such a long separation from Your
face is sufficient punishment for my offence... this, I must stress!
It's in no way proper to act in the opposite fashion to Your opinion,
before whom can I bring complaint against the King of all? Guess!
In no physical form does there exist such reality that is spiritual...
and in no chapter of the *Koran* is found such a miracle... no less!
Perfection of Your body's beauty cannot be adequately described,
unless the mirror would be able to the tale as it really is... confess!
My poetry has attained expression's limits, mind's power is spent;
but description of Your perfection doesn't reach end, nevertheless.

The account of Sadi's separation does not reach the ear of anyone,
on whom his poetry's pathos has made no impression... or even less.

Most fortunate is that one who is Your companion...
he can't grow old because he is in the highest heaven.
Is a mirror placed at door of Your tent facing the sun,
or... are those rays from Your forehead put in motion?
In that direction my prayers shall no longer be offered
if You do not intimate that this is worship's direction!
If all the world was washed off the tablet of our mind,
Love wouldn't disappear for it is a seal, engraved upon.
I sought to retire from the crowd but it was all in vain:
Your eye is causing the recluse a disastrous situation.
Whenever Your beauty beats love's drum a cry goes up
that all hearts are robbed and spoiled in every religion.
Let there be no silver, gold, wealth or property for me:
I have Your face, on earth's surface it is my kingdom.
A true lover doesn't die of a wound at Beloved's hand,
give me liquid poison for it'd be a pure water solution.
If Sadi travelled along another road after he'd learned
the way to You, it'd be a mistake, not to be acted upon.

Like a slave coming to claim Your protection am I!
To be able to fight You I have no arms, so why try?
I made a resolution that I wouldn't lose my heart...
but again I found that becoming Your slave, was I.
Planet Jupiter is not worth the price of Your face...

89

yet in spite of all my poverty... You I want to buy!
I am jealous, but still I am not in the possession of
any power to conceal You from any strangers eye.
And even though I am as week as the feeble ant...
I suppress all my desire and carrying my load am I.
You twisted Your captive in a noose in such a way
it is impossible to break free... no matter how I try!
The exact moment I first saw You, I told myself to
be extremely wary of Your drunken, sleepy, cruel eye.
I must not be opening my eyes while You are away,

or conscious of feeling far away from Your face am I.
You've become bored while Your lovers long for You:
You're fleeing from us while to search for You we try.
These eyes of Sadi are seeing sleep only in a dream,
for You've now banished it by Your fascinating eye.
What do You care about eyes that are always open...
Your eyes heavy... thick with sleep, to open they try!


Until you make hands a belt around the waist of Beloved...
your heart's desire by kissing Beloved's lip can't be fulfilled.
Do you know about the life, of the victim of Love's sword?
It consists of biting an apple from garden of face of Beloved.
This mad passion that exists between the Beloved and me,
has with a pen the story of Khosrau and Shirin obliterated!
Enemy's blood who was not even a victim, to infidels arrow
at crescent moon was shed, by the eyebrows bow of Beloved.

90

A man's body is noble because it enshrines the soul of humanity:
it is not this gaudy dress that you see, that is a sin of humanity.
If a human being is such as he has eyes and mouth, ears and a nose,
what difference is there between a picture on a wall and humanity?
Eating, sleeping, anger, lust, ignorance and darkness are bestial…
animal has no knowledge, understanding of the world of humanity.
Perhaps you are not a real man as you are a slave of the Devil and
your guardian angel cannot get access to abode… soul of humanity?
If these rapacious temperaments of yours pass out from your nature
you would live the rest of your life with the spirit of true humanity.
Have you seen a bird's flight? Then emerge from the chains of lust,
so that you are then able to be one observing the flight of humanity.
Become a Man through advice and help of others, not by yourself…
Sadi also from a Perfect Man, heard true description of humanity.


Your eyes, lovely and still more beautiful from sleep, are:
the taste of Your mouth… is so much sweeter than sugar!
God be protecting me from that sweet smell that is Yours,
for it is more charming than an open, wet rosebud… by far!
I thought of lighting a candle before Your beautiful face…
there is no need for candle, moonlight is more spectacular.
Last night I wanted to indulge in a sweet sleep for awhile:
tonight the sight of Your face is sweeter than sleep by far!
The hard skin of a porcupine feels softer than ermine… on
the lover's bed, on Beloved's breast… for head of the lover.
If in Your kindness You summon me across a fiery ocean;
to go through fire is much more pleasant than across water.

91

Don't speak of pure water, green plants, pleasure grounds
and tulip beds... for me to look at the Beloved is far better.
Don't give me poison by the way of Your cruel guardians,
give it with Your hands, than rose-jam it is much sweeter!
Sadi won't go again in retreat: seclusion may be pleasant
but being in service of the Friend is more pleasant... by far!
You could say that each chapter of this beautiful book you
learn by heart, than another... even like paradise, is better!


Beloved, soul and body be sacrifice to Your soul and body,
selling one hair of Yours for all the world I would never be.
I've never heard of lips that said sweeter words than Yours:
are You all sugar or is Your saliva honey spilling out freely?
Someday do me a favour and at me shoot a glancing arrow
so that Your hand and eyebrow's bow may be enjoyed by me.
Whether You are turning aside or You are veiling Your face,
You through the corner of Your eye looking at me I still see.
The cypress hasn't a face like Yours bright as the full moon:
moon has no stature like Your cypress-like form... naturally.
You are what calamity, to be beyond power of imagination?
We've composed much but aren't able to explain You fully!
If people, ignorant of Your beauty, are finding fault with us,
they'd tell us they excuse us on seeing You in sight plainly!
It's a pity to veil such a beautiful face: it would be a boon to
Your wretched ones, and what harm comes to You, tell me?
Come back... for Your image has remained before my eyes:
sit down... Your features on my mind are printed indelibly!

It's nothing to surrender one's heart to You: I've a last gasp
of life remaining, and may it also a sacrifice to Your soul be!
By abusing me You showed kindness: You spoke I listened.
Heart of Sadi, whose name crossed Your tongue, is happy!


One who has not a Beloved cannot be said to be living:
that one's life is narrow who no goodness is possessing.
That one, in whose mind love's secret isn't conceivable
may possess a physical form… but a soul is not having.
If you have a heart then be entrusting it to a Beloved…
country that doesn't have a sovereign becomes nothing.
The eyes of a blind man cannot see the earth and sky…
because not a pupil those sightless eyes are possessing.
That heart is happy that is in possession of a Beloved…
fortunate is a head, lacking intellectual understanding.
I was asking of Love to tell to me the story of Reason:
the reply was that it was dismissed: authority lacking!
The pain of love is more pleasant than being healthy…
although there is no remedy for it, but to keep waiting.
Whoever is happy in company of a moon-faced One…
wealth that is far beyond any limitation is possessing!
That one who does not possess a rose garden like Sadi,
his house is a prison… and his solitude becomes boring.


As there's no way to escape from love's playground for me,
I just like the ball, have to put up with the polo stick bravely!
I swear by my faith that I will never my hope for You sever:

I swear by our friendship I'll not break promise I take dearly!
Whether You desire to destroy me or grant me eternal life,
Your orders will be obeyed: You want me to I'll do it, really!
O my fortunate *Id* Festival, if You return according to Your
promise if I didn't sacrifice myself to You I'd be mean, truly!
The moon of two weeks has not nearly as much brilliance as
the sun that's shining out of Your collar for everyone to see!
To say nothing of the cypress... if even the Tuba entered the
garden it'd feel ashamed, seeing Your form wave gracefully.
A pious one would not cast one single glance at Your face,
in case Your fascinating eye makes of his heart an absentee!
I am a slave to the generosity of outsiders and mad lovers...
and not to those pious ones who're looking at You secretly.
Come back, though You have done to me every sort of evil,
from blessings, prayer of righteous, You evil eye won't see!
I swear by dust of Your feet that even if Sadi sacrificed his
head it would still not sufficient for Your great kindness be!


I'm so in love with Your hair and drunk by Your fragrance
that of even the Here and Hereafter... I have lost all sense.
My eyes will no longer look at the face of any other person,
all Azar's* idols have been shattered by Beloved's presence.
I haven't any opportunity to sleep because of my thoughts,
for my door should not be shut to stop friends interference.
Wherever a captive exists it seeks door of cage to escape...
I'll not escape Your trap as long as my life's in continuance.

I'm slave of the great generosity of one chained by Beloved,
with one direction in whatever circumstances may dispense.
I'll obey what You order even if You should burn my heart...
I'll be slave to Your command even if You wound me hence!
Whoever's drunk wine on the morning of the Creation will
return on Resurrection Night's prayer-time, to sober sense.
My glance is to You while the others are with themselves...
drunk upon wine, Winebringer takes mystics commonsense.
If You, O graceful cypress, happen to suddenly be standing
among all the hermits, arising would be a great disturbance.
O brothers and friends, do not criticise me... for my will has
gone beyond my control like an arrow thumb does dispense.
Avoid the rain that's falling from the eyes of Sadi, for drops
become torrential when they combine... and become intense.
It is really a pleasure to mention Your name, but the shame
is... that my poetry will be carried from hand to hand hence!

*Note: Azar was the father of Abraham and a carver of idols.*

Like to the beggars kingdom, in the world no sovereignty
there is:
no state, that is more tranquil than resignation's country,
there is.
If anyone can be said to be possessing dignity, then... it is surely
belonging to that one who in the eyes of others, no dignity
there is.

Each one is possessing an attribute, an idiosyncrasy or a quality:
discard attributes, for none better than to be attribute-free,
there is.
You'll be looking at that man who is clothed on Judgement Day,
who today is naked and on whom nothing borrowed to see
there is.
Please tell me the person that is possessing Divine Knowledge?
It's One in Whom no knowledge of anything but Divinity
there is!
A stone or a plant which possesses some special virtue, is better
than a person in whom no use to anyone at all in humanity
there is.
O dervish, what do you know about what is in your best interests?
Be happy if you've nought: that, not without use, you'll see
there is.
That one is not a true lover who complains of his Beloved... and
in that Beloved no pity for state of anyone, including me,
there is.
Do you know what it was that was said by the wounded lover?
"No penalty attached to blood the Beloved takes from me
there is!"
The rule of good manners is that which Sadi has taught you...
if you've ears to hear, no better education than this here,
there is.


There is no time that is more pleasant than love's, I say:
the morning that is that of lovers has no night, only day.

Musicians have gone but Master's mystic dance goes on.
Love has a beginning... to an end it finds there's no way.
The desire of every seeker always has a termination point
but lovers of God's desire is with them... always to stay.
Out of a thousand, the mystical dance affects only one...
because, everyone is not entrusted with the Divine Way.
That One's lovers can appreciate subtlety of this notice:
"No public audience in Special Chamber, upon any day!"
The fragrance of aloes-wood isn't given off until it's burnt:
the initiated knows... that, not for a novice, is what I say.
Every ordinary person with a sweetheart knows her name:
the Beloved loved by me is nameless... and stays that way.
The cypress, in spite of all of its elegance, does not possess
a stature that in any way is comparable to You on any day.
Ask me about intoxication and the mad passion of a lover?
How can anyone know a thing about this who sober stay?
The wind at dawn and the earth of Shiraz are like a fire...
anyone who's consumed by it will be finding no rest today.
Your sleep that is untimely has been misleading you again
because the cry of the morning's passed... in sleep you lay!
O Sadi, since you have shattered the idol, become selfless:
self-love is not less than idolatry, one could accurately say.

You are passing by alone... but You are so joyful:
You leave Your devoted lovers bewildered, pitiful!
Look into the mirror so that You may see Yourself:
You'd be amazed to see that You are so beautiful.

Do You want to hunt or promenade in the garden?
To be Your guide one would have to be masterful!
O graceful rosebush, toss a glance at Your lovers;
fragrant breeze from Your garden to us is merciful.
To Love's plunder You threw Reason's furniture...
You obvious thief, I secretly watch You, be careful!
Each moment Your curls trap captures a fresh prey,
glance's arrows from eyebrow's bow kills each pull!
Know why I don't sleep? You're beauty's sovereign:
to watchman sleep is forbidden, he must be dutiful!
Association of Union with You does not befit me:
bird worthier must be in Your nest, one wonderful!
I do not desire even the Water of Life without You:
let me die at Your threshold, I'm not being fanciful!
I'm the 'wonder of the age' but friends of Yours will
no doubt make You of this 'evil of the time', careful!
O Sadi, since you've the Friend be tranquil, at ease,
though everyone in this world may to you be hurtful.


That One who has just risen moves with inimitable grace:
could it be a cypress who, straight and stately walks apace?
That One's eyebrow is the bow for the slaying of the lover:
that One's curls are a trap for the wise men from any place!
If people should happen to be asserting that such a form is
existing in this wide world of Islam, it's absurd... it is base!
O fire of the harvest of lovers, please come here... sit down,
because a thousand tumults have erupted in this very place.

Kill me though I'm totally innocent… I'm Yours absolutely.
Take, without any religious law, plunder Your marketplace!
I will endure all the suffering for suffering is the cure for me:
I shall eat of Your thorns, to me they are dates full of grace.
It is not nice to be pointed at by people with scorn's finger…
but when it's done by You it is fine… not at all out of place.
It is fitting that You should be the One who is immune…
it is very easy for us to be the one they criticise and debase.
Sadi has now finished this spilling of his life at Your feet…
to do this was the honour that he begged from God's grace.
If You should wish that he was coming alive one more time,
say immediately that he was killed by You… say to his face!


Do You know that in absence of Your face no peace there
is?
I cannot bear separation from You… no time left I declare
is!
What a story it'd be to say a limb of mine failed to praise You,
there isn't a hair on my body not doing this with every care
is!
The only wish I had was to take a look at that dot of a mole,
but, when I saw it I discovered that no way out of its snare
is.
At night I think that perhaps day will never be dawning again:
in morning when I see You, no desire for night in me there
is.

Ever since the day when I opened my eyes and saw Your face,
no wish to see any other with my eyes anytime, anywhere,
is.
If city comes out to fight and oppose me who has that One's
private audience... what care in me for what they declare,
is?
I've not approached You like a hypocrite, leaving if reproached:
I'll serve as a slave, though one losing respect and honour
is.
I swear by God and by all Your body... that from Your love
this one indifferent to enemies and abuse however unfair,
is.
Beloved, don't do cruelty of which no infidel would be guilty,
and even if a Jew did it, then this one no Muslim I declare
is.
I will love You whether You show me kindness or You do not,
not a hope of reward at Your hands, by Your eyes I swear
is!
O Sadi, that one would indeed be a monstrous beast if he says
he having a heart, but not One that easing heart's care...
is.


Last night that One kept me in a state of distraction
by stealing my heart, and my soul laying hands upon.
My eyes scattered pearls over the skirt of my tunic...
you could say that there a load of corals was sewn on.

The pain of separation is not cured by lamentation or
I'd have cried, "What's that remedy I can rely upon?"
I was thinking that it would never change into day…
until in the morning I saw it had an end… thereupon.
The breeze opened Paradise's gate… one might say
that of key of Heaven's guardian it had possession.
I saw the rosebud, that through the influence of the
breeze, held its hand on its collar just like I held on,
for I'm not alone in my madness from love: each rose
has its nightingale singing sweetly on and on and on.
My secret has been divulged and is public property;
how long could it be kept, by patience be relied upon?
O Sadi, one like you must be prepared to give up life.
Two masters in one heart? One, must surely be gone!

It's difficult to keep eyes away from face of the Sweetheart:
whoever tells us to do this a fruitless task will try to impart.
Though in the Beloved's heart there's repulsion towards us,
to see that One in the morning an auspicious day will start.
In the well of that One's chin the lovers helpless hearts are
imprisoned like angels, stuck in a pit in Babylon's rampart.
Before this, I set up pretensions to piety… but again I say
that every such claim made by me was false from the start.
Though in the opinion of the wise ones poison can be fatal,
when it comes from Beloved's hands… it a cure does impart.
I can't remove my feet from Beloved's street. O my friends
excuse me, my feet in the mire are stuck… I cannot depart.

Let all wise men call me mad! One cannot be relinquishing
one's soul in order that others call him sane, not an upstart!
Whoever tells us not to look at the face of the Beloved sees
the physical form: can't see reality, Beloved's spiritual Art.
Camel driver, drive slowly, my heart's ease is in that litter:
camels bear burdens upon backs, we carry ours in our heart.
If separation from Beloved happened for a thousand stages,
the home in my precious soul will belong to my Sweetheart!
O Sadi, it's an easy thing to be falling in love with anyone;
but once the bond's tied tightly it's difficult to pull it apart!

We have never before heard such an uproar that was cried
when that One left home and the market place beautified.
The imagination can't conceive how sweet and attractive
that One is... such charm and beauty, can't be described.
That One takes patience, heart, religion, strength, peace:
from wound can be seen that One's arm is strong as hide.
For God's sake don't conceal Your face from humankind,
so they God's art from right and left hand see... glorified.
Eye that sees You and isn't dazzled by the Perfect One's
power, cannot be called an eye that One truly has spied.
Of what use is the World and Paradise too? From God's
Court there is nothing to wish for but You, this I confide.
I cannot be criticised for complaining against Your love...
because I don't think that this pain only in me does reside.
If we cannot take Your cruelty and injustice, what to do?
Without courage or strength, remedy is to let peace abide.

Patience in absence of Your face isn't patience but poison:
poison from Your hand isn't poison, but sweetmeat inside.
That palate, mouth, lips and teeth of Yours are a delight,
let us see for whom they're prepared, for whom they hide.
Though You may shed my blood and of the whole world,
that we were the culprit... we still would have to all cried.
It is true that Sadi now needs to resign himself... because
whether he submits or not... Your will, his will over-ride.

This sight of Your face is the solution of all difficulties;
patience when You are absent is one of the possibilities.
The introduction of Your wonderful face, is the opening
page of the perfect beauty of all of Your natural abilities.
If Khizer saw Your lips, he certainly would've said they
were both edges of fountain of water of life's properties.
Place Your mouth to a jar of water... then take it away
and see: it will suddenly become a jar of candy to please.
I'm frightened that some day You may lay claim to work
miracles by magic of Your love-glances that lovers tease.
Poison that's coming from Your side to us is like honey:
inappropriate words from Your mouth to us, still please.
I think deeply about Your promise and my repentance of
Love: both of them are baseless is one of my discoveries.
In this city of ours we have never seen a face like Yours,
a face so blessed... that prayers are no longer necessities.
Direct at least one glance our way for alms are obligatory
from such wealth of beauty You are having in all degrees.

When the thirsty soul that is in the wilderness is parched
of what avail is it to him if the world is like a Euphrates?
Sadi is absolutely indifferent to annihilation, because the
renunciation of life is the lover's salvation and final ease.


A heart that's in love and still patient surely must be stone,
for between love and patience... is a million mile no-go zone.
Brothers of the spiritual path, don't give me advice because
in Love's path penitence is like the glass goblet and a stone.
I no longer have to secretly drink wine and do the dance, for
according to lovers' religion a good reputation is overblown.
What criticism can I listen to or what advice can I regard…
I, with eyes on winebringer… ears hearing only harp's moan.
To have something of Beloved we held east's breeze's skirt:
but, no, it was only the wind that into our grasp was blown.
Who'll bring a message to that One who left us so angrily?
Come back, if You wish to fight, shield down we've thrown.
Kill me if You want to… because without the sight of You
this wide world far too narrow for my existence has grown!
Reproaches will never wash away love from Sadi's heart…
blackness cannot leave a negro, it's the colour he does own!


I wish You'd veil Your moon-like face so You people won't see
like they see the sun from every terrace and every door daily!
It's no fault of strangers, for if You saw Your face in a mirror
Your heart would leave Your breast, quicker than 'immediately'.
For Shirin even to talk in Your presence makes one want to laugh,

for water of life flows from Your lips when You smile sweetly.
I cannot let my passionate sighs of love for You rise at dawn
for they may happen to be disturbing You sleeping so soundly.
There is no ornament existing that to Your beauty could add:
no one who dresses, adorns You, could better what she did see.
I have often been telling You not to show Your face to everyone
in case the eyes of each blind person looks at You, to try to see!
Once again I say, "No, not so… for only those who are gifted
with 'inner sight' can see Your physical body and spiritual reality."
I've to give access to a hundred enemies for Your sake: so I might
find a friend who'll give out some information about You to me.
To lose my head would not mean so much to me, my Darling,
as the blowing away of a single hair on Your head… a tragedy!
Sadi does not mind at all to be sitting in the dust of Your street:
but, he doesn't wish his own troubles crossing Your path to be!


There isn't a heart remaining for Your bat's curve, no such ball:
one, power to escape from Your playing-field has none at all.
Since Your hair that's dishevelled has appeared in our gathering,
I know of no peaceful person due to You not mad beyond recall.
I'm bewildered by You, the spiritual attributes that You have;
I marvel at one with any insight not astounded by You at all.
Tell me, is there a defect to be seen in Your beautiful face and
is there any charm that from Your fascinating face doesn't fall?
It is impossible to say that the Water of Life is in this world:
unless it is discovered in well of Your chin, it's nowhere at all!
You've come out from God as symbol of Mercy on His people:

is there any verse of Grace which about You one cannot recall?
If You possess patience or could be content while I am away,
by Your Union to bear separation from You I've no wherewithal.
How can You be complaining about the thorn that's in my foot?
What sympathy can You feel for pain that on You doesn't befall?
I'm afflicted with such anguish from longing to see Your face,
that the physician is baffled… any remedy for it he can't recall.
O You most desired place of worship, where are You… because
it's true there is no direction or limit to Your wilderness at all.
If You send me away what is the slave to do but obey Your order?
If You call me back there shouldn't be surprise You kindly call.
O Sadi, if in quest of dear Beloved you sacrifice precious life,
it'd be fitting if it belonged to Beloved… and not yours at all!

More pleasant than health is love's suffering…
more attractive than wealth, poverty's offering!
Wisdom's regarded as best of all created things:
much better intoxication the mystics are saying.
Egotism rises out of wealth and from position…
but far superior to oneself is oneself renouncing!
Since those heavily laden move with difficulty,
to be unencumbered and active is a better thing.
O Sadi, since land and sovereignty do not last,
more preferable is obedience for it can be lasting.

This is what I'm like, I can't be patient away from beauties:
one can do without rose or tulip but not rosy-faced lovelies!

It's not only myself who's seeking my lost heart in this city:
in quest of the cherished object of my desire are all of these.
I don't know a single soul here who isn't jealously in pursuit
of that angel-born lovely One, my Sweetheart if you please!
Camel driver... bring me news of that Beloved because I am
indifferent to enemies... slanderers, me they don't displease!
A true man should suffer cruelty and still remain grateful...
he shouldn't complain if lacking power to stay on his knees.
Good sir, do not be finding fault with Sadi if you are a man:
he is not a man who has no desire, for angel-faced beauties.


Beloved, last night far from You from love my soul was distraught,
eyes clouds poured onto cheeks from mad desire my heart wrought.
Due to my despair my power of reasoning was crushed by love,
in spite of all this anguish my mad heart the hope of sleep sought.
Separation from You beat plunder's drum around heart's citadel:
police patrol of Your love keeps life's house in turmoil, distraught!
Heart made Your name's image worship-point for life's adoration:
until morning it keeps face on that altar, praising You as it ought!
Quivering of my eyes told me that I'd see the Beloved's face...
but afterwards I discovered that only quicksilver they had caught.
To me Fate did represent the love of beauties as superfine honey,
but afterwards I discovered pure poison... that honey also brought.


O Sadi, this passage through Love's sea turns out to be difficult,
for in the beginning and at end your patience amounts to nought!

On the day of Union I couldn't bear to look upon You:
on the night of separation that I could not rest is true!
In my possession is power to be cutting off my head…
but I've no thought of with my Beloved being through.
The musician's been driven to despair on my account,
because I don't have any strength left to hear him too.
When hand of the helpless one doesn't reach Beloved,
nothing but to tear his clothes that one has left to do.
It's true that we're someone who's weak and miserable:
that no reason exists to set a trap for us… is also true!
It so happens that we have come across a king… a one
who hasn't an idea of loving his slaves as he should do.
You keep Your hands awash in the blood of Your lovers:
there is not a need for You to draw out Your sword too!
I said this to that One, "O You Garden of Spirituality!
To be seeing Your fruits isn't like tasting them! True?"
That One replied, "O Sadi, do not have such thoughts,
for my apple of silver is not for plucking… even by you!"

Do not ask, "In that One's hands how's heart going?"
Ask that One whose fingers into my blood is dripping.
And if I were to tell the tale of what use would it be…
are the healthy, condition of a wounded heart knowing?
They find fault with the wretched one… mad with love,
without ever at the beauty of the face of Layla looking.
Everyone has the image of some face inside his mind…
image of One who transcends all thought I am having.

One whose door You come out of will have a lucky day
for a fortunate omen is seeing Your face in the morning.
One to stop loving You, with well-balanced attributes
and lovely figure, an ill-balanced nature must be having.
Another may avoid love because of Your criticisms but
whatever You happen to say only increases my loving.
Has not the king proclaimed against drinking of wine?
Come... with Your sleepy eyes, lips with wine staining.
You might say Sadi's breast since the day You left him
has been like Oxus river's bank from all of his weeping.
Garden's cypress is low compared with Your symmetry:
Your face causes even market of the sun to dull sharply.
The sky's candle attended by the torches of a thousand
stars in Your presence only some dim lamp seems to be.
In the month of Sha'ban the people repent of their sins,
but see... in Ramadan their eyes from wine are drowsy.
In spite of all his strength, his courage and his bravery,
I know of not a man who from Your noose is an escapee!
This one out of all Your admirers is slain by Your sword,
that one of Your lovers... Your arrows wound grievously.
My eyes carry complaint against Beloved to my heart...
but eyes do not know it is also tied by Your love, tightly.
Tell that one to hold back his hand seeking from skirt of
the Beloved... one with control over his hands, directly.
That person is a beast and a sensualist whose heart isn't
attached to a Spiritual One... such as You happen to be.

Sugarcane be in the bitter mouth of one criticising Sadi:
one who isn't Love's joy feeling, tastes colcynth bitterly.

No journey seems long to the feet of one in quest of Beloved
because Beloved's victim is alive for all eternity! Enough said!
When one who has drunk wine of Truth does the mystic dance,
he'll tear even the skin off his back... even his clothes he'll shed!
One whose face is directed towards the face of our Beloved must
renounce even his own ego for that One's a quarrelsome Beloved.
Be careful not to despise a poor man's tears because successive
drops of rain become a river, when they are eventually combined.
The lover does not move, it is that One's noose that draws him:
what then is use of advice of advisers who foolishly have talked?
When you see one fallen in the playground's dust of that One,
ask that One who is the bat... who is the ball shouldn't be asked.
Devoted slaves don't ask why or when: even if You do everything
that's evil, it's alright for You to do it, for it must be good-hearted.
What straight cypress has any worth whatsoever in Your presence?
What scent has any fragrance if to dust of Your feet it's compared?
The philosopher said not to give my heart to beauties' love glances
as it is like a stone and a clay-pot: he by me would not be heard.
Though a thousand enemies should attack Sadi he swears by his
friendship for that One that he will talk forever of the Beloved.
He's told the circumstances of his condition with tears of blood:
don't only look at page one, the volume is many pages to be read.

Wine from hands of beauties is like a fountain of Paradise,
and it's lawful to make blood drop from wine-drinkers eyes.
I have no idea what the taste of the fresh date fruit is like...
I can only see that the fruit upon the date tree, waiting, lies.
Those charming finger-tips of that One have all been dyed
not with henna but blood from victims... after their demise!
O drivers of the caravan, take care you do not urge forward
that camel-litter because our tied feet don't allow us to rise.
Each night that Majnun slowly passes after being far away
from his Layla's loving face, is like a night without sunrise.
It's that One's noose that is dragging along the lover's feet:
he never asks how much further in that wilderness still lies.
That tattoo's not of indigo but it is made out of fascination:
that's not collyrium painted eyes... but witchery in disguise.
We travel like the ant, sometimes rising, sometimes falling,
and even though our path under the feet of an elephant lies.
Wherever the Beloved dances, if the lover does not sacrifice
his life for the Beloved, he is only a miser in Beloved's eyes.
Even if we render that One service, we are still ashamed...
even though that One does an evil, only goodness in it lies.
Other people may change their sweethearts and dear ones,
but that Beloved that is ours is a Perfect One in these eyes.
O Sadi, be singing of nothing but love, the song of love is
everything and other kinds of talk is nothing but stupid lies.

Who knows how long is separation's night until dawn of morning
except for that one who the prison house of love is confining.

I thought that to try to stop heart's ache I would go to the garden,
but is really a cypress there. Beloved's graceful form is resembling?
Who will carry our message to Beloved who severs love… to say
Beloved broke connection with me but to Beloved I'm still clinging?
To swear by Your soul is not in the etiquette of respect… I swear
by dust of Your feet, and that is a solemn oath that I am swearing.
In spite of the breaking of Your promise and stealing of my heart
my eyes for the blessed sight of Your form continue to be longing.
Come out, for Your street's carpeted with my face which is spread
beneath Your feet, instead of dust upon which You'd be walking.
Image of Your face has firmly planted hope's root in my heart:
agony of my love for You the foundation of patience is sapping.
The wonder is if one pictures Beloved's hair with a calm mind
under every single root of that hair, a distracted heart is lying!
If You were naked so that everyone could see Your whole form,
all would think a garment stuffed with roses You were wearing.
I am not the only one who has been ruined by this mad passion…
how many hands because of You to the Almighty they're raising?
Separation from Beloved in Your eyes can't be a blade of grass…
come, see on our hearts heavy like Mount Alwand* it is weighing.
Because of weakness, the power even to be sighing has left me…
I fear people may imagine Sadi is happy with Beloved's leaving.

* Note: Mount Alwand is a high mountain in Hamadan, Iran (Persia)
wherein a cave according to Firdausi in the 'Shahnama', Zahhak whom
Sadi compares himself with was imprisoned by Feridun. The smoke that
rose from the mountain was believed to be caused by Zahhak's sighs
which is alluded to in the above couplet. For a wonderful and complete

*literal translation see The Shahnama of Firdausi Trans. by A.G. Warner and E. Warner 8 vols. Kegan Paul, Trench, Trubner & Co Ltd. London 1910 etc. Available free online.*

At dawn of day when I open my eyes on the radiant glory,
knocker of Your love on door of service will be struck by me.
The slave wouldn't even deign to accept an empire's throne,
if he could attain riches gained by being Yours in beggary.
Since from behind veil You ravish hearts to such an extent,
what an uproar would arise if veil You threw off... suddenly!
Throw just a sideways glance at the ranks of Your lovers so
night of Path's Wayfarers turns to day by Your face's glory.
No subject will obey an order of a monarch if he does not in
submission conform himself to Your commands, completely!
People request at the door of Your glory reward for each act,
while we're only mentioning Your lack of love... constantly.
If at any time You banish me don't make me a slave in Hell,
tears of separation from You would put out its fires instantly.
O Sadi, the rule of humility and seclusion you won't observe
while piety and asceticism stay in your mind, unfortunately.

At early dawn breeze carried dust to garden from Beloved's street.
pure ambergris filled the garden from Beloved's fragrance, sweet.
If the Beloved would comply with our wishes it'd be a great favour,
and if not, then with Beloved's whim we will have to not compete!
If Beloved accepts me that One will cherish this slave, and if
one is driven off... that One's arm in combat one cannot meet.
That one whose mind is desiring the face of the Beloved has

to undergo much disorder like the Beloved's hair, nothing neat!
If others celebrating the *Id* Festival, break fast tomorrow they
see the new moon, but… we see Beloved's eyebrows, a real treat!
I don't wish any ill on my enemy, for that poor wretch it's enough
punishment to see the lover knee to knee with Beloved on a seat.
Every person even without knowing it is in the struggle of Love:
let us now all see to whose bat the ball of the Beloved will meet.
Everyone's heart is yearning for the pleasure-grounds or garden:
all go in one direction or the other: lover goes to Beloved to entreat.
If this garden and orchard people praise had at least a nightingale
like Sadi, or a rose like the Beloved's face, then it might compete.

Breath of dawn, morning smiles while for love I'm weeping,
what news are you now carrying, of the Beloved's coming?
I'm dissolving in tears at my state and from all your smiles:
you laugh, yet Beloved's smiling lips are you yet knowing?
O morning breeze, speak to that Sweetheart on my behalf,
for I've no one but you to whom that One will be listening.
Tell Beloved, "Don't hate friends so as to please strangers:
enemy's happy when friends in low esteem You're holding."
And say, "It'd be better if You, while staying partial to the
enemy, don't the interest of friends in Your sight be losing.
I'm not the kind of person that my enemy described to You:
You know enemy's heart, lover's condition is not knowing!"
No breeze, don't go and tell that One of my unhappy state,
for sorrow's dust on Beloved's happy heart may be settling.

To each his particular sorrow... but Sadi is always anxious
about this... what with his love for Beloved can he be doing?

We began loving and wisdom criticised us... it said
anyone falling in love can never feel safe... secured.
One who sits in private with a rosy-faced dear one,
from the street of criticism... has never yet escaped.
Love was prevailing... then the name of continence,
reputation and honour of pious hermits disappeared.
I don't understand how 'hundred petalled' rose such
a brilliant bloom dared, brave fir stood tall-statured!
In the garden when that smiling rose-bush sits down
the evergreen cypress doing penance... is one-legged.
Yesterday You sat by Sadi awhile against Your will,
the tumult subsided... when You left again it started.
Ever hear of one who urged on steed of love's agony...
behind which dust of regret didn't rise up like a cloud?

I complain because I am separated from the Beloved;
my laments stem from that beauty by me being loved.
In the absence of the moonlike face of that lovely One,
these cheeks of mine are stained from my crying blood.
Because of my separation from You... the blood of my
heart out from my eyes and onto my chest has flowed.
Not a single person is aware of this pain due to love of
mine: O no, for the instability of the world I've feared.
I'm tormented by the hand of Time, and it's because of

this, that my heart and my soul have been so wounded.
O Sadi, why are you complaining about the Beloved...
for 'neither pleasure nor pain are permanent'... it is said.

I can see no one who I can say is anything like Beloved;
in lovers eyes no image but the Beloved's can be formed.
One being with the intoxicated abandons respectability:
in Winehouse a good reputation, like river water is bled.
Only spiritual reality's possessor is inspired to dance by
Mystic's song: if one has kernel, shell will have dropped.
I am Your slave, place a crown upon my head or an axe;
that is only good, whatever to lovers is done by Beloved.
Reason was once reigning in the kingdom of my soul...
now it is in love with Your sweet lips, just like Farhad.
Search the ambergris-scented polo-sticks of those locks,
you'll find under each hair a heart like a ball, distracted.
O Sadi, however much you may praise Beloved's face...
light on rose's beauty is beyond the nightingale to shed.

Who is that smiling One... who is walking like an angel?
One who suddenly peace out from my mad heart did pull?
Breeze took to garden scent of rose of that One's Union...
glory of garden left, the perfumer's reputation it did annul.
People used to describe Joseph's face before they'd seen it,
but when they saw it... use of tongue was less than pitiful.
After this I will not criticise or fault the God-intoxicated,
for my repudiation of this class of souls was so wrongful!

It was not my intention to surrender heart to Your image:
by Your head... such thoughts I from my mind did annul.
What fault did this ant trying to tie belt of service commit
that it had to leave with head bruised like a snake, pitiful?
What need for one to become intoxicated in a winehouse?
On seeing You all reason leaves head of sober, the dutiful!
On going to pray he saw the prayer-arch of Your eyebrow:
heart lost control, he left wearing idolaters belt, worshipful!
To die in Your presence is better than if after my death they
say I couldn't take pain of Your cruelty: a lover not useful!
O Sadi, you're not worthy of rose of the garden of Union...
for you cannot lie upon thorns like those who are masterful.


I know of none in this city who isn't to Your love a captive:
there's no market that's as brisk as Yours from where I live.
Cypress is elegant but doesn't have elegance of Your form:
honey's sweet but it isn't as sweet as any speech You give.
Who is there on seeing You, doesn't fall in love with You?
One not Your purchaser must be broke... price prohibitive.
There is no one who having caught one glimpse of You...
does not bless and love You forever, You are so addictive!
He is no human being but a body with no soul, who when
asked if he has no love for You... answers in the negative.
You, who have drawn the sword of cruelty over our heads,
we've made peace... no idea of trying to take You captive.
Patience is bitter, but what can I do if I do not exercise it?
For without Your sweet honey-carrying lips I cannot live!

I have a head which I am ready to sacrifice at Your feet…
I'm ashamed of my poverty, to You it is unworthy to give.
I earnestly appeal to You by Your beauty not to withdraw
Your face from me because gazing at it is the reason I live.
Sadi, if you are not satisfied with your lot go your own way,
for the cult of this Love is no affair of yours to away give.

Who exists without the idea of Union with You in mind?
Who does not fix his gaze upon You? He must be blind!
It is not permissible for everyone to be seeing Your face…
it's forbidden to whoever's vision isn't pure, they will find.
It could be that no one else has this love that I possess…
because to that which I can see… others seem to be blind .
Every night's followed by day and each day dims to night:
night of separation from Beloved to end seems disinclined.
A one concerned about the flirtatiousness of beauties is a
weak lover, if to bear their cruelty he patience cannot find.
Examine me a little and You will discover that I have not
a single hair on my body that to praise You isn't inclined.
All know there's no remedy but patience for one mad with
a lost heart… but what to do when powerless is his mind?
Whoever sees the tips of Your dyed fingers will say this…
"If these daggers killed one, not strange this would I find!"
I'd thought that someday I'd tell You of my heart's love…
but how can I speak with tongue when I left heart behind?
It doesn't matter if I'm held in low esteem by the masses.
Don't be imagining that Your throwaway, help can't find.

Sadi's regard is directed to You in preference to the world:
attention he devotes to You isn't less than full in his mind.

Everyone's love except mine grows cold as time passes:
the same love I had at first is now more intense I stress.
If there's no access to Court of Your acceptance, where
can I go? So let me die on the threshold of Your service!
Will I be called on Judgement Day? I have Your Union
and separation… so death or resurrection, seem useless.
I've heard You pay attention to condition of the weak…
expecting Your visit my heart's happy, yet I'm feverish.
If You look at broken-hearted me with Your eye's corner,
I'd be as exalted as the Heavens, Jupiter in faithfulness!
If I can see You, how to  get courage and strength to go?
To stay away from You where's my patience, hardiness?
Some day You will surely see me fall victim to Your love,
holding slayer's skirt with desire's hands… nevertheless.
If the bier of Sadi were carried to the street of Beloved…
how honoured a life, what martyr's death, what success!

My affairs are disordered like Beloved's long, curling hair…
my back curved like Sweetheart's eyebrow beyond compare!
Sorrow drunk a draught of my heart's blood and then said…
"To the health of anyone happy… in such pain and despair."
Is it only my heart that has been plunged in all this sorrow,
or is it really that in this age a happy heart's becoming rare?

Just as my heart does full justice to every sorrow and so the
realm of the world's kingdom of love... is only for that Heir!
Do You know what my eyes image of Your face said to me?
"Please, where's that One who's your companion? Where?"
If you wish to know my condition as clear as daylight, then
ask the dark night for that is also my companion... I swear!
If only it was, that between me and my Sweetheart there is
such a bond as exists with me and sorrow... ah, what a pair!

O Beloved, don't hear I've another Beloved other than You,
 or that other than thinking of You day and night I ever do!
Not only I have fallen into snare of Your long, curling hair,
for... that there is a captive in each curl of Your hair is true!
If I should say that I wasn't with You in any way involved,
the whole house would bear witness, to my affair with You.
 Who finds fault with and criticises me because of this love
won't believe me until seeing You then will declare it's true!
What can I do but patiently endure cruelty of the guardian?
All know the thorn is companion to the rose... it is not new.
It's not only I who's in love with You, I... full of vain desire:
there are many others on fire like me as part of Your retinue.
The wind was carrying some dust from Your home, and put
to shame each scent on every perfumers tray: yes, it did too!
What can I pour at Your feet You may find to be agreeable?
 This life and this soul can't be said to possess much value!
 Someday I'll throw off this patched cloak so all may know
there is an infidel idolater's sacred thread hidden from view.

Sadi's love isn't a story that can be concealed for too long...
it is a tale that in every market is passed on all day through!

Come to me; for I have to talk with You about something...
have I committed some sin, perhaps some fault I'm having?
Is it really right for You to be captivating countless hearts?
Stop doing it, the peoples retribution You will be suffering!
The rich would never be held to blame if they only took the
time to be seeing that in their street someone was begging.
Though much of my time passed to satisfaction of enemies,
I have never heard from my Friend of real intimacy existing.
There is no one left who has any pity on my suffering... and
there's no one saying there's a cure, except for You arriving.
If You should disturb my heart, even for a thousand times...
on my part, I can only keep on trying to be sincere... loving.
My brain is consumed with smoke of the fire of madness...
and yet the vain belief that an elixir exists I am still having.
We've not attained our desire and our life's up to our gullet:
but even if it reached my palate I'd not hope be abandoning.
I swear by the Beloved's soul that Sadi believes there is no
place in the wide world except Beloved's street to be going!

Don't ever imagine that our objective attained can be
without bitterness from Your lips... speaking sweetly.
Separation can often be happening amongst friends...
just as in business both the profit and loss can also be.
If you see someone who's fallen victim to the Beloved,

to Beloved's other lovers… send glad tidings from me.
In Your beauty's empire I do not know of anyone who
hasn't lost his heart unless of spirituality devoid is he.
The corner of Your eyes that are charming are giving…
one could easily say, a sign… to be finally killing me!
If on the day of plunder that sweet-meat falls to the lot
of a seeker, then that one no longer fearing God will be.
I'm still constantly surprised at the hearts of the lovers,
that such heat doesn't burn up their clothes completely!
Beloved's beauty has so thrown into the shade all else,
that Sadi has become invisible because of his obscurity.


Your fascinating movements are symmetrical, harmonious:
but the words that You say are so inconsiderate to all of us.
As patience is impossible I've to put up with Your cruelty…
that one is no real man who due to Your criticism is furious.
If You're my enemy I'll never leave the range of Your arrow:
if You inundate me I'll not avoid flood, however impetuous.
You are beyond my imagination, beyond field of conception:
I'm bewildered by such grace, elegance, beauty so fabulous!
If Fortune should raise me up to the throne of sovereignty…
it'd be worth less than to be serving You a lifetime… for us.
It would be surprising if anyone stayed saintly in this city…
unless not seeing Your face, turning all from being religious.
You don't know what happens outside because of such love:
come out or we will set fire to the curtain: now, listen to us!
O You tree so fair, You've become totally hidden by fruit…

what to do… hands are short, Your apples high, numerous?
You have never sat in expectancy for a single night, so how
can You know impatience of Your lover, waiting… anxious?
O night of separation… O what a long, long night you are!
End, for Sadi's soul is crazed by the terror you inspire in us!

There's a mysterious bond that exists between You and me:
otherwise there are many beautiful faces in the world to see.
I have a body that is melting away because of loving You…
my body has disappeared, but my love for You stays in me!
Do not imagine that this madness of loving You will leave
my mind for as long as bones are still remaining in my body.
If You sat by me, You would cause my heart to be at ease…
when You are away, the impression of You stays inside me.
The details of Your beauty are beyond the power of words…
yet as long as I've a tongue I'll try to describe them exactly.
I don't know if that One's a shapely figure or is Doomsday.
Who can, that such a cypress is existing, ever asserting be?
It could be easily said that You're resembling the moon but
I do not think the moon has a mouth that smiles so sweetly.
I won't die except in Your presence… if there is not a pillow
there is still Your door's threshold to pass away on, for me.
Go Your way O Sadi, for the street of Union with Beloved
is not a market in which one's life has any value, obviously!

That person cannot be said to be having a heart,
who doesn't surrender it to that face, for a start!

That One's neither a sweetheart one can talk to
nor enemy from whose noose one away can dart.
I said to my heart, "Avoid the eyes of that One,
for the sober doesn't go near drunkard, if smart!"
Don't you see the tips of that One's dyed fingers
that twist then tear the hands of patience apart?
One cannot sit with that One with an easy mind,
nor rise from beside that One with a peaceful heart.
If some smoke is rising then there has to be a fire...
and if blood flows a victim dying has to play a part.
Can I sleep when I see that One is before my eyes?
Door in the face of friends must be open, left apart.
Harvest of Your helpless ones shouldn't be burned:
hearts of Your poor ones not left wounded, to smart!
You can never sever affection when the end comes...
You shouldn't have tied them so tightly at the start.
O Sadi, your heart has now gone far beyond control,
an arrow can't return to the thumb after it did depart.

Not only on earth do You not have any equal…
the moon can't compare with Your face when full.
I'll not give my heart to the stature of the cypress
for compared to Your attractive figure, it's pitiful!
You who are in possession of bow-like eyebrows,
all in the city are victims, when arrows You pull!
No one else is able to steal the hearts of mankind
for all hearts are captured… You are so powerful!

If You should choose Your own peer... what to do,
for me in this world... You are the most Masterful.
It has become clear to me now that Your iron-like
heart isn't worthy of Your breast, silken-soft, full.
The name of Sadi that has been forgotten by You,
praises of its gallantry in the world... are plentiful!

That one, around whom its noose Love has thrown...
to the wishes of it he must conform, away or at home.
That one who is not a lover... is not yet really a man:
silver does not become pure until fire it has undergone.
No devotee ever enters the street of Love without first
sacrificing this world here and the next hereafter: gone!
I am so absorbed in praising that One that I'm totally
lost to all thoughts of myself... all is that One, alone!
Just as I do always, I'm offering many thanks to Love:
although torturing the heart, it made soul feel at home.
O Sadi, there's nothing that is better than your poetry:
it is the precious gift of this age, to seekers of the One.
Praise be to this sweet tongue you have which through
the whole world causes furore, though it's home-grown.

A human being who is an adult not everyone can be called...
for Love is one thing, self-love another: a love that's stalled.
It is not every eye that is seen to be black and white or that
can see black from white... that a real 'seeing eye' is named.
Tell all of those who cannot endure the pain of love's flame

not to go near it… a moth's 'bane' its 'wing' could be called.
If I complained about Beloved then my love is not sincere…
one can't really know Beloved, who himself is still recalled.
If one in human form controls carnal wants he becomes one
with a human nature, otherwise a 'beast' that one is called.
What does it matter if a drink from hands of the Beloved is
bitter or sweet? Give, Beloved, soul-thirsty can't be stalled!
My love for Your lips stops comprehension of Your words…
the more bitter You speak, the sweeter the words are heard.
If You strike me with Your sword I'll bear You no enmity…
I'm an enemy of all interfering between me and Your sword.
In all my life I'll never be free because the shackles You tied
on my feet are like a crown You have placed upon my head.
Sadi's hand will not let go of Beloved's skirt due to cruelty:
one can't give up pearls because of dangers on the sea's bed.

Whoever sees the Beloved loses his peace of mind…
he who enters love's snare, again release won't find.
When You talked to me I fell in love, was love-sick:
then You threw off Your veil… our life we resigned.
Moon is not out in day: what is shone into houses?
Cypress is not on terrace: what strolling did I find?
Love's rays lit torch and consumed adepts' harvest…
monastery's novices from it to all else became blind.
Quiet mystic had no power to stay behind patience's
wall: his sense of shame and goodness he left behind.
If during my life's time I pass a moment with You…

life's purpose is attained, for more life I'm disinclined.
One not initiated into love nor tortured by separation,
leaves the world a novice when life's end he does find.
We shall go walking on our heads in quest of Beloved:
one who is walking on his feet might as well be blind!
Sadi's aspirations never was to be inclined to Love...
his foot sank deep in Love, so wisdom you won't find.

Each morning the rose's fragrance drifts from Your garden:
pleasing songs like nightingale's from Your lovers happen.
Khizer saw those life-giving, heart-entrancing lips, he said:
"Out of Your mouth flows the Water of Life's Fountain!"
Joseph belted his waist in service to You, being convinced
that the empire of beauty was now Yours... there and then.
One who has heard of the qualities of the fount of Kauther,
knows it's a mere trace of Your invisible mouth when open.
It's not every heart-ravishing beauty who's appeared to me
that found the way to my heart, for Your abode lies within.
Through envy of the sun of Your beauty every month I can
see moon in the heavens looking like Your eyebrows again.
A soul-refreshing breeze from breath of dawn is one might
say from Your ambergris-scattering hair, that You loosen.
I'd rip open a hundred garments from joyfulness if I could
only see Your hand, like a belt around my waist... tighten.
It has been said You're the One entertaining Your lovers:
Sadi claims such hospitality, a kiss on his lips let happen!

Is there some sugar here that so many flies are around;
or, is it some rarity that so many people can be found?
We've put in so much effort in our searching for You:
no asking of us nobodies that seeking You did abound.
Caravan leader, why go in such hot, desperate haste?
Slower... many a straggler is on mountain and around!
Hundred torches are to be kindled from only one lamp,
Your Light... others with borrowed light can be found.
My heart and tongue are devoted to Your friendship...
while those all speak with You... they only confound!
It's as clear as dawn that they who get no rest at night
from thinking of You, as passionate lovers can be found.
One can swear that those who feel no desire for such a
face... in stupidity and vileness they obviously abound!
Are You aware of cruelty... at hands of Your guardian?
It's a pity parrot and crow as cage-mates can be found!
It's not my fortune to be near You... I invoke blessings
from afar. O... if only personally them I could expound!

Lord of Eternal Faith, in that one's auspicious fortune be rejoicing:
in that one's well-established throne all happiness be abounding;
the Protector of the Age and the Defender of the faithful ones...
the Chosen of God, the religion of Mohammed who is upholding!
You, who are the ruler of the Empire of Solomon and the sovereign,
Muhammad the Atabeg,* who always justice is evenly dispensing!
Down from Abu Bakr and up to Sa'd Zangi... all of your ancestors
every generation after every generation great fame were knowing.

Every renowned and every exalted human being has been bound
by the obligations of your favours that in the past you we giving!
Every person that was famous upon the sea and at all frontiers,
upon the ground at the dust of your feet bow their heads, praising!
O you king of much wisdom, O you asylum of all of your subjects,
may you always be distinguished by God Who you is aiding!
Please be listening closely to an old saying coming from Sadi…
"May your fortune stay young, your dignity in glory be remaining!'
The revolution of Time, for as long as it has ever lasted… has
not been accustomed to be preserving mankind, as one is knowing.
The kingdom of the world is never everlasting… it is therefore
not fitting to place reliance on it or any authority of it be trusting.
Be ruling with justice your empire, do the same with your life…
so eternally in the world your good name and fame be remaining.

*Note: This ghazal is in praise of the reigning sovereign of Fars, of which
Shiraz was the capital. It was written between 1260 and 1262 A.D. Two
Atabegs named Muhammad, father and son reigned in succession. See
Introduction for further explanation.*

The breeze blew and carried with it fragrance of ambergris:
almond tree was bursting into blossom, a metamorphosis!
From being distracted by nightingale the rosebranch raised
its head in spite of all those thorns, what a wonder is this!
The blessed foot of that blessed messenger who is bringing
message from Beloved… let me drop to my knees and kiss!
We consigned to that one's care our letter and that courier
brought back to us a fragrant pod of musk… ah bliss, bliss!

We have never heard of a mother that has ever given birth
to a child as beautiful as You… I say this, with emphasis.
Any female child that may be born in Your time should be
buried alive, as beauty such as You have is the antithesis!
That one who has passed a day until the afternoon prayers
in separation from You, in all truth… totally miserable is!
Sadi, every drop that like an oyster your enlightened heart
has imbibed turned into a pearl… another metamorphosis!
The sweet products of the faculty of your poetic genius…
creates upheaval amongst those critics with their analysis!

Others are like a picture on a wall compared to Your face,
they do not have such a physical form, spirituality, grace.
Since I saw Your rose-like face other roses are only thorns:
since choosing You as friend all are strangers, out of place.
As to the Night of Power that is said to happen but once
in one's life, it's the night when Beloved one does embrace.
It would be a shame if people were to take hold of the skirt
of faithfulness and the collar of hope… then both misplace.
It is not only I who is wounded by Your henna-dyed hand,
many victims by sword of Your love go… without a trace!
I'm astounded at Your eyes enjoying sleep night until day,
while from loving You being awake is now commonplace!
It is a wonderful thing and a perplexing problem because
neither can stay concealed, nor can it be told face to face.
God knows that nothing's left of my body but a shadow;
no, even that itself is a imaginary thing, a piece of space!

Since rose of spiritual reality blossomed in mind's garden,
nightingales, like heron, are silent when hearing my case.
Sadi cannot estimate how sweet of speech You are, for in
the garden of Your nature all birds speak with such grace!

Although the world is against you... stay with the Friend,
that One's a balm: on a sting from others you can depend!
You of such a form, this Age's beauties tuck feet of shame
under their skirts as though magic spell they must defend.
If one morning You moved gracefully in garden, You'd see
the cypress is uprooted from near where stream does wend.
  Cruelty of beauties is bitter to certain people... listen to
this faithful slave say, "They give sweetness, without end!"
O pious one, if you are a devotee, go and shut your eyes for
they are appointed to steal hearts... of all men and women.
  Do one of two things: deliberately put on Your veil or else
be prepared to discover Your secret revealed now and then.
You are welcome in my life, but my poor heart is the casket
with Your secret and I don't wish to have it smashed open.
You could say... "Who sees the beauty of the Beloved as it
really is... unless from the point of view of Sadi it is seen?"

Strike the tent and allow the camel-litter to be moving on,
for your fellow-travellers to other world have already gone.
Your wife and your child and relation, friend and kinsman
are all adopted brethren... of the caravan you travel upon.
Don't go and be fixing your heart upon any companion for

you will be left without them when they are all passing on.
Mortals were only dust in the beginning... and if you think
deeply you'll come to the answer: they'll be the same anon.
So it is better that they should meditate on their beginning
and their end... and appreciate their own value, thereupon.
The earth has swallowed up so many people... and yet so
many are still puffed up with pride... they brag on and on.
There was a certain person who was standing over a tomb,
"These were kings of the world," he cried in lamentation.
I replied to him, "Tear up a coffin from the grave and see
whether they were really kings... or were watchmen, son!"
He answered, "What need is there to dig up the coffin for
I know they're only a handful of bones that rot on and on!"
Advice is a medicine that is bitter... so it must be poured
down your throat just like you a purgative had undergone.
Such a bitter drug as Syrian scammony, mixed with sugar,
is to be got from Sadi's dispensary, that you can rely upon.

It is only the right thing that the rich folk who are living
close to a beggar's house, sometimes of him are thinking.
O You, rich in beauty, You're indifferent to the distress
of the poor... whether they are hurt or heart is suffering!
What do You care if one is in despair from love for You?
The more You kill Your lovers... the more are appearing!
Don't drive me from You because I seem to be a stranger,
'faithful friends are preferable to relations' is the saying.
I'm slave of the generousness of pure-minded reprobates,

who by friendship with You enemies of self are becoming.
Of course such lips that are sweet give a bitter answer...
because as they possess honey, stings they're also giving!
O Sadi... have you not seen true lovers, who with sword
hanging over their heads, their lives as slaves are offering!
They are not like you and me, needy, wanting, helpless...
they have abandoned both worlds... self away are giving!

Trees sprout their buds and nightingales are in rapture of happiness:
the world's become fresh and lovers happily sit in rapt togetherness.
Companion of our gathering is always the stealer of our hearts,
and especially when that One is decked out in such a fine dress.
Those who used to break harp and flute in the Ramadan month
will break vows of penitence when rose's breath their noses caress.
The carpet of greenness has become trodden with the feet of delight
as the Master and devotee join in the dance in a display of oneness.
Those two friends appreciate the value of the time of friendship
who, after parting from each other for a while, re-unite nevertheless.
Not a soul goes out sober from monastery who will declare before
police inspector that these Mystics are overcome by drunkenness.
There's a rosebush in middle of our house that compared to it...
looking small are all the trees of the garden, including the cypress!
Even if everyone in the world is hostile to me, I swear by the
fortune of Beloved, I'm not even aware of all of their existences.
Condition of Love's victim is like travellers on the sea who can
only save their lives by sacrificing goods and chattels... no less!
Someone said this to the cypress: "You do not bear any fruit!"

It replied that, "The spiritually free always only poverty possess!"
O Sadi, many who didn't know way to destination of the mad,
have been travelling along the way via road of wisdom, I guess!

The world is not of such value that people should envy it,
or be concerned in vain of existence or not of it: not a bit!
It'd be right to say that all those who don't pay any heed
to this dust-heap have spiritual insight… this, I submit.
Mystics buy not at any price whatever is not permanent,
even if it's the world's kingdom and everything that's in it.
Don't approve of oppression, don't be guilty of arrogance:
God has many creatures like you that in His Kingdom fit.
This is an abode that truly will always keep on changing:
happy those who their hearts to another home do commit.
Have you ever heard of anyone that the world befriended?
The truth is clear, but some without insight cannot see it!
O you who are on Earth's crust, all Time isn't only yours:
others are in mothers' wombs and fathers' loins… to emit.
The treacherous wolf carried off a sheep from the flock…
and while he did the other sheep in bewilderment did sit.
That one who through pride never set foot on the ground
were dust in the end… now people walk over him and spit.
If only people properly appreciated the value of a breath…
so that they of moments left to them make the most of it.
O Sadi, a man who has a good reputation will never die:
that one is truly dead whose name into 'good' does not fit.

The travellers along the Spiritual Path take no notice of affliction:
those who are captives of love don't flee because of a cruel action.
Upon whom can those who are hopeful of favours be clinging…
if from Beloved's skirt the hand of their quest suffers amputation?
Please  veil Your face, or else it will become impossible for the
followers of Divine Knowledge to on You not plant their vision.
Put on the cloak of the Sufi and bring the cup of wine here because
not harmonising together are a good reputation and intoxication.
Gain the approval of the Beloved and be leaving all others alone:
if they raised a thousand outcries it matters not even one fraction.
I am content… even if the world should rise in hatred against me,
for I have made peace with You who are the object of my attention.
If Sadi should perish by the sword of separation… then the blood
that those beauties are shedding, is really lawful in any situation.
Our rule of life is to lay head of impotence on resignation's threshold:
if people are upset with You, impatience with You is their condition.

You wise boy, the day is rising high and the sun is
now so warm, so fix up the awning, please do this.
Infant grass drunk milk, let the young shoot grow:
spring cloud wept, let the meadow smile with bliss.
Please tell, why should he, who has following him
a figure of a lofty cypress, walk in garden like this?
Wisdom said it is unlawful to tell heart's secrets…
but Love's strong arm pulling up patience's root is!
Heart seeking the desert is indifferent to the road:
one who drained the wine goblet… no hearing is his.

Victim of Love's sword doesn't tell of his condition:
one thirsty for Your face asks not how long road is.
Many are the unpleasant criticisms he must endure,
one desiring a rose like You to look at, to be in bliss.
Honey in presence of enemies wouldn't be agreeable
while the sting inflicted by a friend never harmful is.
One whose head is in the noose is on death's brink:
one holding noose in hand... paying no attention is.
Sadi, if wise, Love is not the path for you to travel:
one can't resist hand of Beloved; impossible this is!

The thought of this auspicious face that people see
as a good omen, kept before eyes... remembered be.
In the whole world no one can ever see another face
unless in a mirror held up before that One's beauty.
Love people have for that One's tiny mole is so great
it'd be amazing if a heart's bird from snare was free.
At feet of that Darling it's right to lose one's head...
a Darling who for Union with, not any hope can be!
It's likely wings and pinions of a bird will be clipped
when it falls into trap, so it can't fly to another tree.
Love for Layla isn't within power of every mad lover,
only those who are attracted by that One's coquetry.
Your love is forbidden to us for Your lovely eyes are
shedding blood of Your lovers and think it lawful be!
How happy is the time of Union, opportunity of joy:
how pleasant is pain that one can tell Beloved finally.

You can't know Sadi's state... not feeling love's pain:
one is aware of his state's circumstances constantly.

Beloved, don't be so impulsive, of spiritual insight are we:
strangers as well as relations are looking at You longingly.
There is not any one who does not in secret, desire You...
I also am doing that which all others are doing, obviously!
The people of spiritual insight are those who look on Your
face with love... all the others are blind, they cannot see!
Some are concerned about religion, others... the mundane;
but concern for other than love for Your face... is baloney!
Winebringer, hand that winehouse winecup to the dervish,
for all of those who have died, now clay for the potter be!
The eye that has not seen Your beauty, what has it seen?
For such ones to pass their time in indifference, a tragedy!
Where do You intend to go and for who are You concerned?
There's a crowd of lovers on each side waiting expectantly.
All of those who aren't beginning to dance on seeing You,
tear garments behind Your back... when You leave finally!
Sadi can't be giving up his love on account of any cruelty:
if You drive us away... at Your door we will sit patiently.

Musician of the gathering, a chant on the harp be striking up!
Attendant of the palace, censer of aloes-wood be kindling up!
The Lot of Grace has turned up and also the Sign of Mercy:
by good fortune, through the door the Beloved is walking up.
Beloved can't be exchanged for the Here and the Hereafter:

Joseph's company is worth more than any treasure turning up.
O how pleasant are cruelty and harshness at Beloved's hands!
Like that done by Ayaz* to Mahmud's heart, never letting up!
It's a day of flowers and the time of spring, how can You sleep?
Get up… so that our skirts with desire, we may be filling up!
The garden is now adorned like the court of Solomon's time:
the bird of dawn, songs as sweet as David's… is singing up.
The reciter of enlightened mind, has scattered threaded pearls
of Sadi's poetry… in king's convivial assembly, he's talking up.
This sovereign of the kingdom of Persia… the mighty Atabeg
Sa'd Abu Nasr Sa'd Zangi*… the beloved. So, be standing up!

*Notes: Ayaz was Sultan Mahmud of Ghazni's favourite slave… and his beloved. Atabeg Sa'd Abu Nasr (Abu Bakr) reigned over Fars whose capital was Shiraz from 1226-1260 and was Sadi's chief patron and it was to him that he dedicated his Gulistan (Rosegarden) completed in 1258. See Introduction.

The nobility of a man consists in generosity and also in devotion:
for those with neither, non-being's better than being… by a million.
O you engrossed in luxury… do not let the world deceive you…
the possibility of permanence in this hotel is out of the question.
And… O you who are distressed by poverty and misery be patient,
for these limited days of life will come to an end… this, I mention.
Tread gently upon the dust of the road over which you are passing,
for it consists of eyes and eyelids and cheeks and form's creation.
It is this same fountain of the sun that illuminates the world
that the homes of tribes of Ad* and Samad* used to shine on.

Don't you see that the pleasant earth of Egypt is just the same
as before, only that it now over Pharaoh and his army lies upon?
The world has not so much of value that men should envy it…
for, brother, neither envious or envied will survive Armageddon.
If you stretch out a begging hand at all, then raise it to a God
Who is beneficent, merciful, forgiving, loving… and on and on.
Earth to the Pleiades… all, through humble devotion to Him,
all… are engaged in praising and in praying and in supplication!
His beneficence is never-ending and His favours are limitless…
no beggar leaves His door without gaining objective's completion.
If you have a firm belief in the Day of Reckoning, do not depreciate
your value by any so-called amusements and acts that are wanton.
No one can profit by the counsel of Sadi, which is the key to the
treasure-house of faith, except the one who is favoured by Fortune.

*Note: Two pre-Islamic Arab tribes. (Koran vlll, 63; xl, 52).*

Under the brand and agony my friends at my patience wonder,
but a brand and pain at Your hands than garden of roses is better.
If You should consign to Hell Your lovers whose poor hearts are
scorched with Your love's brand, they would its fire, cold consider.
You're the Dictator, whether You deal fairly with us or are unjust;
we're Your slaves, whether You seek peace with us or war: whatever.
Wisdom has no power of resistance against love of rare beauties;
if you engage in love, of the carpet of a good reputation be a folder.
If you don't possess the courage of men, stay at home like women,
if you go into battlefield, don't turn away from the arrow-shower.

Don't attribute to lust the cries of learners of the mystical dance;
you know the brave don't cry before of wound they are the sustainer.
Not one of the companions of my crowd sympathised with me…
I see only for me the candle of tears on its pale face being a shedder.
Despite all the complaints I make against the winter of separation,
if the spring of Union should come, 'Of rose… no cold comes after'.
Tell that one who is tortured by heartache like Sadi not to complain,
for the remedy is suffering… when the Beloved of one is the doctor.
All my critics have been telling tales about me to the Beloved:
I continue to declare in public, what they in secret have said.
People have stated before that I'm mad from my love for You…
if they'd have said I was calm only nonsense they'd have talked.
They did not veil any of my faults nor did they cloak my sins…
what's a beggar's offence that they to King should have reported?
Tell me, what bird am I they should carry my story to the Phoenix,
what ant am I that they my tale to Solomon should have related?
People displayed hostility towards me, but it was really good-will,
because they… about my suffering, to its remedy have mentioned.
The story of the passion of Zuleikah was passed on to Joseph…
and to Doorkeeper of Paradise was told how Adam was distracted.
They don't see my hidden wound nor my love that is sealed away,
they have only whatever they have seen on the surface stated.
And if they didn't mention it, there wasn't any need to do so…
my tears and face's colour the tale of my love would have declared.
They've already made a statement that You are loved by Sadi…
it is true that I love You, but even more… than they have said.

Worldly lovers love physically, Mystics know spiritual ecstasy:
let this saying sink into the heart for it in all sincerity is uttered.

The bushes of rose have now decked themselves out…
this has thrown all nightingales into an ecstatic shout.
The reckless winebringers circulating the goblet have
deprived of their senses the wine-drinkers lying about.
We drained only a draught and we've lost all control:
say, what drug's been added to wine to give it clout?
By a single drink we've become lost of all our senses:
how can others possibly… have such a drinking bout?
The initiated ones have caught fire and have burned,
while uninitiated are cold, unmoved as ever, no doubt.
Carry out the tent for the carpet-layers of the breeze
spread carpet of brocade on flowerbeds and all about.
What is life? To be dying in the presence of Beloved!
This crowd of 'living-beings'… hearts of life, without.
Since the world came into existence… rose gatherers
are tormented by armed ranks of thorns… turned out!
People are regarding lovers, as being killed by love…
from Sadi learn they save their lives: without doubt!

For such Ones to go to the pleasure-grounds is not right…
to be friendly with all, to go here, there, both day and night.
It might indeed be right for them to go to those grounds…
but if they should go there without us is certainly not right.

They should not go out and then rob people of their hearts
when they decide that they will go alone and cause a fright.
No one would think it is fair for the gardeners of the rose...
to be made angry by the nightingale's every morning plight.
The complaints made against Love are completely unjust...
when these bold-eyed beauties set out to plunder, outright!
All other cypress trees that follow in the train of that One
should all be bending low before that One's graceful might.
There are many sensible people who enter the street of love
sane... like myself, and then finally leave it mad, one night!
And if all those Ones should be ascending to the Pleiades,
we will be making a ladder to heaven, to climb out of sight.
It is not only Sadi who has drunk deeply in this deep pit...
not one who travels upon this Sea is immune to this plight.

Not all living creatures possess attributes of humanity:
many humans in the world are only pictures in a gallery.
When gilded base-silver's put in the crucible it turns out
to be different, from that which people imagine it to be.
All those people who in the opinion of the wise possess
transcendent merit are in Your eyes valueless, phoney!
Who can be understanding the tongue of circumstance?
The silent of the grave converse with tongues of many,
saying, "Beware! Do not walk arrogantly or proudly on
the earth... there are many that like you in the dust be!"
This passing period of power's really worthless because
passing away is everything... leaving it all to posterity.

They've passed their lives in slumber of luxury and lust:
now that they sleep under the ground it all they can see!
No one will pay attention to excuses now put forward,
for how can seed come to ear... that is sown so recently?
A thousand precious lives be sacrificed for those men of
spiritual insight who count as nil, wealth of the worldly.
Do not take hope from this world… head full of lust and
ambition is not satisfied… until with dust stuffed fully!
I will not be invoking curses upon evil-doers for the poor
wretches are caught in any act their own voices decree!
O Sadi, I swear by life of heart full of life that it is not
worth a kingdom existing to oppress a soul, purposely.

Just above the hills the sun is now rising:
with fingers on door a beauty is knocking.
With bow-like eyebrows that each moment
strike fresh prey... arrows glances piercing!
It's that One's hand, arm that kills dervish:
never think a dagger him down is knocking.
Jasmine-scented One whose graceful form
at the high stature of the juniper is mocking.
My face, eyes are so in love, that the latter
sheds pearls... former gold coins is striking!
Those sallow of face are not fearing the bee,
they take honey while them it keeps stinging.
It's not right to shut door in the lover's face:
You shut it, his head on door he is knocking.

O Sadi, in the future be using a pen of steel
for your poetry any reed pen will set blazing!


That sweetly smiling One, whose mouth is full of honey,
holds the hearts of all in the world and not my heart only.
Who in his house has a cypress-statured One like You…
has no need to be interested in orchard's trees, obviously.
Infidels, what profit are you getting from a lifeless idol?
At least worship Idol with a soul… worthwhile idolatry!
Those arched eyebrows are like a bow… figure an arrow:
another one with such a bow and arrow one never did see.
Reason to believe You've a mouth is it sometimes speaks,
or one wouldn't think You had one and neither would we!
Proof that You've a waist is that it is sometimes girdled,
or one would never think that You had a waist, obviously.
If You wished to speak bitterly to one, it would not seem
bitter… since from that casket of pearls it's spoken softly.
O you who told me not to follow after one thirsting for my
blood, say it to one who can't control his feelings properly.
Whoever bears on his face the mark of the brand of Love,
can't get rid of it, until he finally under the earth shall be!
O Sadi, you can't be taking your boat out of the whirlpool
for it is a well-known fact that… Love, is a shoreless sea.


Who's that with that walk that's robbed heart of patience?
Turk from Khorasan plundering Persia? That makes sense.

Shiraz is fragrant from musk like Khutan's muskdeer's pod,
due to that One's hair... if the spring breeze sent it hence.
If I held a fox robe a moment without that One's body...
it would seem it pricked like a porcupine, giving me offence.
I'll keep watch tonight until morning instead of the guard:
Your sleep-stained eyes rob mine, sleep I can't commence.
I've often thought that I'd not attach my heart to anyone,
but face of such beauties deprives the sage of self-defence.
You robbed me of heart, I gave in. If You kill me... I wait.
Pagan knows no better: kill or plunder... what difference?
Mornings, You put promises of love in my ear like putting
on ear-rings: nights, trample them like hair. Such violence!
You have no need for such violence in order to trap a heart:
I am in Your noose, take me, I'm here not due to accidents.
Whoever offers advice Your beauty's reign will throw into
a new frenzy all who by Your love lost their commonsense.
To describe You is beyond one. You're a sea of sweetness!
Sadi, with audacity to describe You, brings pearls... hence.


Your image is a fresh picture, when exhibited in a different
place, it day by day more charming to our eyes is apparent.
Do you understand what Love is? It's King... sovereignty
on whom, wherever, is established when it pitches its tent.
To others, taste of Love's cruelty may seem bitter: we drink
it from Beloved's hands... it tastes like sweet nourishment.
Give away love of life, take the loving Friend to your heart
if in view of your worth, such good fortune to you is meant.

I never held in my mind any thoughts of Love, but even an
elephant's subdued if he falls into that net's entanglement.
Every moment I enjoy countless delights in this fire which
you can see… for although it burns my heart, it is brilliant.
Don't imagine that my heart's happy with another person:
outwardly I am with others, but thoughts inside are spent.
My jealous spirit warns me not to tell my secret to friends,
but I observe that its record throughout this world is sent.
The tears of yearning flow from Sadi's eyes onto the page,
so when poetry's composed the words become wet I invent.
Acceptable speech proceeds from an anguished heart… for
when aloes are burned, the world from it becomes fragrant.

I'm hopeful my business will be accomplished successfully:
when Union's attained separation comes to an end, surely.
I can never get my fill of You, although You should frown,
an answer that's bitter from one sweet, is like sugar to me.
O Friend, cast Your shadow over my head despite my foe,
because a mole is never desiring the sun rising he will see.
Fortune that's not in tune has now robbed me of that rose:
I'm hopeful the thorn also will come out of my foot shortly.
If I should die this love and longing would keep on going…
though nightingale die the rose bush still blooming will be!
Because the image of Your face appeared before these eyes,
my shadow of a form was only to be seen… with difficulty.
We've cast a thousand lots in Your name... but You've not
turned up: I've no idea to whose lot falls the sign of mercy.

One day Sadi will leave for a mountain from Your cruelty,
and there tears will reach his waist… he will cry so bitterly.

If that promise-breaker fulfils a promise, that One would
resemble a departed soul that the lover's body re-entered.
All nights of Creation would be turned into day by that
One's face if one dawn-like glance the world illuminated.
Every sorrow has its equivalent joy… but I'm afraid that
the poison will slay me… before the antidote has arrived.
We rendered no service but we cherish the hope that due
to Your character, generosity towards us will be exercised.
If the picture of the world's beauties in one book should be,
Your lovely face would be a front-piece of what's collected.
If another lavished every kindness I'd regard it as minute,
but every kind of torment at Your hands… is appreciated.
Cypress is foot-tied, fixed in one place for this reason, that
if it walked with You of its clumsy leg it would be ashamed.
If in Your absence the eastern breeze blows on my wounded
heart, it would be like a fire that has been to tinder applied.
If Your separation does not kill me… I'd sacrifice my life in
exchange for Union with You: odds or evens I'm defeated.
O Sadi, that one is not fit to enter the company of lovers,
who to be sacrificing his life for that One, is not prepared.

Look… someone comes from Garden of Paradise:
is it a star passing, or angel come  into our eyes?

Each delectable attribute from invisible world...
only pain of Beloved's lovers hurt hearts inspires.
Let's see, perhaps Your friendship for a moment
is enjoyed: one moment's added, another retires.
O Sadi, army of Beloved's Royal Love conquers
existence's kingdom... each moment a flag flies!

That cypress that is said to look like Your figure,
could never walk a step before You... never, never!
It is not any sin on our part to be following You...
tell Your glances to stop of hearts being the taker.
Be sure to ask one who's wounded how he is going
when by him You pass by... O You avid traveller!
I am not even given by Fate that one day You'll be
my housemate without knowledge of my neighbour.
One who sincerely thinks about Union with You...
breaks off all connection with all else, is that clear?
How should You know I'm in fire and water today:
when I'm in dust, wind will bring news to Your ear.
Those appreciating the ardent lover's distraction will
tell you what of nightingales complaint one can hear.
Each moment that newly born source of mischief's in
another place... a new crowd of people does bewilder!
All took the rose in their hands and have plundered;
nightingale must complain to try to make rose hear.
I long to spill my life and work upon that One's lap,
in hope all I am and have that One is not a rejecter!

O Sadi, you'll die in these chains, no one will know:
cry, so that One either kills you or of you is the freer.


O Camel-driver drive slowly, for my heart's ease is departing
and my heart I once owned with that heart-ravisher is leaving.
I'm upset and cut off from that One, I'm helpless and I'm sick:
you could say, by that One's absence my bones a lance is piercing.
I thought that by fraud and deceit I would conceal heart's wound:
it can't be hidden for on that One's threshold my blood is flowing!
My uncontrollable Beloved turned away, embittering my life...
I am full of fire like a censer and from my head smoke is rising!
In spite of all of that One's injustice and untrustworthy promises
I still cherish that One inside my heart and when I am speaking.
Camel-driver, keep back the litter, restrain haste to start caravan,
through love for that graceful One you could say my life's departing.
I thought of weeping so camels might get stuck in mud like donkeys,
but even this I can't do for with caravan my heart is soon leaving.
Heart-ravishing Beloved, come back and love and cherish me...
for my wailing and lamentation from the earth to heaven is rising!
I can't sleep from night until dawn nor listen to anyone's advice...
I'll travel with the courier for my grasp of the reins is slipping.
Though it's not my purpose to patiently suffer Beloved's separation
or turn from that One, my purpose far deeper than that is going.
Every sort of statement is made about the soul leaving the body...
with these very own eyes of mine I've witnessed my soul departing!
"Sadi, it's not proper, complaining about us!" "Unfaithful One,
I can't bear Your cruelty and know my love can't stop complaining!"

It'd be the right thing to see that One and not be speaking,
just in case another rival may be behind some wall, hiding.
O Beloved, let me be admitted… exclude all of the others,
so that none of our secrets no one else can ever be knowing.
I desire wine and Beloved and a suitable time and place…
so that One and I can be together… no strangers waiting!
O friend, do not advise me, for one who is mad and drunk
will never become sane and sober by such a one's harping.
It is better to not concern yourself with that Swordsman,
unless you are prepared your head to be suddenly losing!
It'd be easy for You to raise Your hand to shed my blood,
while my life at Your feet is an easy thing… to be giving.
With such a face and elegance You can't be called a moon,
for no moon has lips and teeth that are so sugar-scattering!
And the cypress, that is said to be resembling Your form,
the figure and the sway that You have is never possessing.
We broke our vows because in the religion of us lovers it's
considered proper that a seeker… wine should be drinking.
No foot that's retired into seclusion in that One's house
for the rest of his life, ever in market-place will go seeking.

One can't be surprised if perfumer, reeking of rose-water,
in springtime no regard to the rose-bed should be paying.
It is known by all that in the poetry of Sadi there's such
a musky fragrance that on perfumer's tray one isn't finding.
If God is not pleased with His creatures, the intercession

of all the prophets, will not be able to change His decision.
Creation's divine decree is command of God Most High:
there are no other words that surpass these, in my opinion.
The rust of Pharaoh's heart was inborn, for even polishing
with 'Moses' white hand'* didn't clean its black condition.
God called the wretch, refused him access; so where could
he go? He bandaged his eyes then told him to have vision!
Fire would consume him, Hell-destined, even if he covered
himself with talc like a naphtha-smeared stick… I reckon.
Divine power has predestined good and evil fortune, boy…
whether you are pleased or displeased, you have no option.
People aren't responsible for their sins or their good works:
that one's fortunate another unfortunate is predestination.
Every action done by every single person is predestined…
bdellium  tree neither dates nor peaches has as its creation.
What's ugly can't be improved by woman's tireless efforts:
the beautiful can't in an attractive face… face obliteration.
A negro who is black can never become white by washing.
A fair Greek becomes black by turning lamp out of action?
O Sadi, do not go expecting happiness that is not to be…
because it is so difficult to reap what has never been sown!
Divine Power what is predestined to happen has decreed…
if you resign to Fate, or not… inevitable, must still happen.

* Note: Koran (xx, 24.) God says to Moses, "Press your hand to your side
and it will become white without hurting you, another sign to show you of
our great signs."

That One who is the object of my desire can't be won quickly:
my life will be ending as I quest in hope for what I hold dearly.
Unless You wish it so, it would be futile to be approaching You,
even if I were to use my head as feet searching for You constantly.
Your beauty's lightning flashed, consumed my wisdom's harvest:
did You not say that from all this fire heart's smoke rises rapidly?
O glance like the sun… would it do You any harm if through
You this house of mine became illuminated? Please… tell me!
If You would cast one friendly look in our direction it would be
philosopher's stone, transmuting our copper to gold immediately.
Love, will rob the one who is proud of his wisdom, of his reason…
I've never heard of falcon becoming pigeon's prey: an impossibility.
If You, lovely as You are, should again pass by, the moral code
of the devotee would be changed into the Kalandar's* … instantly.
Unless people assist that one who is stuck fast in the  mud,
the more that he keeps struggling, deeper he sinking will be!
Since the Beloved's image is pictured in my heart, I will destroy…
as though it was an idol whatever else it may conceive: immediately.
The rays of the Sun of Love fall upon every man, but the stones
are not all one kind… for not all jewels each one of them will be.
Admiration's record will sound like a damp drum to one who
listened to Sadi's sayings with acceptance's ear cocked rightly!

*  Note: Kalandars are lovers of God who have given up attachment to
desires and live only for God. The name comes from a Master named
Kalandar Yusuf. The word means 'pure gold.' Kalandars are continually
on the move and care nothing for their own condition… only concerned
with praising God.

Beloved's beauty needs nothing except for one small thing, and it is… that One faith towards lovers is sorely lacking.

Your juicy ruby-red lips possess sweetness that cannot be described, when the topic of conversation they are forming.

Blood flows from my grief-stricken eyes through my desire full of longing that You should by eye's corner be glancing.

Come here, for I call You to mind every moment, although the remembrance of water… only increases thirst's feeling.

A great many people are hoping that You will show them Your face: although a riot should be caused, it's not fitting.

If You're bent on slaughter then You shed my blood first… because, otherwise from my eyes blood would be dripping.

The water from my eyes through my expectation of You… does not resemble tears, but kind of wells up like a spring.

Everyone craves something or other from Your majesty… unlike my ambition which only Yourself of You is desiring.

Don't send me sugar by the hand of a sour-faced servant… although You may some poison with Your hand be giving!

Like the *Kaaba,* You're held sacred because of Your origin: whatever wants Union with You… the world is traversing.

I never imagined that the power of Love's arm would the reins of Wisdom from the hands of the sage be snatching.

Sadi, didn't I tell you not to go looking at beautiful ones? As you haven't given up Beloved, patience keep practising.

Good luck returns by the door through which You enter,
the sight of Your auspicious face opens Fortune's door.
The old Father of the Sky will need so much patience…
before Mother Nature again a child like You will bear.
This grace of Yours is alluring to all hearts… and this
sense of humour of Yours wipes away each painful tear.
I'm indignant with the perfume that anoints Your body
and jealous of the garment that Your breast does wear!
If You should open Your lips…  sugarcane, despite its
sweetness would be envious of Your speech like sugar.
If I had nothing in this world, or in the next one also…
having You I'd possess all, and need nothing anywhere!
I exposed heart to pain after giving it to You: this faith
is unstable for he who cannot at Beloved's hands suffer.
I showed to everyone Your arched eyebrows… that one
who sees new moon to every other person makes it clear.
It may be lawful for You to shed the blood of mankind,
not for You is he who turns from world to face You here.
The lover's eyes can't be closed to sight of the Beloved:
that nightingale hasn't stopped singing to rose is clear?
O Sadi, to look at the Beloved's permissible… but if you
steal one glance that One robs your heart, have no fear!

Egypt's caravan, as much as sugar that One has, doesn't possess:
among all beauties of China, not a one has such sheer loveliness.
Such charm and flirtatiousness can't be found in cypress or rose:
grace and beauty as is that One's, sun and moon doesn't possess.

I thought of taking my courage in both hands and stopping eyes
seeing You, but piety is no shield against beauty's arrows caress.
Our glance when directed towards face of beauties is for good:
whoever is disposed to evil is not a human being, but much less!
Each man you see who is ignorant of Love's mystery may be
classed with minerals… that one is not a living creature, I stress!
There's no way for seekers to go, except to go forward to You:
for they have no possible means of escape from You I must confess.
Mind is not occupied with anyone else… just You: that's enough,
where bewilderment follows, sight and hearing become worthless.
If You should break open the cage of the love-struck nightingale
it wouldn't want to escape because of its heart's great happiness.
You are drunk with sweet sleep until the morning is arriving,
while over me nights pass as if I'll never feel the dawn's caress.
The lamentations of Sadi's passion move many hearts to favour
that One's case… except for that Beast which is totally heartless.
Wood will not burn until a fire is applied to it… and similarly
the vain bragging of the imposter has little effect… or even less!

Love-struck nightingale the descant song is singing:
while the foolish one a vain passion keeps cherishing.
I can clearly see that there's no one outside my house,
and yet still this heart of mine a welcome is shouting.
I have a fire that is consuming the whole of my body
when breeze that comes from the east… it is fanning.
Although I see no shore in this sea with no boundary,
still… a man who is drowning will go on struggling.

The Sweetheart is on the terrace, while this one, his
head against wall of that One's house is smashing!
There is existing a balm for the wound of the lover...
because it is the Beloved that the sword is wielding.
It is a shame that One's hand is lying in my blood...
it is as if a sovereign with a beggar keeps on staying.
I am a slave without having committed any offence:
I'm content, even if innocent me that One's slaying!
I am grateful for favours of that One... whether that
One sends a robe of honour... or my neck is slapping.
One attempting to discuss this, after falling in love,
in the judgement of the wise acceptance isn't finding.
Let the police inspector burn harp of wine-drinkers...
our minstrel a melodious tune can still go on playing.
Fire produces smoke and blood flows from the victim:
also, Sadi this poetry from a higher source is deriving.

May fortune grant that Your views with mine coincide,
so the envier may hear and by an arrow be pierced inside.
Shed my blood and walk over my dust for then all of this
grief and this suffering will become trifling, a mere aside!
Spring's enjoyment's only given to the one who from love
for the garden with roses and thorns are equally satisfied.
Ah... poor man, whatever desire for a treasure you cherish
it is true that your foot over a dangerous path must stride.
Sadi has fallen into this trap because of his insane desire:
he'd be clever if again out from it... himself he could guide.

Many years will pass over our dust as waters of this spring
keep flowing… and the breeze of the east will keep blowing.
During this temporary period of respite granted to a man…
why should he, over dust of others… arrogantly be passing?
Friend, when you pass by the bier of an enemy don't rejoice,
for an experience exactly the same, you also will be having.
Dust of that man's body will be scattered in tomorrow's air
because that one, today upon this earth, is proudly walking.
O you devilish soul… the dust will be filling all your bones
like a collyrium holder, that the salve for the eye is holding.
The world's an ignoble companion, an unfaithful mistress:
since, then, it inevitably must pass away, let it be passing!
This as you can see, is the state of the body under the dust:
take care where your precious soul goes… when it is leaving.
No reliance can be placed on the safeguards of good works:
it could be Sadi passes away, with God's Grace protecting.
God, don't call to account Your miserable servant, promise
help: Your forgiveness is abundant though we keep sinning.


Until You have some knowledge of my condition…
You will pay no regard at all to my present position.
I practiced patience for as long as I had the power…
what more can I do if it can no longer keep going on?
It might be that in Your city the existence of the law
of faithfulness and affection… cannot be relied upon.
People say to me… "Why didn't you close your eyes

so that you would avoid such a dangerous liaison?"
"Good sir, go away… no matter what a man may do
against Fate's arrows, there's no possible protection!"
All of these worries that fill our mind will finally be
vanishing when we leave this world of perturbation.
Where is it possible for the helpless captive of Your
love to go, no way is out from Your street's location.
There is no other face existing on the globe's surface
as alluring and charming as Yours, by my calculation.
I've never seen in all Persia such salt as Yours, and in
Egypt there is no sugar like Yours, without exception!
If You pass an order for Sadi's death… life is not more
important to him than You, he says without hesitation.

It does not matter to You if us You do not see
for following You are many better than are we;
I'd set to travel the world to escape Your power
but in all the world none is like You, obviously.
It would indeed be strange when You stand up
in orchard, if straight cypress didn't bow lowly.
God forbid that there's a sad face in the world
that because of seeing Your face, is not happy.
I knew from the first that the promise that You
made with my wretched self wouldn't stable be!
From this I was convinced that there could not
between a fairy and a human being, be harmony.

O Beloved, don't wound my heart: O please let
me be… as there's no salve in this world for me!
Come, so that I may sacrifice my precious life for
Your sake, for complaining and love, never agree.
I don't wish to live a moment without You… no
pleasure in life without friend known intimately.
People say, "O Sadi, with whom are you in love?
Pain's no pain suffered in Sweetheart's company!"
I'll never tell to an enemy the story of the Friend,
for the false lover a real confidant could never be!

What kind of person are You, that he having access to You
is confused, unless of spiritual insight he has nothing to do?
It does not go with the practice of sweethearts and not with
love's duty that we die of love while ignorant of it are You!
Although You can send me from Your service do not do it;
people do not beat a beggar who has no other door to go to!
I sat on Your path hoping You'd see my state: You did not!
Your drunken eyes being drowsy… You cannot see through.
Every night I am saying this, "That person is happy whose
eyelids are sleeping, but whose Fortune is wide awake too!"
Happy the wild bird not experiencing cruelty from a hand;
while a tame bird and I are killed, having no wings, we two!
I'm not so guilty that I should be dreading any punishment:
the love for which a man will never risk his life… is not true.
All day be fixing your heart on that full moon that you love:
it may become upset one night when it has gone from view!

What difference is between a form of a picture on a wall and
a man to whom people talk of love but never get through to?
The feet of the traveller have to journey both night and day:
upon reaching a safe place they've no more wandering to do.
The page upon which you write some words of Sadi's is like
a leaf from Paradise's tree, so why should it be fresh to you?


Beloved, my Beloved, may my life be a sacrifice for You!
Does it happen that You remember Your lovers, do You?
You have passed on Your way and paid no regard to me:
the cypress never passed on without concern, as You do.
The blessings of God be on the father rearing such a One,
and blessings be upon the mother giving You birth… too.
May good Fortune grant the utmost limit of Your hopes,
and that the Evil Eye is never to be reaching You, is true.
O what a wonderful work He achieved when forming line
of Your face, opening the door of tumult to the world, too!
Someday, I'll be seizing the bridle of the king, and I'll cry
for justice against that One who's my Beloved and argue:
"O my king… if you are not granting some justice to me…
that I will go so far as destroying my precious life is true!"
It is true that wisdom can never be the conqueror of Love:
that master may put up with a slave's cruelty is true, too.
I had it in mind to set off upon my travels far and wide…
I was to take the road leading to Basra or Baghdad anew,

but it was Shiraz's blessed earth that was detaining me:
the clear, sweet, fresh water of Ruknabad... held me too!
That one, who has never set foot down on the threshold
of Love, that he's now laid down his head there, is true!
I've been humbled in the dust and it wouldn't be strange
if my life also was not sacrificed in this desire... for You.
The wild bird that kept clear of the trap has fallen into it,
and this has happened in spite of all its shrewdness, too.
All the people in the world are complaining about others,
but Sadi only complains against himself, all day through.

If the Beloved quarrels it shouldn't upset the lover's heart:
one who cannot put up with it cannot play the lover's part.
If a cry's heard: "A life's been sacrificed at Beloved's feet!"
Don't even mention it for it's a trifling thing, a mere start!
If the light-hearted Beloved puts on lover's heart a burden
the skies couldn't hold, it'd be a load for a minuscule cart.
You will never get a treasure without having difficulties...
dawn will never appear until the night does finally depart.
The long, long night... the anguish the lover suffers can't
be described to one who is not himself awake... as a start.
Ask about my eyes, because the nightly sleep of the drunk
isn't like a sick one's restlessness but... is something apart.
If Your hand takes Your sword my love would not change:
when real Love exists with one's life one may have to part.
A bird that has not been caught can't understand the pain
and longing that is experienced by those caged, kept apart.

The heart can be seen as the mirror of the Chinese picture,
but... this can only be so if there is no rust upon that heart.
Joseph, the Egyptian, will be sold by that one without any
spiritual insight where no buyer with any money will part.
O Sadi, that stupid brute whose head is heavy with sleep
cares nothing about the dawn's soft breeze, its subtle art.

The story of Love a single book cannot be containing:
words cannot do justice to the description, of longing.
Love's mystical song that keeps intoxicating the mad,
the ears of those folk who are sober cannot be hearing.
Making love and respectability do not go together for
one, and any piety into the winehouse is never fitting.
Beloved has so much filled my heart that's so narrow,
there is no room left for a throng of strangers visiting.
Impossible for me to describe You as You really are:
Your garment is too wide in market, to be displaying.
I'll never again surrender heart to another one's face,
there's no room for pictures that to You're comparing.
Who'll be carrying the news tonight to the poor rival:
"The dog into cave's corner, one can't be admitting?"
When the rose blooms it is chaperoned by the thorn:
when taken to breast no room for thorn is remaining.
Such great love and desire exist between two lovers
that the efforts of the bloodthirsty enemy are failing.
I'll snatch a glance at You with the eye of the heart;
eyes are dazzled from Your face's flash of lightning!

There is no place for Sadi among all of Your lovers:
this beggar among Your buyers, room is not finding.

Do you know how delightful to see the Beloved would be?
Like cloud that's raining in the desert of one who's thirsty!
O fragrance of Love! I knew where You were coming from,
for message of Union with Beloved heals spirit... helpfully.
Reason is disapproving of the way I cherish Love's passion:
but Love won't allow me to obey what Reason wants of me.
Perhaps out of pity You will of Yourself bring us to mind...
or else, who is there to take our message to You, instantly?
Fellow seekers in love understand the poor lover's condition
whether a seeker lamenting or lover complaining frequently.
The foot that doesn't stumble one day against love's stone
has not, I could say... life: its heart is not given completely.
If that one absorbed in the Beloved's love is a sincere lover,
he should not on the day that the arrows shower, try to flee!
All of the hours of this life remain completely useless to us,
except that moment when a lover with his Beloved may be!
Poison from sweet Beloved's hand to my heart is like honey,
while in Beloved's absence even honey is never sweet to me.
Do you know why Sadi's now sitting in a corner, secluded?
It is because he can't escape from the hands of such beauty!

Last night, without Your face, I was overcome by sorrow:
the floor was wet as from my eyes tears continued to flow.
In order that my precious life may not be ending in regret,

I bring You to mind at night, yesterday, today, tomorrow.
When night did fall all the eyes elsewhere went to sleep…
you might say, 'Under root of my hairs a needle did grow'.
It wasn't wine I used to drink in Your absence but heart's
blood… that never from eyes into goblet, stopped its flow.
 In whatever direction I was turning my gaze, Your image
was everywhere, like a picture… before my eyes, on show.
When he lay down, the eyes of Majnun only saw Layla…
he would have been a false lover if his eyes sleep did know.
My senses came and they went... I never saw Your face...
nor did Your vision appear here before me… never, no, no!
 Sometimes, like aloes-wood on fire, my sad heart burned:
sometimes, like from a censer… smoke to my head did go.
Sadi, cluster of Pleiades must have broken up tonight... or
else nightly they to sky's collar would climb and out blow!
 Fortunate will be the moment before we fall at Your feet:
to bid farewell to life will be a desirable next step to meet.
 That beggar who has dealings with a One of high places,
has to keep putting up with indignities replete, complete!
O You spiritual form, since Your essence is of this nature
it may be that in Your eyes our existence is… incomplete.
If appearance of all idols resembled Yours… it's likely the
worship direction of all Muslims at an Idol... would meet.
Although You've killed Your captives, making a mistake,
You passing by Your victims is in itself a kindness sweet.
The idea of joining the dance won't leave my mind today,
for our Minstrel does not remain silent for even one beat!

That one who's madly in love with rose all his life, knows
why the nightingale's always madly trying to rose entreat.
O Sadi, no one can ever become acquainted with your pain
and anguish unless you tell it to he who has felt it replete!

I am still working on a habitual vice that won't leave me,
that I cannot live without wine and those of great beauty.
Don't tell me to bear with patience the Beloved's absence:
give up faulting me, it is an evil that in humans you'll see.
If you were to strike with a stone the tame, friendly fowl,
of the master of the house it still never leaving would be!
Are you surprised that my eyes keep continuing to weep?
The wonder is heart's blood doesn't flow from them freely.
I will never be turning back from this that I have started,
whether I succeed in this… or whether I defeated shall be!
I wished to cast just one glance at that One and I'd return,
but that One said there's no way out of that street for me.
Beloved's cruelty can't be compared to that of the guardian:
you might call it… a cloud making the moon difficult to see!
With patience and skill we put some plasters on the wound
made by Your love's sword: they were useless, mere debris!
O Mischief of this Age, since a Beloved like You appeared,
there is not one heart that You isn't always longing to see!
We gave away the world with all its luxuries and pleasures:
Love's a seal that like engraving on stone, removed can't be.
I know of no place in the world today that is existing where
the tale of my poetry and Your beauty isn't told constantly.

You who said, "O Sadi, do not go running after beauties,"
how often say it? Flies will never give up sugar, obviously!

Ever since that time my glance fell on that face so lovely,
all sense of control over myself was suddenly lost by me.
I thought I would succeed in what I'd do by using Reason:
poor wretch became helpless when Love attacked lovingly!
My sight was so engrossed by that One's charming face,
that everything else in this existence I could no longer see.
That One's glance draws a sword over heads of mankind.
How can I stand firm for shield from hand slips suddenly?
One who is burning can't keep concealed fire burning him...
we never uttered a word but tale was told to all and sundry.
Whoever I happened to tell about that One's beautiful face,
became so much in love like me... he quickly lost his sanity!
Beware, that One's lips can rob heart, for one who loving
that One conquered a mountain, fell from top, eventually.
Those spiritually-minded understand that this fiery breath
has consumed my granary, all of a sudden, and absolutely!
Sadi is no match for that One's love: but he, who takes the
field against it, can even fight Zal's Rustom,* successfully!

* Note: Rustom was the son of Zal and father of Sohrab and one of the
heroes of the national epic of Iran, Firdausi's 'Shahnama'.

Whoever dies in Beloved's presence into life is quickened:
that one who has no Beloved has a heart that's deadened.

The candle of that one's heart, whose breast is purified by
mystic desire, cannot dispense with a Beloved in the end.
O seeker of love, get a heart like wax, for the black stone
cannot take impression of a signet it has been so hardened.
Sadi's fallen victim to the face of a stony-hearted Beloved,
anyone killed in this way, does not really die... I contend.

The clamour of the nightingale at dawn is heard...
sleeper's unconscious day is opening... how absurd!
The hearts of helpless lovers are the targets for that
storm of arrows that One shoots... each love-word!
The lovers are victims of the Beloved, and they are
all with souls exposed to danger, haven't you heard?
Tell one who possesses the faculty of really seeing...
"The world by that One's face's beauty is unfurled!"
I know of no one not surrendering heart to that One,
unless it's one without insight... just one of the herd!
That man, whose foot is not pierced by the thorn, is
truly a beast yet to be discovered: something absurd!
Let that One have a frowning face and bitter tongue:
poison from those sweet lips tastes like sugared curd.
The wise will always walk away when trouble comes:
the lovers way is to get involved, his waist he'll gird.
Sadi no longer has the power to escape... because one
that's love-struck with his wings clipped, is a lovebird.

The Beloved has entered the garden and is amused:
a clamour suddenly from the rose and tulip ensued.
I saw the birds of the garden wailing and lamenting
because the rosebud from a jasmine bower appeared!
The water's taken the reflection of the rose's cheeks,
bud of the pomegranate flower a fiery tint assumed.
The cry of the leader of the prayers who has become
a disciple of that One's love, in Winehouse is heard.
Devotee, on seeing miracle done by that Idol's cheek,
came out from his house... with sacred thread girdled.
I became poverty-stricken from that exact day when
the radiance of Your face was for sale finally offered.
It was my heart desire  to sacrifice my life for You…
that desire was fulfilled... mission was accomplished!
Sadi sent flowerbed to autumn's plunder upon the day
a scent of Beloved's rose from heart's garden exhaled.


Cypress-statured Sweetheart towards desert is moving:
watch that walk… see how gracefully that One is going.
Let's see what garden will be happy because of that One:
wherever that One happens to be deciding upon stopping.
As that One walks along the road… the dead man in his
bed of clay shouts out that the Christ by is now passing.
Let all of the seekers beware of that One's eyes, for that
angel-faced Beloved's aim… is to each of them be robbing.
That One... stole the hearts of which ever man or woman
that One saw in the city... and now to the desert is going.

The sun and the cypress are jealous... because they saw a
royal sun with stature of a high cypress... regally passing.
Such a carpet has been spread on the garden that a person
as if it were on a carpet of the finest brocade was walking.
Wisdom has not any power of resistance against Love...
objective of weak only by conciliation one is accomplishing.
O Sadi, you gave up your heart to the Love of that One...
it is gone: no, more... your life too will soon it be following.
That cruel One would not have thoughtlessly gone away
if that One only knew what anguish I would be suffering.

How long the night seems to heartsick lovers: come quickly
so dawn's door at beginning of night to me opens... widely.
It would really be strange if I could leave Your presence for
where can the pigeon fly that's falcon's prey, please tell me!
Because of passion for You I do not want to see Your face,
for the true lover is the one who has given up all completely.
With sideways glance of favour cast a look in our direction,
because prayers of those afflicted are offered in all sincerity.
Every night I keep wondering to which confidential friend I
can be telling about my Beloved and also about our Unity.
What prayers can he, in whose imagination are You, offer?
You O my Idol, from saying my prayers are preventing me!
O Sadi, when you see that One again don't tell of the pain
of love in your heart: Union night is short, long your story!
If you are dreading trouble then the attempts you've made
to be keeping faith with the Beloved are merely... a fantasy.

You can't be blamed for the cruel treatment on us falling,
for where from threshold of Layla can Majnun be going?
If I sacrificed my life at Your feet I would never regret it,
for many a life through love and faithfulness is perishing.
If I am a beggar in Your street it's no matter for surprise:
even if Korah* came to Your house, he'd leave it begging.
If one wounded by love's arrow is menaced by sword from
behind… he is certain to look back at You, before leaving.
I regret that You keep putting Your feet on the ground…
it is more appropriate for them on our eyes to be treading.
I've no inclination to speak in any gathering, except that
place where You are the topic upon which all are talking.
O sober one, if you should pass by one intoxicated, don't
criticise such a one… for Destiny over mankind is ruling.
Our feet are deep into the ground like an archer's target;
enemy is no antagonist whose arrow the mark is missing.
O you frequenter of the street of Love… be more patient:
cruelty always upon lover… at hand of beauties is falling.
O Sadi, if you don't erase from your mind your desire for
the rose… thorn of its cruelty must your foot be piercing.

*Note: Korah was the leader of the rebellion against Moses and was
extremely rich and powerful and… a great miser.

I'm devoted to that light-hearted One who is annoyed with me,
whose answers are bitter yet sugar under that tongue could be.

If my love for that One should take me to Hell it would be fitting,
for I with a heart-ravishing Beloved, am really in Paradise already.
Whoever is free and has his Beloved and a cup of wine, possesses
all he needs of Fortune, life's joy and all worldly desires, obviously.
A human being has an existence beyond just eating and sleeping:
pass your life with Beloved, for animals too are alive… you see?
I make love to a certain One from whose presence I come distraught
like nightingale neglects its nest by delighting in rose constantly.
I am no man if I turn from the Beloved through sword of Beloved's
cruelty: a drum that's wind inside resounds by a finger's simplicity.
In the troubles of the Resurrection when friend flees from friend,
Your lover rises from the dust with the same love for You only.
New Year's breeze blows pleasantly at dawn from faith's garden,
resembling fragrance of the Beloved, not garden's scent, to me.
What does one with head on Beloved's breast, asleep all morning
care for a wretch with head laid on Beloved's threshold, expectantly?
Like Sadi, be concealing your love… and seek pleasure and solace:
one with hidden Sweetheart tastes life's joy, of watchers is free!

Separation must have a heart harder than a stone, but I,
I… have a heart which is never satisfied with only desire.
I bless You still, despite Your unfaithfulness: so… come,
it's appropriate if You shower on me Your abuse and ire.
Here and Hereafter may want to buy You… in exchange
for their hearts: I'll buy You with my life… outbid will I.
Slay me to Your heart's content… for the slave can offer
no opposition to any order that his master might require.

It is not only the living... who are moved with desire and
love for You... the spirits of the dead Your breath desire.
Do not ask the victim of Love's sword how he is faring...
for in whoever happens to see him... pity he does inspire.
The father, who desired from God a darling like Yourself,
had no idea of the fresh mischief... he was about to sire.
O wealthy One, do not shut Mercy's door on face of the
poor... and if You do, that God will open it will transpire.
If You are thirsting for the blood of Sadi, let it be lawful
for You... may You live long: for my life... no care have I.

Thank you, the heavens don't have such grandeur:
the sun and moon are not equal to your splendour.
It'd be strange if soft breeze's skirt did not become
musk-scented when your door's dust it passed over.
There's not a gem in the Pleiades setting anything
like pearls that are in your royal diadem's cluster.
May the dominion of this family be preserved, for
as long as it lasts; our religion will not be the loser.
There is not a single wretch who is more miserable
than that one who of your command is a disobeyer.
Strike your foe who deserves trampling under foot
of elephant, so that his pawn can't be queen either!
Where in the wide world is found such a sovereign?
And if there is, than you he couldn't be any sweeter!
God... grant that this enemy may die in some place
where there's not a friend at his pillow, no one there!

People ask... "O Sadi, how long will your grief last?"
"I'm free of grief in friend's absence," please answer.

Who'll go on a mission for me to bring back the Beloved?
Companionship's pleasure without that One, is clouded.
How's it possible for me to speak in that One's presence?
Perhaps by morning breeze my message will be delivered.
For one to quarrel with the Beloved, a thirsty soul making
foul the Fountain of Life with some mud, could be likened.
Who could tell me to withdraw my heart from that Sweet-
heart to rely on patience, that my passion has prohibited?
May companionship with the Beloved, to that one who is
unable to abandon thought of anything else... be debarred.
The tale of love doesn't come properly from that false lover
who loses hope when a sword before his face is brandished.
My Beloved, don't leave me like this, to joy of my enemies;
one acts like this who wishes friends hearts to be afflicted.
Come, so I'll fall at your feet, and if You should kill me...
one doesn't die whose soul to Your hands has surrendered.
No one can relate the story of the night of separation but
for one who counts stars... like all those Sadi has counted.

Who can have passed exhaling the perfume of ambergris?
Who... approaching with such ravishing gracefulness, is?
The presence of Jacob indicates that lost Joseph is coming,
perhaps good news courier to Canaan going from Egypt is?
I lost my self-control, but the blind do not understand that

173

the wounds of that One's glances fall on the blind like this.
That One is continuing to walk gracefully… while wisdom
whispers in my head, "Shut eyes, a Perfect One coming is!"
Beauty of the Kaaba has urged me to eagerly keep going…
and that the mimosa thorns were like some silken artifice.
O heavenly-faced One, I am so preoccupied with You that
not a single thought about myself ever entering my mind is.
I can't possibly be closing my eyes to the very sight of You
although I clearly see that an arrow very shortly arriving is.
The thousand garments of spiritual reality that I am using
are much too scanty for the form You possess. What bliss!
That One who the false lover imagined would show pity to
the captive, had really come to kill him… then him dismiss.
The lamenting of Sadi has reached everyone in the world…
You've started such a fire, that a loud noise suddenly rises.

All are too involved in their own love affair to criticise me;
because everyone is in love with You… as far as I can see.
You have to be an Angel, not a human... with such radiant
beauty: he is no man who does not look at You constantly.
A son such as You are, is a comfort to his father's soul…
it's right for Mother Nature to be proud of You, obviously.
Curved bow of Your eyebrows stretching to Your earlobe
resembles a hunting hawk that is swooping for its quarry.
Is there a rose in the garden that is looking like Your face?
Is there any cypress that for Your figure is a match to see?
The tree that bears the fruit of my desire is much too high

for these short hands of mine… to reach such a  high tree.
Not even an ordinary human being but a person made of
iron… would melt like wax before the sun of Your beauty.
He is entrusted with the love of that flame-faced One…
who like the moth, is burning and bearing up constantly.
Do not deliver me into separation's hand after Union…
like the harp that the musician plays, after tuning it is he.
Disloyalty to promise with You, from Sadi will not come:
with whom can one be… who to You acts indifferently.

If I called You a cypress, not like this is the cypress;
if I said that You are a moon, the moon is earthless!
Wander the world or traverse the universe… a form
as fair as You among infidels or faithful is foundless.
Is it a ruby or Your lips? Is it candy or Your mouth?
I cannot really be sure… until I'm in Your embraces.
They depict talismans on silk and brocade but there
is 'obvious sorcery' in Your eyebrows: more… or less?
Even though the bee may possess as fine a waist…
the truth is its mouth holds less honey… much less!
Though it's alright for You to shed mankind's blood,
it is not… to put Your kind lover, under such duress.
My heart, if you shed your precious life at that One's
feet, concerning such beauty life has no preciousness!
If that One chooses one in preference to me… let that
One choose, for apart from that One we're choiceless.

May passion for graceful Beloved be unlawful for that
fake who will not risk life for that One... nothing less!
Sadi will under no circumstances take eyes from You,
unless You send him away: it's the only way, no less!

If that sweet Beloved of mine who has left upon a journey
returns... caravan of sugar from Egypt, in Shiraz shall be.
Should You return and then be demanding my blood, I will
be coming to You like a pigeon to the falcon... helplessly!
If my reputation, good name, heart, religion should be lost,
in the eyes if the reckless lover they are valueless, a barley!
I have been eagerly searching for this tone all of my life...
so that this cage may be shattered and my bird be set free!
If You cut the mountain's heart with the agonising wound
that my soul's enduring, the very stones crying out will be!
On that same day that I saw Your face I had this thought:
from such a face as that, one must surely expect coquetry.
That One who is my Beloved surpasses everything that is
comprised within scope of reason, imagination, or analogy.
If You should come back and be walking upon Sadi's eyes,
it would not matter... Beloved is always welcomed by me!

Whoever has seen Your face understands my condition...
for who gives heart to You, patience can no longer rely on.
Perhaps You will be veiling Your face... or else whoever
sees it will not ever be able his eyes to drop his lids upon.
Each creature whose eyes light upon this beauty of Yours

surrenders heart... on You evokes blessings by the million!
If the gardener acquires a cypress like You there would be
no need of watering-spring for his eyes he'd plant it upon.
So many days has my waiting soul passed through in the
hope that one night with You it would find as its location.
I get through the night away from You with much effort...
the days I can't see You seem like nights going on and on.
You can practise cruelty, exercise authority, but… please
refrain from it... if cavalier gallops out, foot soldier's gone!
Lift me from Your threshold's dust with the hand of pity,
if You cast me down no one to me will pay any attention.
Is there a need now to be slaying the lover with a sword?
He will give up life if it is about Beloved one talks upon.
This information Sadi supplies is a message to Seekers...
but a speech's inner meaning isn't understood by everyone.


Anyone who sees Your face at no one else is ever looking:
he's unsatisfied by love, not enough of its joy he is having.
Your graceful strut is so charming that if You strike with
sword anyone before You, he away would  not be turning.
I'm longing so much to die at Your feet that I have lost all
my desire to keep on living… for You I want to be dying!
Such a long time has passed… will not You for a moment
remember a lover who every moment You is remembering?
I don't know who gave You permission or a right to shed
mankind's blood… don't do it: no one such action is doing!

If You don't grant me the bliss don't disallow me one look,
for a sugar-seller even to flies such cruelty isn't practising.
O Sadi, keep singing, if you are longing for that garden…
for no caged nightingale in this way is so sweetly singing.


Who's the mischief-maker passing armed with arrows and bow?
What kind of arrow is this that through soul's armour does go?
This One isn't a creature but a creation of grace and perfection:
O heart, don't waste life, the world is a merely a passing show!
That moon-like face perhaps may not want to show itself again,
if it what was secretly happening to mankind happened to know.
O You Marvel of the Age, please come near me for awhile out
of kindness, because it is true that Time passes and has to go.
Your lovely face, heart-ravishing One, is quite beyond description
and demonstration, just as is the state of me, I'll have You know!
Before the breeze from the east comes back to the bed of flowers,
I see my life passing away like a lightning flash… a quick blow!
You have kindled a fire in the heart of Sadi with Your love…
and smoke of it sometimes passing across his tongue does go.
I'd gaze my fill, then perhaps that One would leave my heart:
taking such a hold of it, only with difficulty will that One depart.
A heart of stone is what one needs upon the high road of goodbye,
to be able to bear the day when that litter's departure does start.
With all my fingers I will stop all the tears of regret, for if I should
let them fall, caravan in the mud would sick fast and never depart.
When Beloved's face left my sight I didn't know where to go…
like eye from which lamp's taken away that anywhere does dart!

The waves this time have so wrecked the ship of my endurance
that I wonder if even its planks will reach the shore, for a start!
It does not even matter if I am killed with the sword of reproach…
it's departure of the Killer that makes spiritual lover's life depart!
It wouldn't be strange if patience and endurance's caravan passed
beyond each eye… when that pure beauty to depart did start.
I know of no one in this city who is not captured by Your charms,
unless it's he who enters the city and leaves it, who has no heart.
If there's one who during his life hasn't given heart to daydreams,
he'll come away lovesick after having seen You play Your part.
Reveal Your face and You will rob the seeker's heart of patience:
raise Your veil and all the wise man's senses will certainly depart!
If Sadi doesn't play the lover's role what use to him the kingdom
of existence? It'd be a pity if all his life he played a useless part!
Only one who feels absence's anguish appreciates Union's worth:
one weary sleeps peacefully when his destination comes to heart.


Who may that bright moon be passing by with such grace?
Thirsty soul resigns life, as pure water nearby keeps pace!
Even if from place to place the cypress were to be moving,
it cannot be said to walk with more than this One's grace!
Is it a black eyed virgin of Paradise that is parading before
desiring eyes, or full moon, or Chinese doll walking apace?
No one has ever gained his desire for that One, except for
the breeze of spring, blowing over hair and brow and face.
The dead, upon seeing that One walk, are imagining that
One to be the sun that is moving across the sky and space.

179

Let that One plant foot on lovers heads, sit on their eyes:
it would be a pity for that One to walk in any marketplace.
Let anyone who possesses a heart or knows religion in the
city beware… for ruin of heart and religion can take place!
From coming… going of that One's image in my eyes and
heart… I am doubtful if it's really that One's passing face.
Whether that One's angry with me or not, that One's will
is law… that One's a sovereign passing by a slave's place,
O Sadi, adopt a life of retirement and practise a lover's role:
that One's a beauty who passing by a recluse, walks apace.

How did this smiling rose grow and become so lovely?
Or how did this immature sour grape taste so sweetly?
And also, how did those birds come out from the egg to
a sweet-voiced nightingale and sugar-eating parrot be?
How did You learn such humour and such eloquence…
that the day You spoke men lost all reason… instantly?
Breeze of the east fostered the sapling on stream's edge:
in less than eye's twinkling straight cypress stood proudly.
I said to Wisdom, "Rest in peace from now on!" Its reply:
"Be silent, that source of mischief's appeared… suddenly!"
The time of Your childhood and instinctual acts has gone:
You've now become a human with the attributes of a fairy.
A mouth's never filled with pearls like a shell, but my eyes
overflow like a sea out of longing… for to it eventually see.
O Sadi, the fresh bud could not be contained in its calyx…
it saw a favourable time, bloomed, became a rose so lovely!

Again today the parlour of our face is like a bunch of roses:
delight of privacy is like a promenade in a garden of flowers.
Wine is legal for one who lives in Heaven, especially from
a hand of companion who like the Winebringer of Paradise is.
What shall I compare Your downy cheeks and ruby lips to?
Much like the outer rim of the Fountain of Life I'd express!
Since I am in love with all those dishevelled curls of Yours,
my existence now resembles Your wild, disordered tresses.
What can victim of Your love do but speak of heart's pain?
Do not imagine You can shed blood, and no one will guess!
God save us from the anvil-like heart of those who did not
become soft like wax before sun that Your face did impress.
It'd be strange if one did not lose his heart to Your beauty,
or if any remained a Muslim in a country of unfaithfulness.
What do You whose smile is like a lightning flash, care if
I weep so many tears they resemble a rainy storm's excess?
It was so unfair of You to taunt Sadi about his mad heart,
for not one who sees such a face remains not under duress.
That one who is not in love with the face and form of You
is only an animal in human form and nothing more or less.


Last night I had the greatest joy of my life, last night:
because that beauty was lying in my embrace, so tight.
I was so drunk seeing that One, so mad with love, that
mundane concerns and religious duties I forgot outright.

To say nothing of sweet and agreeable red wine, poison
from that hand would taste like honey... to my appetite.
From that grace and beauty I knew not whether it was
silver and jasmine or a breast and shoulder in my sight.
I became all eyes and all ears... because of that One's
appearance and voice that refreshes the soul, outright!
I don't know how that night turned into another day...
only one whose senses were sober would get that right.
The *muezzin* repeated the call to prayer by mistake...
perhaps he also like me was outright drunk last night.
We told everything friend and foe could understand...
for we no longer have patience to hold secrets in tight.
O Sadi, perhaps it was in a dream you saw that One:
do not talk of it today because it happened last night.
God forbid that a beggar, who by reason of his avarice
can't remain silent about it, should find a treasure site.


I long so much for face of that sweet One that the desire
to cry bitter lamentations like nightingale stokes my fire.
When in a gathering I remember the red lips of that One
like dew my breast is covered with tears... a ruby attire!
The colour of the tulip reminds me of the Beloved's face:
new grass shoots remind me of down on cheeks I admire.
If a rose like that One's face is mine, it's impossible that
such a spring can within a thousand years again transpire.
The unworthy eat fruit from garden of that One's Union,
while only thorns from that beautiful rose-bed... I acquire.

Don't hope for Union with that One without separation:
obviously after a drinking bout a hangover does transpire.
Fate cast me so far from the Beloved that I'm even content
with the breeze that blows from where Beloved does retire.
Separation from the Beloved tears out the root of patience:
I don't know when Union's orange flower blossoms... afire!
Heart of mine, though the root of patience is bitter to taste,
it's easy to digest for it's eaten hoping Union will transpire.
I still hope for Union, after undergoing separation's agony:
morning springs from night, snake supplies antidote entire!
When the white-poplar arrow of cruel glances fly from those
quarrel-seeking brows, it invades hearts of the sane like fire!
If You passed only a moment with me, like a happy life that
moment I would count in my eyes... as seeing my life entire.
Sadi's ashamed about getting involved in worldly concerns,
even if it is royalty... unless serving Beloved it does require.

If You were to appear... bemused, then the world would be
in confusion and dust of our clay would be alive, instantly.
If one ray from Your face were to penetrate heart's corner,
sigh would escape from his hermit-soul's cell immediately.
Place the bouquet of Hope in the hands of Your lovers, so
that travellers on Love's Path... may eased of their pain be.
I thought one day I'd have a moment with You to fulfil my
desire but that wish is unfulfilled and I fear death shortly.
I fell in love, though I'd known from the first that the seed
of making love would produce regret's branch... eventually.

Friends asked, "Why this mad passion and lamentation?"
"My passion's out of love and lamentation is grief's plea."
My heart is gone and so are my patience and my wisdom:
my soul and I remain; if love makes grief, it too leaves me!
Sadi always laments bitterly through his heart's anguish...
from his burning love, smoke rises from his pen constantly.

My longing for that One is such that it can't be described,
and if I wrote a hundred books, it would not be completed.
You're my sweet soul that in bitter pain has left my form:
O my Soul, come back to my body or I'll become deceased!
If I wrote a chapter about each time I suffer reproaches and
hardships I confront, it would make a story not completed.
What worry should one longing for You have about words?
Nightingale only sings, when rose the garden has entered.
Of what use are the waters of the Euphrates to the thirsty
after death? It wasn't after Majnun died, Layla appeared.
O rose... I hold you dear, because your musky perfume so
intoxicates me one might think scent... is sent, of Beloved.
I said to morning breeze it must be close to You, as breeze
that is wafting from where You are, is ambergris suffused.
Fault is Yours if at any time an impatient lover should cry
lamentations, for You know smoke rises if fire is kindled?
What I said was a mistake made out of thoughtlessness...
Azra was guilty of cruelty but improper what Wamik said.
Reed is peculiar that you can split it, head to breast, and if
you want service again, it runs to you on crown of its head.

The soil of the garden and flower-bed must endure tyranny of autumn's blast… for spring's breeze it has always loved. Sadi… though your heart bleeds on account of the Beloved, it's not right with love, that from mouth… heart is uttered.

Those devoted ones' love isn't inspired by earthly passion: spiritual lovers' journey is not a wrong motive based upon. Mystics enjoy perpetual vision, where others are allowed one look only… a second look is not allowed… thereupon. It's natural for plants to be revived by the morning breeze: minerals and dead bodies are not susceptible, now or anon. If your faith is such that you should die with a live heart… you'll pass into a life with no more death, that… rely upon. Look to that One Who will wipe away darkness from your existence… and not towards a one who of purity has none. To what city do You belong that You do not inquire after Your lovers? Perhaps faith isn't in the land You live upon! Though bones of disciples of spiritual knowledge burn like reeds, like drum to blows they'd be unaffected… thereupon. If You should shed my blood I'll not call You to account at Judgement Day… with lovers, such a thing doesn't go on. Faithless rival who on day of arrow-shower doesn't act as a shield against calamity… is a lover not to be relied upon. Gaze in the mirror… what a charmer You are: but, when You see Yourself, You will not look at us… now or anon. Another may tell the same tale as I, but as he has nothing to do with God… his words would not ever be relied upon.

Don't imagine Sadi can be upset by Your cruelty: should
You shed his innocent blood it wouldn't be unjustly done.

The taste of wine is such that if it once you are drinking
you will be acquiring a new taste for it... every morning.
The root of perseverance will at some time create a tree:
branch of acting rightly sometimes fruit will be growing.
The master of alchemy must be placing much silver into
the black earth, for it... some gold to finally be producing.
One has to exercise great patience for that day when the
heart-healer will through the afflicted's lane, be passing.
The philosopher who tells seekers to close their eyes will
be at one with spiritual insight if our Beloved he's seeing.
It is true that when a king conquers another country the
foundations of the previous government he is destroying.
When a mad one is advised to be careful and sensible, it's
to be feared that such advice... him crazier will be making.
Morning prayer is called, the dervish becomes conscious:
give a bowl of wine... so again unconscious he is becoming.
Bring the cup here, winebringer! Sing me a song minstrel!
Put lips to flute's mouth, so sugarcane-sweet it is tasting!
Today Sadi's poetry may not seem sweet, but tomorrow...
it'll become the talk of all, like Shirin's tale they're telling!

Suddenly, I longed to walk pleasure-grounds of spring's season
with a couple of friends... because one cannot always be alone.
I saw Shiraz's earth looked like a brocade with figures on it...

all those beautiful devices that have been lovingly worked upon.
The Province of Fars under the Atabegs' rule was now at peace,
but there was uproar in the rose-garden from birds cries of agitation.
A sweet One, with mouth small as a pistachio nut, walked by to
amuse us, defying description, such loveliness beyond comparison.
God knows the anemone hasn't such beauty, jasmine such fragrance,
and pine-tree such a shape as that One, beyond one's imagination.
Sorcery of magician Samari is in that One's eyes causing tumult:
the breath of Jesus is in the sugary lips of that life-reviving One.
I was in doubt as to whether it was an idol, new moon, angel,
huri-shaped, moon-faced, angel-featured: I could go on and on!
That One robbed Sadi's heart, no… the whole world, in a moment
on New Year's Day, at ruler's table, when it we plunder upon.

Whenever one who possesses a lovely face is passing,
all eyes nearby towards that one, are quickly turning.
O rose, show even some consideration for nightingale,
where colour and fragrance are there must be singing!
The soul will yearn for You to press Your lips to his...
a thousand years after his dust, a wine-pot is forming.
In every city there is a beautiful one who is fair of face:
none pure-minded and pure-natured like You is living.
O You, who surpass in beauty all beauties of this age,
he feels sick who like ball in curl of Your bat is waiting!
Isn't it a shame to tie in a knot such hair? Loosen it so
Your breast and bosom of musk are fragrantly smelling.
I believe that he who has no attachment to You is not a

human being, but a statue of stone or brass... a nothing!
I cannot take my eyes off You ever again: that one who
has lost his heart to You will his heart be truly seeking!
My heart is so contracted that my breath is stifled like
the cry of one who from the bottom of a well is calling.
O Sadi, offer thanks... suffer cruelty without a murmur,
for all that's good from the hands of the good is coming.

Didn't I say that the time of fasting wouldn't keep lasting,
that austerity would end... and sadness would be ending?
It's true that after difficulty is a time when things ease up,
but it is also true that one must have patience, forbearing.
How long will that Feast of a Beloved hide face from eyes?
Look, there's the new moon, which its crescent is showing!
Why do You close garden's summer-house in this season?
Open its door to me... so my heart You may be refreshing.
Go and tell all the male servants to burn some aloes-wood:
go and tell all of the female servants musk to be bruising...
because I can't help but think that the graceful Sweetheart
will soon enter by this door... and me be suddenly greeting.
All those horsemen are busy carrying off rings from posts,
while our flirtatious One the hearts of heads is snatching.
Whenever the Beloved is talked about during any party...
the minstrel without any hesitation his song stops singing.
And also there isn't any room for poetry in such company,
unless, it is the *ghazals* of Sadi... then it would be fitting!

The fortune of that lover is really a lamp that is unlit,
who is not possessing a Beloved… no doubt about it.
What business does that imposter have in Paradise,
who doesn't feel an attraction for huris… not one bit?
Can one be thrilled with delight by praise, who does
not secretly feel for one he praises a love, passionate?
Among mystics no one is really a spiritual lover who
doesn't fell attached to a Beloved, no doubt about it!
If the Phoenix became ensnared by lock of that One's
hair it would not have the strength of one tiny tomtit!
The Physician that I'm having isn't very sympathetic
because, you might say, that One isn't sick, not a bit!
But ever since Sadi has been tasting the honey he has
not made a complaint against the bee… I must admit!

Whenever that beautiful, roguish One is passing by me,
a hundred caravans go past from the World of Mystery.
That One passes before sober people every moment and
intoxicates with the wine of youth, charm and coquetry.
That One is slaying all the lovers whenever passing by,
but this one is waiting for that One again to pass by me.
I thought I should sit in seclusion like a wise man… but,
that One was driving me crazy when passing like a fairy!
I decided to close the door to the outside world but there's
such pain in my heart I will penetrate walls with my plea!
You've bankrupted the beauty market of all other beauties:
there's no way that customers from You can get away free!

I fear the police inspector will become drunk, love-sick like we are... if he pass the Vintner's house, even occasionally. Be on your guard... one's precious life is wasted, except for that time passed loving the Sweetheart, even momentarily. It is a comfort to suffer pain, in the hope that some day the Physician may happen to come into the patient's proximity. Sadi cannot take his way to the Friend by himself, because that road is not a one strangers are allowed to travel freely.

Whoever desires something sacrifices heart and soul for it; those who worship You, can't stop adoring You, not a bit! Someday I'll fall in dust before You, though my life I may forfeit: one dying at Your feet, an easy death does commit. I'm not such a lover of form to be drunk with desire for one: it's the Painter of form that took my mind... I freely admit. People say to me that I am wasting my life with beauties... but that person without a Beloved is wasting life... all of it! Let that one desiring a tree in Spiritual Reality's Garden... plant its roots inside his heart, and sow it in his soul's pit! Love and self-control are not in harmony: let that one who can't endure criticism withdraw from being involved in IT! If I'm faithless to my pact with You, I'd be not honourable nor a man: despair due to criticism for a true lover is unfit. I wish the garden may see Your graceful form, so roses are strewn at Your feet... Judas tree's petals on Your head sit. How lovely Your walk... how admirable, poetry, a miracle! O Sadi, you composing verse... any end to this book of it?

In my separation from You like night has become this day:
O my eyes, keep on watching for not lawful is sleep today.
I've no longer the power to bear the stone of Your cruelty,
from tenderness this poor heart is a glass cup… not clay!
I hear people ridiculing me behind my back and saying…
"Look at this oldie, over whom a vain fancy holds sway!"
It is not only I who am a prey to the lure of Your mole…
whoever sees it is trapped by Your net… can't get away.
I thought I'd take a look at Beloved from my eyes corner,
but my gaze upon that One does stay and stay and stay!
O heart… didn't I tell you to turn back your love's reins?
It'll toss you down since bridle slipped… grasp fell away.
This poetry of mine is produced from love of Your face…
parrot has eaten sugar, now it is a sweet-singer each day!
That imposter who never surrendered to anyone's control
has fallen on this occasion into Your trap, tamed, to stay!
Particulars of my love for You cannot be fully described…
for I've done my utmost effort and book is finished today.
The people of this Age are purchasing slaves with gold…
Sadi's voluntarily Your slave, freedom he has given away.

A week of my life's gone; no, gone are ten days in number
since from Purity's Garden, Love's scent was the exhaler!
That One who spurned me was cruel, for nothing sold me,
can't be bought from me even if world's offered by a bidder.

Let that One say anything about me even if bitter it be,
from such sweet lips it would be so witty, nothing better!
If I should dread the thorn I'd not gain a bundle of roses:
if object of desire's in crocodile's mouth, still be a seeker!
Do not leave me Beloved, for without You I cannot stay:
don't desert me, for I'll not my connection from You sever.
I'll not occupy myself with my concerns and neglect You:
impossible for one seeing You of himself to regard as finer.
It's an easy matter to bless You than to be hearing abuse,
for what than to converse with You... could ever be better?
I tried hard to stop revealing the pain that's in my heart;
in the end at death's door… my strength was no longer.
O please, O minstrel, stop playing your melody of love!
How long sing it? Your harp, of my veil has been a tearer!
Those who thirst for You died on brink of Life's Fountain.
How long can they gasp like fish on land… and so suffer?
Give an ear to Sadi's poetry, O You who are so beautiful,
especially when You put pearls in ears… and be a listener.

Whoever his whole life without that one is passing
if death does not take him, he feels life's depressing.
I was determined not to surrender heart to anyone,
but that graceful cypress me of my heart is robbing.
I am madly in love with the form of that One... but,
that one who is so cruel, me so unkindly is treating.
The snow of old age began to settle upon my head,
but my nature that's within me young is remaining.

I was not revealing to anyone the state of my heart,
but all of a sudden it all of my tears were revealing.
One who keeps struggling against Fate of Heaven,
continues against an iron that is cold to be hitting!
Wisdom has no power of resistance against Love…
it puts up with it from the lack of power it's having.
The eyes of Sadi expecting to see the Beloved's face
pours out pearls just the same as his mouth is doing.
Without doubt there must be delirium in this mind,
because such sweet poetry as this it keeps producing.

The Beloved towards me is so completely unfaithful…
that One leaves me without a reason… it is so pitiful!
That faithless One has extinguished my life's candle,
and is displaying everywhere a brightness so beautiful.
That One's acting like a stranger to all who are family;
while to strangers showing friendship, isn't so unusual.
That cruel Beloved One is really just a seller of barley:
makes a big show of selling wheat to me: so bountiful!
My Beloved's a reprobate, winehouse haunter, a rogue:
in front of lovers Beloved acts like an ascetic… fanciful!
O Muslims, come here, help me, for such a One as this
has to be guilty of impiety, or at least of being unlawful!
Ship of my life is wrecked by that One's love… and that
One is now abandoning poor me, it is all so very pitiful!
Whatever cruelty and oppression is falling to my lot is a
calamity that's now happened, because of Fate's cupful.

Sadi who is sweet of voice is begging just one kiss from
that One's lips... for the sake of Love that is so merciful.

Customers so swarm around the sweetmeat seller, that he
must either pin the flies wings or must cover up the honey.
And, whoever accepts a cure or listens to counsel is either
not a lover at all, or if he is… not a sincere one, obviously.
If You command a slave to profess infidelity, he'd do so:
he would take it if You prescribed poison to Your devotee.
A candle in Your presence is like a light in front of a fire,
rose in Your hands is like before Joseph a show of beauty.
Gain can't come to merchants of the sea without danger:
one who desires You struggles as long as a breath has he.
Eyes leaves are not dry in winter of separation from You:
it is so strange for fresh leaves wither in winter's tyranny.
Whoever doesn't have a Beloved wastes his life, just as a
thing that is not boiled on the fire, cooked cannot ever be!
Unless there is hidden grief one's feelings cannot be told:
Sadi has also seen a rose, so like nightingale crying is he.

That one without a peaceful heart in diversion is never engaging:
friend journeying once with friend, never alone again is travelling.
Breeze from the Peaceful Place blows not on my wounded heart:
the true dawn won't appear 'til the long dark night's disappearing.
The area of the world seems restricted to heart-ravished ones…
for one stuck fast in the mud in one place, elsewhere isn't going.

Thoughts of Beloved will never leave the heart of the love-crazed
because seeing the rose and the tulip in the garden is so pleasing.
With You as companion I would go walking on mimosa thorns…
yes, as willingly as that one who upon silken-brocade is walking.
The pheasant, despite its elegant gait, can't compare in grace
of movement to You, however flirtatiously in garden it is strutting.
O Throne of Solomon, should You pass over us in this way…
it'd be strange if a poor, tiny ant under foot You were not crushing.
How do gardeners fare at night from annoyance due to nightingales?
For during rose-season their clamour from garden isn't disappearing.
My poetry's circled the world though it's not come to Your ears…
indeed, words of mine to that place where You are, are not reaching.
Tell that one who tries to induce us with advice to forget You
"Use the sword"… for Your lover won't leave You by his advising.
O You idol of Yaghma,* You'd better veil Your moon-like face
or the hearts of the people of the city You could be easily plundering!
Precious jewels are possible to take from the mouth of the shark
but no one who is concerned about his life upon the sea is voyaging.
O Sadi, be bearing your burden and do not go forgetting Beloved…
Wamik's love because of the cruelty shown by Azra, isn't ceasing.*

*Notes: Yaghma… a town in Turkestan celebrated for its beautiful
women. Wamik and Azra are two famous Persian lovers.


One with a little flowerbed doesn't walk out in the garden:
he who's happy at home won't leave with mind mad again.

195

That one whose skirt's caught even by a thorn from There,
will not again yearn for a bed of roses: here... now or when.
Journey to worship-point is long... where attendant is with
Beloved: one facing that Point, need not with desert reckon.
Soul of the lover won't yearn for the delights of Paradise...
even if the keys to all of Heaven's doors were to him given.
If scent of spiritual Truth should some day intoxicate your
brain, heart will never desire rose, tulip, sweet basil again.
That one with knowledge of where Beloved is… would be
an imposter if he did not face the arrows to get there then.
The attribute of the sincere lover is surely this, that he will
not be false to his promise, even if life he pays! That even!
That heart that is in love should say to the one criticising:
"Good sir, it is a sickness without cure, so go away then."
The image of love won't leave my heart due to reproaches:
the engraving into stone even by a flood away isn't taken.
It was never the desire of Wisdom to be looking at Love…
but it so happens that all cheats eventually go into prison.
O Sadi, if you describe your love for that One all through
the night, the night would end but not what's left for pen.


O my God, last night how blessed was that sorcery,
when separation's victim that One passed so quickly.
Perhaps Beloved, on whom we look with love's eyes,
will give us one look that one can only call, 'kindly'?
One cannot say what beauty of that face resembles:
one could say at midnight Day's door opened widely.

None would approve if I said that One's a full moon:
more, garden of trees full of moons hanging brightly!
Never say I'd any consciousness of myself or anyone
else anywhere, at time when You were known by me!
In stages of praising You I have reached such a plane
where in my eyes both worlds are naught, I guarantee!
Beloved exists and I... no, remove me, for in Beloved's
presence it cannot be said that there is another entity!
Against loving glance of Beloved, drawn like a sword,
we turned to patience: as defence it was a catastrophe!
O Sadi, you cannot again close your eyes because your
heart, which had a little patience, is taken... suddenly!

It's only right for the lover to be preferring
Beloved's actions... to what he is desiring.
Beware of one who complains to strangers
of pain at Beloved's hands he is suffering.
Bear any burden Beloved gives: one gains
shirt full of roses who thorns are enduring.
The Abode of Love is in that Winehouse.
The need for reputation there, is existing?
Do not be a slave to your carnal desires...
that cur of the city for a bone is searching.
Being intoxicated by beauties every night
causes a hangover when sober at morning.
That king of the city of the lovers should
himself... only a single Beloved be having.

Promenade of Sadi is palace of the king…
it is not often that there's anyone passing.

It is true one can do without everyone else… but You
are indispensable: that none can match You… is true!
A well of sweet water is such because of some stones;
the banquet of a rich man is attended by beggars, too.
Is that sweat from Your body or is it really rosewater?
Is that breath from Your mouth… or perfume I imbue?
I've lavished on You my body, my reason and my soul:
I've consecrated to You my heart, eyes… my mind too!
What is the heart? It's the vital spirit making me live!
O Beloved, ask me to give it and I'll say, "Take it, do!"
The comfort of soul is coming from Your sword's hilt…
heart's balm is from Your quiver's arrows, shot so true!
Who shall I talk to of my hidden pain as no one knows
about my agony except the One Who knows all: You!
I am reproached by people who say to me, "What is it
you see in that one?" Blind know not what sighted do.
How can that helpless deer that is bound by the neck
fail to be following behind one who trapped it? True?
It's only enough for that one who has a mad heart like
me to be giving expression in poetry… that charms too.
Do you know why Sadi's lament pleases one so much?
Agreeable scent rises when aloes-wood burns through.

Patience be constant, for promise my Beloved has broken:
I am finished, undone... yet Beloved has not yet been won.
Sighs rose from my heart, eyes were congested with blood.
O God, my Beloved stays far from me... what have I done?
Beloved has no pity on this body of mine... bent like a bow:
that One's quickly passing my side like an arrow does run!
All my life I laid face of devotion on Beloved's threshold...
I thought maybe that One will open door for me: not done!
An enemy would do just as You have now done to a friend,
in fact a friend more friendly with my enemies is that One!
In my love for Beloved I don't ever hold back silver or gold,
but apart from tears and heart's pain companions are none.
O Sadi, since unfaithfulness of your Beloved is confirmed,
break off all hope in your heart as promise to you is broken.

Who's that One who goes hunting with the feet
of lovers hearts bound in chains of total defeat?
That One's foster-sister of Babylon's sorceress,
equal in flirtations to Kashmir's beautiful elite.
That One's a paradise, that if you have seen it
sight of an old man becomes young... I entreat!
Out of love for the bow of that One's eyebrows
a victim from those arrows doesn't even retreat.
The painter when he sees that One's lovely face,
tosses his paintings away... he cannot compete!
O You, a powerful archer, but weak of promise,
You've left me... but Fate forced You to retreat.

Those short-sighted people vainly criticise and
are reproaching me for my love being indiscreet!
The blood that my nature has imbibed with milk
will only leave this body when my death I meet.
If the ardent lover's Beloved demands one's life
from giving it up one is not allowed any retreat.
Let that one who is wanting to act according to
Beloved's will... make his own desires, obsolete.
O Sadi, since you've become the captive of love
all that's now open is to as obsolete all else treat.


The time has arrived when fragrance of the rose-garden
overpowers the scent of the perfumer's rosewater again.
The sleeplessness of the nightingales who are now fully
awake has out from hearts of all sleepers slumber driven.
We have abandoned the cell of austerity because who is
it that will be bringing a prayer-mat into a wine tavern?
Let's be sincere and divest ourselves of this patched coat
that's concealing the thread of infidelity that lies within.
Get up, for Your dreamy eyes are heavy with sleep... and
many more than a thousand tumults are waking up again.
A beautiful One might sometimes be stealing a heart...
but, You've robbed all mankind of hearts, there and then!
Do one of two possibilities... either give Your heart to me
or else release of my heart from out of Your control begin.
We have no road to go, and we cannot face staying here:
our Sweetheart is tired of us while we are captured again.

A wound by Your hand is best, if I have to be wounded...
Your load is the best if I have to be carrying some burden.
I have made this one resolution: to be wallowing in blood,
but... never to be turning away from Beloved, ever again.
If I were to be offered the Here and also the Hereafter...
and told to choose these two and give up Beloved... then
I would never be a one who would sell his Joseph... never!
So you can be keeping all that base silver of yours! Amen!
O Sadi, if you are a real man you will not turn away from
Beloved in spite of cruelty and injustice, again and again!

The moth cannot bear to be very far from the light
but if she tries to approach it, it will set her alight.
All are engrossed with some attachment or other:
spiritual-minded on love of Beloved set their sight.
When the Day of Resurrection happens, the Court
of Account is held, Royal mandate told forthright.
We will live again when the Beloved is mentioned:
all others will come to life from the trumpets might!
We are completely intoxicated by love's pure wine:
we are not hunting for Salsabil and Kafur's* delight.
*Huri* seeing Your heavenly face on Judgement Day
would admit her limitations... if she had any insight.
Our night will only turn into day... when You come
from Your bedroom like dawn after a very long night.
It's not strange if the living are smitten with You...
even the dead from love from their graves will alight!

I, as well as all of the heartsick lovers, can appreciate
the prolongation of the long and dreadfully dark night.
Please tell me, what's to be gained by our destruction?
What can the Anka* do with a sparrow, a mere sprite?
It is also to be feared that a spark from all the sighs of
the ardent lovers will set the veil of self-control alight!
To all outward appearances You aren't anywhere near,
but You are never far away from our mind's eyes sight.
I cannot travel along the road leading away from You:
Your noose is better than separation, however slight!
O Sadi, because you have such desire for the honey…
you also have to  be enduring the bee's stinging bite!

*Notes: Salsabil and Kafur are two fountains in Paradise. The Anka (the
Phoenix) is the bird that symbolises the Beyond state of God.*

Light is illuminating the sky from Your sun-like face…
say, "He alone is God," evil eye be far from Your face.
One can't point to a human like You in the Universe:
not in Paradise's Garden can a *huri* ever You replace.
If a *huri* saw such a heavenly face on Judgement Day,
if honest… would acknowledge she was commonplace!
Our night will only turn into day when You come out
of Your bed-chamber like dawn that night does replace.
It'd not be strange if the living felt attraction for You,
for even the dead will rise… through love for Your face!
The beasts not filled with love for such a beautiful One
cannot be said to have souls… that a body does encase.

Veil of horse's hair can't stop fascination of Your eyes,
drunkard can't hide how much himself he tries to efface.
As You possess such sweetness it'd not be strange if...
bee wears yellow patch, infidels thread it does embrace.
O Beloved I cannot ever be telling what I am suffering
in Your presence, except that when I'm there's the case.
You and I today are centres of attraction of all mankind:
I'm famous for sweet poetry... You for beauty and grace.
I feel aggrieved that You should be looked at by each eye:
Sadi, it's not strange you're jealous, it Sa'd* did embrace!

* Note: Sadi here makes a word-play on his own name and that of Sa'd
who was a great friend of Prophet Mohammed. At his funeral the Prophet
turned his face away while Sa'd was being lowered into the grave. On
being asked why, he replied that the huris of Paradise had come to receive
the spirit of Sa'd and as they belonged to Sa'd he couldn't look upon them
and so the following saying came from that event... "Sa'd is jealous and I
am more jealous and God is more jealous than either of us."

For as long as I have lived I have accomplished nothing:
truthfully, all of my life in profligacy I have been living.
At the Resurrection hour I'll have nothing to depend on
except for the one hope: that God me may be pardoning.
Reproaches one's precious soul will suffer will be many
from tyranny of lust when Judgement Day is happening.
Sometimes I think how fine it would be if there was not
a Resurrection Day so... bad the good won't be shaming.
But... I realise again it'd be wrong to give in to despair:
what's forgiveness of millions like me to His Forgiving?

My friends tell me to repent of my sins, but as soon as
I make a vow never to sin again, that vow's not lasting!
My judgement's eyes can't see the road of expedience:
forgive my sin, or with Your grace set lamp for guiding.
Shamed by my sin I cannot be lifting my head up, but,
if You tell me to, I'll it… to highest heaven, be raising.
Though my disobedience and offence has gone beyond
every limit and reckoning… I hope for Your pardoning.
God, what work can Sadi do Your Majesty approves?
Grant me strength or over my weaknesses be passing!

It's one to the lover whether he sleeps on thorns or brocade
if his plans to be able to embrace the Beloved are waylaid.
Although another may be patient without seeing Beloved
I cannot be staying peaceful in this fire that doesn't fade!
My sighs are a fire the smoke of which is rising to the sky:
my tears resemble a spring whose waves the shore invade.
We're not indispensable to You but we still ask Your help:
though You're independent of us we're hopeful of Your aid.
O You who are happy and engrossed with the companions
of the cave we look to door like seven sleepers' dog, unafraid. *
All of this burden I'm enduring and I proceed upon my way:
a rutting camel goes fast though loaded, its joy being made.
We have thrown down the shield and submitted our necks:
it is Yours to command... whether You kill us or give us aid.
If You strike with cruelty's sword, Your blows comfort me:
You frown, 'Your bitterness sweet my soul will have made!'

O Sadi, if you happen to be cauterised with Love's brand...
brand of the Master to the slave is seen as a glorious trade.

* Note: Dog of the seven sleepers'... see previous note.

Relationship with a Master is good fortune that is soul-inspiring:
communion with pretender absent is unexpectedly, entertaining.
The time of night is ending with the first gleam of the dawn...
O Beloved, raise head from collar if You desire a second morning.
If You happen to display at night Your face that is like the sun...
all of the people would probably believe that the day was dawning.
One should be kindling the torch and be undertaking a real enterprise
so the torment of drunken hangover in one's head may be leaving.
Get up, and be counting as gain the rustle of the spring breeze...
birds harmoniously sing and pleasant fragrance tulip bed is emitting.
In the estimation of the wise man each separate leaf of the green
trees can be seen as a page of the Infinite Book God is knowing.
It is spring's season... get up, so we may go out to enjoy ourselves:
we can't rely on Fortune as to whether we will see another spring.
You made a promise that You would spend one night with me...
countless nights have gone, number of days are beyond reckoning.
Time of youth has passed and the raven-black hair turns white...
a flash of lightning has gone, dust of a horseman is  disappearing.
Wipe out the volume of all your thoughts and recite Sadi's poetry:
bring a lap full of jewels and them on all assembled, be raining.

Road to Winehouse is taken by the non-imbibing seeker:
he's spent cash of a whole lifetime on a day as a drinker.
I fear, O you of good repute, your reputation is at stake:
secretly bring me the wine bottles, openly be an imbiber!
If we go to the Resurrection without load of good works
it's best when load one has is opened, no shame to suffer.
All of this reputation and good name are like bad money:
gilded brass cannot stand touchstone's test or any other!
Judgement Day: when devotion, good works are brought,
what to Gracious God but all our poverty can we offer?
One's objective isn't attained by policy, fortune by force:
wealth, honour is His to give: let us see who is receiver!
Many the cell of a Sufi's been turned into a Winehouse:
many library's been turned into bench of a wine-drinker!

Who is a one truly alive… in the wise man's opinion?
It is that one who dies in street of Beloved… that one!
The wise man's advice isn't really helpful to the lover
who is one who is mad and is one full of intoxication.
If you should offer your life as a sacrifice to Beloved…
it's better than wandering the world, lost, in oblivion.
O You thief of my heart and the consumer of my soul:
my life's passed thinking about Your love… on and on!
If You give me a poisonous drink, it'll not taste bitter:
if You put me on Uhud* Mountain, it'd be no burden!
Captive of Your desire is never escaping and he who's
drowned in Your love will never the shore, land upon!

A secret pain consumes my heart that is so afflicted…
this love is such, it must be quite obvious, to everyone.
Don't be imagining that my heart can ever be at rest,
and do not expect that sleep my eyelids will fall upon.
If You've any grounds for reproaching us declare Your
complaint… if it's Your fault, pay the price thereupon!
I can't allow You to stand until You are sitting down,
and my sorrow will never be lightened, until it is done.
What's the value of pearls… what's the use of money?
I'd be an imposter if for Your sake my life wasn't given.
Another Beloved like You is impossible to be obtained:
for You, countless lives like Sadi's… would be undone.

*Note: Uhud is the name of a mountain about three miles from Medina
where Prophet Mohammed was defeated by the Quarish.*

To suffer cruelty from the Beloved is a condition…
as hangover follows wine-drinking, rose has thorn.
I am convinced that whatever You happen to say
is coming sweetly from Your lips, yes… thereupon.
One cannot be approaching another, and so… I've
come to You, so that from You I'll gain protection.
The garden is surely smiling when during season
of spring, clouds of March are weeping on and on!
You departed and no attention were You paying,
You left behind many heart and eye… now gone.
If on some occasion I am dying in Your presence,
it would not hurt me… nor grieve me, thereupon;

207

except for the deep longing to be alive again… so
that I'd be dying again before You… why go on?
I thought that I should be staying in a corner like
a stone with heart's face turned, the wall upon…
but, I know that this wouldn't be practicable for
You'd be able to make the stones talk on and on.
Sadi will not leave You because of Your cruelty:
where can captive take himself… if already gone?

Bright full moon, I'm confused by Your form and long hair:
a form or doomsday, ambergris or musky curls… I see there?
I've lost my way on the path of Love: O You Guide, please
show me the road, my patience is gone: O help me, Helper!
If You chased me away from You like a dog from a mosque,
I would no more disobey Your order than that of a Master!
Arrows of my cries pass each moment from heart's direction
through Highest Heaven… like a needle through gossamer.
What to do? I am able to lose a heart, but not a Sweetheart.
How to act? I can give up my life, but not that One… ever!
If I'm in Paradise without You Salsabil's water is tasteless:
if I am in Hell with You, even a blast of ice is better by far!
If bird of Union with You flew off in zenith of my Fortune,
would to God that I might be through joy, arrow's feather.
As long as I live I'll keep Your name turning on my tongue:
as long as I exist I'll keep Your image in my heart… forever!
If the gracious rain of Your bounty fails to fall on my head,
I'd send up a request to Heaven like a Jew at the Passover.

I am greatly upset... though You kindly overlook my faults
I'm now terrified: in Your mercy of my sins be the Forgiver.
Although the heart-rending sighs of Sadi pierce the skies...
they don't impress Your infidel heart. Help me, O believer!

We're strangers in this city... beggars in this country;
captives in Your noose and snared in Your net are we!
The door of the Universe has been flung wide open but
Your long hair our heart's feet enchain, we're not free!
I can never take these eyes away from gazing at You...
My Monarch, do not hold back Your glance from me.
Although there are many better than us following You,
we shall not be meeting Your peer in the world... truly!
I thought of sacrificing my life for Your sake... but then
it occurred to me that all my possessions are unworthy.
The story that I am telling is the outcome of my pain...
aloes gives no fragrance unless on fire it lies eventually.
If I should say my condition is not of one who is upset,
cheeks colour would betray mind's secrets, indubitably!
I'll not stop gazing at those bow-horns, Your eyebrows,
even if both eyes are pierced by Your arrows... directly!
I'm wondering at the good sense of those giving advice;
be off... a lover's not one to accept reproof, even mildly!
O Sadi, it's the truth a lovely face is made to gaze upon:
what use an eye that can see if it can't look, occasionally.

He is a  lover who patiently endures the Beloved's cruelty,
and sacrifices his wishes to those of Beloved's completely.
If the life of the true lover is put at risk by the sword, then
he sees it as his own fault… not as Beloved's does he see.
It is wrong to be taking a beautiful one for the sake of lust:
so be subduing our passions for Beloved's sake should we.
I have heard of lovers who take themselves to the desert…
helpless from folks criticism and their sweethearts' cruelty.
I'll make myself take the way to the street of the Beloved:
I'll be laying down my head at the feet of the Beloved only.
You said breeze from the garden in rose season is pleasant,
but the love of the Beloved won't leave mind in any degree!
The garden without seeing the Beloved is like a penance…
even if you plant a thousand rosebushes, matters not to me!
O breeze, if you should pass by the rose-bed of the seeker…
convey blessing of a lover to the Eternal Beloved instantly.
We will never speak to anyone of the pain of loving You…
lover's condition should only be told to Beloved… secretly.
Everyone passes life among others, but Sadi is in seclusion:
the lover of the Beloved is from all of mankind an absentee!

O You, who surpass all of mankind in nobility of character,
the world's eyes gaze on Your face that couldn't be lovelier!
It's right that people patiently endure that One's flirtations
because that One of such gracefulness is the sole possessor.
O You, through the love of the tree of whose physical form
all the birds of my soul are now taking flight, into the ether!

That one who shut the door against such a face as Yours…
has never been endowed with any spiritual insight… either.
I would even drink date wine if Your hands offered some…
I'd neglect prayers, if to Your wishes they were an opposer!
If I should weep like a candle I might be excused because no
one who is in the fire says, "Don't be melting me, kind sir!"
I didn't say a word about the fire of love that consumed me
until those tears of my tell-tale eyes of me was the betrayer.
Water and fire are certainly opposed to each other and I've
never heard that of patience love was ever the close partner.
Everyone is trying hard to get a glimpse of a beautiful one,
but it is also true that love can be true or false for the lover.
It is indispensable for one who wants to visit the Kaaba to
put up with the ups and downs if he wants to be a traveller.
O Sadi… that lover is one who is truly alive who dies upon
Beloved's threshold… after he's been an earnest supplicator.

That breeze, heavy with musk, to the spirit brings healing…
get up friend, it's time for the sound of the drum of morning.
O musician, chant your song, light your candle, bring wine,
bruise the ambergris, burn the aloes, the roses be scattering!
If Beloved should offer a hand to you, nothing else matters!
Bride who is beautiful without a trousseau is more pleasing.
If clouds are to lavish their bounty they should do it today…
tomorrow when the thirsty are dead, rain may not be falling.
I am not so remiss in fulfilling my promise as to be relaxing
my hold of Your skirt… because a sharp sword I'm fearing!

But, kill me with Your own hand, for one is told to practise
forbearance with friends, with one's enemies to be fighting.
If You strike me with a sword here is my body as a shield…
only that faker who pretends love, being killed is avoiding.
Tomorrow when I raise my head from dust, if I saw You…
not an iota of concern about Judgement Day I'd be feeling.
Let's see how far many prayers reach on Judgement Day…
my face turns to You while all mankind to Mecca's turning.
Sadi remains foot-bound in this love he has for Your face…
You've never captured anyone with possibility of escaping!

O silver-bodied Winebringer, why are You sleeping, why?
Get up… sprinkle the water of joy on our grief's fiery sigh!
Be imprinting just one kiss upon the edge of the cup… and
quickly be circulating that honeyed wine we'd want to try.
Because the clouds of March are all busy scattering pearls,
and the breeze of a new spring sends the fragrance on high,
we are endeavouring to prevent the skirt of soberness from
being defiled in all of the winehouses: O how hard we try!
But the power of love is finally prevailing, and now it does
seem obvious the power of wisdom to resist has passed by.
I exclaimed this… "O you powerful one, O you wisdom…
tell me this: why, why is it that you fled from love… why?"
That one replied, "If a cat should become as bold as a lion,
it does not dare to take on a leopard… and it then to defy!"
Sweethearts are the demolishers of the house of continence
and musicians are raiders: on Mecca's road in wait they lie.

That sweet of mouth Beloved who causes many upheavals
is rendering repentance bitter in the throat of one such as I.
O Sadi, be holding fast to the long, curling hair of Beloved:
whenever you get the opportunity to hold on, you must try!
Be leaving all of your enemies to their own devices, and let
them raise their uproar... the din of doomsday... by and by!

About the long dark night what would that one know
who is wrapped in luxury's garment... and is all show?
The man who is wise knows the outcome of love so he
does not make a beginning of it from the very first go!
I tried hard to avoid surrendering my heart to anyone,
but with both eyes open how's it possible not to do so?
Look out for calamity from arrow of that One's glance
for it will never return again... once it has left the bow!
It must surely be because of coquetry of the pheasant,
that the destiny of the falcon's eyes is to never let go.
Police inspector's on the track of the drunken outsider,
but never bothers the Sufis' flirting, that all now know.
Tell everyone who is loving the rose to leave and to be
enduring the cruelty of the thorn... tell them all to go!
O you, you who have yielded your heart to the Archer,
you've to take off your shield... down it quickly throw!
Whatever you expect at Beloved's hands is a kindness,
be it disdain or honour, whatever Beloved does bestow.
The hand of Majnun was grasping at the skirt of Layla:
head of Mahmud lay in dust at Ayaz's foot... long ago!

There is not another nightingale able to sing like me...
there's no minstrel who with a voice like mine does go!
Everything of value is derived from a particular source;
sugar is coming from Egypt and Sadi, Shiraz did grow!

How blessed is the night, even more joyful is the day...
auspicious Fortune has come out to welcome me today!
Drummer, a double roll on the kettledrum for last night
was a Night of Power... today's like New Year's Day.
Is this a moon, or is it an angel, or is it a human being?
Is it You I'm seeing or the sun's world-illuminating ray?
Didn't You know my enemies are waiting in ambush?
You acted well when ill-advisers You told to go away!
You enemy, I am one who is united with the Beloved...
shut eyes if your heart is not wanting it to be this way.
I knew that for many nights heart did not rest from my
world-consuming cries... due to separation's bitter tray.
If those nights hadn't been so truly terrible Sadi would
not have appreciated the true worth of this day: today!

It could be that tonight untimely is the cock's crowing,
lovers have not had their fill of embracing and kissing.
The Beloved's breast among the curls of that long hair
resembles a ball of ivory... in ebony polo-sticks curling.
Tonight... when that eye of mischief is still fast asleep,
be careful to stay awake or your life you'll be regretting!
Until you hear the morning's call from Friday Mosque,

or roll of drums from gate of Atabeg's palace booming...
it would be a mistake to take your lips from that One's
red mouth, when the stupid cock at morning is crowing!

May your life be prolonged though my breath you shorten!
I will call upon the Prophet to intercede for I cannot go on!
Please, don't all my cries and appeals against your hatred
cause your bell-like head to ache? Of me, is it very brazen?
Tell the house's master to open the pigeon-cote's latch, or
else to kill me, for in this cage we're as good as dead, again.
I'll go, because there's such a callous person as you are here,
if you should stay a moment longer the roof will have fallen.
Although it's night and brutish men are waiting in ambush,
can the head of the police than this make any worse prison?
People desire to listen to their friends and to be with them,
but when in your company, I wish my death would happen!
Formerly I wished to see my friends, now that desire left me
and this is all because of this ill fortune of you... once again.
If anyone should hear that you were there beside the Kaaba,
he'd from Mecca without performing the pilgrimage, return.
If that old vinegar which is upon your frowning brow should
ever become honey, it even the worst blowflies would spurn!
O Sadi... the death agony of a sage would be more pleasant
than to live with one with whom there's no sympathy, even.

Fragrance of springtime is released O sweet-voiced nightingale,
sing your plaintive note and if like me you are caged, just wail!

People take sweethearts, kind and unkind… each day their hearts
are fixed on another one, but only One all my interest does entail.
Camel driver, on my behalf tell that One carried at front of the
caravan to keep sleeping on camel while bell's ringing does prevail.
However harsh the vendor of sweets may be to flies… fanning
as much as ever… they are still swarming, it is all to no avail!
Now that my bonds are tied fast what use is advice of the wise?
In future I'll be vigilant if I get a chance to flee from cage's jail!
To me it's no difference if Friend comes or sword falls on head:
I fell in love with One whom I can't leave and walk another's trail.
All the others that I have known I could forget in one moment:
I'm like a sunless morning, no sigh escapes my heart in the pale.
I am poor in middle of caravan, let whoever wants, attack me…
minstrel left me less than night patrol would accept as 'a sale'.
If You want to chain me, do: You want to advise me? Give it!
Infatuated lover will die when in his love for You he does fail!
O heart's ease, You've sent Sadi's lament throughout the world!
How long make him complain? Come, he went beyond the pale!

That One who wants to destroy me, for whose safety I'm concerned,
no matter how much flirting… no one ever that One has blamed.
That One never gives fruit to any man… is only a pleasure garden:
apple of that One's form's tree can only be seen and not tasted.
I don't apply a cure to my heart because one who is made sick
by love will not back to health by any medicine be ever nursed!
Tell one not ready to sacrifice the joys of both worlds and wealth
and life, not to love sweethearts or he will repent for being misled.

I'll not fight with that One although that One grasps the sword…
even at the Resurrection I will not ask retaliation for blood spilled.
O… if only I could see that One just once again at the Resurrection,
then I would become responsible for what sins that One committed!
O Sadi, do not expect to hear news of the safety of that person
who has fallen in love… and is wanting his heart to be gratified.

One who has his own Beloved does not take a strange sweetheart.
O you with hands so nimble, chop away at your wall for a start!
To whom You give orders instantly girds loins in service, but…
it'd be better if commands to only Your servant You did impart.
From the very first I thought I'd sacrifice my life for Your face:
it's inconsistent with being a man to one's promise break apart.
Everyone I ask about love's pain is answering, "Why ask me,
because I am also helpless when it comes to affairs of the heart!"
O you who are aspiring to intimacy with one who is above you,
you have to exercise patience like moth… in love's burning art!
As You have shown me Your face, You either ought not to have
broken my heart or not revealed Your face to me from the start.
All these Monarchs of Beauty have not a limit to their loveliness:
ah no, for they never any sympathy for their close friends impart.
I once imagined that in Love, reason would be worth something,
but I'll never again place reliance on imagination… that upstart!
Anyone wishing to say anything about me let him say whatever,
I'll never withdraw my hand from off the skirt of that Sweetheart!
On Resurrection Day when people pay no regard to each other,
on no account will I not talk to my Beloved… take that to heart!

217

O Sadi, don't be boasting of self-restraint in the street of Love…
there's a purchaser for each chattel in its own market, for a start!

O poor little fox, why haven't you stayed in your lair?
You have fought with a lion… suffered then and there.
Even an enemy would not act towards his foe as a fool
treats his own soul, to satisfy his desires: do you hear?
What complaint can he possibly bring against others:
with his own hand he slaps his own neck everywhere?
What claim can a thief make against police injustice?
Tell him it's his own doing… send his head elsewhere.
Your blood will be shed for stealing the king's carpet…
you fool! Why not lie upon your own mat? Take care!
Better that both eyes should be blind at the same time
than that they should fail to see their own faults glare!
There's a pit on a road: a man has eyes to see and sun,
so that he is able to watch his feet and avoid the snare.
He has so many lamps but still keeps on going astray:
let him fall, experience hurt, perhaps he'll learn to care.
Point out to others how the oppressors fall in their pits:
digging pits for others, themselves they'll find in there!
If one were to apply the ear to the heart of Sadi's words,
of God's will, before that of his own he would be aware.

Moon appeared from horizon of that One's clothes… said I:
"Breathe 'Glory of God' around that One against the evil eye!"

Let us see which of these Time's revolutions will make for me:
Beloved will place arms around my neck, or my blood will fly?
Tell that one who doesn't know who killed the devotee to look
at finger-tips and nails of the Beloved... obvious for one to spy!
If flowerbed should tell me the tulip says it has the same colour
as that One's face... its tongue be pulled like lily's for that lie.
I can't say that One is a moon, the Pleiades, a cypress, the sun:
that body has soul's beauty... in those clothes a body does lie.
Granted, that One withdraws sleeve from grasp of poor lovers:
but, is it possible to go when so many hearts grab skirt and cry?
I've given over to Friend my share of having any kind of reputation.
In this world he is my enemy who to hurt that One does try!
If my body is hair-thin through Fate's cruelty I could bear it more
than a hair's breadth of woe to that One's body anyone may imply.
See what a face that is that is baffling all my power of speech!
Is it dawn shining in the east, or Beloved out the window I spy?
O my Beloved, when in the future a list is made of wise folk...
quickly erase my name from it, if in it my name happens to lie.
This patched cloak of piety and asceticism doesn't become Sadi!
Winebringer, give a cup and strip this cloak off him... this lie!


You've done wrong in listening to the words of my enemies,
You have forgotten promise You made to friends like these.
Who asked You to display Your face that adorns the city...
and when You've done so, who said to veil it, tell... please?
Is Your cruel heart not even aware that I am boiling away...
just like a brazen pot does on a raging fire... with such ease?

I see no escape from being obsessed with thoughts of You...
unless it's when I become intoxicated and my senses freeze!
Outwardly I am listening to the advice that people give me,
while secretly inside love tells me to listen to none of these.
That One is the Winebringer, from whose hands I take the
cup: that One is the Minstrel, whose song gives heart ease.
Give me a goblet of wine... be taking off this cloak of mine:
set sweetmeats before me... sell this patched cloak, please!
I sat and I waited until You finally came out... gracefully:
You came out... I went out of my senses with absolute ease!
The world's far too small to be able to contain Your beauty,
so how can I, a poor wretch, ever be held in Your embraces?
Those wise ones keep giving advice to me, always saying...
"Sadi, stop vain lamentations like an empty drum, please!"
But as long as the drum continues to be beaten with a drum-
stick it will never stay silent... just to please such as these!

Fortune does not allow me to hold to my heart that Sweetheart,
never letting exile be forgotten by a kiss from lips sweetly apart.
The noose that One likes to use to trap victims from far and wide
I'll steal away so one day to my heart I'll lure that One's heart.
Yet I don't dare stroke that One's hair with a hand that's bold:
snared in that hair like birds are lovers hearts, too many to chart!
I'm a slave to that most beautiful form which in my imagination
is clothed in grace measured by a rod tailors apply to their art.
O cypress with Your silver limbs, the scent and colour of You
put to shame myrtle's smell and made eglantine's bloom depart.

Use Your eyes, see it is time to walk in the garden without concern,
and step upon the jasmine and flower of Judas tree… that upstart!
Full of joy, happiness is New Year's Day, especially in Shiraz:
here a stranger forgets where he is from and loses to it his heart.
Over the garden's Egypt, like Joseph, the beautiful rose is ruling…
eastern breeze scent of Beloved's garment into city does impart.
Don't wonder at how during spring-time out of jealousy of You,
clouds are weeping and flowers are smiling… playing their part!
If over the dead Your feet should tread with that walk so graceful,
it is not absurd if a voice is heard that from a shroud does depart.
All distraction is banished from our land in the reign of the king,
except for Sadi by Your beauty… and people, by his poetic art.


You have gone but You are never forgotten…
You come here and my senses are gone again.
Your eyebrows bow that is always stretched
as far as Your earlobe, is worthy of magician!
It is an impossibility for me to embrace You…
but allow me to kiss Your foot now and then!
Oppression at Your hands is only just, right:
like honey, is sting of Your every expression.
It'd be quite useless in the season of spring,
to tell the nightingale never to cry out again.
Morning breeze was divulging heart's pain
which last night I tried hard not to happen!
Flood that last night came up to my waist,
tonight will pass over shoulder, what then?

A whole city would talk about Your beauty
but it bewilders the tongue-tied, unspoken.
Sit down... a thousand upheavals arise from
those bewildered seekers when You've risen.
Impossible for this cauldron to stop boiling
in the fire that by You is now kindled again.
Nightingale that fell into Beloved's hands
instantly forgets its companions in garden.
Good sir, go purchase Beloved in exchange
for everything you have. Don't sell! Listen!
If anyone asks you to repent of your love…
listen: don't lend ear to that one ever again!
Every day Sadi is heard to give such advice,
but… to such good advice he does not listen!


Indifferent to everyone else in the world is that one adoring You:
that one cares nothing about worry and grief others cause, too!
That one can only seek Your love who abandons self-love…
none can think of Union with You unless with life he is through.
Don't call him a true lover who can't be patient with the Beloved;
don't call him 'man' who for love's sake can't take criticism too!
When you have lost control of heart, as if an unmanageable colt,
that you can't regain power over it, not by any means… is true!
Sincere lover doesn't forsake Beloved due to cruelty and criticism:
he wouldn't even wince if at him spears and arrows You threw.
If You should suddenly approach one lying in dust of the tomb,
it'd surely be strange if his soul didn't re-enter his body anew!

The garden is ashamed because of Your beautiful, tall figure,
because it was never possessing such a graceful cypress, as You.
I thought that by patience I might escape Your love's whirlpool,
but again I look and it is a shoreless sea that comes into view.
My promise with You is not a promise that's subject to change:
it is a garden that the blast of autumn never is coming through.
What fault have I or You saw in me that You would leave me?
Your slave is blameless, so dismissing him is not right to do!
There's not a creature in the whole world who hears Sadi's wailing
that doesn't acknowledge his cries to be totally sincere and true!

A certain one the hand of regret on his ear-lobe is laying,
while another one in the embrace of his Beloved is lying.
Lying shoulder to shoulder with my rivals, One doesn't
know how this lonely lover slept last night: One, loving.
All of those well-wishers keep on giving me good advice,
in reply I'm shouting, "Be silent all of you, stop talking!"
My ears are so full of notes of music and sound of songs
that no more room in them for criticism is now remaining.
People keep on urging me to close my eyes to that One...
to which I reply... "Hey, let that One a veil be wearing!"
For as long as an image of that One remains in his mind
this mad lover will not ever again his senses be regaining.
It is an impossibility to seal the fount of my eyes because
the sea of this heart of mine is… boiling, boiling, boiling!
Come and let us drink from the hands of the Loved One,
whether poison or honey... whatever that One is offering!

Leave me lying in the dust of that street of the Beloved…
please go away… allow my enemy to me be finally killing!
Sadi is not a lover who is 'slack' in the performance of his
promise and forgets Beloved because cruelty is impending.

Beware of the mouth of that One that is smiling,
and that One's red lips and those teeth flashing!
It has to be that milk of the wet-nurse's breasts
who reared that beauty was with honey dripping.
If the gardener saw that One's swaying saunter,
all the cypress' from his garden he'd be uprooting!
And if such a huri* were to be entering Paradise;
Paradise's paris'* that One's slaves are becoming.
There is not a pit in the path of the true Believers,
the dimple of the pit of that One's chin excepting.
How long shall I sit, thirsty for the water of Life,
that upon the lip of that mouth's well is awaiting?
It'd be fitting if the Beloved made that face freely
available to the distracted sightseers for viewing.
Camel driver… where's the beauty of the Kaaba?
For in its wilderness all us are now away passing!
Many are the ones who struggle in the dust like a
ball because of that One's bat-like hair… striking!
Of course Wisdom and Patience fled unnerved by
that One… that One they were not withstanding.
We've no patience to bear Your absence anymore,
for only so far is limit of its endurance continuing.

The ardent lover has to withstand all of the many
reproach his friends at him may keep on throwing.
What difference would the rain ever make to that
person who in the Red Sea is hopelessly drowning?
What does Sadi care for the criticisms of anyone?
Dead man with a lance don't try to be frightening!

*Note: A huri is a female beauty of Paradise; a pari is a female jinn.

If a person because of his love should utter a cry,
it'd be strange if fire didn't cause pot to boil dry!
If one tears his garments from passionate desire,
cover sin with Your skirt's forgiveness by and by.
The breeze of the east wafts the scent of the rose,
the love-sick nightingale does not silence his cry!
If the musicians should keep playing in this way,
all friends to get their senses back would not try!
If the winebringer should give wine out of the jar,
winter would carry off dervish's coat, it would fly!
Bring me some poison because every limb of mine
is crying out with eager longing… drink, and die!
People will not ask you about length of the night:
only he knows who to sleep last night didn't try!
It'd be a pity to die without Love… so try to win
it for as long as a breath and soul in you does lie.
The head that doesn't lie at the feet of Beloved is
a heavy load that on shoulders does lie, I testify!

Even if Sadi should become one with that dust…
his lamentations will again be heard, on that rely!
Whoever has a heart will be hearing the sound of
his sighs until Judgement Day… sigh after sigh!


No one has ever seen such grace and charm and sweetness
as which that One has: one seeing once wants again access.
How sweetly our minstrel is singing because of his anguish:
the song of lovesick nightingale, exciting pleasure to excess.
It often occurs to my mind to be hiding the pain of love, but
the glass discovers it's impossible its secrets not to express!
If the bird that flies should happen to grow old in its cage…
it is in its nature that memory of how to fly, it does possess.
Please tell what have we done that the Beloved's sweet lips
do not open in speech again or eyes look with Love's caress?
If You should heap every kind of abuse on me, I would only
bless You. A humble servant renders service… others less!
A last breath remains for one drowning in Your love's sea…
now that You've killed him, at least him to the shore press.
The blood of Sadi isn't really worthy of the honour of being
smeared on Your hand: falcon doesn't try locust to possess.


Sinning in secret than worshipping in public is better:
if you adore God of vain desires, do not be the idolater.
Don't regard other men with eyes of pride and disdain,
it's possible a friend of God may be a drunken outsider.
In this earth you see are people with the nature of kings

226

in whose eyes a Universe isn't worth a corpse's bother.
Illustration of sun and a bat's eye isn't comprehended
by the so-called vision of that one... who is a stranger.
They practise generosity, don't see themselves giving
favours, endure chastisement, with none are an arguer!
They flee like smoke from hearth of vile, wretched ones,
and from them even for a bowl... they are not a beggar.
For the here or the hereafter their heart's aren't longing:
one must sing Beloved's praises or of trash be attender!
Acceptable in God's presence because of their honesty,
they're notorious for loving and their drunken behaviour.
Saints walk and are never boasting. It's because of its
being hollow that the pod of the poppy is a loud rattler.
The height of the fortunate mystic's pride is to refrain
from arrogance towards the drunkard, the wine-drinker!
Position of righteous and dissolute man isn't clear yet:
pay regard to final state, not the present, a do-gooder!
If you prefer the external husk, to the kernel of Truth...
wear a Sufi's blue cloak or shave head like a Kalandar.
Aim of Path's People is not to wear clothes for show,
gird your loins in service of King, be a Sufi who's truer.
And since the grace of the Almighty Lord is with you,
also in footsteps of the servants of God be a follower.
When Fortune favours you, fulfil the desires of people
and refrain from hurting any heart when you've power.
Sadi's creation is not a picture outwardly embellished
like painter that door of Turkish bath is the decorator.

No... it is a veil studded with rubies and pearls that is
let down over the face of such a Beauty who's a teaser.

Some business that occupies him every one is desiring:
vagabond like me the passion of his heart is absorbing.
I never imagined that You would associate with me...
O Morsel when I won You, You proved to be so filling!
Is it really You with me, behind me guardians clamour?
Road to desert in Your company I am truly following?
The brand of Your separation still sears my soul, but...
perhaps hand like balm to my heart You'll be applying.
I cannot expect from Fortune bliss of You as my guest:
a poor man's courtyard would be a royal tent in spring.
None can apply balm to wound of Your love's sword...
I am a golden saucer that with glue one is not repairing.
  One cannot tell lovers to be abandoning their love...
impossible to tell infidels their faith be relinquishing!
Today I enjoy You with the minstrel and winebringer;
let envious... themselves on chamber-door be hanging.
As for me, I've no apprehension about wiles of enemy;
but a scorpion by vileness even stone will be stinging!
O Sadi, you've gained your heart's ease... drink wine
and be indifferent to friends and also enemies abusing.
You warning against giving heart and falling in love...
I'm what I am, be off... your own business be minding!

That one who has a beautiful Beloved who is also unkind...
has to endure the cruelty of whatever that One has in mind.
 And if that One can say anything that is even more bitter,
let it be spoken from those sweetest lips one could ever find.
 All the power of being able to move did suddenly leave me,
at the first time that I ever saw that One's walk, so refined!
That One would easily revive a victim of the arrow of love,
if that One happening to pass near the victim, him did find.
I'm so intoxicated by the conversation of that One that I'm
lost in answering that One's speech... nothing in my mind!
My love was concealed but my patience became exhausted,
I was then forced to reveal my love's secrets to all mankind.
 O... if only I could render some service to that One, but...
what service could I do... that would be of the worthy kind?
 Human beings are in danger of becoming... because of the
angel-like movement of that One... quite mad in the mind!
O if only that Sovereign had decided to come out... so this
 beggar of the market might be brought back into his mind.
 O Sadi, it is better not to be seeing the face of the Beloved,
than to be seeing it in the presence of strangers... that kind!

Let that one who has a Beloved with a heart that is tender,
be careful of that One's delicate feelings: this... remember!
The lover of the rose cannot be considered as being faithful
 if he is not even able to endure the thorn's sharp reminder!
 O you who claim to be a well-wisher, let me remain in the
fire of love and of me to be shunning it don't be the adviser.

Although I am as weak as the feeble ant, I am still able to
annihilate the self... and the whole load of that One I bear.
O... if only our heart has at least a thousand lives, so that
I could sacrifice each one of them... to see that One forever.
Don't regard that one as a sincere lover who gets annoyed
with the Beloved when Beloved of that one is a reproacher.
Not a one is able to attain the peace of mind that we enjoy
who has not first been reduced to the final gasp of despair!
Whoever wishes to strike his head against the wall of the
hard-hearted Beloved, this is where to be... a head-butter!
Please tell, is our blood having any consequences in terms
of any value in the eyes of the Beloved... any whatsoever?
O Sadi... if that One should demand your life then to win
the heart of that One, it you should completely surrender!

Win a Sweetheart to hand and through hope of the happiness
that One will bring: bear patiently hurt causing unhappiness.
Who will be giving to us some access to the pavilion of Union?
O breeze of dawn, give us a message from Court of that Empress.
That One's face whose bright beauty obscures the morning light,
has made abundant tears that look like stars flow from my eyes.
Whenever I should think that this wounded heart's finally healed,
that One is scattering salt all over it, by showing such loveliness.
The amiable Beloved knows only too well that however badly
an action is... it will never be seen as such in the lover's eyes!
That poor wretch, who formed in his mind... a picture of Your
face, could never remain at ease with having seen it... I stress!

When I happen with Your dreamy eyes to be comparing them...
I become angry with the unparalleled impudence of the narcissus.
Such a charming, swaying walk, smiling lips and beautiful face,
how's it possible for any man not to be longing for such loveliness?
Tongue of eloquence of Sadi is helpless in describing You, though
to Beauty of all beauties he's rendered full justice, nevertheless!

Get up, and let's now amuse ourselves in the garden's flowerbed,
since the opportunity for a moment's enjoyment itself has offered.
For this raging torrent will one day be uprooting the tree and
this unfavourable wind will finally... the lamp be making dead!
The green grass grew then withered, rose blossomed, shed petals;
and the nightingale must eventually let the crow have its head.
Dust of many a garden owner... has been fashioned into the
clay of the garden walls, by revolutions of earth Time has led.
You have heard of the branding at the Resurrection with gold
and silver? It is the past that brands you... after you are dead!
Many a season will pass on mountain and plain and the clouds
will keep weeping on gardens after we are dead, let it be said!
If you were to open the graves of the dead you would find that
all the pride of pomp in one's brain is not worth even one shred!
O Sadi, do not pay any regard to worldly wealth and honour,
they're an inheritance left by rich men... crows pick at each head.
Whether you listen to good advice or not, we have told the truth,
and a messenger is only responsible for delivering what is said.

O You Winebringer... give to me that red wine!
O Musician, play me on harp that tune so fine;
for I've never gained any access from asceticism,
how long against stone I'll strike glass of mine?
My heart is broken without getting its wants...
my reputation and honour they now all malign!
Love came near me... and Reason fled far away
from my presence... like the wind it did whine!
You devout wearer of the coat of many patches,
how long be arguing with this poor lover's line?
The lover wanders through both lovers worlds,
but look... those ascetics stay at home to pine!
Because of Your love I threw off patched-coat:
it's possible I'll attain Union with the Divine!
Sadi, keep on playing the lover's part forever...
and in all worlds to single-mindedness incline!

Don't ever imagine a heart-sick lover will accept counsel:
I've not an ear that listens, to whom advice will you tell?
For as long as I was wise I didn't follow the path of Love:
heart's now in such a state, my senses in confusion dwell!
After all, isn't it natural that one heart rushes to another?
Why am I desiring Union, but You tire of me... please tell.
You're never absent from my thoughts, not for a moment:
a big difference between a thought... and when it does jell!
Someday I will kiss Your hand and then fall at Your feet:
moth's needing permission for itself into a flame to propel?

232

See how the sparrow keeps longing to relate to the falcon?
Poor little bird only hastens to its death… it knows well!
My life will perish in Your Love at last… ah my Desire!
The fiery memory of You in my heart death cannot quell!
We've no friend in all the world except for You, Beloved;
whether You reject or accept the worthless goods we sell.
O illustrious courier, who is taking message to Beloved,
O if only in your place for me to be the messenger befell!
The revolution of Time has finally turned my head white,
but in this old mind of mine these vain fancies still dwell!
O Sadi, as you have become a prisoner… bear its burden,
for the wretched rogue has to suffer until he bids farewell.


If silver-bodied, hard-hearted Beloved would come back to me,
thorns would leave rose and foot: foot from mire would be free!
O morning breeze, from desire to turn this night into day time…
fling back camel-litters covering off that Sun burning so brightly!
That One from ownership may be making ready to slay the lover:
thousands of victims would come forth to meet their death happily!
A group of associates, giving no thought to my reason or religion
have clutched my sleeve, warning me: leave that One immediately!
What would a wise one say to the lover's critic? "He who lies
on shore knows nothing of condition of one drowning in the sea!"
Beloved may, having full-ownership, smear hands with my blood:
because death by hand of a slayer like that One would please me.
If that critic were wise he'd know patience is impossible for Majnun:
he, makes his camel kneel at the place where his Layla will be!

233

Wisdom's creating many worries that keep wearing out the mind:
if you want peace, go away smart-arse: don't be a lover like me!
As long as my feet can move they will look for the Path of Love:
let Wisdom say, "A curse on such a business, without profitability!"
If you'll sit in Beloved's company careless of the Here and Hereafter,
wonderful pictures like those in Greece and China you will see.
To touch on this such expressions are needed only Sadi can compose:
what comes from the soul... for it to sink into the heart is necessary!


The evil eye stay far from You, One of attributes so rare;
my moon, crowd's candle, Ruler of nations... everywhere.
You moved away flirtatiously and You didn't come back...
I have never seen a cypress sway so gracefully, anywhere.
All Your attributes indicate points of spiritual knowledge:
Your face is demonstrating Divine Omnipotence, I swear!
Don't read the story of the anguish of Layla and Majnun,
Your love has wiped away memory of back then and there!
What veil exists that can separate the lover from Beloved?
Even Alexander's forts could not be a hindrance, I declare.
Your fame's been shouted abroad and the mystics know it:
speaker and listener are moved to join the dance, wherever!
Let the whole city stand gazing and see me, for I've locked
my arms in Beloved's embrace, like shoulder-brace to wear.
Time's revolution is complete, my life has reached its end:
desire for You is unsatisfied, love for You... still an affair!
If You should send me off I've no one to intercede for me...
I've a path to You but I've no means to be going elsewhere.

To whom can I tell tale of the anguish loving You entails?
We've told all of this story and still a solution isn't there!
Sadi in future will not be wise and will not be sensible too,
for Love triumphs over each branch of science everywhere!

Look, here I am standing… engaged in service to You:
what does it matter to me whether it's acceptable too?
I have no strength to cling to You, no power to escape:
no patience away from You… no option of Union too!
Was not the noose of Your love and Your twisting hair
enough without spurning lovers, victims who love You?
Don't reproach me though I may deserve it! Thousand
precious lives be sacrificed to humour humourless You!
If I have to endure Your reproaches it is even my fault,
Love is a heavy burden… I'm 'unjust and ignorant' too.
If I fully described all that I've suffered at the hands of
separation from You, it would be a long story and true!
I can't compose a letter to You because of my tears, for
when I write it's immediately wet all the way through!
What concern do I have with the babbling of advisers?
Philosopher's claim to better mad Bahlul,* is stupid too!
No one can learn the way of Love only through talking,
unless of course it's in his nature to be a talker, to You.
Kindly summon the captive of Your Love, if You drive
him away in anger… where can Your chained one go to?
Powerless to grapple with You, not only is Sadi's arm:
lion's clawed-arms yield to sword's glance of Yours too!

I had finally sat myself down and was in my self-absorbed,
door of my house to any entering or exiting I had closed…
night slowly passed, eyes fixed on expectation's threshold
that in the morning Hope would at my door have knocked.
That One's head is filled with drunken stupor, hands dyed
with blood of lovers and dreamy eyes with magic anointed.
Winebringer, come here… let my neighbour close his eyes,
for both ears against the righteous traditions, I've stuffed.
My mind contains such a picture of the Beloved that all of
the objects of sense… can no longer by me be apprehended.
Words of Wisdom during time of the Empire of Love were
as ineffectual as commands of official who was dismissed.
I have no complaint to make against You… no, one should
be grateful to the King… for taking beggar's house instead.
Only a glutton would pay attention to food on the dinner
table at which the host's the object that everyone regarded.
I swear by Love… that the stroke of a sword by Your hand
would be just as agreeable to me… as music being played.
I should whisper my tale into Your ears with my own lips;
it's a pity message by hand of messenger has to be relayed.
In Sadi's heart is only room for You: how pleasant it'd be if
to exclusion of the world… he could with You, be occupied.

We have a Master so forgiving… that despite our heavy
load of sins we still remain hopeful of that One's mercy.
Who can open the door that the Almighty keeps closed?
Come let's make supplications at His door immediately!
O God, whether You call us to You or if drive us away,
we have no other door to go except Your door of bounty.
If You happen to forgive Your servants… we're exalted:
otherwise, we're unable to lift heads from sins so heavy.
You have created all of us from just a handful of dust…
for such a great blessing, how can we truly grateful be?
Day and night You're in intimate communion with us:
of You we are passing our days and nights neglectfully.
We do not claim to have rendered You devoted service:
we're ashamed of shortcomings of our service, heartily!
May the day never dawn when we're filled with despair
when we come to the Court of Your Grace, eventually.
O Lord, please reform us through Your Grace, because
indeed so miserable and distressed is state of poor me!
See us as beggars of Your street… if we are excluded
from those who at Your Court are treated intimately.

I cannot ever conceive attributes of that One's vision
except in that I am mad from that One talking to me!
That One gave us a sip on the Day of Creation: now
we are still drunk from that wine's power, its divinity!
Sadi, since that One can't be understood by Reason…
come, let's now raise our heads in this drunken frenzy!

God be praised that we didn't die without seeing our king's face,
that we had the opportunity to serve him with love and grace.
Many a Fatiha we have recited and often we whispered the Ikhas*
at the departure and the return of your standards to this place.
So... now we shall hear once again the roll of the drums of good
tidings and the jangling of bells as the camels pick up their pace.
A face we have longed to be seeing as much as the new moon
has appeared from the east that looks like the full moon's face.
Today we expressed thanks for the happiness of your safe return,
with smiling lips... for we have tasted separation's bitter base.
We were not sitting in the shadow of the palace of safety until
we had travelled across the mountains and deserts of the chase.
The time has now finally arrived for us to fulfil our desires as
occasion for any regrets has finally passed on more than apace.
Hand of Heaven on that day had kindled such a fire of separation
in this granary of ours, that we became like wheat was the case!
God be thanked that the pleasant breath of the spring has returned,
and that we were delivered from winter's tyrannical cold face.
We have torn, like a drum by a drumstick, the skin of that enemy
who did not want such drumbeats of happiness taking place!
O Sadi, in the presence of the sun it is always the best of manners
to say that... we have not yet seen the dark night... is the case!

*Notes: The Fatiha is the opening chapter or sura of the Koran and Ikhlas the penultimate chapter which are recited as a charm to avert the evil eye. This ghazal is in praise of Sadi's patron Atabeg Abu Bakr (d. 1260). See Introduction.

If on one day at Your hands some justice I succeed in obtaining
I'll dance one night to make amends for past life I've been wasting.
I love You so much that if some time I am separated from You,
please bear my absence: to be without You I could not be bearing!
Heart warns a hundred times to shut eyes to this source of mischief,
but… once again my eyes, that form that is bewitching, are seeing.
You should never sit in the garden in front of the cypress or the
gardener will say that he will never another cypress be planting.
My companions travelled, each friend of mine, to distant places…
unlike me whose garment in the mimosa thorns of love was catching.
I have fallen into such a sea that I cannot see any limit to it…
I've measured my strength with One against whom I'm a weakling!
Your absence is hard on me but I must continue to try to be patient,
for I would be a faithless friend if from Your cruelty I was fleeing.
Don't ask me how I was last night in my darkness and loneliness!
Why ask of separation's night, when of day of Union I'm worrying?
My laments at night are silent so my heart's pain stays concealed…
but my secret cries the ears of everyone in the world are reaching.
Secret company of Beloved is preferable to society's for a century…
I do not want any freedom, for Joseph's company me is imprisoning.
I am that sweet-singing nightingale whose voice even after his
body is dust, "I'm Sadi in the garden," will be heard to be saying!

I can't pursue my own interests because of love for You…
I'm like the moth, I burn but the flame keep flying through.

If You wish to be kind to me please be kind to me today…
or You may often look and not find me… then what to do?
I'm not so needy that I'll be satisfied with only one glance,
nor am I so thirsty that the Oxus River… it would subdue!
I'm like the harp, with head bowed in submission and love:
come, strike up Your pleasure and play on me, won't You?
Although You may place me on the fire a hundred times…
and pull me out, I'm pure gold: if I melt, I'm the same too!
And even if You approved of such cruelty as to stone me…
I would not be guilty of the offence of trying to resist You.
What can I do as I cannot give to that One proper service?
That my life is worthless to lay at Beloved's feet… is true!
I'm a winehouse hunter, a lover, madman and a drunkard…
what worse can those gossip-mongers say who me pursue?
I described to the physician the state of my mad heart and
that my eyes door stayed open… from thinking about You!
He replied, "O Sadi, complaint of this kind that you have
is Love's disease… that a cure for it I don't know, is true!"


I'm truly most fortunate today because my glance
has fallen upon the beauty of that One, by chance.
Give all praises due to Almighty God in Heaven
that my fortune has caused another circumstance.
Perhaps it's a vision that has appeared before me,
or is it possible… my imagination it did enhance?
As such good luck didn't fall to my lot on any day:
such a rose never bloomed for me… not a chance!

Today, I've seen what my heart's always desired,
while my ill-wisher saw his desire… not advance.
What more can one expect from Fate and Time…
because my new moon's reached its full expanse.
Now that You have revealed Your face to me…
my condition's greatly improved its circumstance.
O come back to me, because through my longing
for Your face I feel disgusted with this romance.
I am so tormented by separation from You that
heart does not give Union with You any chance!
And because of the extreme thirst that I suffer I
cannot swallow pure water in any circumstance!
Helpless… I come back to Your face when other
resources fail… and patience I look at askance.
I cling to You to protect me from Your injustice;
it's to You, complaint against You I'll advance!
O Sadi, when Beloved's friendly then cruelty of
others in the world is easy, in any circumstance!

You came to me and from desire I became quite senseless;
but since You left me I have become one who is… lifeless.
It is not forgetfulness that stops me from praising You…
no, it is contemplation of You making me mad… I confess.
While You left I slept not on rose-bed's fringe for a night
when I did not find myself in desert feeling thorns caress.
Hope of Union with You revived me every moment, or…
Your absence would've killed me, seeing You less and less.

Due of Your friendship it was like lying in a tulip, a sweet basil field, even when like Abraham I felt fire on me press. All night long I expected the bird of dawn to crow, hoping that from the morning breezes Your fragrance I'd possess. Through separation's cruelty Sadi is saying each day that while he has not broken his promise… You have. Confess!

The Beloved that is mine and that Sweetheart that I know has a sweet mouth beyond reach of my lips and teeth… so why won't fate allow me to sit, and seat that graceful One by my side… while on the head of that One, roses I throw? You with a heart-ravishing face, You're the sum of beauty: why worry Oneself, heart at ease, with me mad with woe? Take this opportunity, only a bit of my existence remains: when I remember You I no longer remain myself… I… go! I don't grieve about Union with You or Your separation… whatever You order me to do, as Your slave I'll remain so! O You… more fair than Layla, the fear that I have is that Your Love will make me, like Majnun… over the hills go! If a whole world rises up in hatred against me… if I should turn my gaze from Your face, hatred for it… may I know! I am imprisoned in Your snare, conquered by Your power, drunk by rapture You inspire… true praise I can't bestow. I'm mad from Your love: foot's stuck in mud chasing You. I can't bear this patiently… I need You Your face to show! In secret I keep crying out and it remains a matter of great wonder that over the world lovers can't sleep, I cry out so!

You've seen how fiercely fire will take hold of a dry thing?
You are fiercer than a fire and I am much more than aglow!
People say "Sadi, don't waste your life in this mad fancy!"
"If I lose my life no matter: Beloved's the only life I know!"

O You balm of my wound, O You… my soul's solace!
Do not make me suffer separation from Your fair face!
O You, who are the One who eases my wounded heart,
that You are the comforter of my mad mind is the case!
People tell me to take my hand from off that One's skirt
so that One may hold back grasp from my collar apace.
That one who is inviting me to any garden of pleasure
takes me into a prison if it is a place without Your face.
It's strange that I cannot find my way to Your presence,
nor have I any knowledge of any road to any other place.
Please, be accepting me as Your slave during one day…
and by the next day see how I am king of the populace!
O You, You rosebush of the garden of spiritual insight:
You've made me indifferent to the rose-garden's grace!
Since that same day when I saw Your cypress stature…
I've forgotten garden's cypress, can't remember a trace!
That double-string of pearls made conversation's topic:
bleeding tears gushed from my eyes… all over the place.
People say, "O Sadi, be patient in that One's absence."
I bear that One's load: as for patience, I haven't a trace!

You came in through the door and all of my senses left me:
one could say from this world to another I went, suddenly!
My ears were turned to the road to hear news of Beloved:
messenger finally arrived and my senses from me did flee!
I lay like a dewdrop before the sun when Love descended
on my soul, and I ascended to the star Capella, instantly.
I lost all power to enter into the presence of the Beloved...
at times I walked on my feet, at times on my head, crazily.
In order to see that One's swaying walk and to hear that
One, from head to foot I was eyes and ears... desperately!
How could I stop my eyes from looking at that One for it
was in seeing that One that I 'saw', when I first did See!
May I always be in despair of Your faithfulness if even for
a day or moment without You to see, contented stays me!
That One remained indifferent to the fact I was captured:
it was I who from that One's glance's noose, was not free.
They say, "Sadi, what happened, your red face is yellow?"
"Love's elixir thrown on my base metal, it's gold you see!"

O You of such a straight stature, we too are not worthless,
who of all in the world is better... we too are not worthless.
You said, "No nightingale saw rose with colour as mine!"
You certainly are a truth-teller... we too are not worthless!
How often will You say, "We are incomparable?" O You
whose beauty is unique by far... we too are not worthless!
O Sweetheart of each gathering, heart's ease of each soul,
though You have many a lover... we too are not worthless.

You did say that there was no creature on earth like You...
beauty of humanity without peer we too are not worthless!
If You are famous for beauty, unique pearl, why stay away
so far away from us, my Dear... we too are not worthless.
I thought that You'd have seen us, inquired of our welfare:
why be upset with us, You hear? We too are not worthless.
And even if You're a rose-bed or sweet singing nightingale,
though in world none are fairer... we too are not worthless!
O Sadi, if that lovely One's chosen one in preference to us,
tell that One to select whoever... we too are not worthless.

Please let me before Your face be slowly passing...
and all of Your noble attributes be contemplating.
Desire's from absence, cruelty from Your presence:
cruelty is preferable as desire we can't be enduring.
You don't turn Your face to mine, it's Your choice:
come back to me so at Your feet my face I'm laying.
We're in love with You: even if all the people were
against me and my life took... You I'd keep loving!
You've said Your lovers are greater than the dust...
it is not so, for we less than the dust are becoming.
We are with and without You: what state is this?
We're in Your circle: still outside, us You displace!
Complaints against enemies are brought to friends:
if Beloved is enemy, where complaints to be taking?
How strange I cannot indulge in hope of Your love,
nor dare for even a little affection to be cherishing!

We do not voluntarily run in the pursuit of anyone:
Beloved pulls us, in Beloved's lasso we're dangling.
O Sadi, tell… who are you? So many are caught in
this loop of that lasso that we're lean prey, waiting!

I am devoted to You and Your companion am I,
"From Your hands I crave Your bounty," I sigh.
All who are strangers are well aware… that at
Your court the word 'intimate' to me does apply.
But… I am afraid, O You fruit of a lofty tree…
that You beyond reach of these short hands lie.
I discovered in the last few days of my life that
wasting my fifty years so far in neglect have I.
I swear by Your being… since I've known You
I have had no knowledge of me… this, I certify!
Others ask of You things that conform to their
views… ambitions: from You only You want I.
I am the nightingale of Your beauty's garden…
how could my songs fail to be famous on high?
People drag me away, saying: "Give up Love,"
beating me for being the King's pawn they try!
If you should slice me into a hundred pieces…
I would not change my colour, I'm 'God's dye!'
O Sadi, they say not to look for Beloved… but,
the Beloved carries me off no matter what I try!
I don't have option to turn from Beloved's side:
go… tell amber, that the straw to draw in am I.

I swear by God that even if I die from You I'll not turn my heart:
leave my bedside, physician, for your medicine I'll have no part.
All my life I would have associated with the witty and beautiful,
but You've come and Your image has been inscribed on my heart.
O wise man, don't advise me, for I will not put it into practice:
although I may do without me, from the Beloved I can't be apart.
O shield, leave from my front, for the dart has pierced my soul;
let me be seeing now who it is that strikes me with that dart?
If You should see Your movements in the water… You'd say
with Your own lips, that they're the perfection of beauty's art.
I take no delight in the garden, nor have I any desire for friends,
set out on your journey companions… I'm captured, I can't start!
With joy and happiness You were refreshed by sweet slumber…
while I and others didn't sleep last night from noise I did impart.
Don't the rich show any compassion towards the helpless beggars?
Give me a glance, O rich One, I beg for a sight of You, Sweetheart.
If You burn me like aloes let my body be sacrifice for Your soul…
each moment of my life would be pleasant from the scent I impart!
Didn't You say that Sadi would not win release from Your power?
I swear by Your feet's dust, if You slay me… I will still not depart!

Although gazing on You is forbidden me who is so sinful,
what can I do, since to keep eyes off Your face I'm unable.
I suffer cruelty from Beloved from whom I have to bear it:
I have not staying power nor power to sigh, it's so pitiful!
I've neither the opportunity of staying nor patience to go:

247

I possess neither place to stay, nor asylum that's merciful.
Neither would that One look at me in pity, if I did stay...
nor do I have any refuge... if away from You I should pull.
My body be sacrificed for You: Your threshold is a resting
place for slave's head: beggary's best as You're Masterful!
Since one with such beauty as Yours treads path of virtue,
it wouldn't be manliness for me to have eye that's lustful!
I've enough of crowd's approval, virtue of good reputation:
as I am prepared to lose my head of my cap why be careful?
God, what a night I had tonight when such a star showed,
I no longer felt love for sun or a desire for moon that is full.
You afflicted, don't complain of the darkness of the night:
in my opinion bright morning than dark night is more dull.
Since in the eyes of Sadi it's no sin to look at a lovely face,
you'd have surmised that I have been guilty of being sinful.

Get up and let us abandon formality's path and appraise
the shop of spiritual knowledge: two barleys is all it pays.
If that tunic-wearing Beloved should again be passing by
then we also would tear off garments... of mysteries maze.
Seventy small affairs being hidden from eyes of mankind
are better than one act of devotion in which hypocrisy lays.
It may be that One who lavished so many favours on us in
the past will forgive us if we commit sin one of these days.
O Sadi, Time that is not kind, is unfaithful to everyone...
come, let us praise faith in this short life of ours... always.

It's not a night when the eyes can be closed in slumber,
the Blessed don't sleep in the garden of Paradise, ever!
The influence of the spring's fragrance revives the earth:
one's heart must be of stone not refreshed by the zephyr!
I smell scent of skirt of that One who was lost long ago,
if I mentioned this all would shout, "That's an old error!"
The lover doesn't possess ears that will listen to advice:
ours is an illness to which physician can't find an answer.
People are urging me to repent of thinking about Beloved:
it wouldn't be real repentance but sin much, much deadlier.
O all you fellow travellers, please, please leave us alone…
for we want to remain stationed here at the Beloved's door.
O brother, regard pangs of love as being like Nimrod's fire
because to me its flames are as like to Abraham they were!
The dead would rise, dancing from the dust of the ground,
if You happened when their bones were rotten to pass over.
I'm longing for Union with You, keep dreading separation:
regarding everything else in the world I've no hope, no fear.
It'd not be strange if I'm found slain at Beloved's tent-flap:
how the living could survive… is to me the greatest wonder.
O Sadi, love and lust can never come together in harmony…
the accursed Devil, the Angel glorifying God, can't go near.


How pleasantly the rose-scented breeze blows in the morning.
Get up, O friend, for many a breeze over our dust will be blowing.
You who for as long as you lived didn't follow the straight path,
will be afraid when on the Last Day when the bridge you're crossing.

A coin of gilded brass won't be accepted in Resurrection's market…
it must be pure to be emerging from the fire, without any scathing.
You may hide sins from strangers but the All-Seeing sees them…
hide misdeeds from neighbours but knowing is the All-Knowing.
Cherishing carnal desires is opposed to judgement of the wise…
the child loves dates, but the doctor some constraint is advising.
I surrendered myself to despair but Your mercy's giving me courage:
O sinners, there's still always hope of pardon from the All-Forgiving.
If You burn us Lord, it'd be a fitting punishment for our misdeeds…
if forgive, Your mercy is universal… Your bounty goes on, giving!
Although accursed Satan has led me away from Justice's Path…
I still am resting my hopes upon the All-Merciful and All-Forgiving.
He Who bestowed on me life and granted subsistence and lavished
many favours on me, will also forgive when my bones are mouldering.
O Sadi, superfluous speech is a waste of life, and now is the time
to offer some excuses, and may the Almighty God us be pardoning!


Get up and let us keep 'our trust', the vow of faithfulness,
atone for our past sins through service and trustworthiness.
It was a stupid thing to do, humbling ourselves before men:
from now on let's practise humility at door of His highness.
Door of the hospital of penitence has not yet been closed…
we can still cure the disease of sin, by begging forgiveness.
We turned from God to the people, but it was all in vain…
it would be better to turn to God from all others, I confess!
Let us put aside lust and desire and heart's vain passions…
let's bend the back of devotion with our single-heartedness.

It is a pity hearts of men should get into the Devil's power:
how long to surrender home of Friend to enemy's evilness?
Since even the exalted rank of angels is below our position
why should we yield so humbly to Satan's powerfulness?
Base silver will only bring shame and an evil reputation…
get up O sage, so that we can seek elixir of Truthfulness!
O Sadi, the rich journey far afield for the purpose of trade,
while we like beggars, pray at door of His Holy Kindness.
O God, lend us Your aid, for favours and forgiveness befit
You: while our deeds are always worthy of us, more or less!

Since You've come I've had enough of about myself talking:
it'd be good manners for me to fall down… You're standing.
If such a graceful creature as You enters by the garden door,
red rose, ashamed, would say… "Why am I still blooming?"
When rose reaches end nightingale's peace of mind departs:
all the world now knows this heart's pain, I was concealing.
I have swept all the dust of Shiraz with my eyes in the hope
that You might, some where, Your foot have been planting!
In a few mornings more when scent of the rose is exhaled…
separation will kill me quicker than it nightingale is killing!
You obviously heard of how Farhad would perforate stones:
but not stones of Your threshold my eyes tears are piercing!
It is no wonder my night is long for my eyes are wide open
thinking of You, O Tyrant! Strange, if I had been sleeping!
I excuse Your servants if Sadi's blood is shed many times:
tell them to spill it, and deny You gave to them the ordering!

When the nightingale sounded dawn's kettledrum one morning,
out on balcony from repentance-chamber of solitude I was coming.
I am able to see now that before the high standard of the sun
the black tassel of the darkness upon the horizon is slowly fading.
When the radiance of the day is emerging from the black quilt,
white-bodied Beloved in absolute unveiled beauty will be sitting.
My heart is a captive to Love and my soul is pledged to desire;
that charming easer of the heart through my doorway is entering.
My brain is still so intoxicated by fragrance of that One's breath
that ambergris and roses scent to sense of smell can't be reaching.
I'll never again feel any anxiety about the night that is dark…
for day is fated to be terminated by each night that is coming.
I did not fully understand whether that One's sleeves contained
Judas-flower and roses, or hands and arms that roses were staining.
If you were to imagine that One as water in a glass you couldn't
the difference between water and the glass ever be distinguishing.
O Winebringer, quickly bring the oceans of the east and west…
for the habitual drunkard a long time to get drunk is taking.
I'm not one failing to distinguish between what's lawful or unlawful;
wine with You is allowable, water without You one is not drinking.
In no city can such sugar be found such as You are… O Beloved;
for You are the One who compels parrots to talk like Sadi's talking.
This poem that is elaborately constructed, like a chain-mail is…
for enemy to draw from sheath sword of criticism it is not allowing.

O my Darling, a thousand blessings on Your whole soul, forever!
God Who made such a being from Not-Being, is the great Creator!
I have never seen anywhere the sun upon a moving cypress, but...
Your attributes defy description and Your features are the definer!
You seemed like a peacock, every part of You still more beautiful:
now I see You are head to foot like sugarcane... only even better!
However much I'm tortured by Your cruelty I am hopeful You'll
be faithful... Your eyes say, "No!" "Yes," Your eyebrows utter.
Please look at me at least once again, then begin Your reproaches:
show arrogance as much as You like, like king to slave, no matter!
You've robbed me of heart, don't take religion too: don't deprive
me of my senses: don't slay unlawful me, don't hate Your lover!
Both roses and thorns can be found in the garden: whatever that
One does is good... to endure cruelty at such hands, is easier.
That One has gone and my soul goes, while my body is tortured
with grief: to the king who falls asleep, does a watchman matter?
That One hit me with cruelty's sword, quickly departed while
saying, looking back, "Sadi complains of us! A real man? Never!"

My feet by the bonds of Your love are so chained...
that one might say I'm a deer with its head trapped.
Sometimes I weep about my pain with no remedy...
sometimes, I smile at my state that is so distracted.
Your love has so deprived me of sense and hearing...
I can no longer on advice of the sensible act matured.
Patience's scope has all of a sudden been narrowed:
into the desert the story of my love I've now tossed.

I'm not so mad as to give up love for the Beloved…
if you are wise, from giving me advice be restrained!
No painter can possibly draw such a picture as You:
I cannot conceive that it's possible to ever be created.
How many souls, bodies are tormented by Your love?
I am not alone in being a captive and broken-hearted.
You might come back again… but in Your own time:
if You did, my Fortune would be one having ascended.
If You should call to me while I'm asleep in the tomb,
my soul that's stricken with grief would be comforted.
I hold my life as a sacrifice to the dust of Your feet…
whether You give me comfort… or me make afflicted.
And if Your joys should lay in Sadi being sorrowful…
I'd even welcome this injustice placed upon my head.


When I look at You, the eyes of the envious I pluck out:
thanks to God my fate's eyes are opened without doubt.
Fling back the tent flap, let both friend and enemy see…
the Beloved is so kind to me, despite the enemy's clout!
Tell city's wise men not to preach to me: I will not listen.
Tell area's boss don't cry "Repent!" or of it I'll break out!
If you struck with dagger to warn not to pursue that One,
as long as breath was still in my body, my love I'd shout!
Useless advice: "Be more reverent about Beloved's love!"
It would be wicked to turn from Beloved by being devout!
In the past I had a heart at ease and also a sound intellect:
Your love set such a fire my granary burns, it can't go out!

If the whole city was united in their wanting to attack me
I'd draw sword against all: for You… I'd throw shield out.
For how long will You reject me and this destiny of mine?
Love, that's seized my coat will not let me from it get out!
Whether You act to my wishes or not, You are the judge:
kill me if against Your judgement I say one word of doubt!
Sadi is enduring this pain and keeps on pressing forward:
if You are what You are and I am me, blood will spill out!

It's no difference if words said from lips of sweet-mouthed,
silver-bodied Beloved are a blessing or curse! Enough said!
The false lover who thinks of himself, has not fully drunk
of the pure wine of Love, so he will continue to be insipid.
Whether You're weary of me or reproach me… the captive
of Your love's indifferent to Your ennui and being abused.
I am not one to shun my desire's object because of cruelty:
the bird cannot fly into the sky who in the trap is foot-tied.
It won't be long before this sage of fifty years will quickly
become notorious throughout the city for being infatuated.
I, who am Your associate, have no fear of anyone existing:
close companion's not afraid  by a rabble to be reproached!
I don't sleep all night through, for friends taunt me, saying:
"Such a strange lover, how can he let sleep enter his head?"
I dare not be hoping that You might come into my embrace,
for Your beauty cannot even in my imagination be pictured!
Perhaps these pages will have to be burned someday soon
for no pen can ever bear the heat of Sadi, it'll be consumed!

From this thorn that we have planted dates can't be eaten:
from the wool that we have spun, brocade cannot be woven.
We've not eased the tablet of our sins by using any excuse:
we don't do good works, to weigh against faults so brazen.
We are destroyed by our passions; and what lamentations
we'll cry on Resurrection Day... as them we haven't beaten.
Alas for this precious life that has now almost passed away
while we are still cherishing thoughts of sin and acts rotten.
How unmanly we are to set our affections upon this world,
in which the men of God have never found a single haven.
They, like the locust, are engaged in devotion... while we...
like an ant, loins girt, are in hall and field, busy like denizen.
Youth and old age have passed away like a night and a day:
night has ended and the day has appeared, but we doze on.
For how long can one remain like a bird on this battlement?
Because... some day we shall become bricks here and then!
It'd be strange if on that Judgement Day we are protected,
seeing that we gave not protection nor shelter to any men.
If the Master does not intercede on that Day it'd be just...
one doesn't blame the mid-wife, if one is an ugly specimen.
His bounty may fall on us... otherwise do not be imagining
that with all these hellish sins, Paradise will be flung open!
O Sadi, perhaps an ear of corn from Saints granary of grace
will be bestowed upon you... for its seed we have not sown!

Last night in seclusion's desert I boasted of my aloneness,
I pitched my tent above those esteemed for their goodness.
When I was glorying in the Oneness in the street of Unity
the duality of devotees of the hermitage was made useless.
So deeply I was searching the mysteries of the Universe...
that even Universal Reason was confused... full of stress!
Reason had been my guide, but when Love did come to me
I hit back of my hand on mouth of Reason's feverishness.
I'd tied so many knots on the line of conceit and self-will...
at hands of Creation's Tailor like a thread I was in a mess.
I put on door of my heart lock of patience against desires...
so I'd not wander to other doors like key looking for access.
If anyone feels a desire for wisdom, let that one not speak;
for since I inclined to wisdom I keep silent, this... I stress!
Like a Mystic I'd in my breast spiritual knowledge's pearl:
so, having that jewel ocean's pearls I'd no wish to possess.
After this I will only move straight forward like the sun...
formerly I'd wander loosely like heavenly sphere... no less.
I obliterated the sayings of Sadi from records of existence
before presence of the Perfect Master... trying for access!


Two weeks have passed by without seeing that moon so full,
and I'm reduced to despair for to that One I've not been helpful.
My Friend has broken our love pact while staying faithful am I...
my Friend has cut off love's root while I am remaining faithful.
O my Beloved, in the end You have treated me as my enemies
wished, in return for me not listening to friends trying to be helpful.

You sold me for nothing despite Love's conditions: despite Your
cruelty I would still buy You: give heart and soul… I am pitiful.
Darling, I swear by the dust of Your feet that since I have adopted
You as my Sweetheart, like foes I have left false friends so plentiful!
I look at You and wish that I might become Your feet's dust…
You see me, leave like the wind say, "I've not seen him!" Unfaithful!
Haven't You seen how I ran after You amongst all the people?
That on my head I didn't go after You, was to everyone… shameful!
Sugar's nice, although You can't appreciate the sweetness of it:
it is something that I know… as I have tasted bitterness so plentiful.
It is permissible for me to lay claim to sincerity and to love…
for I've preferred the Beloved above all in the world that's wonderful.
Sing, O minstrel of the gathering, and recite the poetry of Sadi…
bring wine of perfect Love, of date-wine… I'd not drunk a cupful!

Heart's devoted to You though eyes are turned elsewhere
so that the enemy may not know that it is at You I stare.
Someday, I will emerge from this veil of respectability…
if I see an idol like You I will be worshipping it, wherever!
Praise be to God that my heart's become prey of Beloved:
I've been saved from suffering pangs of a distraught lover.
You have broken the promise that You made to remember
our love… while I've stuck to the promise that I did swear.
I swear to God, as long as heart's spiritual sense reminds
me of Friend, I'm indifferent to enemies taunts, anywhere!
I wished to give a present that was worthy of Your help…
even my life's a contemptible offering, so what can I offer?

When I did see so clearly that You had no love for Sadi...
I laughed at Fortune while over myself I wept everywhere!

I can't take being separated from You for another moment:
that I have no desire to see any face than Yours is evident.
On that first day that I met my Shirin I knew like Farhad
to sacrifice my precious life then and there... I'd be content.
I spite of everyone in the whole world I love You, although
my wisdom may be scorned... my religion an impediment.
If You raised sword I'd drop shield before You, but with no
sword You have slain me... with Your silvery arm-ament!
Show Yourself O You bright dawn of lovers, if day is here;
long night makes hatred of moon and the Pleiades ferment.
I existed, then had to undergo punishment of non-existence
and now I beg Your bounty: I'm poor, helpless, discontent.
I need a sincere friend like candle who would pity my state,
it's the only one I see burns nightly at my pillow until spent.
Because of Your smile Your lips remain open, like the rose:
You think Your nightingale should be like heron, sad, bent?
Gardener is upset... "O Sadi, close your eyes!" "Gardener,
don't worry about rose: look and not pluck is what I meant!"

Winebringer, give wine, for dreg-drinkers of Winehouse are we,
we're familiar with the Wineshop and strangers to Reason be!
We burn ourselves and like candle sacrifice our lives this way:
in whatever crowd there is a candle, we are the moths to see.
All those wise ones are not concerned with us in this discussion,

how can it harm those who are sensible… if we senseless be?

Though piety and good reputation some people have on show,

we're famous in the world for downright drunkenness and sensuality.

In this Path, if you understand it properly, we're after the same:

in this street, if you see, we're members of the same house, obviously.

People say that dignity and position are both gained by wisdom;

we don't care a fig for them, we're drunkards and fools, indubitably!

The fault's yours if you haven't the eye to tell what is the jewel…

otherwise, each of us is a unique pearl, in ocean of spiritual reality.

From Nought's desert we came yesterday, tomorrow we're gone…

so in this one night we are in the world, let us seek less of sensuality!

If what you need is the pure wine… O Sadi, then let the Winebringer

give wine again, for we are Winehouse dreg-drinkers… permanently!


We're happy with the Beloved's face... of garden oblivious:

whether spring comes or an autumn's blast, content are us!

If we win our desire, One of cypress stature, we're content:

though if all world's cypress' died, we would make no fuss.

If others go to the gardens of pleasure for sake of diversion,

we… O hearts ease, are content to be with You… only us!

If a tulip is in his garden let the gardener give it elsewhere,

we are happy being in heart-ravishing Sweetheart's caress!

If the king and magistrate punish us, they have the power:

if the old and young disapprove of us we don't care, not us!

If You are the only one pleased with us, then being content

with what the Here and Hereafter has for us… is obvious!

Whether the waves lift our boat to the height of the sun or

plunge it into depth of sea: we are on shore, happy, no fuss!
We have endured many sorrows and our life has had no joy
and we've given up all ease but now at peace you'll find us!
O Sadi, wealthy folk are frightened of loss, but, if cry of…
"Thieves!" comes from caravan, we are not fussed… not us!

For ages in pursuit of our object of our desire we were wandering,
Beloved's in our house while searching the world we keep roaming.
Even the might and majesty of the Being Who is beyond limits
of space: everywhere searching for that One we were wandering.
We thought that we should not be looking at beautiful ones…
they stole our hearts, we were compelled upon them to be gazing.
Like the nightingale we keep lamenting all through the night
until sun shows his face… then, like a bat ourselves we're hiding.
People used to describe to us the beauty of the unseen Joseph…
he appeared before us, we lost our sense and the power of speaking.
We used to say that we would never again drink wine in secret…
Winebringer, give us wine, because that idea we're now abandoning!
Let everyone in this city come outside, to be witnessing how we…
who were at one time seen as old… young again are becoming.
O Sadi, be informing the army of the beautiful ones not to hurt
my heart, for we've become the prey of the Beloved… out hunting.

At the moment of my death, I will be longing for You:
give up life in hope of becoming Your street's dust too!
On Resurrection's morning when I raise my head from
dust I'll rise talking to You… to look for You too I'll do.

In a crowd where are gathered beauties of both worlds,
I will gaze at You... and become slave of beauty of You.
I will not talk of Paradise nor smell the roses of Heaven,
nor even seek *huris* beauty but Your street I will rush to.
I'd not drink wine of Paradise from winebringer's hands:
what need for wine, when I am drunk on beauty of You?
"It's easy to cross thousand deserts without selfishness,
but if I oppose, O Sadi, I will at least be beside you too!"

I pass the long night in wakefulness, for dawn I'm hopeful;
perhaps morning breeze will waft Your scent so bountiful.
It'd indeed be strange if the root of Love shouldn't give me
any fruit, seeing I pour all desire's rain on it to be merciful.
I cannot leave threshold of Your service, even if You refuse
me admission to the house of Your intimacy so wonderful.
You killed me with sword of Your separation... and turned
away: come back again, give me immortality. I'm hopeful!
How many days have I passed in this hope… that I might
be spending just one night in Your company, so delightful.
What fault have I committed that You don't speak to me?
What did I do to deserve separation from You? Be helpful.
I keep on blessing You despite all of Your unfaithfulness...
I look for You, although Your unkindness is still plentiful.
I will not tell the story of the Beloved except in Beloved's
presence, then only One person will know my secret in full.
Tale of Your separation and story of Your parting haven't
been finished… but my book has reached its end, it is full!

It is impossible that I should cease telling the story of my
love for You... unless Fate my speech's tongue does annul.
O Sadi, if you pass your life in this enterprise... thinking
that the tale of your love will ever reach its end, is fanciful.


Sit down again Beloved for the candle will keep burning
and sight of Your face at night, full daylight is revealing.
Lovers' minstrel's gone, drunkards' winebringer's asleep:
Beloved's always the same and our meeting's everlasting.
Court garden's nightingale's now proclaiming the dawn:
morning cocks' crowing through palace they are hearing.
We have devoted to You our house and all that is in it...
whatever's pleasing to You all the world I'm forbidding!
Either release me or be tying me even tighter, because no
one from the trap of hunter such as Yourself is escaping.
One not passing through the fire knows not how I burn:
one burnt, what it is to cherish a vain desire is knowing.
First I was anxious my reputation should not be sullied:
now I don't care about stone as goblet in pieces is lying!
Sadi, it matters if name and fame go... loving this One?
One loving them, is unfit for Love's path to be treading.


We promised in Beloved's absence into desert's space
we'd not go,
and to any pleasurable place without seeing Your face,
we'd not go.

The garden of Love's abode and flowerbed are pleasurable places,
but unless enjoyment is provided; there, happy to grace,
we'd not go.
Others may play at love with everyone, but not for us… we are at
Your special table: for their theft of food in this place…
we'd not go!
One can only be walking in the footsteps of that darling Sweetheart,
but if that One cannot put up with our annoying chase,
we'd not go.
Even if our Friend was cutting our body to pieces with the sword,
over to enemies place to be complaining about our case,
we'd not go!
Let that One place a foot on our head and eyes as though a carpet,
but even if the figures on this rug that One did efface,
we'd not go!
Do not out of harshness and cruelty turn away Your face from us
for unless You slay us, from Your sight even a trace
we'd not go!
O Sadi, it is the condition of our faithfulness to Layla that even if
any of the people should call us mad, with an angry face,
we'd not go!


Will I take the blows of Fate, or separation from Beloved?
Which load can I carry when of strength I haven't a shred?
I have not any strength left to keep away from that One…
nor the power to embrace such a One, now let that be said.

I possess neither patience to gather support from wisdom,
nor do I have the wisdom by tranquillity to be inwardly fed.
It is not being a man to tire of beauties, from their cruelty:
I'm a woman if Your hardness like a man I'd not endured.
Constantly I've drunk wine from the pure goblet of Union
and so I also have to put up with cropsickness' heavy head.
If in the flowerbed some rose should appear like Your face,
I'd stick its thorns into the worthless eyes in Sadi's head.

If that One drew sword and to kill all lovers threatened,
I'd still be the first to glory in my love… on that depend.
Tell that faithless, obstinate, treacherous One to accept
my head… because it down at that One's feet I will send.
It's impossible for me to close my eyes to Beloved's face:
it is better to shut ears to advice that my way did wend.
It's said by people that the society of sweethearts is fire:
I don't care one fig if they burn all my harvest's dividend.
I'm a quick-witted bird who feels so happy bound by that
One… no memory about my nest do I now comprehend.
Heart's so full of pain that if I didn't stop their flow with
sleeve… my tears would pour to where my skirt does end.
If I were to strip the clothes off my frail body… you'd see
whether beneath them a ghost or a body there did attend.
I have to bear the cruelty of enemies for my heart will not
ever be allowing me to withdraw my love from the Friend.
What difference does it make to one free from pain that
a poor soul like me suffering anguish, his shirt should rend?

The long night is banished from the throne of Jam: so well
I know this tale… for I'm in the well of Bizhan* in the end.
People say, "O Sadi, do not keep doing it… give up love!"
My reply is, "Hard for me to do it, my vow I can't rend!"

*Note: Bizhan was another Persian hero from the Shahnama.


Darling, if I should look at Your moon-like face from each side,
I should certainly see traces of the Divine Art that there reside.
In a hundred ways I gaze all the time upon Your whole form…
  in this hope, that these eyes Your face may happen to guide.
You're harsh in the lack of regard for the condition of poor me,
while I am devoted to dust of Your feet's soles, I must confide.
You're the sun, while I'm an insignificant mote in Your beam…
You're too exalted to look at this creature whom himself is beside.
Your long curls are the Land of Darkness, lips… Water of Life:
that raven-blackness of Your long hair, I see immortality inside!
May my infidel eye not see again Your lovely face if I should
look in any corrupt manner at the plaits Your hair does divide.
The way to gain Your love is long, but like Sadi I will travel,
and like him I will be looking back with regret… at the wayside.


If it happened that I did die because of this love for You,
that I would not blame You at Resurrection Day is true.
One can have nothing to do with this world or the next,
but one can not to the Beloved's company say… adieu!

O You, the balm of the wound of all the afflicted ones...
there does not exist for me any other cure but You! You!
I'm one of those poor wretches who doesn't have a friend
except for You… in this world, and in that next one too!
O police inspector, what can you expect from the young?
I... someone who is old, will never repentance go through!
Someday I will kiss the bow of the eyebrow of that One:
let that One strike me with an arrow's glance, shot true!
O ambergris-scented breeze of the spring, when you pass
by the land of Shiraz, say of this place I'm a devotee too!
I cannot go to sleep, because with Beloved being absent,
I'd feel uncomfortable on the finest silk worms ever grew!
O You solace of Sadi's life, You've gone away from here,
but never been passing out of this one's mind have You.

My eyes are on Your path, ears for Your message listen:
You remain without worry while my days in grief hasten.
There is not one day or night existing when You inquire
how Your lovers try to pass days and nights that remain.
Love of sweet idols, wherever... used to ravish my heart,
now I've a direction to worship with idols I've no concern.
I pray to spend a moment with You to fulfil heart's desire:
I have drawn many a breath and my desire I didn't obtain.
I've not joy of Your Union nor power to bear separation...
I've no strength to leave this quarter nor chance to remain.
What kind of enemy are You, that from my love for Your
hand and its sword my feet still refuse to flee this domain?

I am not reproached by anyone who has spiritual insight...
for Love is quickly taking from wisdom's hands… the rein.
I no longer possess an ear of knowing or sense to question,
so that I might talk with You or hear You speaking again.
If Fate sealed my tongue all of the fragments of my bones
would burst into speech by my love that still does remain.
What heart would not be consumed in fire of Sadi's love?
If his poetry circled all the world all would find it profane!

No one ever saw a moon so sweet of speech, so gracefully walking:
cypress of such a wonderful stature, moon auspicious in its rising.
The cypress would fall down if You moved from where You are…
and the moon would sink if on the terrace You were not appearing.
As soon as my heart had become Yours I began to close my eyes.
Forbidden to all the world is what to You happens to be pleasing.
My heart's ear turns to door to hear what news of You will come:
eye of hope is fixed on road to see who Your note will be bringing.
The friendly gathering that lacks a candle has no illumination:
a meeting without the Beloved is simply defective in its arranging.
Enter my door unannounced just for one night in all of my life
so that the morning of the lover's night from darkness is emerging.
I bear burden of Your love and dispense with everything else,
although neither attention nor honour to me are You paying.
The Master's will is law, being Ruler and Sovereign: if He slays
us we're His slaves, if He cherishes us we're Him always serving.
O you who are criticising the crazy seeker, our Beloved is present,
even though you, who Beloved really is may never be knowing.

Let Beloved come to greet me in spite of harshness and cruelty...
and in answer to it let Beloved, soul of my love-sick self be taking.
O Sadi, if you're seeking then go your way and suffer anguish:
you will either attain heart's desire or perish while attempting.

Upon that same day I saw that One's mole I thought that I
was in danger of being lured in trap by grain, that I did spy.
I never had disordered looks and unruly hair until now when
my wits are as scattered as my hair from Your face and eye.
This affair will doubtlessly end in separation if people know
I am united with Your face... that love's vision does supply.
The colour of my face discloses to everyone my heart's pain:
it has divulged what revealed to strangers I wished to deny.
Before this affair of mine ended in madness... wisdom kept
giving advice to me but I didn't listen, to me it didn't apply.
Who happened to see face of that One would quickly flee if
he happened to know how much unrest because of it, had I.
A fire kept falling on my head from brand of separation and
such a flood came from my eyes, I pierced the earth thereby.
It is strange that in spite of annoyance of so many thorns...
I didn't smell dawn's scent without opening like rose in sky.
Formerly, my heart was a house full of turmoil, but now I've
filled it with You... and swept it of all the world can supply!
Sadi's unable to compose poetry that is worthy of You, but,
I uttered whatever came to my lips... with all I can supply.
I've never seen anyone of such charm as heart-ravishing
as You... and I've never found a rose-petal so refreshing.

269

Another human being like Yourself is impossible to find
in the Universe: also, such a fairy I've never been seeing.
And such a wonderful marvel and so much fascination I
have never, even in the art of Samari,* been discovering.
It is impossible for me to discover a possibility of rivalry
between Your face and the moon that in sky is glowing.
In any shop of any jeweller… I have not yet been able to
discover any ruby that like Your lips is sugar-scattering.
I've never seen a composition in pure Persian poetry like
those two rows of pearls, that in Your mouth are laying.
Please tell me, who would be buying the moon? For I've
often seen the moon, but never saw anyone purchasing!
Neither have I found anyone who tears veil concealing
secrets of the ascetics as successfully as You are doing.
I've seen all of the beautiful ones of the Universe… but
one endowed with charm like Yours, I am never seeing.
And I've never been observing, even in the lands of the
heathens… such cruelty as in Islam You are practicing.
O Sadi, for the role of you being a monk you are not fit,
because a bigger vagabond than yourself I'm not seeing.

* *Note: Samari made the golden calf for the Children of Israel.*

I was not the man to come to hand-wrestling with You;
but, still I contested and tested if my bravery was true.
I observed that You carried off hearts of high and low…
I also decided to show my strength and my bravery too!

That spear, with which I planned to carry off the ring...
on the battlefield it knocked me down, ran me through!
I was one who amongst all of the people was notorious,
even though no advantage to me was had by loving You.
I'll not, on this occasion, mention others shortcomings,
as I have often listened to them... and about myself too!
I thought of how against You I could bring a complaint,
but what use is any complaint that You won't listen to?
Do not ever deprive me of hope of gaining Your bounty,
because... from the very beginning I was turning to You.
If my head has to go then let it be sacrificed at Your feet!
That death must come sooner or later... is certainly true!
I'm reduced to such dire straits today through Your love
fire's reaching sky through smoke of heart burnt through.
And on that Day of Resurrection when I raise my head
from dust, I'll still be Your lover as I always was. True!

For as long as I have silver I will be squandering it:
for as long as You have a kiss, to take it I'll see fit;
and if I happened to be tossed in a prison tomorrow,
it happens right now that I'm in a garden, exquisite!
Let the world's end come as far as I am concerned...
for You were everything that I had desired... from it.
What skirts full of roses there would be in the garden
if only the Gardener didn't object to what I commit!
I was never expecting from Fortune that's auspicious
that Phoenix would enter my nest, just the opposite.

You've taught all of us in the city, love... only Love:
come, so I may declare to You too an analysis of It!
I have much to say in my heart that is against You;
when in Your presence my tongue does the opposite.
I'll speak out, so friend and enemy may understand
no difference between the drunk and sober... I admit.
If You, silver-bodied cypress, should be coming out
to drive me from Your presence, contentedly I… sit.
Don't say that Sadi's attained what is his objective;
but though You are cruel I love You, do not doubt it!
As long as I live I'll be worshipping the form of You,
and if I happen to die I will a greeting to You submit.

It's so, with a passion enslaving me I'm drunk, as before:
O Winebringer, send me out of myself with one cup more.
Be serving out the wine to those who are short-sighted…
my rivals get drunk on wine… I, with seeing One I adore.
I swear by this Love and Faith existing between us, that
I've not given up love for You, nor another do I love more.
Before my physical form was created love for You was in
my heart: I brought it with me, and this is so… I implore.
It's true that I'm Your slave, although when You are here
it can't be really said that I even exist, as me You ignore!
You're tired… I haven't the strength to be alone: You have
practised cruelty, while I kept promise... faithful as before.
To be alone was a habit of mine but since You have come
I have never stopped my searching for You whom I adore.

O Sadi, did not I tell you to stop pursuing heart's desire?
I will not again, if this time I escape free... not like before.

Let everyone know that I'm in love and intoxicated...
the rumour's true that I've not done what I promised.
If the enemy hurts me, or if friend is reproaching me,
I am indifferent to everything that about me, is said.
O spirit of desire, who wants good name and place?
I am free from your bondage and in peace I've rested.
May I be hating Your face that's so beautiful if I am
happening to take even a look at anybody else's head.
Back in the past I used to be seen with all and sundry,
but since seeing Friend, door to strangers I've closed.
O Winebringer, I became drunk from looking at Your
form, even before with wine You made me intoxicated.
I spent many a night thinking about Your lovely face:
I never slept and caused neighbours to stay out of bed.
It's a pity that those lips of Yours talk with everyone:
please abuse me with them and I'll bless them instead!
Sadi... for a long time, in his heart out of love for You,
"It'd be strange, if I didn't worship such an Idol," said.
Chains of sorrows of the world on my head were laid,
but... now I'm bound to You, I'm freed from all dread.

Shut the door of friendship in people's faces... permanently, we have:
turned away from all of the others to only with You be... we have.
We've broken off all other attachments except the one for Beloved...

obliterated all promises except with Beloved… obviously, we have.
Those people, who are sober, always keep aloof from this business…
it'd be only proper if they criticised the 'drunken stupidity' we have.
Anguish keeps always afflicting that one who is his own proprietor;
escaped from that, by being that fair-faced One's property, we have.
We are grateful for Your favours on whatever path we may travel…
we are praying for Your welfare, in whatever place we see we have.
Though held in honour by others, in Your eyes we are contemptible;
although the world may exalt us… in Your eyes obscurity we have.
O You Idol of all who are pure of mind, reveal Yourself to us…
so that we may see You, then a way to of self-love be free we have.
We've guarded our eyes, to prevent our hearts from being stolen;
despite our precautions, fallen into Your noose quite easily we have.
We have placed our precious lives on the palms of Your hands…
until permission to spill them all at Your feet, obediently, we have.
O Sadi, love consists in our maintaining the promise of faithfulness
on the same firm foundation that established it originally, we have.


I do not have the patience to endure Your separation…
I can't prefer any other to You in any kind of situation.
At least ask how I am someday as You're passing by:
how I'm going, how poor me is, still the same location?
I should be doomed to Hell if I stay alive without You;
God wouldn't give Paradise's bliss to a sad companion.
I do not know what to call You… You are both my eyes:
without Your presence… I would be blind from then on.
When Beloved's face is veiled from you, better be blind:

place no candle near my pillow when I know separation.
I have to fulfil promise of faithfulness to You although
a thousand times more cruelty to me falls heavily upon.
I am not a mortar that'd complain against Beloved for
pounding me: put me on fire like a cauldron, I'd stay on!
Revolve around my head, O mill of Time's revolutions,
with every cruelty... for I'm the millstone, so pound on!
Like a nightingale to rose I came to sing Your praises...
like tulip You made my tongue dumb, now song's gone.
O Sweetheart, the leopard didn't kill me with its claws:
You killed me with Your fingertips, henna painted upon.
Like musk-deer's pod my blood's burnt in my mad heart:
musky scent's left me to fly into the sky and further on.
O Sadi, practise virtue and stop all of this endless talk:
why should sugar say, "I am the sweetest composition!"

We've relinquished all hope, expectation of reward have abandoned;
we have cast aspiration's shadow like Phoenix over places desolated.
Whether He delivers us to the flood or He bears us to the shore...
we've cast hearts on ocean, ourselves to mercy of waves committed.
If police inspector forbids evil-doers to perpetrate what is wrong...
let him come, for veil from face of the Inviolable One we've removed.
We have made the seeker join the dance, thrown Sufi into ecstasy;
the Beloved we've compelled to dance, wine with opium drugged.
There's no one without a skirt that's wet but others it are concealing:
while we have a skirt that outside to the sun we have exposed!

O Sadi, those pious ones are indulging in worship of the self…
while we've thrown kettledrum over neck and ass into mire dumped.

We are all eyes and You are all their light, my Darling:
evil eye be far away from Your face's sight, my Darling!
Do not veil Your face, for whoever sees a huri like You
would instantly up to Paradise take flight, my Darling.
In Your kindness, careful You don't be criticising me…
I don't know joy of Your presence's delight, my Darling.
Your face is the reason for the uproar and all the worry
in the whole universe, everyone in sight… my Darling!
A cypress plant that looks like Your form has come…
so how can we remain patient tonight… my Darling?
All of this great storm keeps on passing over my head
from a heart that is burning O so bright, my Darling!
All this fascination and beauty belonging to You are
a source of arrogance, a flirtatious rite… my Darling!
Sadi, who drinks from this Fountain of Life will never
be satisfied, even if Time stops outright, my Darling!

I will never go away because of any kind of reproaches…
for I'm attracted to stay here hoping that Union comes.
If anyone should speak to me on the subject of wisdom,
it is my fear that because of that I'll embrace madness!
I'm incapable of listening to any kind of advice at all…
my heart's ear is occupied with music of mystic dances.

Let the wind carry off all the whole harvest of my life…
both worlds without You aren't two grains, worthless!
O my friends, don't go blaming me or reproaching me,
for whatever I may have sown myself, I'll reap: no less!
What can I do but be following that One as I have my
neck in the noose of that One? I'm completely helpless!
That One said, "O Sadi, you'll see me in your dreams,"
but if I should fall asleep I'd be a lover who is faithless.

How could I, who have no means at all, ever purchase You?
Isn't it a shame that I'm Your lover, You my Beloved, too?
You are surely the shadow of graciousness… take me under
Your protection for I haven't that, which is worthy of You!
I will not become attached to You as I wouldn't on my own
think it right that You would be my rose, I Your thorn, too!
I never imagined that Your noose would fall on me because
I do not possess sufficient worth… to be captivated by You.
It's impossible to go along Your street due to the guardian:
unless it is at a time… when Your protection covers me too!
I'm never feeling any sorrow or happiness in any place at all
unless in sympathy with You… then… I feel them like new.
If God Almighty should call You to account for any fault…
let Him forgive You: I will be responsible for Your sins too!
People are in love with my poetry, O eyesight of beauties…
and why not, for that I'm in love with Your face is too true!
How could I deserve to call You so as You I'd get to know,
unless You forgive… so that I may become worthy of You?

Though I well know that I'll never Union with You attain,
still I'll not turn back, so on road seeking You, dying I'll do!
To keep my faith in You I am just as determined as ever…
not only in the present world but in the one still coming too!
Better for Sadi not to exist if pleasing You he does no more;
for it's not right that You are my Glory and I disgrace You!

Because of rivals I do not cast a single glance Your way,
just in case that I was lusting after You they could say!
The only prey that I'm after in all the world is that One:
with my envious rivals I will not share that One today.
Secret pain of separation from You passed endurance…
or else sound from my heart would find tongue to relay!
You've caught me like a pigeon in trap of Your long hair:
You have sealed up my eyes like I am Your falcon today.
None in this age has cried like me from that One's love,
my words from Shiraz, entered the Universe… to stay!
Often they have said to me, "O Sadi, return to your self!"
"It's not right to be absorbed in me… not Beloved," I say!

Do not keep talking about China and Greece to me,
for my heart is given to a Sweetheart in this country!
At the moment that One is brought into my mind…
I forget existence… and what non-existence may be!
Suffering grief is what has fallen to me in the world:
a man eats only what he has been given… obviously.
Dates are sweet, but hand is too short to reach palm:

278

fresh, cool water is there... but the thirsty cannot see!
I don't know a single devotee in the city who is proof
against my Sweetheart, who's in my mind constantly.
Nothing I have ever seen can equal that One's face...
no fragrance that's known is smelling O so fragrantly.
I do not want to live without that One and not with:
for it'd be shameful... if that One was seen with me!
O friends, close up your eyes to this physical world...
because in our midst we have... this hidden mystery!
Though the world may see this One's outward form,
no one could ever understand this One's inner reality.
I'm so burnt up that I can't be seen by the uninitiated:
one fever-stricken is never appreciated by the healthy.
Whether You give Your heart or take my life, devotion
I still have to do... and the slave must serve faithfully!
From this enterprise Sadi can't win safety for his life:
it's... thirsty wayfarer, poisoned rosewater, obviously.
If like iron this lover cannot bear the heat of the fire...
he must make wax of his forehead, quite deliberately!

I have neither the ability to win the Beloved,
nor the strength to await that One, instead.
I regard every cruelty that comes to me from
Your hands as from Fate's wheel on my head.
Whether I had one heart or a thousand... I'd
treasure Your love that in it has made its bed.

I keep this wasted body of mine thin like a hair
as a memento of Your hair gracing Your head.
I, having undergone grief love entails, regard
worldly grief as contemptible, never to be fed.
Due to You I'm drowned in waters of my eyes:
I still hope for Your embrace, lips of ruby red.
You have stolen my heart and still are silent…
I've an account with You that must be settled.
If You should continue to be abusive to Sadi,
all I'm concerned with are Your lips, ruby red!

It is so strange that I burn fiercely in Your absence:
with a single spark I could consume a world, hence!
Every moment I am burning with such a fiery flame
that in presence of lovely Beloved's face I'm incense.
I was completely consumed, though I didn't confess
I burned in love for… (with name one can dispense).
Be merciful, for I am one who is totally distracted…
extend sympathy, for deep in my soul fire is intense.
All lovers enjoy ease and comfort in Your company:
I am heavy with sin, and so my burning is immense.
People say to me, "Sadi, stop all of your lamenting!"
If I don't, who'd know I secretly burn? Make sense?

I made vows again and again in love not to be falling,
but the vision of Your sweet face keeps on appearing.

I didn't want to tell the story of my love: what to do?
My tears of blood and pale face the tale keep telling!
I reached a rosebush, saw no scope left for patience…
I've not yet picked rose but many pricks I'm suffering.
Let Time roll up the carpet of my life, but I've not yet
the story of the Beloved's fair face finished describing.
That one who is advising me to be practising patience
is like one who in vain on my cold iron keeps blowing.
I swear by Your eyes that as You've not left my sight
I've not looked on another beauty with eyes of loving.
I never used to count days expecting union with You,
for I thought being far from You wasn't really living.
What animosity exists that Your nature hasn't tried?
By our love… to friend about it I'm not complaining!
At first I fled in fear from Your trap like a wild beast;
now I'm with You, I'd not at sword's point be leaving!
Who was it told You Sadi was 'no man' to be a lover?
If I left this faith in You, then… "No man" be saying.


I made many efforts the secret of my love to be concealing:
on the top of the fire I could not help but to keep on boiling.
At first I was careful not to surrender my heart to anyone:
all sense and self-restraint left me when You I was seeing.
A story from Your lips reached my soul's ear… ever since
people's advice is merely a tale in my ears that I'm hearing.
Perhaps You'll veil Your face and so put down the uproar,
for mind cannot stop my eyes… from at You to be looking.

In my heart I'm upset: best I don't join the mystic dance;
if I fell... people me, out upon shoulders would be carrying.
Come, make peace with me today... embrace me tonight,
for from expectation my eyes last night were not closing.
You gave me away for nothing, while I'm still determined
that not for any world, a hair of Your body I'd be selling.
I'll tell story of my pain to one who has suffered a wound,
as I'd be reproached by a healthy one if... out I was crying.
Don't offer Sadi advice... he hasn't an understanding ear.
What profit is in preacher's advice when I'm not listening?
It's better to die on road to the desert than to remain idle;
for if I fail to succeed... to best of my ability I'll be striving.

Is it You who're by my side or do I just imagine You?
I can never imagine such good fortune could be true!
You're like sugar in my embrace: if I should be placed
like aloes on a blazing fire, with all cares I'm through.
As my request is given I no longer have fear of death:
let arrow of calamity fly... for now I'm its target too!
Sky, close for a moment against the sun, dawn's door,
for tonight I am so happy with my full moon... You!
Sweet is breeze from rose-bed and to sleep in garden,
if at dawn there wasn't one nightingale's hullabaloo!
It'd be a shame if I were to look at others tomorrow
with these two eyes... with which tonight I see You!
Soul of the thirsty is comforted by Euphrates bank:
Euphrates is over my head, this thirst grows anew!

When I failed to see You I lost all sense from Love:
I'm beside myself with joy now that I sit with You!
Speak to me, for there is no stranger near us but for
candle whose tongue I will now cut… blow out too!
Nothing shall remain between the two of us except
this shirt… and if it is a barrier I will tear it in two!
Don't say Sadi won't win soul's release from pain!
Where to take a soul, cut off from the love of You?

O please, cast one glance over here in my direction…
cure my pain with a little sympathetic consideration.
You have broken Your promise so many times, so do
now a single act of faithfulness… without hesitation.
Every day that's passing You remain in my thoughts,
even for a single day remember me with deliberation.
Abandon Your habit of obstinate hostility… and give
up this custom that You have of complete opposition.
Get up and close the door of Your mansion: sit down
and open Your bodice You wrapped without a notion.
Make that one whom You want to destroy be familiar
with Your service for perhaps a day or two's duration.
When that one has become intimate and love-bound,
then afflict upon that one the suffering of separation.
Sadi, as Beloved is rightly regarded as indispensable,
be resigned and rest your hopes upon Predestination.
If that One strikes You with sword be a shield for it,
and if that One abuses you, give that One devotion.

"It is not fit to always complain about the Beloved!"
Fine! Let cruelty to me, daily be Beloved's vocation!

O You, whose face to my heart brings happiness…
and whose eyes are my abode's lamp of brightness!
It would be quite right to say that Your love is the
water that was mixed with my clay, yes… no less!
I am happy through You… may heaven bless You
and God be with You, my Fate of auspiciousness!
When You happen to be here all my affairs are so
well arranged, but in Your absence I am worthless.
One could say that You sit opposite me night and
day and wherever You happen to go I have access!
That perhaps the pain that afflicts my heart from
Your love might possibly be hidden… I did guess;
but, now that You have gone… ah no, a thousand
times, for my life's passing, that is now worthless!
Wherever there is a tale and also an audience You
are the subject and I'm the audience, this I stress!
If that One would wield sword with those silvery
arms, causing blood from me to flow, nevertheless
do not let anyone cry out in revenge for my death,
because I have pardoned my killer… whom I bless.

O my beautiful One, this poet is far too bewildered
to fully describe all of Your attributes: enough said.

I've never heard that the cypress ever achieved what
You with that graceful, swaying walk have achieved.
Who in the whole, wide world could ever believe that
the sun rises from a human being's collar: Your head!
We are patient… separated from everyone and thing
in the world; but, distant from You, patience has fled.
O harsh and faithless One, have You seen that You
have broken Your promise that to me You have said?
The end of separation is no longer apparent to me…
but, the hope that I have for Union has never ended.
I am fearful that… in the end the Water of Life will
remain for me like it was for Alexander, in the head!
That one who keeps suffering because of separation,
won't revive 'til smelling Herchim's quince up ahead;
so let us see to whom You will be throwing the ball
of happiness and bliss… on the polo-field outspread!
I had a heart but it fell into the Sweetheart's power;
I had a life but I gave it up to Beloved's face instead.
The wise man does not complain about love's pain…
as long as hope keeps existing, a cure lies up ahead.
It's impossible for treasure to exist without a snake;
no garden can ever bloom without thorns… it's said.
If Sadi is consumed before Your eyes… the moon is
not at all concerned that the fine lawn may be dead.
The moth has gone and it has killed itself… so why
should retribution be placed upon the candle's head?

Is that a quince, or a chin, or an apple, all silvery?
Are those lips, or sugar… or sweet life that I see?
I have an Idol, the wrinkle of whose eyebrows are
resembling the idol of the temple of China to me!
The Pleiades declined sharply in my estimation…
the hour that those earrings of that One I did see!
The whole world becomes to my eyes each day on
which I don't see that One's face, dark as can be!
I keep longing for sleep… but how could my head
lie on the pillow when the Beloved's far from me?
Who saw such a form made of water and clay said,
"A human out of clay created our God Almighty!"
The arrogance of beauties is not so great: towards
their lovers, cruelty is not really so much cruelty!
I shall not turn from the love I cherish for You…
whether You're bent upon loving me or hating me.
O lovely One, what need do You have for sword,
Your henna-stained hand could kill me, expertly!
It is best to be killed by the hand of the Beloved,
for one should leave the world with some dignity.
Kill me, so that my critics can't have the chance
of saying the royal falcon… the locust didn't see.
Religion of Sadi consists in looking at Beloved…
God forbid a day comes Faith is lost completely!

Hey, get up! Because the winter is passing away
and the door of the garden pavilion is open today.

Place upon the dish the oranges and the violets...
place chafing bowl in bed-chamber without delay,
and tell to this curtain to be quickly moving aside
immediately from where upon balcony it does lay.
Hey, get up! Because breeze of New Year's dawn
is strewing all the roses... along that garden's way.
In this season of the rose it is totally impossible to
expect the love-struck nightingale in silence to stay.
The sound of the drum cannot be silenced under a
blanket, nor can love be shut away anywhere today.
Fragrance of the rose and dawn of the New Year...
and sweet sound of the nightingale... singing away,
have brought about sale of many garments, turbans
and many are the houses and shops now in disarray!
Our head is lying upon that breast of our Beloved...
so now let the rival's head upon anvil forcefully lay!
The eye that the lover is raising towards his Beloved
does not flutter if a shower of arrows comes his way.
O Sadi, if your hands are able to be reaching the fruit
then let the cruelty of the Gardener come what may.

Ah... let me weep like clouds in spring for even a stone
would cry out on the day that Beloved left me... alone.
Tell the camel-driver of my tearful condition in case he
is binding litter on camel on a day of rain and hailstone!
Those ones who tasted once the wine of separation know
how difficult is the disappointment of hope... now moan.

You left us while our eyes were filled with tears of regret,
crying like sinners' eyes when Resurrection Day's known.
However much I tell circumstances of my love for You…
I could only say a thousandth part of heart's deep groan.
O dawn of vigil-keeper, soul has reached endurance's end,
because You… delay like the night of fasters have shown.
It is only Fate that could force Sadi to drive out love that
has been implanted in his heart, for years away have flown.
How much do I tell you of the story? This must be enough:
whatever is left… only to the Beloved can I make it known.


How can one go on without seeing a sign of Your Union,
my heart can no longer bear to feel Your absence going on.
If this happens to be the whim in Your street, then I must
brace myself for I will have to bear many a cruelty later on!
For how long will I see reason driven mad by Your love…
or myself without a heart, or my heart without peace anon?
It's quite possible to see my body as dust beneath Your feet
but I am not even allowed to see dust Your shoes are upon!
Last night I dreamed that I had Your hair held in my hand,
let us see the use of me having such a mad dream going on!
In presence of Your face and form, it is short-sighted folly
to go to the garden and the graceful cypress to stare upon.
If Khizer had taken this road to the dimple of Your chin…
he wouldn't have Water of Life kept looking for, on and on!
One couldn't see a finer ball in curve of polo bat than each
burning heart falling into Your hair's curl… or, thereupon.

Picture of Your loving glance in my eyes will not disappear at sight of the rose, tulip and sweet basil... that I gaze on! O Sadi, stop all of this vain regret of yours... do you know remedy for your affairs? Sacrifice life... Beloved look upon! How pleasant it is for two lovers to sit together with their hands upon necks... enjoying sweet reconciliation, I swear! And... I swear by lives of Saints it is a great pity to waste our precious time without those sweet of heart being there!

The cypress of stature may do a thousand acts of cruelty... but, it is only right to excuse One, when you are together! O musky breeze of union... how is it possible to thank you, because... garden of my hope was just beginning to wither. Separation for Your face the other day was a hurtful trial: a sight of Your fair form today of my spirits is the reviver! Let that one who doesn't appreciate value of Union's time the separation for only one day or perhaps just two, suffer. If in spite of my innocence my head falls at that One's feet, it's unnecessary to feel hurt by trifle, hands of exulted offer. It's granted that You'd scourge such a one who is lovesick: where can one go with Your noose around neck, as it were? Lovers, who are capable of patience, still have not reached height of desire: it's impossible for one frozen to be on fire! O Sadi, if you've attributes of a human being, die through love: for to die in the ordinary sense is in a beastly manner.

For how long can we patiently keep our eyes closed?
What's left but to let harvest of our lives be burned?
If the look of pure love could be called a sin then my
only harvest are all of the sins that I have garnered.
How many nights I rip clothes in the mystic dance
under desire's spell... at dawn make them patched?
Asceticism won't provide a remedy for the love-sick:
not being hypocritical with You, is way to be cured!
How can we express Your Union? It's impossible as
yet to discharge our thanks for You being envisioned.
How can my sweet voice compare with Your mouth?
It is like kindling a torch, as the sun is being viewed!
Envious heard Sadi's eloquence, was thunderstruck:
his only hope is to be silent... or of poetry be learned!


How sweet is love's fragrance from breath of servants, humble!
Heart bleeds from desire, mouth smiles, hoping... You fill full!
It is possible that one... whose eyes are closed every day, may,
through his piety, escape that One's fascinating witchery's pull!
I was allowed to take one look and a thousand murders I stopped:
that One stole away mystic's heart, sage's mind that was peaceful.
The street of the beautiful ones is the scene all day of rioting...
because of quarrelsome drunkards, close friends, rakes... plentiful!
If I escaped from Your love's snare... where would I be fleeing?
Liberty away from You is bondage, life without You impermissible!
If You do not like me, don't give me over to the enemy's power...
I will not leave You because of cruelty, of those wishing me ill.

Come and sit here by me for a moment and please talk to me…
because even a little speech from Your smiling mouth is, a miracle!
If all narrators about Shirin happened to see this piece of sugar…
they'd gnaw hands with teeth as they would at sugarcane pull.
O Sadi, all the Sweethearts of the world are in love with you…
because now between the wolf and sheep… it has become peaceful!


If you fix eyes on Beloved, do not lend your ear to the enemy:
make resignation your only protection against a fate so stormy.
Let that one who is not content to be burnt like the moth is burnt,
avoid all this hovering around his Companion who is so fiery.
One should avoid passing through the street of the sweet of lip,
bid farewell to your heart… or that One's window do not see!
Who is it that is testifying to our deviation from the right path?
Let him look at that beautiful face, cease finding fault with me!
Lovers never turn from Beloved because of cruelty of that One!
No! God forbid that you judge Friend with standard of an enemy!
For one to die in Beloved's street would be sweeter than life…
until you die never taking love's hand from that One's skirt be!
Beloved is a looking-glass, so let everyone whose face is ugly
beware of looking into that mirror that's always reflecting truly.
O Sadi, don't grapple with the silver-armed, and even if you
have a powerful arm, measuring strength with iron you'd be!

You've done wrong to Love by Your lovers abandoning:
it is wrong of You to show Your face… then it be hiding.

With a King an impudent beggar is claiming friendship:
he can't exist without him, with him he can't be talking.
I suffer a thousand pangs which I think I can't conceal:
my lips can't close like a bud at the time of blossoming.
It is not in my power to exact compensation from You:
You think Your faults lawful then me You're criticising.
Who declares the garden cypress resembles Your figure?
Bring to orchard a cypress as graceful as You in walking.
I love You so... heart doesn't even want Union with You;
perfect Love is not from You, one wants to be extracting.
All Khusrau wanted of Shirin was to enjoy her embrace;
love was Farhad's aim, and Mount Bisitun to be cutting!
It's so easy to give advice to the lover who is distracted:
to whom will you offer it since it he cannot be accepting?
In the past I used to complain to my relations and friends
about sleeping too much... now I complain of not sleeping.
Sadi, you're not magnanimous if you turn from the sword:
if you are hurt by a sting... no honey will you be gathering.

The days of lovers are so pleasant and so delightful...
from morning's fragrance, nightingales singing, joyful!
At such a time the lover sits happily with Sweetheart
for the disturbance caused by guardian... is uneventful.
It is an adequate punishment for the enemy to suffer...
seeing lovers face to face with sweethearts... eyes full!
With two bodies in one garment like a pistachio nut in
a shell... the two heads up from one collar, ah blissful!

Your lot in this life consists of this present moment...
wise man, don't be one missing opportunities, rueful!
Since you know you cannot perform a shepherd's duty,
give up the sheep to the wolves... your hands are full!
I feel love for all these rogues and all these drunkards,
rather than devotees and preachers... who at one pull!
I say let all of these friends and all of these strangers
say of me whatever, be it complimentary or resentful.
It's characteristic of the lips of sweet spoken beauties
to take from the hearts of the wise until they are full!
I went with the outsiders, ruffian youths: I wiped out
all I had learned from learned scholars, so masterful.
Who has any knowledge of any cure for Sadi's pain?
Even physicians, of this disease... have had a cupful!

That one who sleeps with head on breast of the Beloved,
can't know how to a watchman night seems long ahead.
You'd laugh at my wisdom if for love of that One I wept,
but such a difficult problem is the path us experts tread.
What's the use of rebuking those who give up the heart:
such advice should be given to the heart-stealers instead.
O You, lovely of face, sweet of disposition! Lift skirt from
Your feet, by hands of impure mystics it may be clutched.
I'm unable to abandon love for that One no matter what:
I don't care... let me with that One's cruelty be afflicted!
Don't believe that I will let go my grasp from Your skirt,
for my attachment even by the sword will not be severed.

I'll not lift eyes from Your face even if guardian slays me:
let lover of the rose humour caprice in the gardener's head.
 I have surrendered my willpower over to Love… just like
the camel's nose-ring in the driver's hand, ready to be led.
Lover with enlightened mind complains not in the night…
 knowing eventually a night turns to day for the shepherd.
What does a sugar-seller of Egypt know of the fly's state?
Former flaps his sleeve, latter puts desire's hand on head!
O Sadi, it may be that they'll on your head flap sleeves…
 so that, like the fly, you may not approach sweet Beloved.

Again that cypress with the graceful walk is going… where?
A One whose skirt is grasped by hearts… spiritually aware!
From eyes of the captives of that One's snare, blood flows…
that One not even once asks… who, or even what, they are!
Let the people know that I'm in love… that I am also drunk:
in Winehouse's street no such thing as a reputation is there.
What's left but to place head at that One's guardian's feet?
That one who wants the king will kiss the slave anywhere!
 Heart inside breast of Sadi flutters like a pigeon, from this
coming and going of a gracefully walking cypress… I swear!
O friend, when shall my sleep and my peace of mind return:
how can this be, since both are forbidden as a lover's share?

To describe how sweet that mouth is, is an impossibility:
this much is clear, it is far from the lips and mouth of me.

One can't call this a face for it's the circle of a full moon:
nor can that be described as a figure, more a cypress tree.
That One's the rival of the cypress but that One truly is
better than it... because that One also has a silver body!
There never was such a body with such beauty and grace:
you could say that in that One's garments only a soul be!
Is that a mole on the silvery surface of that earlobe or is it
a speck of ghaliya perfume on a jasmine flower... so tiny?
In short... in this world today You are a marvel and it is
clear Your eyes are a gate wherein You act mischievously.
I thought I'd free my heart from that loop of Your curls...
I fear that is them lying curl within curl, an impossibility.
One longing to gain Union with You at cost of his soul
finds success hard, as the price is one of contemptibility!
Don't call that one a man who turns his face away from
the sword of cruelty in the street of Love, a woman is he!
If one with wounded heart cries out in that One's street,
you could not blame him, for beside himself he must be!
In my opinion whatever offence or fault is committed by
the possessor of a beautiful face... is really a virtuosity!
Sadi is passionately attached to You... not to himself:
each coat a vagabond wears, a shroud will prove to be!

To surrender one's life is an easy thing to be doing...
but to give up the Beloved is impossible, I'm saying.
However bitter Your speech may happen to become,
from that mouth of Yours it'd seem... sweet-talking!

We have stopped talking about the garden's cypress
when in the presence of Your graceful form, swaying.
Imagination is so bewildered at You… that it cannot
make any impression at all upon what I am thinking!
I've been trapped in such a snare that it's impossible
for me to ever win my release by me for help pleading.
I was caught up in my composing of a whole volume
that was on You: but, that to discuss, I'm hesitating:
because, You are sweeter than even famous Shirin…
whom in a story it has been possible to be describing.
The nightingales have so much courage when to the
garden they come and of the rose keep complaining!
But that one whose gaze is fixed on Beloved in the
camel-litter, to the camel-driver cannot be speaking.
I'm not even able to complain to the kindly Beloved
about the guardian's cruelty that I am experiencing.
It would be a pity to divulge to an interpreter that
sealed message that a friend to a friend is sending.
There are a great many who would wish to publish
through the whole world this story Sadi is telling!

Say from me to that good advice giver… "Good sir, enough said…
flood overwhelms this one you try to scare with mere rain instead!"
If sober folk saw drunkards' Winebringer, they would break vows
of repentance like me, under spell of those eyes… just out of bed!
If I could be carried to Heaven tomorrow in the company of saints,
better to be taken to Hell with the sinners… than without Beloved.

What fragrance is it that has deprived me of wisdom and patience?
I do not know if it is from Garden of Paradise or perfumer's market.
You are with those short-sighted people in the well of Canaan…
come to Egypt so that the purchasers of Joseph may come forward.
O morning breeze, please say this to that moon of the gathering…
"You are free, while the world by love for Your face is captured."
If that city-distracting flirt should someday inquire of my condition,
say that he doesn't sleep at night because of his capricious Beloved.
If any time You should happen to pass this way look in our direction
for I do not think that the reward for good should be evil instead.
Folks say to me, "O Sadi, since you have experienced cruelty you'd
better bear it!" But, I go further, "Let me die in street of devoted!"

Breeze gives us an intensely delightful impression of the garden;
morning has dawned, day is here… get up, the lamp now darken.
If You would make all of mankind lovesick and drunk like me,
show Your face to devotees, make ascetics taste of wine a specimen.
There is a class who sneer at the mystical dance and at Love…
sing us a sweet chant so that the discontented may leave again.
Wear the patched coat, pass cup: bring wine and banish sorrow;
they're ignorant of, indifferent to, joyful lives of conscious men.
The sighs like smoke of lovers consumed by love reach the sky…
these words have no weight to those whose passions are frozen!
If you can join in the right dance according to the mystical tradition,
you can trample on this world and the one to come spurn again.
I'm wounded by a hidden sword and I am heaving sighs in secret;
where is an ear that can hear the bitter weeping of us silent men?

I have not become broken and old like this in my own time…
it is those eyes belonging to the Beloved that my hair does whiten.
Paradise's fragrance is exhaled while we are pledged to torment;
water of life streams past while of thirst we die there and then.
I hear them saying… "O Sadi, do not again go after that One:'
can I help it, for passion drags me along, in spite of myself again?

No parrot utters more heart-ravishing speech than You:
words flow from Your mouth with honey… into the blue!
It is only right for all people to be praising Your words…
but they've no opportunity to talk if You are talking too!
No garden has a cypress like You… almond eyes, mouth
small like a pistachio nut and speech all sugared through.
It wouldn't be fair to tell my love's story in Your presence,
I therefore make a vow I will not tell it again, this… I do!
Your charming eyes are working magic with their glance:
though I can't say that my eyes have power to speak too!
Breeze, if you have the opportunity to talk, then whisper
into the ear of that bored One words of mine, just a few.
No description is possible worthy of that One's beauty…
for the words of the mad lover as credible they don't view.
I'm ashamed to call You a full moon in regards to beauty:
has one heard of talk that from mouth of full moon flew?
Beloved might not realise state of lover who drowned in
the sea… but might find a freshness in these poems anew.
Pearls are shed from the mouth of Sadi in place of poems,
and if he'd money he'd have written his words in gold too!

If Union with You could come within the scope of imagination,
I shouldn't begrudge spilling my life at Your feet in any situation.
To depart and return does not satisfy the demands of desire...
it is not the rule of Love to make and break promise relied upon.
My perplexity's not about You, but concerns Pen of the Divine
Art... that such a perfect form as belongs to You could fashion.
Who can place some balm on the heart of one who's been wounded
by Love... without power to stay, or means to escape later on?
One who by night sleeps like a lamp in Beloved's presence does
not fear extinguishment in daytime and to be hung up... thereupon.
The flowing flood of tears and blazing fire of sighs are like the
wind blowing dust over one's head... as nothing in Your estimation.
It happens to be Your habit to utter bitter words to Your lovers...
the remedy of Sadi is to mingle his speech with a sugar concoction!

For me to try measuring my strength with Love... is
impossible, when its power overwhelms me, like this.
Whether You grant me access to Your form or fail to
pass by me, is in Your hands... to kill me, or cherish.
And if You should happen to attack me with a sharp
sword... to surrender to You, no choice left for me is!
Condition of a ship at sea is one of two alternatives:
it is either all gain, O sage, or loss: everything amiss!
If the creed is Love what then is the code of the lover?
Our heart, Your shrine, take from thoughts... but this!
The sun is not worthy to shine in Your presence... nor

can the cypress exalt form before You, it'd be remiss!
Whoever looked at such a face has torn coat like Sadi:
madness is caused by state of knowledge... know this!
Like a candle I must either melt or be put out at dawn,
my only resource left is to burn and accept whatever is!

It was not fair of You to at first a promise be making,
when You had an idea You'd the promise be breaking.
It is wrong to bring up one in the luxury of kindness...
then him, with the sword of separation, be wounding.
One should never expect faithfulness and love again
from those who are angel-faced... but deceit showing.
If one more time I should gain access to a corner I am
determined then that in early retirement I'll be living.
Ah no... but patience and being alone are impossible
for in Beloved's face the door one cannot be shutting.
Sometimes I think I'll weep bitterly from loving You,
but... that You would laugh at my tears I'm thinking.
Whether You are my enemy or see me as Your friend,
my hold from off Your skirt... I will never be releasing.
The inference, dear Sadi... is that you can only escape
from that One's snare by your whole life surrendering.
Whether You set me free or You call me Your slave...
it's quite impossible from this bondage, to be escaping.

If the prey of Love's desert should be pierced by that One's arrow
it can't free itself: foot-bound, that One's chains it can't overthrow.

I thought that to avoid Love's torture I would travel the world:
that One's world-embracing beauty over the Universe did flow.
The vanquished one has no alternative available but to surrender:
how can that one withdraw one's head from that One's arrow?
The victim of the Beloved doesn't suffer pain… other folk are
alive through their souls, but we live by that One that we know.
The wonder is while that One complains of this haste of ours,
we are reduced to despair because of that One being too slow!
I let my eye wander through all the world then it finally returned,
no one's face seemed fair beside face that One to me did show.
Why all of this loud noise on the part of sweet-talking Sadi?
Beloved of mine is a Koranic verse and I am interpreting it so.
The melody of Love's mystery was filling the heart of David
so there was rising to Heaven music of his Psalms… long ago.


Whoever takes the road to self does not travel in our direction:
by beauty of that One's face power to see experiences annihilation.
O breeze, the bed of the violet and the jasmine have no fragrance…
prepare perfume from that One's musky hair, a heady concoction!
Ordinary people want from that One according to their rank,
but we aspire to nothing but to fulfil that One's every direction.
I'm in that One's snare, while that One goes wherever: if that
One does not adapt to my state… I will help that One's situation.
To try to allay suspicions of enemies so no information is theirs,
while my heart is on that One… my eyes I'll fix in another direction.
That One's skirt I will be grasping on Doomsday… while my
present life will be spent in thinking about that One's explanation.

O Sadi, if you stumble against a stone do not cry out, for from
the first I warned that head is unsafe in that One's street's location.


How that elegant cypress walks along the road so gracefully,
and how sweet the glances of that One's deer-like eyes to see!
When have you ever seen a cypress that has girdled its waist
or a full moon that's placed a hat on its head? Please tell me!
A rose in that One's presence is resembling a weed on the earth:
moon before that face is like a star before the moon, you see?
That One is walking with majesty, while a hundred thousand
hearts are accompanying… like a sovereign following an army.
I am told to be on guard and flee from that One, but… I reply,
"Where am I able to go because there's no place to hide for me?"
You might say that at the very first glance that I was casting
at the chin of that One, into that well my heart fell, uncontrollably.
I don't begrudge the fact my heart has gone beyond my control:
this precious life of mine to give if that One demands it, is ready.
O light of my eyes, please place upon my eyes the feet that You
have placed upon the dust, for better than road's dust they be.
It is a pity that a bitter answer is from such a mouth as Yours
and that the white breast of Yours has a heart black as can be!
The wretched are consumed on the fire of Your love: ah… no,
for You are wrapped up in the morning… still sleeping peacefully.
I thought I'd complain of You to some friends and acquaintances,
in the hope You'd stop ill-treating Your innocent lover… me!
Again a sense of humour seized the skirt of my resolution, saying,
"Sadi, seek no protection against Beloved until Beloved be kindly?"

You hid face with sleeve having thrown to us a picture of You.
You keep Yourself hidden while a world goes mad for You too!
You're still hidden in bud but filled the heart of the complaining
nightingale with tumult... because of Love's irresistible glue!
Everyone without seeing You describes Your face, O You who
have thrown mankind into perplexity: lift Your veil, please do!
It's not right You show such a lovely face to the helpless ones:
You've made it the topic of general conversation, haven't You?
I am hoping that like the oyster's shell, the drop that You have
cast to me from the cloud of Your grace will become a pearl too.
No painter that sees You can draw Your picture and whoever
has looked on You... flung pencil from fingers amazed at You!
It's this regret that kills me... You allow Your attributes to be
told by the rabble and You forbid the initiated to tell them too.
You are hard over Your servants and whatever You order is right,
and You have used violence against one too weak to resist You.
I bowed my head in homage to You: when looking again I realised
You had flung many heads like Sadi's from Your threshold too!
O Beloved, You've done wrong by cutting the bond: was this
the way to keep faith, still not seen You'd make such promises?
I'm known in Your street though not allowed to see Your face:
You're the bloody-mouthed wolf that didn't tear Joseph to pieces!
We didn't catch a glimpse of that One though all the city talked:
story of Majnun the ears of Layla never reached, what's this?
In his dreams Farhad had kissed the lips of rose-bodied Shirin,
but nothing but deep regret ever came from those dreams of his.

We made so many useless efforts looking for You, like a child
who will run off after a sparrow that flying away suddenly is.
You have not yet made a prey of the bird of the seeker's heart,
except with the catapult of Your arched eyebrows full of bliss!
What does the graceful walk of that One resemble? It like the
strutting of peacock: glance like gaze of frightened antelope is.
If I set down my foot outside the centre of Shiraz there's no way
that I can travel, for You have drawn circle round me as emphasis!
One could not come to any hand-grips with Your crystal hands…
we left blessing You, listening to Your abuse as us You did dismiss.
May the eyes of Sadi not see Your face ever again if he should
open those same eyes on anyone after sight of Your face is his!


O You, though out of my sight, are firmly in my heart:
Your beauty shows in spite of veil… Your covering art!
You've stolen hearts of the herd… You've drunk blood
of devotees… made prey of all, yet kept Yourself apart.
What can I gain from another… to cut off love for You?
You are also my balm, O You who wounded my heart!
If You have broken my heart through painful wounding
what's it matter, for I hear breaking hearts is Your art!


Best that you don't test your strength with that arm of silver:
it is best not to wrestle with that tough athlete… any further!
You gave heart to that One, accepting love, you've no alternative:
if that One doesn't adapt to you, put up with that One, no other.
Care only for Beloved so Beloved will be interested in Your life:

that you were not absorbed in your own life would be much better.
The shield of patience can no longer endure the arrow of separation:
if you didn't fight against Beloved with archer-eyebrows, is safer!
Partnership with One with whom I have executed Love's contract
would be right, even though of my stock that One is now owner.
It is better for the slave to place the head of submission on the
mandate of the Absolute Ruler, than to be exalted by some honour.
I wouldn't raise my head in Your presence even if You should
strike me like a harp: it's up to You to cherish this faithful lover.
O my precious Darling, there can be no doubt that I will be felled
by the arrow of doom, so it is best of me You be the over-thrower!
Our gathering again today is beginning to resemble a rose-garden:
minstrel is surpassing love-lorn nightingale… as the sweet singer.
Lend an ear to the lament of the minstrel and leave the nightingale,
which than Sadi of Shiraz, isn't a singer who is in any way better!


The sun is flashing out its beams from the eastern horizon:
Winebringer… a morning cup of last night's wine, come on!
Take for a while my reason: must I bear wisdom's tyranny?
Take for a while my senses: must one worry about Fortune?
If calamity's stones rain, make my head's crown shield me;
if criticism's arrows hit me, my life be a target from then on!
I've lifted Wine-jar to my lips for it contains Water of Life:
it not only tasted of fire… pomegranates seeds colour shone.
How is it possible for the seeker to look for that pure wine?
Anka, that Phoenix, nest of tiny sparrow cannot rest upon!
If you are offered the wine in exchange for your life, take it!

Winehouse dust out-sweets Life's Water in Sage's opinion.
Let Sufi take himself to his retreat, Sadi will wander in the
desert: the virtuous one does not criticise the wicked person.

That One's a Sweetheart, merry with drink, graceful figure,
unadorned by art… who in hand, a goblet of wine does stir.
In the friendly gathering of wine-drinkers that One's waist
is girdled and that One's blouse is open… wider and wider!
That Sweetheart's lips, full of pearls, resemble a cornelian…
that One's flowing curls are like nooses… twisted together!
In the rose-bed of that Sweetheart's face's garden are moles,
young negroes that are born of the moon, there they gather.
In the presence of such a One as this the earth bends low…
while the sky is standing… waiting to be the humble server.
The sun, which is the sovereign and the lord of all the sky…
in the vast open field of that One's beauty is a foot-soldier!
Sadi has never been recalled into the memory of that One,
even though he is a modest and upstanding… sincere lover!

Morning breeze, you move along joyfully, full of happiness,
you bring balm to my soul bringing Beloved's note, no less!
Have you passed in a garden or have you been in Paradise?
You're welcome, may you be happy, may fortune you bless!
Since being in this abode, I never saw such a door as you've
opened today, before these eyes, into the garden… I confess.
Beauties and saucy sweethearts come and go like the rose:
You've remained there standing before me, like the cypress.

306

At first You were a hand-lamp, then slowly a wax candle…
I did not take it seriously and this granary burned to ashes.
Since Your beauty appeared in the world, many a calamity
is upon us. O You mischief-maker who bore You? Confess!
I wish some morning You'd go out to the pleasure-ground…
so the garden might shed its morning roses and You caress.
A lover forming an attachment with a sweetheart will often
remember her; but, each moment my thoughts You possess!
How joyful would be my fate if I died from my love for You;
I always gladly take love's pain due to Sweetheart: no less!
The pain of a cautery can be relieved wherever it is applied:
but not Sadi's brand… which Your first glance did impress!


O lightning, if over the corner of that One's terrace you're passing,
carry news from me to there, where the wind dare not be approaching.
O bird, if you should be flying over to the street of that Sweetheart,
the message from that One's lovers to that angelic One be taking.
If that Beloved with the attributes of Jupiter should ask about
news of us, reply that to win Beloved our lives we would be selling.
Although the thirsty of the desert are reduced to their last gasp,
You… upon that camel-litter, in the sweetest of sleeps are lying.
O lovely One, not a day goes by that You do not pass at least
a hundred times before my heart, whether present or absent being.
Have You any idea what befalls us at Your hands? Have You?
Until You come to Yourself and see Your state, You're not knowing!
You, though absent from sight are near us in spirit: come back
to us, for we are consumed by patience in all this endless waiting.

Either give Your heart to us, since our heart is in Your power...
or, this love that we are feeling for You... be instantly expelling!
Since You are exposing secrets of our love in such a way from
behind veil, let's now see from outside the veil what's happening.
Sadi, who are you to be boasting of love? Make claim to service,
and... acknowledgment of servitude in all sincerity be making.

O You, whose essence is holy, and whose body is spiritual!
You're my heart's ease and of my soul the balm so merciful!
Happy is that one who is attached to You, and also is that
brotherhood... in the midst of whom You are most powerful!
I also will be tying my belt... girding my loins to serve You:
it may be that You will call me to be Your slave, so dutiful.
The sugar that I see on Your tray is really useless, because
You are driving away all the flies where it is most plentiful.
Wherever You are passing with all of Your great beauty no
one doubts You are a garden's cypress: even more beautiful!
And if that one who sees the hands and the arms of Yours
doesn't give heart to you... You will get it by being forceful!
Walk on my eyes for You're Master over me: give the order
for my execution, for You're my Sovereign... so Masterful!
I'll not turn my head away from the mandate You gave me,
even though You turn me head down like a pen that is full.
Do You see this dust that is on my face and have You any
knowledge of the pain that at my heart continues to pull?
It is clear that the smoke which is arising from the heart of
Sadi is produced by the hidden fire that nothing can annul!

O You, You piece of Paradise and You, symbol of mercy!
In Your time the favours of God comes to us... assuredly!
I thought there might be some end to this pain of Love...
but, it begins afresh every morning and this I did not see!
The story of my love is notorious throughout the world...
but I have not the power to tell it again to You, obviously.
We bore Your absence patiently to the utmost limit of our
power, but there seems to be no limit to loving hopelessly.
There is no room for wisdom where love pitches its tent...
an uproar would be the result of two kings in one country.
In point of beauty You're distinguished among Your peers,
like the held high standard... in midst of a victorious army.
I don't criticise You because You rule with absolute power:
it is only right that You kill a slave, though he innocent be!
As soon as Love began to practise tyranny... then Wisdom
seemed devoid of the capacity of resisting it, even slightly.
It's to the protection of Your grace that I'll flee tomorrow...
where everyone who is desperately seeking asylum will be!
I am helpless, where can I take my complaint against You?
I've an accusation against You... I must make it personally.
O Sadi, how long can this tale of your love stay concealed?
This wound of the heart will become infectious, eventually.


O You, who are passing by Your lovers in such a way...
that with each flirtatious glance You steal a heart away;

You will be slaying all Your lovers who are so afflicted:
let us see if You will pity one of Your victims one day!
We have come over here from the street of the lovers...
we are not mere idle sightseers, who drift the highway.
As long as You with Your radiant face are in my view,
nothing else ever falls within my vision, one could say.
I imagined that I would not surrender my heart to one
because of the fear of falling in love... losing the way;
that I would draw a magic circle around myself so that
no heart-stealing fairy into it could come... on any day.
These angel-faced ones, these ear-ringed adorned ones
are true adepts at beautifying, flirting come what may!
Have You ever heard of a patient nightingale when the
rosebuds are beginning to blossom at the dawn of day?
Wisdom is throwing a veil over the threshold of love...
but the tears quickly expose it when they fall that way.
Do you know, O my son, why you suffer pangs of love?
So you escape every other grief the world makes one day.
One moment in the Beloved's company is dirt-cheap if
in exchange for it even both of the worlds for it you pay!
Is this a pen that is in the hand of Sadi... or could it be a
thousand sleeves full of lustrous pearls? Now please say!
And please say, what is the city this candy comes from?
You're no pen made from reed but from sugarcane today!

Whether You grant life to me or You'll be my destruction,
I'll submit to Your commands, You're beyond my station.

I'm still a sinner though I do a thousand acts of devotion;
You can slay many better than me, be guiltless thereupon.
I cannot complain against You to anyone... You're sought
everywhere but You still go which way You want to go on.
You are like the sun because of Your face's perfect beauty:
the eye cannot see You as You are, You it can't look upon.
If it is so that looking at the Beloved is forbidden, I would
have repented all my life... for obeying such a prohibition!
I swear by God, if You slay me angrily, I'd not turn away:
how can one flee from You as You're his asylum to rely on?
Darling, I am like a wild animal that did not sleep all night
while birds and fishes did: for Your face I waited on and on!
If this long night kills me through all my yearning for You...
it wouldn't be strange if morning's breeze revived me anon.
If I should endeavour to conceal from friends love's pain...
my burning words would bear witness to it, from hereupon.
Khizer, like Sadi's pen is engaged day by day in travelling...
it'd not be strange if Life's Water from darkness flowed on.

My heart's at ease since You all my thoughts were filling,
whether You send me a crown or with sword me are killing.
You, in the attributes of Your face, Reason's eye dazzled,
like the bird of night which nothing but daylight is seeing!
You wound all people with the sword of Your blood-thirsty
glance and ruby lips... then on it, salt You keep scattering.
We are gleaners of the harvest of the rich and the powerful;
You, You the Lord of the harvest, one look at us be taking.

I grant You may root out love for me from Your hard heart,
but... You can't out from mine, my love for You be driving!
If You want to slay me without fault, You have the power:
it is wrong if You, faith's promise, with lover are breaking.
There is no end to this love... because in it we are pure and
because it is the truth that You are chastity... forthcoming.
Don't imagine that I'll engage in opposition to the wish of
the Friend, even if the world hatefully against me is acting.
If You desire not to surrender Your heart to anyone... close
Your eyes: iron shield to stop love's arrows one is requiring!
Tell our adversary we are helpless... and there is no need for
that One, strength of that One against us to be measuring.
O Sadi, since one cannot gain mastery, submission has to
be practised towards those that powerful hands are having.

If You cannot hide those long curls and face with a veil...
You are trying to tear away the veil of the Mystic's tale.
I'm devoted to the silver circle of Your ear-ring... for You
are the Master of all of Your obedient slaves in Your jail.
Enter the retreat of the pure and pious and see what acts
of drunkenness and intoxication that in private do prevail.
I swear by Saints Fortune You are forever in my memory,
and it is not a memory that after forgetfulness does pale.
You are so congenial to my nature and so firmly fixed in
my heart that I imagine being in Your embrace, in detail!
How fortunate are those having conversations with You:
I have not courage to speak nor patience to silently bewail.

How can the unfriendly guardian be worth Your company,
as his nature is all sting while You with pure honey assail?
I said to the morning breeze by way of instruction, this…
"Tell rose-bed don't send rose to thorn, this guard curtail!"
Sober one, can you know heart's anguish of the drunkard?
As you have no fire… how then can you boil… until pale?
You, who have no heart, cannot understand what Love is.
You with no ear can't hear the Mystic's song, Love's tale.
O Sadi, don't give up love for Beloved in exchange for both
worlds: it'd be a pity to, for the price of Joseph, make a sale!


If You lift musk-scented forehead's curls from off Your face…
Your lovers for sacrifice… their heads at Your feet will place.
Cypress of silver form… if You would only join in the dance
see the rapture and sacrifice of souls that now is commonplace.
You have a beautiful form and a face so fair that the cypress,
tulip… the box-tree and the rose, Your form's grace does efface.
Is there a garden existing, growing a flower like Your cheek?
A cypress grows that compares to Your form… even a trace?
If You did see that beauty of Your ear's lobe and Your mole…
You would never again glance at another face, only Your face!
I am a devotee of that breeze that blows in from the north…
that northern breeze that playfully Your face's curls displace.
O musician of this gathering, sing out… chant out your song:
nightingale of drunken lovers sing sweetly and fill this space.
Who said that You steal hundreds of hearts with one glance?
You would easily hunt down a thousand prey in a single chase!

Due to the elegance of the sweet language of Sadi's verse…
that all Shiraz's poets are my devoted slaves, is now the case.

O You cypress of the garden of the spiritual realities…
You are the soul and best thing in the world of frailties!
All are agreed that to be dying in Your presence… is far
sweeter than to live after You have from eyes like these.
Your eyes work the magic of the ancient magicians and
You seduce the adepts of the end of this age, with ease!
When Your name comes under discussion You could say
that You are present in person, everyone You do please!
And that one You return to after a journey has no need
to receive from You a traveller's present… You are his!
If the morning breeze brought a message of Your coming
I'd give up my life as a reward to that benevolent breeze.
The sorrow of the heart can only be dispelled by the hope
that joy will eventually come and finally this heart ease!
And if You should happen to be seeing Your own face…
amazement at Your own beauty Yourself it would seize!
If it happens that You become reconciled with Your lover,
how fine it'd be: love in springtime everyone does please!
Sadi is loving that dark down around Your rosy cheeks…
look at this old man, remembering his youthful fantasies!

The beauty of Your down is a chapter of the book of Your beauties,
whose sweetness is only a single letter in the book of Your qualities!

The musk deer would have become overwhelmed by Your fragrance
if one twist of the curl of Your long hair unwound in the breeze!
You've banished sleep from eyes of possessors of spiritual insight,
through fear they might see in a dream Your phantom them tease.
Under the spell of Your mouth that is witty and smiles so sweetly,
my heart that is wounded is overflowing with grief and unease.
Be unveiling Your face like Joseph did so that those who criticise
Your lovers may then the excuse of Zuleikha plead with ease.
Not seeing Your face all the time I don't want Paradise's Garden,
because no wine can ever quench this thirst… my heart's disease!
If one absorbed in remembering You is placed in Hell… its torment
wouldn't cause him any suffering because of memories like these.
Call me Your slave only one time by way of doing me a favour…
so that You can from each hair-root of mine hear me You please!
Don't look at me in case others may become hopeful like I am…
for because of beggars habits none can be helpful to such as these.
The smoothness of my poetry is derived from my fiery genius…
which is like the fire of Your face from which sweat does squeeze!
All lovers unite with sweethearts while I seek with aching heart:
all others at the spring of water while Sadi only the mirage sees.


What kind of walk is this that my heart of peace You're stealing,
that my mind of patience and body of its senses You are robbing?
What worth is a garden of tulips? Shake Your sleeve and tell
the gardener to come if a shirt full of roses he wants to be carrying.
Both day and night are occurring at the time when like the sun
You show Your face and again when the window You are closing.

Your hair from Your head to Your waist is a sheaf in a granary:
careful to hide that sheaf or my stock-in-trade off You'll be carrying.
You have subtly stolen my heart by deceit… the thief commits
robbery by night but in the broad daylight my heart You're stealing!
If You, without cause or fault of mine, left me without the notion
that I shall also leave You, You only a false idea are entertaining.
Why shouldn't smoke not rise from the granary You set on fire?
Wouldn't blood flow from where without need to, You are prickling?
You follow the dictates of enmity and come not acting in conformity
with Love's obligations, when to the foe freedom You're giving.
Blame not a poor one for with halting steps not following You…
for You, his poor neck with the chain of Love, are tightly tying!
O Sadi, in uttering sweet speech before that palate and mouth,
you are sending pearls to the sea, and gold to the mine are carrying.


If only you'd appreciate true pleasure's in its renunciation
you'd never again call soul's lust 'pleasure'… never again.
You would close a thousand doors of people against you,
if only a single heavenly door… to you, is allowed to open.
If you from the chains of lustful passion released the bird
of your soul it'd be able to make flights into the empyrean.
But you do not possess the self-restraint of the Phoenix…
for you're like a sparrow in the trap of such fierce passion.
I fear that from your worship of the physical appearance,
you will not know spiritual Reality's Path, to walk upon.
Even if a weed from your garden of devotion does grow…
a weed like yours would seem like a rose from the garden.

You'll be regretting your attempt to purchase both worlds
because such time doing that is a waste of life... a burden!
This is all you will gain from what remains to you of life...
if you will finish your life in the same way, that you began.
Something better than life was yours while you were alive?
Appreciate it, you can't buy a moment of it, for a kingdom.
You move so slowly, and with such a stagnant brain, that
I'm afraid that you may fall way behind the Caravan, son.
And this is my order to you, dear brother, it is this... that
you should never waste a moment if it's possible, not one!
It is right that you should hold your tongue like an oyster,
so when the necessity comes you will scatter pearls, anon.
Sadi has been putting up with bitterness all of his long life
so he might be winning a name for sweet speech... later on.

That One of the beautiful face who of the soul has purity,
purges life of its darkness by means of the light of divinity.
If evil passions were to be banished from your thoughts...
whatever you looked upon would become that One to see!
The rapture inspired by music of Love's gathering will only
reach the heart's ear when you close the gross ear instantly.
One who is enthralled by evil passions will forever have all
his friendships eventually turned to relationships of enmity.
If you do not wish to become foot-tied in the heart's snare...
don't become nest-mate of birds without shame, obviously.
Unless you are lopping off the branch that trespasses upon
your neighbour's house, it shall give rise to feeling bitterly.

Beware, I have warned you not to step upon sin's pathway,
or else it'll not become you to boast knowledge of divinity.
O Sadi, there is no virtue in getting the better of people in
a fist fight: you'd be a real man if lust you beat completely!


I've had enough of flying since I've no longer feathers or wings!
Escape from Your hand? You don't let me move or do other things.
I can't pursue escape and I can't follow love's road… where are
these sufferings of the victim who with him such patience brings?
It's useless to speak to you of the sadness of my lot… who may
never have experienced a night that to it a year's length clings.
All my life has been passed in separation and it would be easy
to bear if there's chance of Union with what the Last Day brings.
How pleasant it would be to feel patient under separation for
all one's life, in hope that some day Union from Eternity springs.
There'd be nothing strange in You failing to sympathise with
this one's pain: such a plight in Your life isn't one of Your things.
O You source of such commotion, why do You continue to sit?
Show Your stature to cypress that no such form to garden brings.
Speak only one word to me who is so captivated by Your love
that my self is effaced by Your existence from which Life springs!
For there won't be tonight any mystical music where the drum
is thumped only once and the lute escapes with only two zings!
Do not again display to the sky that sun-bright face of Yours,
for the full moon would wane to a crescent feeling shameful things.
One night say that because of Your musk-scented down and
mole, the fine pen was worked and a drip of ink to cheek clings.

O Sadi, do not be saying that even to look at that One is a sin...
it would be a sin to take eyes off from where such beauty springs.
From whatever door You come back with such grace and beauty
it would be a door which You opened to mankind out of mercy.
Vain one criticising can't distinguish his hand from an orange
in that crowd where, Joseph-like, You let all Your beauty see!
Beauties are sometimes seen to be adorned with many jewels;
You, silver-bodied One, make jewels more valuable, obviously.
When nightingale sees face of the rose it then begins to sing...
my speech is always stopped by Your face... that amazes me!
You can't veil face from all, endowed with beauty as You are:
You are sun riding sky, Paradise's virgins letting clothes lie.
You're exalted in rank, care nothing for condition of destitute:
You're sleepy and feel for the eyes of the wide-awake no pity.
I grant You're an evergreen cypress, born of Paradise's water:
don't hold Yourself aloof from us, You know You're our property.
If You don't bless me, honour me with Your abuse; for although
it may be bitter, what pleases Your lips to say is sweet to me!
The thirst led me to believe that the flood would reach my waist:
now that I've gone beyond my depth I know that You are a sea!
Whether You are driving me away or at me You are frowning,
the fly will never be flying away anywhere from the confectionery.
O Sadi, you cause a furore by reciting this sweet poetry of yours:
in your day, parrot not allowed to be pecking at sugar... will be!


You've never made a promise that You didn't break in the end;
You've sent me in the raging fire, but in it Yourself don't send.

You've shown the foundation of Your love won't remain stable;
You tied in the trap, while from noose Your way away did wend.
You broke my heart and then went away despite love's promise…
so now that You've broken the glass, be careful how it will end.
There is no lamp like You in any house, in any place… anywhere:
but no one shuts door of house like You do, on that I can depend.
If You should torture me with the brand and the pain of separation,
I can't bear it… shed my blood, You will be exempted my Friend.
Come, we've trampled under feet thoughts of conceit and pride
and have now placed these feet upon existence itself, I contend!
If with corner of Your eye You glance at captives, let me be first
cured of pain, for You wrongfully hurt one who cannot defend.
It would be right for everyone who sees You to say that any
one who sees You has truly looked upon Paradise without end!
Don't think it strange that Sadi cries while remembering Beloved:
Love brings desire, wine drunkard into drunkenness does send.
If You should lay claim to loveliness... You've the evidence;
as You've beauty of the moon and garden cypress' elegance.
I do not open door to anyone so no one may enter my mind:
my heart You can enter… there You have an open entrance.
Are You an angel, are You a moon? I do not know what to
call You, neither can I suggestion what You're like advance.
I cannot take a complaint against You to anyone because to
You belong prestige, power and rank... beauty You enhance!
The flowers of Your garden's face are resembling red tulips:
but what to do with rosy face, taking black-hearted stance?
What fault do You see in this slave to break faith with him

except we're weak and You're strong in each circumstance?
Perfect beauty's spoiled by sour expression on a sweet face:
don't be against us, all mankind wish You well in advance.
By uttering one fine saying You steal a thousand hearts...
this is not as nice as to give to one heart one helpful chance.
By God, if like Sadi your heart only one way went, you'd lie
awake all night, like him... in expectation of just one glance.

You strutting along with such grace, who're You, what's Your name?
Lovers blood is shed by You... You oblivious, play assassin's game!
I'm always afraid of being consumed like moth's burnt to nothing,
through jealousy at You being favourite of all... like candle's flame.
You stir commotion, are shedding blood while all mankind looks on:
how harmoniously delectable Your movements and speech the same.
Your sweet looks surely have formed the topic of every conversation:
sugarcane said, "Look, I've girded my loins, in Your service I came!"
If infidel were to see Your form resembling an idol made from silver,
unfaithful would never again call in praise of a marble idol's name!
You are crowd's affliction, arena of man and woman's destruction;
mischief in mansion and market and You set the household aflame.
I've sacrificed to Your love heart, religion and all of my learning too,
in truth today I'm the wily bird and You, You're snare for the game!
I can't bear stone of reproach by each and every one who is ignorant:
for You are like a light behind a glass that inside Sadi's breast came.

What blessing will I invoke on you, blessed shadow of the Huma?*
O God, grant that this protection be always over Islam, O ruler!

Your bounty's apparent while you are hidden from man's sight…
you are famous, while you Divine Mystery's shadow are under.
You are engaged in devotion within the royal tent of chastity…
kings are kept standing in waiting outside your pavilion's door.
The sun with all these candles behind it and torches in front
can't enter your royal presence by sign: 'Get permission to enter!'
You are the rising place of the constellation of felicity, a heaven
of auspicious stars, an ocean of royal pearls, shell… a pearler!
May the sanctuary of chastity and virtue be adorned by you!
Knowledge of Islam is kept by your son Muhammed,* the other.
O envious one, if you don't become as dust in that one's service
then you have the wind in your hand… go and measure it, sir!
Let whoever wishes to complain at any defect in this kingdom
go his way and give vent to his vexation somewhere or other.
Endeavour and bravery don't give what wealth and fortune do;
treasure and army don't achieve what zeal and prudence gather.
I was unable to render you adequate service… my pen inspired
by my love and my regard for you… up upon its head did stir.
May the palace of your sublimity for ever be so lofty that no
bird could throw its shadow over it except for one bird: Huma!
Your well-wishers have a crown of honour on their heads while
all of your ill-wishers upon their feet have nothing but a fetter!
O successor of the son of Salghar,* supreme in state and Islam…
the angel of the sign of mercy and the realm conquering ruler!

*Notes: The Huma, like the Anka or Phoenix represents good fortune as
it is a symbol for God in the Beyond State. This ghazal is in praise of
Atabeg Muhammed Shah who reigned over the province of Fars whose

*capital was Shiraz and was a child who reigned for two and a half years*
*(1260-1262) under the regency of his mother Khatun (Princess) Tarkham,*
*the widow of Atabeg Sad's the second whom this ghazal also praises.*
*Salghar was a Turkish general in the employment of the Seljuki monarchs*
*and founder of the Atabeg dynasty of Fars.*

Better for cypress to keep standing when You are moving;
the parrot had better remain silent when You are speaking.
No one ever voluntarily surrenders his heart to Your love:
You've set Your snare in which that one You are catching.
What a plague You are that plunders wisdom of the sober,
with those lovely drunken eyes of Yours, glancing, taking!
By reason of the love that I have and the jealousy I feel…
I am angry that at those strangers You are often looking.
You've said that to look at You is a sin, You steal hearts.
Is it right You… guilty of an offence, others are accusing?
Will You never forget that You have a record for hostility,
that You with all Your lovers always keep on quarrelling?
Your hands are dyed with fresh blood of Your wretched…
does anyone ever act like You do, O You of such cunning?
You're friendly towards Your enemies, angry with friends:
this is not friendship, that to Your lover You are showing.
If You should wield the sword here then be taking my life:
there is peace inside this one with whom You are fighting.
As long as I hear mystic's song I'll lend no ear to criticism:
O imposter, advice you give is useless, it I'm not hearing!
Take care that you don't turn away from Beloved's face to
look at the sun, for you are from a sun to the wall turning.

O Sadi, be wary of that One's hard, cruel heart, because
what does that Infidel care if one for clemency is crying?

You're looking at everyone with the eye of approval and mercy;
when it finally comes to my turn You practise all this coquetry.
O you who continue to advise me not to pursue that One anymore,
you only blame Ayaz... not Sabuktegin's son Mahmud,* obviously.
The straight-statued cypress passes in front when I am praying,
saying, "I'm lovers' worship place, you repeat prayers mistakenly!"
Yesterday I said to that One hopefully, "I pray for Your welfare,"
and that One replied, "Pray for yourself, but do it with all sincerity."
I said to that One, "If I bite Your lip I'll drink wine, taste sugar!"
That One... "If you come to my feast, you'll tell of it incessantly!"
You call me Your own Sadi and then You cruelly repel me again...
if You don't lay the table why are You opening the door so widely?

* Note: Ayaz and Mahmud... see previous note.

That One is a Darling who finds it fine to ill-treat me:
that One's so powerful who goes against me violently.
I endure a heavy burden from an antagonist of whose
cruelty I cannot approach any judges to judge harshly.
Wisdom is helpless when it comes to Love's bondage,
like the believer who is in an infidel's power, suddenly.
I am often thinking that I will reveal all this to people,
so that perhaps a heart out there may have pity on me.
Again I say, "What does a king really care if a servant

who is in his household happens to die, occasionally?"
O You who does expect from me patience and sense...
You are only placing a heavy load on a weakling, see!
People are flinging treasure at the feet of sovereigns...
but I've a head to offer if You care to take it from me!
It'd be a pity if the eye which is accustomed to seeing
Beloved looked on another... after that One it did see!
I am lost in wonderment at Your perfect loveliness...
Your great beauty is needing no adornment, obviously.
It is only Sadi who is able to compose poetry like this:
it's not every beggar that has such exquisite jewellery!

Cast at least a backward glance at us when You pass by,
or does pride stop You remembering lovers... do You try?
All of Khutan never saw a face of such seductive charms:
there never was in any garden a cypress so fine and high!
If You lifted the veil from Your eyebrow's deep green bow
in public, any rainbow no buyer would again want to buy.
The garden cypress doesn't have such heart-alluring form:
on sun, despite its looks, Your perfumed hair one can't see.
Since Heaven started creating none has elegance like You:
I don't know if You're a huri, angel, human being, or fairy!
Since surrendering heart to Your love I am in care's ocean:
when at prayer it could be said You are where I pray: there!
I no longer know my way, I'm sinking like a drowning man!
Look, Your lips are like cornelian from my blood You share.
When I've passed from this world my spirit would return if

only You pass over my dust... proudly sweeping past there.
Fire leaps from that One's ruby lips... disturbing my spirit:
if such a One gives Life, you O Sadi, for it gratefully care!
If another lays claim, one could say he vainly wants to vie
with you like Samari's calf in Moses' time... gold not true!

What has entered Your heart that You Your love have uprooted?
What has happened that from Your sight Your old lover is rejected?
O Beloved, separation between us has passed beyond all limits...
hasn't the time come yet when again to me You will be attached?
It could be I'll meet my death in Your presence if the opportunity
arises... or in Your street by me for You, having too long longed.
O kindly Beloved, open me a door to Your face because no one
else will open the door if You shut it... so, please open it instead!
Even if the whole of the Universe were peopled with only beauties
no face but Your face would please both these eyes in my head.
I often thought that I would not open my eyes upon a fair face,
but You have gone and on us a spell You cast: it's now completed!
Perhaps You'll happen to see Yourself in a mirror, or else I don't
think You in any way resemble anyone else in the whole world.
Sadi's sayings, even if all of the creation appreciated them, would
be worth absolutely nothing, if by You they were not to be approved!
No adequate service can ever be rendered by all of my endeavours
unless there is still a hope of a pardon at the hands of the Beloved.

O breeze of the New Year, what is the state of the garden
that the nightingales utter cries of anguish out in the open?

O storehouse of antidotes, cast a glance at Your wounded:
the salve's in Your hand but the wounds You won't lessen.
Either bring about a private interview or lower the veil... or
the sweet face of Yours will make a riot in the world of men.
Now and then Your face perspires owing to such delicacy...
just like when spring showers fall on rosebuds as they open.
Are those aloes under Your skirt, or roses in Your sleeve, or
musk in Your collar? Show us whatever it is You have then.
The rose cannot be compared to Your heart-ravishing face:
You're in midst of roses like rose among a thorny specimen.
At times Your noose of long hair drags me along by force…
then bow of Your eyebrows are killing me with humiliation.
Even though You may release it from the snare, Your prey
wouldn't escape: Beloved's jail is better than freedom again.
At first when You stole my heart You seemed faithful, but
as soon as my love waxed, waned was to me Your affection.
We're in much need of a fresh life after separation from You
for this life has been spent by us in the hope of Unification.
I fear the mystic's prayers using Your image are not valid...
for even his point of worship with Your face has been riven!
Every pain that one experiences has its cure and its remedy,
but the salve for Sadi's pain is harmony with Beloved again!

When you're able to be of help to a man crushed by misery
you'd take care of his heart if you'd any kind of humanity.
You can't go to Paradise from Judgement Place tomorrow
unless you give up this world: both ways, an impossibility.

It is neither generous nor manly to observe others faults...
look at yourself, because that you're not sinless cannot be.
Rule of seekers and perfect men is generosity and virtue...
what sign of true manliness have you but a cap of a Sufi?
Happily, proud Haman* would carry off stakes from you,
 if possession of wealth and dignity were your only glory!
What Tuba trees in Paradise have been planted for man,
while you, like some beast, are desiring only grass to see!
Who knows 'circumstances language'... so he whispers in
corpse's ear, "How happy life of your successor must be!"
 By what righteousness can you, whose register contains
many pages that are black, hope that Paradise you'll see?
O one of such poor spirit, seek to be close to God's portal,
for access to kings that you now have has no permanency.
You're a traveller, world resembles a caravan in a mirage:
not an asylum or retreat in which protection's found easily.
Call yourself to account and stop railing at others O Sadi:
for your stock in trade for Doomsday is in deeds of devilry!

*Note: Haman: Pharaoh's powerful minister in Moses' time.

How can that ascetic not be the Winehouse inhabitant...
when Sweetheart at night visits him there to him enchant.
So let the police inspector look at the face of the Beloved...
it is like the mosque's niche while I am a worshipping ant!
Ever since the time that I've discovered the Water of Life,
I don't care in the slightest if my rival dies... I'm adamant!

We cannot keep on explaining to all the hard-hearted ones
what this heart continues to suffer from loving... we can't!
There may happen to be friends, there may be sweethearts,
but... that the lover will only acknowledge Beloved I grant!
A more spiritual guest than You does not pass before this
heart upon the night that it, knowing anyone else... shan't.
Settle down there in the street of the dervish, so that then
an ascetic to be remaining in Your street's quarter... can't!
If you have a heart and are not in possession of a Beloved,
tell us the difference between a rational being and a plant?
If You want someone to stand up in Your service it is me:
and if You do not want it then I will sit down... reluctant!
O Sadi, if Destiny should slay you, then allow it to be by
hands of that One with arms of silver, who does enchant!

What face is this, that seeing... deprives me of patience?
 That figure so beautiful, it good qualities does dispense.
O my Darling, answer me as harshly as it pleases You...
though a chance to be bitter, with sweet speech commence.
I will never again blame those who are miserable and mad,
even the wise seeing that One's face... lose commonsense.
You're present in my heart like life in body, blood in veins,
You are not forgotten by me now, then thought of... hence!
One wishing to pass a night pleasantly with the Beloved,
must spend many gloomy nights and with others dispense.
Winebringer, bring it... Minstrel, sing it: for the Sufi is in
the dance and dualism believers say, "Unity makes sense!"

O Sadi, the limitations of poetry are obvious: remain silent because the object of your praise has beauty with no fence!

Why shouldn't ring-dove's heart be wrung with anguish,
when its loving song-mate is caught in the trap's mesh?
I spent my whole night with head in the bosom of peace;
but today I spent all day longing for a message, I stress.
That scent of rose and hyacinth and that complaining of
nightingale were sweet, but... they had to finally finish.
Don't ask me for patience in separation: it, I don't have!
Absence is like a stone, sick heart a glass goblet, a mess!
Never will a unhappy heart of one used to the Beloved's
society who's lost his high position, be comforted, unless!
It's unlawful for the ardent lover to use eyes in Beloved's
absence... extinguish candle, so I may set out in darkness.
I'll wait until breath of morning stirs... for it is then that
a message from the Beloved the heart of the lover reaches.
It is useless for me to go where You are... unless in Your
generosity You favour me with a welcome full of kindness.
Of that entity which You did see not a trace is remaining:
my life's come to the last gasp... in longing for Your caress.
Sadi doesn't tell to strangers tale of his Sweetheart's love:
never does one experienced in love tell his story to novices.

You plunder the house of those who are spiritually-minded,
You tear aside the veil of those who to abstinence are wed.

O You, You angel-face, if You are not wearing a veil You
will the penitence of the Sufis make permanently impaired.
Please, of what manner of a creature is this? I do not know
if You're a human being or an angel or even a fairy instead.
Even though my whole stock-in-trade could be involved in
a loss because of it, such a customer is profitably sighted.
Take to the painter a copy of this face so that he'll in the
future decide painting pictures to totally have renounced.
With this glance of Yours You have no need for a sword:
You make one assault and by storm our hearts are carried.
If You'd gazed steadfastly at Your own face in the mirror,
in our direction ever again... You never would have looked.
If Khusrau had lived in Your age, because You are sweeter
than Shirin… he would his heart to You have surrendered.
Although I may shut the door in the face of some people,
I can't close it against You, in my thoughts You're planted.
If Sadi happened to fall victim to Your Love then his spirit
would instantly come alive when over his head You passed.

I long to fall at that One's feet like a ball and say nothing,
and even if that One me... with that One's bat be striking.
Let a tempest pour on the heads of that One's lovers and
let arrows in path of that One's ardent lovers keep raining.
If that One cauterises you with that One's brand, submit,
and if that One slays you with pain, no remedy be seeking.
And if the eye-ducts of the lovesick were to overflow, then
blood out in a gushing stream would continue to be rushing.

331

Gathering of spiritual lovers, hail! I wonder who can have
drunk this wine the mere smell of which I find intoxicating!
Let whoever has written a record of Sadi's love delete from
it the chapter where 'Upon self-control' reads the heading.
And let whoever has never smelt the pure fragrance of Love
come here to Shiraz and our dust they can then be smelling.

That one knows nothing of Love who has not a Beloved:
a heart which You do not prey on, a heart can't be called.
Someday I will sacrifice my life for only one look of You,
just in case I should ever at some other face have looked.
God knows I'll not save my soul from Your love's power:
by You many much better and much worse will be slayed.
The pain of Love followed and swept all other pain away:
to take out the thorn from Your foot the needle is required.
Wine isn't allowed, but You with those two drunken eyes
will never let anyone leave Your presence not intoxicated.
You passed on happy and smiling, and You don't deserve
the looks at You from every side by those who're dejected.
You are unaware a whole people are mad from Your Love:
one who has yet to fall can't know state of all You've felled.
The evergreen cypress resembles Your figure perfectly, but
it never the graceful, swaying walk like Yours has attained!
It seems Your drunken eyes are bent upon creating trouble:
one won't sleep until one's done harm if one is intoxicated!
O Sadi, you'll not see the Beloved nor win Union with that
One... until to put any value upon yourself you have ceased.

News of You, has made worse the wound of separation...
like mirage of clear water with Your thirsty ones You con!
What traveller's present can You be giving to Your lovers?
What gift would be better than You coming home... anon?
You've gone, carrying my heart, making me a prey to grief:
night and day I think of You, know not where You've gone.
When I took You as my Beloved I said to my heart... that it
wouldn't be strange if beauty practised infidelity on and on!
What can a subject do but be patient? You... can practise as
much cruelty as You want to do for You reign, as sovereign.
I addressed the morning breeze the message I have for You:
I know of no other to take it my friend, so please carry it on!
I'm past listening to advice my friend... be off wise doctor...
and be making no display of your abstinence to us hereupon.
You who said you cannot be patient under beauties cruelty,
you would become so... if you like Sadi at One looked upon.
To open one morning the door of the eye on Paradise, would
be nowhere near as pleasant as to it at the Beloved, open on.

Happy is that one's morning by whom You've passed:
auspicious is that one's day at whom You've glanced.
The slave who is in Your retinue is truly a free man...
and happy is that country... in which You've travelled.
No purchaser would again buy sweets at any cost...
if even only one time at him so sweetly You've smiled!
O You... You bright sun and shadow of the Huma, we

are longing for a look from You… if it You've promised.
I will never lessen love and faith towards You, however
much enmity and such cruelty to me You've intensified.
All I have is a head that I can throw down at Your feet,
if such a mere trifle as this mind is… You've considered.
Do You know my face faces You, away from the world?
So be careful Your face… not to another You've turned!
It's a lifetime since I nightly started thinking about You;
are You asleep or all of my sighs at dawn, You've heard?
You said that sooner or later You'd help my condition…
You will only do so when over my dust… You've passed.
O Sadi, in field of Love of Beloved it's your duty to make
sure against arrow of reproach… yourself you've shielded.
But, O you sage… you will be needing a far better shield
than wisdom, if dart of glance of beauties you've avoided.

I know why Your beauty with Your sleeve You're hiding;
it is usual for a fairy… face from humans to be concealing.
Your attached friends and lovers await on right and left…
pride's preventing You from before or behind You looking.
I came to be looking on You and then to look into myself:
I couldn't gaze fully, each aspect Your beauty is fulfilling.
The goal of Fate's desire is performance of Your service…
I, one among Your slaves, girdled loins to You be serving.
I am ready to place my face in dust if You will destroy me;
I'll place hands in chains if me a captive You'll be making.
Whatever You do is right and Your power's also absolute:

334

You're defendant and judge, to who can I be complaining?
If I walked on my head searching for You, where can I go
unless the grace from the Master on my behalf is coming.
I thought that if I did not see You I'd forget Your love…
You leave me, are beside me, absent… yet in my thinking.
If Sadi should perish may Your life be preserved and that
of Your friends! If You killed Your slave, You'd be caring?

Have You noticed You've failed to observe faithfulness?
You've departed and done so despite of Love… confess!
You've counted as worth nothing all this misery of mine,
You've paid no regard at all to my hopeless helplessness.
I am still pleased with You in spite of all of Your cruelty:
You're upset with me although I am completely faultless.
To commit faults Yourself and to see them in friends is a
custom in the world that You have brought, nevertheless!
I will put up with Your flirting as You are a delicate One:
I'll bear burden, You're a creature nurtured in tenderness!
I who have a wound that bleeds will banish pain of You…
since You're the One who of love's pain couldn't care less.
I thought I would not shed tears on the dust of Your door
anymore because You have drunk my blood, more or less.
This love for You must have been created in me… because
the gold, the yellow, is never leaving the saffron… I guess!
You, who are a mote drifting around in the sunbeam, what
can you do poor wretch, is this insignificance of your mess?

Sadi will not be giving in on account of all of Your cruelty:
rose is companion of thorn... pure wine is mixed with lees.
It is better for one to be dying in the field of the battle than
for one to flee because of cowardice: this, I can only stress!

Do you know what that nightingale of dawn said to me?
What kind of man are you then that of Love ignorant be?
Even a camel's in ecstasy and delight from Arabs' songs:
if you get no pleasure you are a perverse beast, obviously.
I'll never turn my eyes from You and direct them to me...
the wise man never commits himself to one blind, to see!
O my Beloved, You're so lovely in my eyes that wherever
I look You may be said to be everything that's seen by me.
I'll never look again at the stature of the garden's cypress;
I'll never again praise the way snow-cock walks gracefully.
Strut of the partridge is nothing, nor the sway of cypress,
nor can peacock display itself in You presence, obviously.
Whenever You pass I gaze at You: who does not want to
turn to look at You because of Your form that's so lovely?
I am so fascinated by Your walk that it is no wonder You
are a hundred times more fascinated with You... than me!
Be generous just once... pay some regard to our condition;
it could be that next time passing over our dust You'll be.
Sadi won't give up love for You from cruelty or oppression;
I'm Your feet's dust, You're drinking my blood constantly!

Your drunken eyes have annulled the habit of soberness...
or one wouldn't have seen trouble in sleep or wakefulness.
How can the sky ever compare with You in treachery and
also... how can Time be rivalling You in such unkindness?
Your teacher has instructed You in sauciness and charm:
the wonder of it is that You were not taught faithfulness.
You are as precious as gold but in the possession of rivals:
You're as charming as the rose, but go with the worthless.
How saucy and sweet You are in hunting down hearts...
treacherous in murdering men, but innocent nevertheless!
You have stolen my heart and I willingly sacrifice my life,
for the solace of the dervish is lying in his load's lightness.
If by chance You should pass by the body of Love's victim,
speak a word so You'll restore life to a body that's lifeless.
If You are proposing to disturb the hearts of all the people,
loosen Your hair because in each curl a heart You possess!
Beauties of the city of Farkhar would lie prostrate head to
dust before Your face like an idol from the Kaaba, no less!
Your mouth that is all sugary could be compared to a point,
because Your face that is like moon... is like a round discus.
I've written to You a thousand letters in succession though
Your answers are bitter, Your speech sweetness dispenses.
You have surpassed all mankind today in charm by reason
of Your beauty... and Sadi, through his poetry's sweetness.

My life's so lacking in taste in absence of the Beloved
that from this hidden fire... smoke is rising to my head.

Shiraz has yet to be closing its gates to the caravan…
but we from the bondage of Love have never been freed.
The camel, that is lacking in power of being in control,
must carry a load… for it is powerless and must be led.
You've drunk blood of a thousand Wamiks because of
Your attractiveness: thousand Azras in charm excelled.
A Chinese painter would become distracted if he saw
Your physical form which is Reality from foot to head.
O You, at door of whose mansion clamour of love rises,
like an uproar in a caravan with sweet water up ahead,
You're a cypress when dancing, a moon when speaking:
dawn from afar, and in our company… a candle lighted.
At first You were not like now… at least You are real:
yesterday, You were the senses pleasure, let it be said.
City is Yours: You're the Sovereign, pass Your orders:
pardon me without good works, or send me off instead.
Face of Sadi's hope is laid upon Your threshold's dust:
after You he has not a one who is a Goal to be desired.


One day I said to that One's chin, "A silver quince you are!"
The reply, "If you really saw me you'd see me as better by far!"
If I were to call You a sun or a rose it would also be bad manners,
both the sun and moon, garden of roses and eglantine You are.
A face that is truly beautiful is not in need of any embellishment:
You, O angel-faced moon, are handsome, You're beauty's star!
It's not right people ask after me on separation's bed; does one
ask one whose wealth of joy is gone, "Why, sorrowful you are?"

You be sitting down, for in Your days we've cried lamentations:
many an uproar will rise where You sit or something similar.
If You call us, Your slaves, we will all become kings… and if
You turn Your face from us… completely in misery we all are.
No one dares to find fault with him of whom You approve…
no one can reject that one whom You select, near or from afar.
The face of Sadi's hope is laid on the dust of Your threshold:
after You he has no one, O You Goal: that is what You are!

Unveiling Your face, Beloved, You deprive mankind of self-control
and when You go behind the veil You take their patience… whole!
I call You a huri of Paradise; I talk of You as a moon that's full…
for I haven't seen a human being with charms like Yours, O soul!
You have imparted to the mirror the reflection of Your face…
or else how could it have the audacity to Your glance then extol?
If I were to carry a copy of Your eyes and eyebrows to a painter,
I'd tell him, "Portray in some way Sagittarius and Jupiter's aureole."
It'd be a real shame if such an attractive, freshly blooming, flower
scattering tree as You are, didn't over our heads its shade roll.
I shall never raise my eyes from Your face to take a look at another;
for when You are in my house the common herd outside can patrol.
I haven't the option to take my eyes off You and onto myself…
whether You look at me or not, is completely up to You to control.
Counsels of the wise do not affect me anymore, so who is there
to strike up for a while the Kalandar's* chant, to sing their barcarolle?
O Sadi, love and lasting peace of mind are obviously incompatible…
that one who does not travel as a foot-soldier, should not enrol.

Please, veil Your face, O moon of our household,
so Reason will not end in this madness manifold.
Wondrous beauty of Your image in my mind, has
put on eyes of prudence and wisdom... a blindfold.
By what good fortune, am I able to be with You?
By what courage... can I escape Your strong hold?
I am longing to be enjoying only Your company...
and be shunned... estranged from the world's fold.
Either that One's image will destroy Sadi's house,
or the Beloved will adopt him... into the household!


O silvery cypress, You are heading for Love's desert...
You are totally perfidious to leave and so to us desert!
No one has ever walked so saucily, with so much grace:
are You really like this or are You just a malicious flirt?
A fairy is usually hiding her face from all of mankind...
You, O one with a fairy's face unveiled are an extrovert!
If it is entertainment You desire then look at Yourself...
could You have a more pleasant time to Yourself divert?
Listen... are You going to cherish Your slave or kill him?
Are You going to sit with him for a while... or him desert?
My heart goes with You but I'm afraid in case You now
should depart from an uproar that is caused by an expert.
We honestly stay obedient to what are Your commands:
where else are You going to go to flirt, subvert and hurt?

There is no heart that is capable of saving soul from You,
having conquered city You are now moving to the desert!
If You'd only set Your foot down upon these eyes of mine
I'd place them on the road so dirt will not soil Your skirt!
Though our hearts have no peace... still keep on moving in
that same way, for in gracefully walking You're the expert.
The heart and eyes of Sadi are going to accompany You...
never be thinking You walk alone... for we walk in concert!

Are You a cypress of the garden, a moon or a fairy?
Are You an angel or a painter's portfolio? Tell me!
You've such a graceful walk and work such magic...
before it Samari the magician would lose all sorcery.
You'll pass a hundred times more inside that one's
mind when You only once that one happens to see.
You walk away and all our hearts follow after You:
when You return again our souls revive immediately.
If You, O Beloved... were amongst us like a candle,
many a moth would be attracted to You... instantly!
How long do You wish to keep Your face concealed?
You wear a veil, but ours You tear apart deliberately!
One day in the future be appearing to all of mankind,
so who ever may happen to see You will see... a fairy.
The sun will fall from its watchtower up in the sky...
when it sees You who possess a face that's so lovely.
Day and night heart and soul are occupied with You:
Your image on heart... on signet ring Your name be!

To such an extent You exceed all limits of sweetness
that Sadi will be consumed by his desire, You to see.


O faithless One, You have left all our hearts, suddenly.
Please, why have done this, You a promise-breaker be?
Beauty's sovereign has committed some kind of mistake
that You took Your favour's shadow, from my begging?
You've said that You'd drink with me the cup of Union:
before I'd drank a drop You raised Your sword of cruelty.
It was for Your sake that I withdrew heart from others...
when I was Yours, You Yourself renounced love for me!
Friends are far from each other by an offence or a fault…
it's wrong to take heart from me without me being faulty.
For ages Sadi has put the feet of patience under his skirt,
but I never saw You raise head from the collar of fidelity!


It's night... sweetheart, a candle and wine and sweetmeat;
it'd be a gift if on this night You Your friends should meet:
on condition I, like a slave… should be girding my loins in
Your service, while You sit like a Monarch, I at Your feet.
What to do... for patience in Your absence is unattainable?
I went away in anger, came back to You meekly to entreat.
No Master that I can obey like You is my destiny… while
You can choose a thousand better than me... from the elite.
O dervish, be content with colour and fragrance of spring...
for Gardener won't let you to pick roses and apples sweet.
Your frowning would not make any difference... were You

to say even a thousand bitter words, You'd still be sweet!
At dawn of Creation love existed between all us and You:
a thousand years pass, You're still as You were: complete!
The force of Love can place a bridle upon the head of lions
and Love's force is like nose-ring that leads a camel's feet.
It's from good fortune that Sadi is bound in Love's chains.
How lucky a pigeon that King's falcon's claws does meet.
O believers, I don't have any patience far from a fair face;
you've your own religion... and I mine, however indiscreet!

Is it a rose or is it an idol or is it a moon... or a face?
Is it night or jet or musk or that One's hair like lace?
I don't imagine that in the Garden of Paradise grows
on the banks of any stream a cypress with Your grace.
Your lips are so sweet and so eloquent that the poet's
baffled describing You... all words just fill up... space.
"Help! O Lord!" escaped from our lips from fragrance
of that One: "Breeze, where's scent from, what place?"
Hey there, beautiful winebringer with face that's rosy!
All sense from us with wine's water wash out... efface!
Perverse charmer, what a disturber of the city You are!
Rose-petal of pure beauty, ornament of feasting-place!
O my heart, since you have fallen on Love's polo-field,
you'll have to become like ball, of sense having no trace.
O my heart, if you're in love keep burning, be resigned.
O body, if you're a seeker keep asking, begin the chase!
You say, "Sacrifice your life in this Path or give me up;

either place head at my door... or seek another's place!"
Those ill-wishers are reproaching me with, "How long
will you endure such a One whose temper's a disgrace?"
But it is impossible for Sadi to ever desert the Beloved,
my enemy! Say whatever you want to say... to my face!
The Sufi cares nothing about having a good reputation...
what concern has such a one for the ordinary population.

O black spot on green down what a pretty mole you are,
but you are much too near the edge of a snare's location.
A huri is never leaving Paradise... where are You now?
Moon is not on earth, moon-face why do You shine on?
If cypress of the garden sees how gracefully You move,
no one would see it being so proud again in the garden.
The parrot wouldn't again think it is right to peck sugar
if it saw Your pistachio-like mouth during conversation.
You are perfect in beauty and are of such infinite grace;
You're fickle in love... in promises such a faithless one.
Captive in Your service is even worthier than a prince:
a slave with You is happier than he of a king's station.
I gave up earthly concerns... won safety by being apart
from the world: a beggar never fears a robber's location.
The learner is burned tomorrow with Hell's brand... for
today Love's fire has not removed his youthful emotion.
Each moment my imagination lifts its head elsewhere...
let's see what's coming to me from such an imagination.

O Sadi, when you escape from existence you are free of
mankind: once goblet is shattered, no more fear of stone.

For a long time we were in suspense in expectation of the Beloved,
but as time elapsed and we waited all of our hopes were unfulfilled.
Not a wish of mine came true in relation to the joy of Union...
while a load was laid on my head by the misery of being separated.
Each moment the grief of separation seared me with the brand,
and absence's hand broke the thorn that in my heart was lodged!
O You whose long hair is a noose and whose eyebrows are a bow!
O You whose figure is the cypress... Your face is spring-tided!
I know that You are not concerned about the anguish of Sadi...
whose eyes, in expectation of Your coming, a river have bled!
Please... help us lovers, because it will be enhancing Your joy...
and give an ear to this saying... because it is to be remembered!

Value of the rose is lost when the garden You're entering,
and when You are speaking the Water of Life is trickling.
The peacock and partridge will no longer be on display or
be showing grace of movement when You begin walking.
Tell me, O heart of mine... how often have I advised you
to keep closing your eyes or you may a captive be coming?
A moon so lovely does not exist... perhaps You are a sun?
No heart can be so hard: perhaps You're a flint... striking?
If You should approach Love's victim a hundred times...
he'd still cherish hope... in expectation of Your returning.

345

Forbidden to draw shield over face to ward off Your sword,
I would never fight You even if to me You're in opposition.
None remains who doesn't become distraught at the sight
of You, O Beloved, when out from veil You are appearing.
O breeze, you wouldn't speak again of rose and hyacinth,
if on that One's curls and cheeks roses, you were blowing.
I wish that I could monopolise Your love… for it would be
a great pity if You should hearts of strangers be entering.
O Sadi, your poetry's stolen many a heart with such form
and such thought… that with it you are expertly adorning!

If I should lose my life in this love I have for You,
such a trifling loss would be easy to suffer through.
O You whose purpose is my complete destruction,
have a little patience until I take one look at You.
It is not Your beauty that I'm finding so amazing:
that I have a small amount of wisdom is quite true.
I am so astonished at the attitude of the Almighty,
Who made such perfection in a human being: You!
It is true that it wouldn't be right to look at such a
face as Yours, and later take a look at another too!
If You went in people's houses You'd rob men and
women of their senses: of control they'd be through!
I'm longing to be the dust at Your feet… so perhaps
passing over my head… is something that You'd do!
That foolish 'guardian' may have right on his side…
that he protected You from me… his enemy, is true!

Because You are such a beautiful mirror it would be
a shame if You fell into the hands of the blind too!
Sadi sighs, making an impression upon mountains:
but makes not one impression on hard-hearted You!
I have been calling a stone hard all through my life:
that You proved to be harder than any stone is true.

No one's appeared anywhere endowed with such beauty;
no mother ever again will produce a child like You to see.
The sun will be setting if You are not veiling Your face...
it's said that there's no room for two suns in one country.
I am the very first one in whose two eyes You did appear
to be the most beautiful sight in all the world, obviously.
I was never before taking myself to Love's Winehouse...
today my desire for You... a cup for me is guaranteeing.
Either anyone in the world with face as lovely as Yours
isn't existing or there is: for any but You I'm not caring!
I never heard cypress produced such fruit as a rosy face
and almond eyes Your cypress-like figure is displaying.
Yours is such a face that if the bright sun were veiled...
it'd as much effulgence as star on dark night be shedding.
Don't be associating with me, because people would be
filled with envy if jewel in beggar's hand they're seeing.
I'd not lessen a  hair's-breadth of my love for Beloved...
even if that One with each hair's-tip this one is lancing.
Someday perhaps You will be setting out to visit Sadi:
he will put head on steps on road where You're walking!

I thought that I would practise being intrepid for awhile
and never surrender my heart to any sweetheart's guile.
Any person, whose eyes have looked upon Your beauty
will never listen to advice... not even, for a little while:
especially ours whose connection with and attachment
to You dates back to when Creation was only infantile!
I swear by Your head that I will not tear You from this
heart... a more solemn oath than this I cannot compile.
Put aside Your veil at least for a moment so that Your
lover that yearns may at least be comforted, for a while.
Mother Nature can't be so very old since that one has
produced a child such as You to all of us totally beguile.
The wound of Farhad might have been a little better if
Shirin had not sprinkled so much salt on it meanwhile.
If only I could be the dust on Your path so that perhaps
You would then cast Your dear shadow over me awhile.
What can a bond-slave do who's failing to perform any
loyal service whatsoever for his master in any domicile?
O Sadi... the time for having a good reputation is over;
now it is the time for you to be making love, for a while.


What person looks like You so I can say You're like that one?
You've surpassed in beauty whatever is possible to one's vision.
You're subtle in essence and soul and grace of figure and form,
You dress elegantly, have delicate body, of beauty are a phenomenon!
A thousand eyes like moths are in love with Your stunning beauty;

I'm all for that one's luck, candle of whose group You are companion.
What difference can my suffering make to You who feel no pain?
How can You, on stream's bank, know about this thirsty one?
I've never seen a human form with such grace and of such purity:
You're Water of Life's Fountain, clay of scent that does stun!
O breeze of Paradise's garden, what kind of a breeze are you?
O breeze of Beloved's rose-garden, what scent have you spun?
If I should draw a breath of Love from my heart that is sincere,
do not be surprised if the passion set fire to any insincere one!
Don't tell anyone that your foot stumbled against Love's stone,
he would criticise you with, "Why don't you on your head run?"
A heart can't be with two sweethearts... nor admit two loves...
if you are attached to that One then your very own self abandon!
Even while I'm alive pour Water of Life down my thirsting throat;
and please, don't be washing me with tears when my life is done!
O Sadi, what desire of yours can your own will possibly fulfil?
If it's not granted, who are you to think by you it can be won?

Why have I given my heart to You, who'll only break it?
What did I do, that You a look my way won't commit?
Heart and soul are with You while I look right and left
so rivals won't realise You're my Beloved, You're... IT!
Others pass out of the mind when passing out of sight,
but You're fixed in heart like soul that in body does fit!
You are a Phoenix and I'm a miserable, helpless beggar:
I'd be a king if You cast Your shadow over me, I admit.
Like a slave I come to do obeisance to You and service:

if You don't answer me You're being arrogant, admit it!
A true man is willing to fall at Your feet like a ball, so
that You may that one with bat, Your silver arm… hit!
Drunkard losing sense from wine is 'unjust, ignorant':
intoxication from Love and selflessness is right, is fit!
If You move gracefully in the garden with such a form,
gardener seeing You, "You're a cypress," would say it!
I can't eat fruit from the branch of my hope in You, for
I feel certain that You will destroy me… if You see fit!
A poor man's food is eaten because it's sweet and rich:
O Sadi, practise a quick tongue, sweet talk, exquisite!

Do not keep asking, "Haven't you at all remembered me?"
That I've never forgotten You is what I can say truthfully.
How lovely You are, yet so faithless that in love with You
is a whole city while You care for none… You're care free!
O flirtatious Beloved, why is it that we are at peace with
You while You are up in arms against us quite obviously?
The givers of cold comfort are handing me advice, saying:
"Give up love for that One, before you become… sickly!"
They don't know that the fever of the lovesick because of
that One won't be subsiding through that One's frigidity.
No resource is existing against any of Your guardians…
while they resemble thorns You're the rose, indubitably!
If you associate with beauties, carpet of your good name
be folding up and putting away… it again you won't see.

Rose-scented breeze, with me hold no further conversation
for like the nightingale you have driven me into insanity!
Why has not the suffering of Sadi's life been plucked out?
It's because You are his pain and also You are his remedy.


If You draw the bow against us our shield down we will throw:
let all our hearts be unhappy if that is how You wish us to go.
If You slay us we're Your slaves: You cherish us, it's Your right.
We're attached to You, why You are far from us we don't know!
You have said, "If you can't stand the pain of Love then go away!"
But how can I go, as Your noose around my neck remains so?
I close my eyes because He may suddenly send me into Hell...
I open them again and find that I as a Paradise inhabitant go!
The supreme excellence of Your sword's handle O my Beloved,
is this... if You kill me with it, I'd be envied by high and low.
The enemy has no understanding of why we would cry out...
the one wounded by Love only the resource of silence can know.
O You, fancy-free... how long can one possibly quench the fire?
My ruddy face has lost its complexion due to Your face's glow!
A man with his sense can't enjoy pleasure for he's prey to caring:
Winebringer of the gathering, let him cup of insensibility know!
O Sadi, don't blame that one intoxicated with the wine of Love
for if you too tasted some of that... into drunkenness would go!


I wouldn't turn my face from You though You torment me;
to suffer disgrace at hands of a Dear One hurts pleasantly.

I've allowed You to use whatever weapon You wish to use
to kill me, except sword of acting towards me indifferently.
You are much too dear and much too sweet to my heart for
me to be turning sour at Your words You spoke so bitterly.
It matters not whether Your purpose is a blessing or abuse;
keep uttering it from the sweet lips of Yours raining honey.
If You went hunting no beast of the chase would flee from
You because to be caught in Your trap a pleasure would be.
In expectation of a sick-visit that the Beloved might pay…
illness of love-sick patient's heart, grateful You would see!
If You should give me poison I would quaff it like honey on
condition that You don't give it to that guardian, only me!
You go away while my heart and soul are devoted to You;
but, what is the good because me You never take seriously.
If Fate would affect You with the pain of a love like mine…
You'd after count as nothing mankind grieving dreadfully!
Ask the length of the night from the eyes of the afflicted…
whatever is easy in Your eyes You think for others is easy.
My story and that of Majnun's are resembling each other:
we have both failed in our quest and died trying, fatefully.
O Sadi, keep on lamenting if you have no way to Union…
the helpless lover has no recourse… but weeping profusely!

I did not know at first that You were unkind and faithless:
better to make no promise, than make and break, I confess.
Friends criticise me asking why did I give my heart to You:
they should be asking You why You such beauty possess?

You who told me not to run after the beauties of the time...
what a difference is our opinion in this time of great stress!
It is not a mole nor a chin nor dishevelled hair that's stolen
the seeker's heart: no... it is a Divine Mystery and no less!
Remove Your veil, for the outsiders cannot see Your face...
You're too big to be in a small, slotted mirror and impress.
I dare not knock at Your door, out of fear of the guardians:
this, I'm allowed... visit Your quarter to beg, but no access!
Love's anguish and poverty and notoriety and the criticisms
are all easy to endure, but I can't bear separation's distress!
It's the day for pleasure-garden and music and riverbank...
in all this city not a heart is left for You to steal... possess!
I'd thought that when I came I'd tell You heart's sorrow...
what to say? When You came, grief left my heart! Ah, yes!
Candle must be out of this house of ours, be extinguished,
so our neighbour may not know You are here; nevertheless,
Sadi is not one who'd ever flee from that noose of Yours...
knowing slavery to You is better than liberty he'd confess!
People tell me to go away, surrender heart to another love:
can't have two loves, especially in Atabegs' reign, I stress.

    You are my precious Soul and my Friend: any order
    You like You can give me, O my existence's arbiter!
    May neither sorrow nor harm nor pain come to You,
    You're heart's comfort, soul's solace, grief's repeller.
    Do a thousand violent and harsh things against me:
    easy bearing cruelty at Your hands... old benefactor.

I don't know the more beautiful… Your head or feet:
why discriminate, from head to foot You are lovelier!
Though my heart suffers many pains at Your hand…
You're still balm of my wound, You're pain's soother.
You move and eyes of infidels and believers follow…
You're their point of worship, make them an idolater.
It's unfitting such beauty should be seen by each eye,
unless around You of God's Name, You be breather.
I don't say You're a rose on top of a swaying cypress:
no, rather, a world-illuminating sun seen on a banner!
Who can capture You, dark-eyed, musk-scented One?
Like the musk deer, of men You are scared… You are!
Though noose of Sadi may make prey of the fierce lion,
You do not fall into his snare, for You're a sacred deer!

Welcome, O you ambergris-scented eastern breeze…
tell me quickly some news of that angry One, please!
That One's a Darling: weak in love, strong in cruelty,
with a friendly face, inimical personality, all of these!
The next time that One wants my destruction let that
One kill innocent me, not think of excuses to appease!
I'm afraid that those thirsting will die unless the water
that has flowed down stream comes back like a breeze.
I have observed that Love when confronted by patience
is resembling fire and cotton, stone and jar… all these!
Let one whose purpose is to be engaged in Love, wash
both his hands of any self-interest whatsoever… please!

For as long as you remain the captive of the curve of the
bat you have to suffer fate like the ball… not displease!
Sovereigns have much treasure, cavalcade and a retinue!
Mystics have the dance and ecstatic cries: both of these!
O Sadi, your poetry keeps describing the tumult of Love
in a style that is harmonious… with much ease to please!
Such great eloquence isn't a gift that's given to everyone:
aloes doesn't give off its fragrance without a fiery breeze.


Blessed is that hour when you sit with your Beloved…
if you come near or sit far, by that One you get burned.
Eagles rip out even the talons of the iron-clad falcon…
best trick for you is with the sparrow to be associated.
If you're burned it isn't fit for a cry to escape from You,
if like moth to stay near flame is what you have desired.
If You've been happy in our company be reckless like us;
as long as You sit Your friends won't rise… intoxicated.
Drink the wine now so you renounce all worldly desires:
He will come to wake you, drunk you'll not have stayed.
The belly's lust will someday make you the ants prey…
if like the bee you every place of sweets have frequented.
You're chained by the physical by not seeing their soul…
this demon you'll forget if with a huri you are associated.
I do not think that you'll win Union with Beloved unless
you remain cut off from all that in the world is contained.
You'll only tell difference between sleep and wakefulness
when like Sadi the dark night in loneliness you've passed.

This heart You have brought close with love don't drive insane,
this heart You have trampled on with Your absence must complain.
You said You'd not with Your pen cross out Your lovesick admirers,
but You did: and never be cruel to Your lovers… You did, again!
You spoke ill of me, I am content. God forbid, You spoke well!
You called me a dog, I'm pleased. God reward, You were humane!
God Almighty, what a face is that which annihilated my existence,
as soon as its fortunate manifestation its Mother couldn't contain?
What kindness You've shown: perhaps it was a slip of the tongue;
what sweet words… perhaps a slip of the pen You've made again?
Your favour would be fitting as I've been corrected by Your cruelty;
scatter roses on my head… You've pierced feet with thorn's pain.
O my heart, consider it a rare piece of luck if some day you are
with joy, after suffering for so long under burden of Love's domain.
It could be that the dawn will break on the night of Sadi's sorrows,
for You made him wasted like a candle in the early morning rain.


Darling, the time is here for You Your heart with love to be linking,
for my desire for You the last limits of endurance is finally reaching.
It's strange that You, of agreeable nature, veil face from us slaves…
it is incredible You, so well-balanced, door on friends be shutting!
You're so happy and patient that You imagine we're just as happy
and just as patient as what You keep on continually experiencing!
Didn't You say, faithless Beloved… that You would never break
up with us? Perhaps You are now thinking we're not worth knowing?

Much comfort and mercy that one is given who can see You!
Great the favour and faith of a father who You as a child is loving!
The prey can be killed when it's caught in the trap... You uprooted
Union's tree when I firmly the roots of Love had finished planting.
Before this, alone, I used to enjoy peace of mind and tranquillity...
You suddenly entered the gathering and peace You were disturbing.
Often You said of Your own accord You'd be true to Your promise:
now I've discovered You break Your promises that You're making!
If I were to spill my life at Your feet I would still offer excuses...
for that wouldn't be a service on my part worthy of You accepting.
Assume a depressed attitude and show Your anger... this world
wouldn't seem so bitter. How can You talk so sweetly: I'm melting?
Perhaps Sadi's complaints are wind in Your eyes; for his groans
sound like thunder, while Your smile is like lightning... flashing!


Didn't You say You would and I say You'd not, keep Your promise,
and be true to Your pledge of faith, affection, love: not be remiss?
Wound of the sword of doom is preferable to separation's sting;
it'd be better for You to slay me, than You to leave me like this.
No one has such a lovely face as Yours: are You a Paradise virgin?
No one gives off such fragrance: this One a deer of Tartary is?
What does the moisture on surface of Your lovely face resemble?
It is like a drop of spring's rain on a rose's petal... for emphasis!
I have seen parrots but never heard a sweeter voice than Yours:
that must be sugar that You have, not a mouth and lips to kiss!
O sage, who declared that you would not look at lovely ones...
what use is that heart to you, a sweetheart can't fill with bliss?

357

I am longing to be in Your company for a night and for a day...
or are You passing a night and day like me in a state like this?
If I live long enough heart's desire's skirt may by me be grasped,
for rose always comes from thorns, dawn from a dark night is.
Sadi's nature is not that he should feel annoyed at Your whims...
whatever You say is sweet and only sugar from Your lips drips.

I have not found that You to Your promise faithful have been:
You opened the path to Union, I came, You left... how mean!
You pretended to be faithful to Your promise, stole my free heart:
I gave myself to You, You took Your love back, picked me clean.
You gave me the undertaking that Your love would be firm...
with these eyes I saw You break every promise, it was unforseen!
I tried in a hundred different ways to become Your companion;
but, You are too strong to fall into my trap, always have been.
It was not just the idea of Union, but then to snatch it away;
why not hold it back from the beginning... from a lover so green?
You'll not appreciate friends and sweethearts, except on a night
when like Sadi you lie... and branded by separation have been.

It is not the way of sweethearts nor consistent with affection
that You should scorn Your sincere lovers who admire perfection.
Why should not my heart not be grieved... since it is unimaginable
that You would utter a bitter answer from such a sweet location?
Come for a moment, sit, engage in a little conversation because
we're dying of thirst at the Fountain of Life that's flowing on.
I'll not tell my heart's love to anyone, as my face's colour has...

take then a look at my complexion and learn my secrets thereupon.
It would not be strange if heart-burning words escaped me…
it'd be a wonder if I didn't burn, such a fire You set me upon.
Beauties steal mystics hearts and devotees peace of mind with
their forms: You did that, spirituality You have also relied on.
I wasn't untrue to my promise by speaking of anyone but You:
the rest are on tip of tongue while You're in my soul and beyond.
It'd be a pity if You were sold for all this world contains, and
it'd be a gift if You were bought for the Now and the Later On.
It'd not be strange if I described Your perfect beauty with a hundred
tongues, but I'd still lack the words to praise You properly thereupon.
O friend, please offer me no advice for I have looked at that One…
because you're ignorant of what between us secretly goes on.
It has surpassed the story of Layla's beauty and Majnun's passion:
if you saw my writing on that One their tale you'd read as gone!
Sadi's afflicted heart overflows with blood from loving You…
You neither slay him with separation's sword nor give him Union.

I cannot say that a spiritual being is water and clay,
because no human beauty is so perfect in every way.
If You are water and clay like the rest of mankind…
You're heavenly clay made by Water of Life's spray.
I surveyed the loveliest things on earth to compare
them with You but You surpassed all, in every way.
The substance of everyone I see is composed of soul
and a body, but You're soul from head to foot I say!
If Your face in the mirror steals Your heart, You'd

become like me, helpless to help Yourself each day.
How should a heart which is chained to Your long
hair be peaceful... in view of it tumbling every way?
It is impossible for You to either cherish or torment
I who entered into a pact to serve You, or not stay.
But, do not act against the advice of wise men who,
"Do what is proper... and not what you can," say!
Does it matter if I perish as a sacrifice for Your life?
Sheep of sacrifice is destined for Id Festival one day.
Sadi's luminous soul that's the candle of Your party
would be worthless if he did not make it alight stay.

I don't know to whom in the world You bear resemblance:
world and all in it is outward forms, You're soul's expanse!
Lovers enter Your snare of their own accord... for who ever
You should captivate Your release from self, with a glance.
Don't ask me how I am... whatever pleases You, I'm that:
do not ask my name... to whatever You call me, I'll dance!
You steal the person with that first glance so completely,
that one becomes powerless to any other look You chance!
You've hidden Yourself with a veil, while through love for
Your beauty my hidden secrets are told like some romance.
I sat upon the fire when smoke of my love began to rise up,
You did not stay a moment, so fire You did only enhance!
When image of Your beautiful form comes into mind's eye,
I am lost for any words... how Your attributes to enhance?
It's no sin on my part to be looking at those who're young:

old men appreciate value of youthfulness... with a glance.
What can You, whose eyes are open in a drunken slumber,
know of hardships I suffer... awake in every circumstance?
Breeze of the east, I can't find access to street of Beloved:
travel in safety, to Beloved my greetings take and enhance.
Sadi will not turn his head in any direction from Your trap:
You captured a prisoner, slay him when You get a chance!

The time has come when the brook's green bank is pleasant:
thinking of pleasure-ground... cypress-like Beloved, evident.
If you could have intimate communion with the Beloved...
you have a garden in your house, let outside grass be spent.
O pleasant breeze from my Beloved's street where have you
been that my spirit by your fragrance has such refreshment?
Minstrel's song quickly passes, drunken dance mystically...
sweethearts are in ecstasy, their mad cries of rapture spent!
O you whose footsteps falter and road to Union is narrow,
it's wrong to turn back, keep feet going where you are sent.
If you were to see my great weeping you would not be able
to tell whether it's a flood of tears or river that by you went.
The wretched ball is told not to be distracted... but, what
fault is the poor ball's? To speak to the bat is quite evident!
O you who told me to forgo my love for the cruel Beloved...
I'll never take heart from that One's Love, better you went!
O Sadi, flirtatiousness and restraint are not compatible...
beauties are naturally flirtatious, ascetics... sad and spent!

Every day the wind carries off a rose from the garden,
wounding the heart of the poor nightingale once again.
One who is accustomed to society of contemporaries,
should endure the tyranny of Time... where and when.
Because the falcon of Death is carrying off in its talons
every one and each thing that's ever born, like a pigeon,
O friend, don't set any affections on this present world
for undisturbed security is not possible here, ever again.
Every tulip and hyacinth that blossoms from the dust
is a moon-like face, musk-scented hair... there and then.
There's not an edifice erected on the earth that has not
sooner or later undergone change, it's a matter of 'when'.
This world that's full of deceit and in appearance is foul
impudently showing beauty each morning is its regimen.
Yesterday... garden, pleasure ground, tulip-bed were full
of delight, and clamour in orchard rose from birds again;
while today, the mimosa thorns have drawn their swords
you could say that a rose never blossomed in this garden.
This world is nothing but a bridge that leads to Eternity:
a home upon a bridge is not made by the discerning men.
O Sadi, if sky should pamper you with sugar, it does not
possess any real help... in the end it kills you with poison.

No painter would ever draw such a face as this...
such great beauty in any country as this, never is.
With the grace of a cypress and figure of fir tree...
with a face like the moon... such an angel of bliss.

That One trips along and out of self-adoration...
and that One not even looking at anyone else is!
In Beloved's stirrup, hands of a hundred thousand
hearts are... a ruler passing with an army is this!
Those cheeks are a garden, mouth is a rosebud...
no... a Paradise around Kauther's fountain of bliss.
Moon-faced One, be practising kindness because
such fair-faced beauty in need of some ornament is.
In Your absence there's helplessness in each corner,
because of You in each house there's some distress.
Cast a shadow over my head like Huma so through
Your good auspices my lucky star... soon shining is!
What harm can accrue to shadow of a master if the
master happens to inquire after any servant of his?
It might be advisable on my part to be making some
complaint... if the judge other than the defendant is.
O Sadi, it's better to take bitter medicine from that
One's hand than sweets from a hand other than this.
In the world the only thing of men remaining is dust,
but remaining of bodies of lovers there only ashes is!

Everyone has a body and has limbs and youth and beauty;
none have Your grace: perhaps You are a cypress, stately.
I glance here and there, to see if anyone looks like You...
only names, You're a body; bodies... You are a soul I see!
If You lifted Your veil, You'd rip veil off all, immediately!
You will not understand why a person is dazzled by You

until there is one like Yourself, by whom You dazzled be!
You pierce soul's armour with arrow of Your eyelashes…
I'm not thin-skinned, You're a more skilful archer than me.
Whatever is said in praising You, truthfully You are that;
Your failing is You aren't kind in regard to us, constantly.
Your love's captive has reached his last gasp, how long can
You leave him wounded? Kill him outright, to set him free.
I can't bear that You are always sitting with some people,
while as far as I'm concerned You set me on fire purposely.
It'd really be strange for that man to die and never revive,
whom You drive away from You then call back eventually.
O Sadi, if to reach end of your journey you happen to fail,
you can at least end your life in quest of that One, finally.

O my lovely Beloved, when You pass before these eyes of mine
You seem more beautiful than ever if one has to draw that line.
To tell the truth I've seen much beauty and many beauties, but
not a one with such charm and grace as Yours, You're O so fine!
It was the badge of the infidel that I bore all of my life… except
when I wore the sacred thread and to serve You stood in line.
The truth is this… that the fairy will hide away out of shame
when a human being like You comes among the people, to shine.
I have yielded up my head to the sword of Your power and know
that if You kill my body You'll still be keeping this soul of mine.
There is not one being in existence who can rival Your look except
for when You see in the mirror Your face… from time to time!
O vain imposter, you'd be pitying, commiserating with my state

if you had for even a short time suffered this condition of mine.
The prey has fallen and the traveller's foot is stuck in the mire:
will it ever happen that near Your victim You could pass sometime?
Stock of patience that Sadi has, has now been totally exhausted;
don't treat him badly, his buyer emptied his purse the first time.

Everyone to the pleasure-grounds has gone for amusement
but You're our Beloved and our thoughts there never went.
That one who is concerned about his own existence and not
with You is either blind or ignorant of any Mystical intent.
The eyes of one who is driven mad by Your love have lit on
an object that's beyond even the sage's wise enlightenment.
A cypress does not seem beautiful in memory of one whose
attention towards lovely form such as Yours recently went.
The one hope has driven from my heart all the other hopes:
the one passion has every other passion in my mind spent.
Really, I do not wish You to grant me a pardon from death;
to see You move perfectly a moment's grace in me augment.
I am afraid in Fars (since its birth it's been free from wars),
a disturbance caused by Your beauty… could turn violent!
If I should ever have access to a table full of plunder… then
I'll not clutch for anything but for Your long hair in descent.
People say, "O Sadi, why not ask a favour of the Beloved?"
I ask nothing of Beloved, but Beloved in form and content!

We are all eyes awaiting Your revelation:
to Your command, all ears in expectation.

Yours isn't a form, without sight of whose
face patience can enter one's imagination.
I'll kill myself on account of You, so Your
hands with my blood won't get a smear on.
You've said that this crowd of mad lovers,
"Will see me only on Day of Destruction."
A heart-ravishing face as Yours, when You
show it causes the next Day of Destruction!
All we are is some sort-sighted sightseers...
and You... are a tree of such a high station.
Whether You drive us away or show us pity
our heads are on threshold of Your location.
If You are fair demand from me as thanks...
an offering of my life as sacrifice thereupon.
It is unfit Reason is measuring its strength
against the power of Love, as it can't go on.
What can you know, who have never passed
a day of loneliness or one night of separation?
This tale would become as clear as the day...
if you spent only one night at Sadi's location.

Keep exercising as much authority as You like, as You are agreeable
to my heart... sovereignty is being bound by hands of the beautiful.
I knew that I had to sacrifice my life in Your street in order to get
to see Your face... but, You are cruel although also indispensable.
Power and authority are Yours, so what resource has a slave
whether You burn him although innocent, or be unjustly critical.

If I don't utter a word in praise of Your face and Your hair, Your
  mirror would declare in secret… that You're the fairest of all.
It's natural those ones who have not seen rose in midst of garden
for the petals of Judas tree and the red mallows to them enthrall.
 I thought that You'd gone away and were hidden from my eye,
but You haven't left me… because nothing but You can I recall.
O morning breeze, take my message of Union with the Beloved;
  you are a pleasant breeze bringing scent of ambergris over all.
That One cannot be seen, because of that One's supine beauty:
  we obviously are not seen, because of our insignificance to all.
If the Beloved is wishing to associate with the young reprobates,
we too have given up asceticism, spiritual teacher we won't call.
 O Sadi, cease to look at that One or lay aside the patched coat
for dissipation is not permissible in the dervish's patched shawl.


There was never a cypress with form such as You possess;
  any moon the beauty of Your lovely face did never express.
If the night of heartbroken lovers was lacking any candle…
  the brilliant radiance of Yours would illuminate it, I stress.
Those virgins of Paradise who steal away hearts of men…
  would never rob us of our hearts which stay in Your caress.
It is quite clear what the strength is my grip's possessing,
  compared with Your powerful biceps… and forearms press.
Magic of my poetry has pervaded the Universe, but what
use is it compared to the luminous hand that You possess?
Do not let the likes of You be ever ashamed of our society:
  the sweets of Yours are the place for us flies to transgress.

One turns his face to the pleasure-ground, and another to
garden: I turn my face to where Yours turns, nevertheless.
O Sadi, you will never rest nor relax your efforts until you
are losing your head in this mad quest of yours… I stress!
This longing and desire that you feel will be fruitless until
the Beloved an inclination for Union, does finally express.

Never will that heart die whose life You are becoming:
he is happy in both worlds to whom You are belonging.
It's the truth that sorrow and care won't enter the circle
in midst of which You are like the central point, turning.
The autumn blast will never scatter the garden's leaves,
in which You its cypress that is so stately are becoming.
All look to see on whom lies auspicious fortune's glance,
when for only one moment… You at that one are looking.
A cruel spring of water You are, where one like Harut is
dying of thirst, while You near to his mouth are staying!
If it was possible to begin anew the sky's revolution You
would again as wonder of the cycle of its ages be coming.
Your attributes are beyond a poet's imagination… and
if anyone's described them Your tongue did the describing.
How could one not bear the burden of Your separation…
for of heart's pain You are the solace, You're the healing.
O you who cannot exist without the Beloved… it is only
right that you the heavy burden of that One be bearing!
Sadi hopes that You will be the Beloved of the soul upon
that day when tumult of the Judgement Day is occurring.

O Beloved, fill a goblet with that intoxicating wine so it
can remove from mystic's mind consciousness, every bit!
The sage is the one who is anxious to see into the future,
but upon entering Love's path… all this he wants to quit.
Mischievous One, new from the world of the beginning,
do not disappear from my eyes… for in my heart You fit!
You have robbed heart of peace, deprived me of fortitude
and You've now exhausted my patience, every single bit!
The state of my eyes that have never been closed cannot
be described to You who are sleeping soundly… I submit.
The passionate one attached to You and indifferent to the
world gave up his heart to You when You robbed him of it.
I thought to say a few words about Your face… then You
unveiled it… closed the door of my speech. So… exquisite!
If the wine is from this jar and minstrel is from this street
then surely we will break our vows of penitence… over it!
O Sadi, the purpose of the body's casket is God's wonder:
you've a hundred mysteries in you… but not found one yet!
The Painter of Creation perfected this phenomenal world
in order you might see the painting and adore Who did it!


Do You remember… You were contemplating fighting with us?
The decision rests with You… whether it is war or it is peace.
It was quite wicked being false to promise made with Your lovers:
You made it worse by doing it, then thinking it is good for us.
It was never Your custom to regard Your friends as Your enemies,
except on occasion when You looked at friend as enemy… plus!

My heart doesn't let me become estranged from You for an instant,
although I know You've utterly forgotten me… whom You nonplus!
In the same way Your tinctured fingernails still bear witness
against Your fingers, that You've dipped in lovers blood… thus!
Since You have departed no one else has come into my thoughts,
for over them You've deputed Your image as a viceroy: over us!
Do what You want with us, for we dare not fight with You…
best we lay head on that spot when Your sword's raised for us.
Fresh fruits are taken every moment from the branch of my tongue,
gardens have grown from seed that You plant in our heart thus!
Sadi's lost all interest in the Here and the Hereafter since You
painted Your image on the wall of his thoughts, so… marvellous!

I have had many but never seen one to compare with You…
such a candle as You has never come into the gathering too!
It's not generally my good fortune for You to remember me,
such ready cash rarely comes to one… and me a beggar too!
An association more refined, face more lovely, or a conduct
more blameless than Yours? Is it possible to describe You?
Tell the maid-servant of the house to shut the chamber door
so no slanderer may come and peek in… to see what we do!
On the day of Union with the Beloved… the heart does not
yearn for garden or look at rose, or beauty of narcissus too!
No one I tell my tale to proves to be of any use whatsoever,
for Love's problem is one not one geometrician can ever do!
Sadi is enduring all this anguish and is bearing the burden.
Whoever has a faithful Friend doesn't go elsewhere for You.

That is love, for the sake of which, you'd drink poison...
it's not when you worry the Beloved you'll forget again.
Brush off nobility's mark from your shoulder and if told
it with infidel's badge to replace... to be free, do it then.
Mortar is treated cruelly by its mate but is resigned to it.
What lover boils over like a cauldron from heart's pain?
O wise-arse, you who reproach me who is beside himself,
the way of sage and path of lover are always the twain!
The Beloved comes to you when you have become ready.
Minstrel will sing to you when you become silent again.
If you're not ready to take reproaches don't seek Beloved:
the bee will sting you when you're seeking honey to gain.
Foot-tied should feel the same enjoyment in Your love...
as if You put Your hand on his breast... again and again.
The true man should look on locust and the ant with the
close regard as love for Beloved's earlobe and hair's train.
As long as you're chained by evil lust Truth's door's shut:
one can only talk to you, when you from words can gain!
Careful what sort of form you have in front of the mirror,
you'll see same... Beloved is your mirror, if you see plain!
O Sadi, ask for spiritual wisdom from the Master's circle,
and it'd be well advised if you heard what they did explain.

*Bayadi'...*

Praise be to God, the Lord of both worlds, for His great bounty!
may the name of the Almighty be honoured and glorified eternally!
He is security for sustenance because of His unlimited beneficence:
whether we do good deeds or not we still receive His generosity.
How wonderful His greatness, His power, His ever-lastingness:
the Creator of mankind, generation after generation... eternally!
Genie and men and all created beings altogether are prostrating
themselves before Him in adoration... with great loving humility.
Blessed is one who is seeking Him, cursed is one forsaking Him!
Damnation be his who any substitute to Him adopts completely!
So many indications there are of His might among all us creatures
and in the heavens there are signs for that one who does wisely
know... because clear to him is all this, clear to that one whose
eyes are anointed with knowledge of God's inexhaustible mercy.
He is moving among the clouds wherever the hills are all barren
making them become fresh spring pastures of abundant greenery.
In His great mercy He has produced trees from out of seeds...
and by His power He has created from a clot, mankind to... BE!
He's our Father, before whose comprehension power of imagination
remains helpless and whose apprehension we cannot a way see!
There are no bounds to obligations created beings incur for His
bounty and will angels ever weary of singing His praises eternally?
God, Protector, is too exalted for His real nature to be understood:
you cannot compare that One... Who compared to none can be!

O Sadi, let it be sufficient and cut short your extravagant language.
Do not give expression to any claims that will end shamefully.

O you… you whom the realm of the dervish do deny…
cannot understand the mad desire that in him does lie.
Freedom's corner, contentment's treasure… are realms
a king can't acquire with sword, no matter how he try.
The wise do not go searching after a transient glory…
that one is truly wise, whom upon his action can rely.
Those enjoying illusory world have no sense of reality:
what they have here is difficult to leave when they die.
One leaves the garden feeling sore and sad at heart…
the other breaks his prison with joyful arms held high.
Dervish hasn't wealth, causing anxiety on Final Day;
he's like a water-fowl, that storm him does not terrify!
The Angel of Death carries off by force that alien soul:
no need be violent to lover who to sacrifice self does try.
Aspirations of the dervish… a frenzied, distraught lover,
are not centred in this world, no… in the next they do lie.
On Creation's First Day, the Divine Love pact was on
offer to all… the Man would not break it even if he'd die.
I saw a helpless lover consumed with passion and I said
to that one, "O my friend, to worry, don't you even try!"
That poor wretch heaved a sigh because of his suffering
and he answered me with, "Let me be, for helpless am I!
I hear that advice of yours that is so attractive but what
use is a cure to me, who longs for pain causing my sigh?"

O Sadi, life is so precious... so don't waste it in neglect:
it's only a fool who 'misses the tide': that you can't deny.


In this love of You our longing and patience are limitless:
heal our mad hearts with Union with You... nothing less!
The ordinary physician doesn't know a cure for lovers pain:
only Layla can cure the anguish of her Majnun's madness.
If You'll not sympathise with the wretched, grief-stricken,
at the first You should not show us Your face's loveliness.
Since You deprived reason of stability... heart of patience,
You should now help this impatient lover, who is helpless.
In the past my mind was free of desire for those of beauty,
as soon as I saw You... I instantly chose path to madness!
My desire of the Here and Hereafter is Union with You...
or else in Your absence this world and the next are useless.
O Beloved... I long so for the sight of You that if some day
a sigh escapes my heart, it'd burn the seven seas... no less!
Ah, come to me, so that for awhile today we may be happy
in secret communion... what comes next we can only guess.
O Sadi... you keep on saying sweet poetry in spite of foes:
how long can any patient with dropsy like such sweetness?


This silly old fool is happy in a young person's company:
it's silly for old to measure strength with youth's vitality.
How strange that I who haven't strength to break a hair,
should be arguing with one who can snap a chain, easily!

When that cypress-statured, silver-bodied takes up a bow
my desire's to be a target for that One's arrows, instantly.
If eyes of the prey should light upon that hand and bow...
it would advance until it fell into the trap by itself, happily.
None saw a human being with sweeter speech than Yours:
sugar or milk did You drink from mother's milk, originally?
The period of youth's splendid days last only a short time;
enjoy the passing hour, dear boy, delay ends disastrously!
You, who warned me to close my eyes to seeing beauties...
I can apply such advice as to all but to fate, can't you see?
Our asceticism is known, our infidelity's been concealed...
we've now thrown off our head the veil of all this disunity!
O Sadi, even if you lay head in homage at Beloved's feet...
you must still want pardon for your shortcomings, finally!

Winebringer, give that liquid ruby, ruby wine... what is it?
Give me that other wine, food for the soul, and keep it lit!
Let the old Master take the lead in quaffing cup after cup,
so the imposters may find fault with youngsters, not a bit!
You can't bear burden of Beloved's love unless intoxicated:
truly... the rutting camel is carrying the heaviest load on it!
O You, whose face is the heart's ease of mankind, that any
folk should look upon the world without it, is really not fit!
How can one describe Your physical and spiritual charms?
Your beauty tied tight the tongue of praise, it You've knit!
Beloved... even the bee's stitched on infidels yellow badge
for honey of Your lips: Your waist a slim wasp's would fit!

Because it is true that Your face deprives me of my heart...
I'm afraid in the end You will take my life, I won't save it!
Either, strike my wounded heart with arrow of destruction
so I may resign my life... or, let 'security's arrow', me... hit!
And when You are to shoot me with Your arrows, give me
notice so I can first kiss Your hand and bow: this, I submit!
Sadi has suffered so much grief due to separation from You
that he cannot even in happiness of Union, be forgetting it.
If an arrow should inflict a wound and it should be healed...
the scar cannot be effaced from the place of injury, not a bit!

Who has in archery to that delicate armed Beloved given such skill,
that an arrow from that One's loving glances is enough a deer to kill.
The prey of a thousand hearts will be returning to face Your arrow
if shot from this kind of eyebrow's bow Your eye's quiver does fill.
It is true that You have no need of body armour or a horse any more,
as on the day of battle You can put on armour of Your hair at will.
The realm of India and the empire of the Turks will be surrendered
to You when they see Your lovely eyes and Your black curls that kill.
It is certain the Magian priests who attend upon the idols in Fakhar
cannot with their eyes of that lovely Sweetheart have had their fill.
Don't subject fortifications of rebel's stronghold to bombardment,
just throw over roof of citadel the noose of Your curls... if You will.
You have captured this one... who all of his life has continued to
observe seclusion of the Anka, as the falcon the quail does, still.
I looked upon Your lips and blood-stained tears fell from my eyes...
You then began to talk and value of pearls collapsed to become... nil.

The lustre of Your face has depreciated the market of sun and moon,
just like power of Moses did overcome those sorcerers magical skill.
One can't gain a treasure through exerting toil that is quite useless:
Fortune belongs to right positioning, a strong arm won't pockets fill!
O Sadi, it is only that one who can put up with a fickle disposition
that to loving One fair of face surrenders his heart and also his will!

If that moon of mine should such a face be unveiling,
the sun because of such beauty would itself be hiding.
One could say Your fascinating, recluse-alluring eyes
by spell of their magic have deprived mine of sleeping.
The first glance took reins of wisdom from my control:
can one who lost reason, right course now be following?
I thought through Union I may win release from Love:
can patient with dropsy, get relief from water drinking?
Claim to Love is worthless, unless you from Beloved's
hands pure poison readily as pure sugar are consuming.
Love's an attribute of Humanity: if you don't have this
mystical sense you're a mere beast, eating and sleeping.
Bring fire and burn up the granary of the spiritually free
so King on what's destroyed taxes won't be demanding.
I'm always afraid I'll be consumed by the fire of my love:
how long can a kebab, this heart, be on the fire, roasting?
Some folk are drunk on wine but lack having a beloved...
I'm so drunk with that One, wine I've no need drinking.
Sadi... didn't I warned you not to walk into Love's trap?
Beloved's arrowed glance even Afrasyab* is overthrowing!

This longing and this patience of ours beyond all limits has passed:
if You've self-restraint, our strength to endure is totally exhausted!
Look even only once with the eyes of kindness upon our condition…
because from the table of the king relief for the beggar is secured.
A king, of course, has the power to become angry with his courtiers,
but… a limit to the cruelty he can hand out must be finally observed.
I do not care for life without You, because there remains no pleasure
in prolonging our existence… during the absence of the Beloved.
If I should happen to die because of thirst then what is the good if
with a million tears the grass on my grave happens to be watered?
The state of this miserable condition of mine is baffling description:
when You finally do come back, of my condition You'll be informed.
Please come back and take this precious life of mine as a gift…
for what other provision for a quest by a poor beggar can be offered?
O Almighty God, be granting this lover some respite and security,
until eventually, once again, his eyes see the face of the Beloved.
Ah brother, in the eyes of beautiful ones neither the power of a king
nor the asceticism of any devotee has any value, please be informed!

O if only that the veil could be falling from off the face of Layla…
so no one may be left to oppose the claims of Majnun, the afflicted!
Sadi, it's a well-known fact, predestined are misery and happiness…
and so… whatever lot may fall to you, submit to what is destined.

I've never seen a face that had such beauty and loveliness...
I've never seen such curls having charm and attractiveness.
If that hard-hearted, delicate-bodied One were to hide face,
musk would tell the tale, for its fragrance it cannot repress.
O You who're equally attractive physically and spiritually,
such a beautiful face and nature... my eyes did never caress.
If I become dazed from my helplessness do not blame me...
for it's You who wields the bat, ball is not at fault, I stress!
That one sometimes experiencing rapture and intoxication,
delights in the cries of partying drunkards, their joyfulness!
We look for criticism with all our hearts in Love's market...
seclusion's corner is for the pious ascetics loving loneliness!
Garden needs nothing to enhance its beauty: no, I'm wrong:
it's lacking a cypress such as You on stream's bank, no less!
O sweet-scented rose, if spring goes on for a hundred years,
you'd not see a sweet-tongued nightingale like me I confess!
O Sadi, you cannot place a kiss upon the hand of that One;
your alternative is to on that One's foot rub face... I guess!


What good is a whole book of wisdom be to a reckless lover?
Mind of a man crazy with love being preached to can't bear!
O preacher, even if your words can mingle water with fire...
it is true that your words will never patience to Love adhere!
The only use for the eye is to catch a glimpse of the Beloved:
if it does not look at that One what's the use of vision, ever?
Lovers are indifferent to the rebukes of friends and enemies...
endure torture of Beloved's love or disgrace's rebuke in the ear.

All are knowing that I'm loving Your cheek's fine green down
and not like the other animals... the plains high, green verdure!
On the day that I was trapped by that Sweetheart of Yagma,
I instantly surrendered my heart and my faith... up to plunder!
I grant the cypress possesses symmetry and a stately stature:
  tell it to look at the movements of my graceful One… closer!
If You should drive Your lover away he wouldn't go... or, if he
did he'd return, for fly can't do without confectioner's counter.
No one can excel You in beauty, and not a rival me in poetry,
because this style of mine and Your beauty are by far superior.
Sadi, drummer whose duty was tonight hasn't beaten dawn's
drum, or maybe following night of loneliness, it beats no more.


If You happened to throw off Your veil in middle of the city,
 You'd consign to torment a thousand who believed sincerely.
 Who has the power to look on Your face that is so dazzling
  in beauty… from behind veil You could ravish hearts easily.
 Not for a moment does our heart remain completely empty:
  do not permit its destruction now You've conquered the city.
 You have tied the feet of my heart with Your plaited hair…
O Beloved... turn plaits of Your hair, but never face from me.
 My love's story falls flat on Your ears for You don't realise,
  dew drenched rose, condition of Your lover, thirsting greatly.
 If lamp's blown out what does breeze care... and if fine lawn
  disintegrates, to a moonbeam does it matter, even slightly?
 If that Beloved was to accept me as a slave, here is my ear…
  and ring of bondage to that One 'til Judgement Day we see.

380

And even if my dust was to be scattered all over the world...
the wind blowing it from Beloved's street is an impossibility.
If my doom should overtake me upon the night of separation,
on Resurrection Day I'd pitch tent beside Beloved, hopefully.
Each ghazal of mine is a letter containing the tale of my love;
what's the use of writing letters that the Beloved doesn't see?
Sadi, don't indulge in boasting, your poetry is indeed magical,
but magic won't buy you one glance from Beloved... obviously.

Every city is a home for one who has as home no place,
wherever night overtakes the dervish will find his space.
Do not call that homeless one who has nothing except
God, a beggar... for his baggage is an empire of Grace!
The Man of God is not an alien in the east or the west,
for however far he travels the Lord's domain is his place.
That one who is a stranger to wealth and greatness and
power that he is a friend to all who he meets is the case.
The short-sighted seek ease... dervish wants affliction,
because he knows that real comfort lies at pain's base!
When the lover finds an opportunity to see the Beloved,
every one he sees afterwards is wearing a dragon's face.
Give up all you possess and pass on, for this transitory
life which is terminated by death, of worth has no trace.
That the Kingdom of delight and of eternal bliss will be
blood-pay of who falls victim to Love's sword is the case.
That given to you from Beloved's hand is sweet, O Sadi:
don't seek self-pleasure... Beloved says that's a disgrace.

May Your soul God be always blessing:
Your lips and teeth need no sweetening!
Let he who has lost his Joseph-like heart,
for it in pit of that One's chin be looking!
There's no sedition that is in Fars except
what from Your seductive eyes is coming!
Even if the cypress were able to saunter...
it'd never Your graceful ease be attaining.
Your night is like the day to other people:
because in your bedroom the sun's shining.
O You garden of spirituality, for how long
against gardener must we be complaining?
We are Your nightingale... so please allow
us to for a while in Your garden... be crying.
If You practise a thousand acts of cruelty,
I'd a thousand times more... You be loving.
We have tested the strong arm of Patience:
it's a glass vessel upon Your anvil, waiting.
Whether You remain faithful or You don't,
our promise to You we will still be fulfilling.
From me accept good tidings of Union's joy,
if by pain of separation from You I'm dying.
O Sadi, you'll become a dervish who is alive
if your life in this quest to its end is coming!

The station of the dervishes is fixed on that One's polo-ground,
in the curve of that One's bat my heart like a ball can be found.

There's no road that lovers can travel outside of Beloved's street,
the long curls of that One's dishevelled hair their feet have bound.
How long will those who are ignorant tell me to exercise patience?
O wise ones, patience is no cure, for no cure has ever been found!
Whether that One is bestowing a glance on me or decides not to…
that One can command me for as an obedient slave I am renowned.
If that One slays me through no fault of mine it'd be my usual
bad luck… and if I am favoured, it's that One's kindness, unbound!
I've no inclination to go into the garden nor any love for the cypress:
if cypress I find attractive, that One's form leaves me spellbound!
How can that one still sit who has lost his heart to that One?
How can that one escape who to that One is completely bound?
Those spiritually blind criticise the ardent lover for his bewilderment;
one not bewildered by that One, as not being in love can be found.
No one has seen a rose like You in garden of this present time…
especially as song of one, Your nightingale, in garden does resound.
If skilful archers were to shoot every bird with all of their arrows…
alas for the nightingale that is uttering all these songs, so profound!
O Sadi, if you are seeking Beloved, tread the Path, endure pain…
for the Beloved's face is your Kaaba and patience is desert, unbound.


O You, whose mouth contains the water of life… the arrow
aimed at my certain destruction has been fixed in Your bow.
You will be responsible for the death of everyone in the city,
unless You draw a veil over all Your beauty that You show.
I will never be comparing Your face with that of the sun's…
that would be praising the sun, Your stature wouldn't grow!

If You would grant us one look with that corner of Your eye,
it'd be a favour; but if not, then it's Your prerogative I know.
Most people think of their friends and companions each day,
while our head still at Your threshold we so happily bestow!
We have witnessed many trees that are laden with fruit, but
we've seen none better than those that in Your garden grow.
If hands of the lover can't reach fruit, is it the garden's fault?
The gardener is to blame... for protection is all he does know!
Many the thoughts that have been passing across my mind...
but the picture never leaving my heart, is Your form on show!
If You, O Beloved, should be hurtful to me a thousand times,
my heart would never cease its loving You: this, I truly know!
O Sadi, cherish a wish for Union in proportion to your worth:
our Simurgh isn't a fit mate, that in a crow's nest should go!

O Beloved, if it's Your will that we should be without any will,
then without Your consent our desire's not permissible to fulfil.
Whether You are receiving us or are driving us from Your side,
it is contrary to our religion to ever be one opposing Your will.
If Your feeling of kindness towards us has undergone a change,
the love for You that we're feeling remains near to perfect, still.
You will never hurt my feelings no matter what You do to me…
what Beloved approves of regarding this lover is good, not ill!
Even though there was hatred and strife among the Arab tribes,
love and friendship between Layla and Majnun remained, still.
A thousand hatreds arise because of the words of the slanderers,
between lover and Beloved friendship remaining… always will.

I am devoted to the figure of that Sweetheart wearing a blouse,
for love of whose face a thousand garments are being torn, still.
I cannot be patient even for a little while without the Beloved,
because I can never give up the will to be alive… or, the thrill!
Beloved's beauty stays in my vision and my desire is the same:
if the beggar were given the whole world he'd be a beggar still.
Faults and virtues make no difference in eyes of generous friends
when the objective is to really please and not have any ill-will.

I thought I would not be criticised because of my love for You…
if people criticise me then in that respect it is 'run of the mill'.
You said it was wrong to be looking on the face of such beauty…
it's not wrong and I consider this idea of yours a 'load of swill'!
Sadi is happy in spite of the anguish of separation from Beloved,
for although pain wrings in his heart of a cure he's hopeful still.
Misery and distress are weighing upon the dervish's heart today,
but he is happy for he is hopeful tomorrow bringing mercy will.

O You whose figure is more agile than the moving cypress,
heart seeing Your face feels more joy Your face can express.
I am no longer afraid of the cruel arrow of one's own death…
it is not any more terrible than Your glance, You murderess!
The garment of spiritual Reality has always fitted me well…
but that it sits more gracefully on Your lovely figure I stress!
If my enemies are complaining of the purity of my looking…
the skirt of the Beloved is even more pure… I must confess!
Since the rose of Your face bloomed in the garden of beauty,

my patience's veil is more torn than the rose's petalled dress.
If You desire to strut along proudly, set feet on Sadi's eyes,
they're a hundred times lower than Your door's dust, or less!

That One is kind to everyone but spiteful to me;
what can I do, my fate like this… happens to be!
O my soul, you shouldn't measure your strength
once again with that One's arm that's all silvery!
That one who is prudent does not place down his
foot until the ground in front he can properly see!
Those wise ones in love's bondage resemble boys
playing with a prettily-coloured snake... foolishly!
That one afflicted with pain of separation, sleeps
only on that night when a grave his pillow will be.
Don't let people lament over my destruction… for
this isn't the first time that it has happened to me.
All of this cruelty I must continue to be enduring...
my love's a thousand times as great as any cruelty!
Even though a man may capture a lion in his noose,
if caught in Beloved's snare he's helpless, obviously.
If You were to give me a thousand bitter answers…
that they were all so sweet, my belief still would be.
O Sadi, submit to your annihilation, for that this is
only resource against Beloved's arm is its certainty.
My heart is gone and my eyes are filled with blood;
only my life is left to sacrifice, if Beloved wants me.

O courier with auspicious feet holding the Beloved's letter,
nothing but that One's heart-alluring message to me utter.
How pleasant to hear Beloved's state from Beloved's lips...
or from one who from Beloved's lips was that news receiver.
O my close friend, where's the high standard of the caravan
so we'll sacrifice our heads at the feet of the message-bearer.
What regret and what sorrow that we have been so helpless,
because to seize the Beloved's reins is far beyond my power!
I'm so afflicted by love of the Beloved that whoever sees me
pities my condition due to Beloved's heart's cruel behaviour.
Whether the Beloved slays lover or is cherishing that one...
submission is slave's duty... authority is in Beloved's order!
If that sleeve of the Beloved should not fall into my grasp...
head upon Beloved's threshold while still living is this lover.
None except Love's martyr leaves the world with no regrets:
that martyr finds the arrow from bow of Beloved is the killer!
Since Your departure nothing's passed through Sadi's mind:
is there another in the world, who can replace Beloved there?
Where did this minstrel come from who said name of Beloved?
For sake of Beloved's message, my body and soul I've offered.
My heart is revived by the hope of the Beloved's faithfulness:
hearing Beloved's words my soul dances from what is uttered.
Who succumbed to intoxication of love from the Beloved's cup
won't return to his senses until Trumpet's last note is blasted.
After this, if I should be travelling abroad I will not bring back
any souvenir except for a greeting from that One, the Beloved!
The lovesick one will only recover through Beloved's fragrance:

if he has to die he'll not... unless Beloved's name is last uttered.
Once, I used to be the ruler of all of my domain... but now I am
in bondage to Beloved... as far as will and purpose are allowed.
If the Beloved should care for another and is indifferent to me...
I do not have another in mind to ever take the place of Beloved!
If it is impermissible for me to set foot on the Beloved's terrace,
only alternative is on the ground below it to lay down my head.
Who's daring to mention a beggar in the presence of a monarch?
Big difference between my poverty and such pomp let it be said.
And, if it is the Beloved's will to slay Sadi, unjustly... to perish
in fulfilling wish of the Beloved, is life enough for him, instead!

The world was thrown into such an uproar by Your beauty...
to take Your eyes off You for an instant was an impossibility.
What anguish You've made in the hearts of your kind lovers
by those unkind glances that You've given so mischievously.
I became so completely divorced from reason and wellbeing,
upon that day when those people talked about You... to me.
Nothing remained of garden and orchard when the cypress-
tree of Your form grew, throwing them into chaos and worry.
Be friendly towards and take care not to cast us out of Your
sight because on Your account the foe defames us constantly.
I swear by Your eyes that it would be a great pity if eyes that
were withdrawn from You are directed at the moon suddenly.
Some day this story will reach Your friends, that Sadi went
in quest of Beloved and lay down his life for Beloved, finally!

Winebringer, many hearts You stole with mischievous eyes of Yours,
if I could snatch a few kisses on chin, or what above it lies, of Yours!
Tell, how long will arrows of Your loving glances be darted in secret?
Reason has surrendered because of murderous eyes… fires of Yours.
You're with us then leave us: show Yourself, then snatch You away.
Your anger's covered with kindness: poison in sugared lies, of Yours.
If Shirin saw Your sweet lips speak she'd have been under obligation
to offer You Parviz's* kingdom for those lips one desires… of Yours!
World might've rest for awhile from all of the turmoil and the tumult
if not for that city-disturbing face and the mischievous eyes of Yours.
How could any person have attraction anymore towards being sober,
if he saw in breast of early-rising drunkard, hand there lies, of Yours?
O Sadi, keep quaffing cups of pure wine for out of tune with party's
happy drunkard's is asceticism's and abstinence's disguises of Yours.

*Note: Shirin was of course married to King Khusrau Parviz.

There's no beauty in flirtatiousness to  heart-ravishing Sweetheart,
to compare that One's curls to Frankish necklace one cannot start.
Although you may not see that One's mouth except when speaking,
if you look closely you will find it's not as constricted as my heart.
You are slaying an army of lovers with all Your murderous glances:
keep on slaying… no opponent to stand up to You can even start!
I've firmly seized in my grasp the skirt of Union with that One;
but what's the use... Fortune's not gained by a strong grip's art!
And if that One doesn't favour me it would indeed be quite strange,
as there is no slave of Sa'd Abu Bakr* like Sadi, who is no upstart!

389

*Note: Sadi's patron. Shiraz's ruler 1226-60. See Introduction.

Whose face is that... which the caravan is preceding?
Perhaps it's a torch the camel-driver's hand is holding.
You could say that it is Solomon, seated in his litter,
whose throne on the eastern breeze is slowly moving.
Beauty of that One's face that's like the moon seated
on high... the moon that is in Paradise, is resembling.
A heavenly face in a litter like the sun in a zodiac sign:
O sages, see this marvel: a sun in a canopy is shining!
Like a lotus in the water and the sun behind a cloud...
that One's angel-like face, silken veil keeps concealing.
That One who is hidden behind the veil, has suddenly
the veil from off the face of my love affair been lifting!
The camel has in speed by far out-stripped me because
than it, a heavier load, I am now having to be carrying.
How treacherous and faithless are You, O cruel One:
if this is how You regard us, our loyalty... is remaining.
O camel-driver, please stop your caravan for a while...
for this is the last moment of the time for the Uniting!
We have been faithful to our promise but You haven't.
Sadi... be off! For this is Your reward for that, coming.
Did you not know that the last stage of old age is not
the time of one's strength with youth to be measuring?

Your eyes, like swords, have flashed murderous glances...
so they all at once deprive mankind of reason and senses.

390

Your love has completely sapped Reason's foundations...
Your cruelty completely closed Hope's door to any access.
The lover from the anguish You cause is loudly lamenting,
true believer from loving You in idolater's girdle will dress.
An uproar's in the monastery from Your face's description,
the Sufi has taken himself to the winehouse... under stress.
I am told by all I consult about that Sweetheart's cruelty...
that I should be weaning my heart from this affair, no less!
I can free my mind from all of this worry about my life, but
I can't stop myself from looking at the Beloved's loveliness.
Sadi has been often grieving, deeply, in secret... but, on this
occasion he's thrown off the veil from his secrets, I confess!

That one is a king who with his Shirin is associating,
that one who has a black-eyed huri in bed... awaiting!
Faithfulness is that, allowing freedom from worries...
if one's pillow is lonely... then it cannot be happening.
Everyone is telling stories about the idols of China...
in each twist of our Idol's hair there's an idol waiting.
If that One with silver ear-rings unveiled that face...
all say face is the moon, ears the Pleiades sparkling!
Even if I did not love that One, all of the world does!
See that Wis, with all of those Ramins congregating!
From kindness please turn a hair's breath and glance,
in Your hair's tips hundreds of lover's hearts are lying!
My eyes are only opening to be looking at Your face...
one might say by my love of You the world I'm hating.

Who calls You 'moon of Khutan' or a 'moving cypress',
only the outer form of Your face and figure keeps seeing.
Call me Your slave and it would make me a monarch...
the fly make ascend, a royal falcon it is then becoming.
Sadi's fame for gallantry has penetrated to everywhere,
he is not sinful... in our religion it is good to be praising.


Sun is canopied under the shade of that One's night-black hair:
Paradise's Tuba tree serves that swaying cypress form, so rare!
Can that be a figure? No, it truly is the Resurrection Day coming:
it is like the Final Day's confusion, when that One moves near!
In this affair the idea of death is a pleasing thing to my mind...
for that One's ruby lips are promising the Water of Life to share.
Is that the fragrance of spring in the air or is it the morning breeze?
Is it the north wind passing, or a message from that One I hear?
In the past my heart kept on boasting that it was a wise bird:
now... look, it has fallen prey to that One's snare-like, long hair!
I have always been helpless... caught in that snare of that One:
now see, I'm reduced to poverty, that One wants me to be there!
My heart in my chest is tormented each moment by its anxiety
to know, whose slave is that One... and whose, is Sadi? Declare!


Last night before my eyes kept passing the vision of Your face,
that my suffering body was senseless due to love was the case.
The Huma of my physical form, far away from its happy nest...
rolled in the dust like a bird with its throat cut, lacking in grace.
My feeble heart heaved many a blood-reeking sigh because it

was immersed in a torrent of blood… from my liver's dark base!
Such groans I was uttering because of all of my love's suffering
that the planet Venus mourned in sympathy… with my case.
The carpet of the dust was well watered from all of my tears,
the ears of the sky were deafened by my cries filling that space.
Guess what kind of Love's arrow must have pierced my heart,
so my life is a shield against darts of separation from Your face?
Be patient, O Sadi, and submit to this pain, for at the beginning
that in my mind that this day was soon coming… was the case!

Ah no, that Fate our long-standing friendship has been disturbing;
and the claims of this, our intimate relationship, has been abolishing.
Two friends never enjoyed comfort from their lives for a moment,
for their period of close friendship Fate quite suddenly was ending.
Since hearts must necessarily be broken and ties of love severed,
happy is that one who wasn't attached to anyone from the beginning!
Our hearts cannot be withdrawing from the love of such company…
who their hearts, from their attachment to us, they are disengaging.
The means of enjoyment were at the disposal of loving friends,
but Fate to our sincere requests was unfavourable to such pleading.
Sadi gave up indulging in the society of people from the day that
he realised about the unfaithfulness of the sky's quick revolving.
If Fortune should hug you to her bosom like a harp place no reliance
on her, for she is punishing you when seen to be kind and loving!

The agony of Love is a pain for which there is no physician:
if one tormented by Love cries out, it's no strange situation.

The wise know that those who're madly in love care nought
for advice of a counsellor... or the sage's wise proclamation.
One who has not drunk the wine of Love, nor pain's dregs...
he has no part nor lot nor any place, in this worldly location.
There is no sweeter smell than the fragrance of the Beloved,
even compared to a musk, aloes... and ambergris concoction.
It'd be strange if the prey were to escape that One's noose...
it wouldn't be surprising if that one in snare finds extinction.
If the Friend knew what I suffer I'd not mind enemy's cruelty,
neither would I be concerned about the guardian's oppression.
Even the eyes of my enemy are shedding tears over my story:
a proverb, 'Kindness from a stranger, treachery in a relation!'
The rose fell on its back with so much laughter, that it didn't
notice that the nightingale was in such a state of perturbation.
How's it possible for Sadi to be complaining against Beloved?
He must put up with Beloved, in the other way is stagnation.

Who has seen a heart that keeps on courting danger,
or wastes like a candle and like a moth is a wanderer.
A thousand kinds of sorrow come from each side and
in pursuit of other kinds of suffering it's a fast runner.
Its head is always drunk with tumult of Love's wine,
of trouble and mischief... it like a drunkard is a seeker.
From ill-fortune it was unprincipled, lawless, helpless:
due to Love... dejected, insane, non-eater, non-drinker!
Like one love-sick it's only working at love's business,
and like a fool it turns from wisdom's path, altogether.

Thousand times I offered it advice before this, saying:
"Don't pursue vain fancies so," but... it was no better!
Do not give it advice in any form whatever because it's
only worse from any word from any kind of admonisher!


One can do without everything... without Beloved: an impossibility!
According to advice, don't stop loving Beloved, even momentarily.
If you are accepted as a slave and as being inferior... be grateful,
for even that would be a great boon from Beloved, don't you see?
If you were offered everything in the world in exchange for Beloved,
don't agree: everything is valueless compared to Beloved, obviously.
The world and all it contains with even the added bliss of Paradise:
riches enough to entice dervish from Beloved, would never be!
It's not a case of offering thanks or from Beloved accepting you,
for if you died you'd still be under obligation to Beloved, eternally.
It'd be wrong for me, who raised eyes to look at that One's face,
to wink at the arrows that Beloved continually shoots at me!
And if it is so that that it becomes possible to flee from Love,
where to go? For I could not dispense with the Beloved, obviously.
One can ransom the prisoner of the infidel in one way or another,
but to redeem a captive from that Beloved is truly an impossibility!
Who in the whole of Creation has the ability to enter my thoughts
when I've not begun to stop thinking of Beloved, even momentarily?
It's true that You've no peer, but suppose for example, You have...
I'll not take an exchange or substitute for Beloved, to any degree.
O Sadi, seek to please Beloved and exercise much more patience...
for love consists in not only of Beloved's treatment, crying bitterly!

This separation of ours all limits has exceeded,
O Beloved!
Come back to me for I'm Your slave... devoted,
O Beloved!
What does it matter if I sacrifice myself to being rebuked…
for 'back-biting of the enemy is kindness' is said,
O Beloved.
If You walk with such graceful gait You'll destroy the world:
look here if You thirst for Your sick lover's blood,
O Beloved.
My condition is so from the brand of love that if I should die,
divine law's blood-right from You'll be extracted,
O Beloved!
Be faithful to Your pact... give up all cruelty in consideration
of the fact that I am no unfaithful lover! Agreed,
O Beloved?
If You were to return to me a thousand years after my death,
from my grave a welcome cry would be directed...
O Beloved.
Your love has triumphed and these eyes shed tears of blood...
don't, if You do, to God my hands will be raised,
O Beloved!
If You've come to drink my blood, here I am, waiting! Get up,
if You have come to take this life! Come forward,
O Beloved.

O my Darling, sympathise with me, afflicted and powerless!
Have pity upon me, I'm poor, helpless, distracted,
O Beloved!
If You will not listen to the tale of Sadi, what then can he do?
Because, to enemies this cannot ever be uttered…
O Beloved.


My heart from the power of Your Love has taken itself to the desert:
although Your heart may be far from me, Your Love I'll never desert.
Why has Your musky mole changed its colour on account of me?
Perhaps Your face is clouded because of the smoke from my heart?
Last night when the torch of Your Love set fire to the whole world,
it cast a shadow on my heart and every single atom of it did hurt!
Every lamp that was lit upon the earth from the hearth of red wine
was extinguished by the cold morning sighs that I at dawn exert!
O hard-hearted One, the cry of help from me… Your afflicted lover,
has no effect on You, though it would make blood from a stone spurt!
Our distracted heart is our whole world of thought and that world
is so tormented by its desire for You it's in chaos… smashed apart!
The grief You cause has robbed me of patience and has robbed well…
such sorrow takes my life and it did it so completely… from the start!
The heart of Sadi is always shrinking from such troubles as these…
I don't know why he was bold enough to hold Your hair, this upstart!


Companion of that cypress-like figure of Yours, is  happy;
for on that one is bestowed the Divine favour and bounty!

Whoever in all his life has won even a moment with You...
he has it in vain if after that he wants something else to be.
His judgement is faulty, he who's ascertained Your views,
and then draws a single breath, on his own... purposefully!
He is no lover whose eyes are hourly towards another one...
no true seeker has thoughts moving elsewhere... ceaselessly.
Leave me to my memories of You... give me a lonely corner:
but no one is ever alone who in communion with You will be.
One can't voluntarily exercise patience when You're absent:
but, necessity might enforce patience... if it has to be for me.
The sight of Your face each morning's like New Year's Day:
night of separation whenever, is a winter's night continually!
O God, grant release to all Your captives, except for that one
who is a prisoner held tight in the noose of Beloved's beauty!
Take a look at that sage who has manifested love's madness!
That sage, who has lost control of his heart, a madman is he!
But... one can be excusing the feet that to Sadi are belonging;
for they are not the first, that sinking into such quicksand be!


We've bowed our heads in submission to request and pleasure from
You:
from Your world-adorning judgement, what is our measure... from
You?
Wherever You have got down and then You've pitched Your tent
there,
no one else could ever take Your place (this I can You assure)... from
You.

Any more than thirst of a patient with dropsy can by drinking spring water…

one cannot get satiated by seeing Love's unlimited treasure… from You.

I have been fostering Your Love in my mind for such a very long time…

I'd rather part with my life than give up Love, in any measure, from You.

I do not possess in any way the worth of the dust on which You step…

for that dust has been given right to kiss Your foot: a pleasure, from You.

My friends criticise, saying that I could not have been in my right mind

to let my experienced feet sink into 'such a morass'; they infer, from You!

But, of what use are the eyes in the head of a person or the soul in the body,

if they don't see coming that face's look, soul's great comforter, from You.

There is no one else on whom we could fix this love for You we are feeling!

One could look in a mirror… then it's only reflection in mirror from You!

It is a day today when the people are going to the grounds for pleasure…

get up, so cypress is ashamed by being given form's measure… from You.

Last night, I saw in a vision that the Beloved was saying this to me…

"O Sadi, don't lend ears to words of enemies… keep them far from you!

You will only then become a true lover of this face of mine at that time

when indifference to this life and one coming after, is a sampler from you.

A real seeker of the Beloved is that one who does not turn from obstacles…

it's not right that resolution should by fear of sword, disappear from you!"

The coils of Beloved's hair are the noose of calamity's snare:
who isn't trapped by this noose of this business doesn't care.
If I should, without pity, be slain in the presence of that One,
one glance my way would be the blood-right for many a lover!
If our lives be sacrificed in quest of Union with the Beloved it
doesn't matter: worth more than our lives is Beloved… by far!
Divine Law does not require any evidence of the lover's claim:
pale face is proof and bitter lamentations testify… he's a lover!
Abstinent man's stand-by is strength of his wisdom, patience:
but wisdom's caught in love's trap, patience in passion's snare!
The foot-bound, helpless and heartsick lover… whose soul is in
the snare doesn't ask why it has happened or even gives a care.

The Lord of the kingdom of existence is the supreme arbitrator:
nothing He does is from tyranny, if you complain you're unfair!
Draw the sword from its sheath and pour poison into the cup…
for we're agreeable and we're content with whatever's in there!
And whether You cherish me with some kindness or You leave
me angrily, Your orders can't be wrong, Your rewards just are!
  He who forgets promise on account of guardian's oppression,
or because of Beloved's cruelty… is really a faithless imposter!
Only good can come from Beloved's nature… so let that One
abuse me in every way: sweet lips give a blessing to the eater!

It is a happy fate for the beggars of the Beloved's street,
to sit on road in the hope that One's face one may greet.
I thought I'd sit in a secluded corner, but my heart can't
rest as my thoughts are drawn to the Beloved, to meet!
Patience in absence of face of the Beloved isn't possible:
how to put up with Beloved's whims? A way… discreet!
That one's affairs are disordered like the Beloved's hair,
who's surrendered his heart to loving that face so sweet!
The season of spring is drawing my heart to the garden,
so that I may sit by a rose with Beloved's scent, replete!
Tomorrow when the dead are raised at the Resurrection,
look for my dust, O breeze, only in the Beloved's street.
Sadi extinguishes the lamp on the night of separation…
in case his eyes on something other than Beloved's meet.

O heart, be patient, patience is the ornament of dervishness:
the cure of love is forbearance and duty of love is faithfulness.
That One is Judge and we must respect that One... the Lord.
If that One kills, that One rules: if cherishes, it is lawfulness.
Though that One summons us, hand of impatience still prays:
if we're driven away, our face of hope looks back, nevertheless!
The bright lightening has flashed and the spring breeze blown,
Majnun's strength's gone... "Where is Layla's tent, confess!"
In opinion of philosophers it's a mistake to neglect love's days.
Dawn breaks, wake up! End of world is annihilation... no less!
The society of the precious Beloved is sole objective of this life:
both worlds are the cost for glimpse of that face I must confess.
If the suffering of the heart of Your lovers is what's pleases You
it is agreeable to us... our desire is to fulfil Your wish, I confess!
What claim can a slave make? It is for the Master to command.
If You plant a foot, see... my right eye waits for You to impress!
Do not drive me from Your door for that isn't the way of fidelity.
In every city are strangers and in every country beggars, no less!
In spite of my faults I still hope, apart from my fears I still hope:
if my coin is base, Your grace is elixir for gold, and not baseless.
Ah Sadi, if you are a lover, why do you love the idea of Union?
He who tries to please Beloved, his own wants doesn't express!

Love is fixed in my heart... while that One has forsaken me!
O friends, please help me for I am one finished, completely!
It'd indeed be strange if I should realise my heart's desire...
how can I accomplish this, for Fortune has abandoned me?

I possessed good fortune and wisdom...power and wealth.
Ah no… through this love all four have become lost to me!
Love and passion and desire… all remain fixed in my mind,
and patience, tranquillity, peace of mind left me completely.
I am only half alive, for that One drains my heart's blood…
but this heart of mine has been out of control… ceaselessly!
If I should perish, it doesn't matter, for a hundred thousand
better than me have succumbed to the Beloved, completely!
What is the use of giving rein to the steed of passion, since
the reins of its control have left the hands of me... obviously?
O Sadi, love was so easy in the presence of the Beloved, and
it is remaining quite secure now that the Beloved has left me.

Being with friends is pleasant, more so… on stream's bank staying:
wine's pleasure is enhanced by hearing nightingale's sweet singing.
Sleep of the morning is a delight by the side of a bed of jasmine…
no, it's more pleasant in embrace of One who of jasmine is smelling!
Pleasure of sleep, induced by luscious wine drunk in the morning, is
enhanced by enjoyment when on bed of wild anemones one's laying.
Don't turn attention from Beloved's beauty to the pleasure ground…
because it is much more pleasant a faithful companion to be facing.
I'd not give a fig for sound of harp and the sweet singing minstrel!
To us, conversation of companion with sweet nature's more alluring.
If the greenery around the rose-garden is quite lovely, then the down
on cheeks of rosy faced sweetheart is by far much more fascinating!
Water that by blowing of wind is clothed in chain armour is a sight,
more so to fall victim to Beloved's hair… Beloved's face is covering!

The fountain of Kauther and garden of Paradise are pleasant enough;
but, to us it is far more pleasant to in street of Beloved be staying!
O Sadi, how to appreciate One without knowing that One's cruelty?
Heart's desire, from strenuous effort its pleasure is often enhancing.


I thought that I might in a dream some vision see
of the Beloved:
in the morning my eyes alighted on the beauty…
of the Beloved.
People look for the Id's new moon… we believe the Id is seen in
eyebrows like crescent moon, rising flirtatiously,
of the Beloved!
We will never again pay any regard to the tall cypress, because
of our love for the cypress-like figure, so comely,
of the Beloved!
I am unconscious of myself for the reason that a sincere lover is
unconscious of self, by being absorbed, in Unity
of the Beloved.
O sleep, do not be paying any more visits to these eyes of Sadi:
in his eyes is only room left for sleep, or imagery
of the Beloved.


If anyone has ever heard of a cypress that walked, or fir-tree
with a silver ear-lobe and breast, it is that One… obviously.
Is it not that One's apparent height that you are perceiving?
That One's real stature is beyond short-sighted folk, to see!
Let it not be that sleep comes near to my eyes in Your time!

Love's nothing to do with head on a pillow... unconsciously.
All others are asleep and night's beyond the midnight hour...
but the eyes of the poor lover are wide open... that lover is me!
I grant you it is practising idolatry to look at beautiful faces;
but, I'll never give it up because this is my religion, Idolatry!
It's the season where people head off for the pleasure ground,
especially now it's spring time, month of March... obviously!
The garden is like Paradise today, but You're not entering it,
so that people would exclaim, "There... is a black-eyed huri!"
Whatever we've said in describing the Beloved's perfection is
just as if we'd said nothing... for it, a hundred times more, be!
Talons of the falcon are not used with such violence against a
pigeon... as that delicate grip You have been exerting on Sadi!
I do not care to write any more poetry because the flies would
begin to bother me... because of the sweetness of this poetry!

If my life as a sacrifice for Yours You should be demanding,
the answer to Your test would be easy... just be commanding!
I swear by Your soul that I would not part with a single hair
of Yours, in exchange for everything the world is containing!
In spite of the fact that You don't have any love for anyone,
there is not a single person who love for You isn't professing.
And, notwithstanding this intention of Yours to be like this,
O cruel One, many a life upon Your threshold is now laying.
Many are the upheavals that are arising on the earth because
of Your face that of course the moon in Heaven is resembling!
It's impossible for me to overtake You by my strenuous effort;

for as far as swiftness goes even the wind You are surpassing!
Even for a single moment I'm never ceasing to remember You,
so that at another moment… You I'd have to be remembering.
It's a pity the short-sighted compare You to garden's cypress.
What eyebrows, O huri-born! You need any bow to be killing?
You could easily be saying this… that this emaciated body of
Sadi could be a model that from Your waist this one is taking!
And if it happens that You should have an occasion to speak,
one couldn't imagine that You, Beloved, a mouth was having!
It can't be possible that there could ever be anything sweeter
than this poetry… unless it is Your mouth… sugar-scattering!

Your teacher has instructed You in every kind of charm and flattery:
Your teacher's taught You cruelty, flirtatiousness, banter, treachery!
I am totally devoted to Your smiling lips and Your fascinating eyes,
that taught beguiling deceptions of magic to Zuhhak and Samari!*
Surely the violet-scented breeze that is blowing in the garden must
have acquired its fragrance from that curling hair of Yours, so musky!
Where on earth could that teacher of Yours have learned this charm,
unless that one went elsewhere, of all magic's art made a discovery!
Straightness of Your mouth must have been acquired from my heart,
and the slenderness of my body must be from Your waist so tiny!
O my Idol, why should You be having the need of having a teacher?
China's idol-makers go in Your hair's curls, learn craft… perfectly!
Thousands of melodious poets, love-distraught nightingales, must
have learned from You the art of speaking our Persian in its purity.
Calamity of Love so sapped foundations of purity and moderation

that even the Sufi has adopted the Kalandar's loose code of morality!
I've never seen a human being with such form and such a disposition,
or figure and temperament… perhaps they were acquired from a huri?
Popularity of the market of the sun and also the moon has departed,
because all customers have learned the way to Your shop suddenly.
All who were in my family were adept in the path of religion… but,
I was one who was with Your Lover as my teacher taught in poetry.
Not a single person who has been able to gain access to Your street
will ever make a decision to travel again, or… remember his country!
That One drenched hands in blood of people saying it was henna.
I don't know who taught that One how to do murder… so cleverly!
If you should have occasion to be crossing the stream of Sadi's tears,
you're under obligation first to take lessons in swimming, obviously!

*Note: Zuhhak was a cruel tyrant who conquered Jamshid and became king of Persia… he was also a black magician, as was Samiri of Israel who made the famous golden calf. See 'Shahnama'.*

Surely the morning breeze brings scent of Beloved's hair…
because it delivers my afflicted heart from all pain and care.
My fortune's eyes won't taste sleep throughout all of my life,
if in my dream I see that One trapped in my arms, my snare?
The truth that is my precious life is not worthy of that One:
but, it is all I have the power and ability left to give, to spare!
This is not even a matter of me having any choice in it at all:
the Beloved's will takes precedence over my wish, anywhere.
If heart suffers a thousand pangs through Beloved's cruelty…
I'm still my Beloved's slave for Beloved dispels my every care.

407

There is no room for strangers in our private place... so be off!
As they're saying, 'Who's not my friend is a burden I declare!'
O cruel One, Sadi's heart has been badly hurt, seeking You...
Your heart is not even touched by hope in Your lover's prayer!
And if it's Your wish that I should have no more wishes left...
it doesn't matter to me for only for Your will, do I really care.
My heart's not attracted by the tulip-bed and the rose-garden
for memories of Beloved are rose-garden and tulip-bed I share!

What do I care if there is a pleasure ground outside of the city?
To be near Beloved, wherever, is the place of pleasure for me!
I'm surprised that any person who has seen Your face should
ever again in all that one's life care for any amusement to see!
If you're too concerned with yourself to remember the Beloved
don't hope for Union nor of that One think even momentarily.
As the armies of Love have conquered the realm of your heart,
be on your guard, they will plunder it each morning, eventually!
I take much pleasure in the breeze because of that fragrance of
Your long hair even though I'm often reproached for such folly.
How can You, each twist of whose curls is a noose for the wise,
have time to spare to give to the company of the mad? Tell me!
Where ever I happen to go to escape the tyranny of Your love...
I experience the same distress and the same torment repeatedly.
A thousand cypresses cannot ever attain Your stature in point
of inner significance, though outwardly the cypress rates highly.
Who said to You... 'Give me sweets by hand of the guardian'?
Give me with Your own hand, even poison then tastes sweetly.

I am not the only person whom Love in this world has assailed,
every human you see… to Beloved's Love is pledged eventually.
How can you justly be criticising Sadi… seeing that you are on
the shore while in the centre of the whirlpool of Love is he, Sadi!


In the world You are the limit of what I'm desiring,
O Beloved.
Thousand precious lives to Your soul be sacrificing,
O Beloved.
The bird of my heart's remaining so attached to Your snare that
it is no longer remembering even its time of nesting,
O Beloved.
And if You are not even opening the door to me where can I go?
Let me, there upon Your threshold finally be dying,
O Beloved!
Tell me to bring You my broken heart and a life devoted to You
and I'll reply, "Yes, both of them please be taking,
O Beloved!"
Don't be cruel… the great aren't so inconsiderate and arrogant
on account of a slave's fault, really a small thing…
O Beloved.
If in Your kindness You would drink my blood, it'd be proper…
but, out of Your sight me do not ever be sending…
O Beloved.
You should utter speech befitting the ruby lips that You have:
bitter answer from Your mouth is always pleasing,
O Beloved.

I must work to fulfil Your will and to see my life as nothing...
if Your wish is to slay me, by it... me free be setting,
O Beloved.
Who said that Sadi would shun this misery... caused by Love?
I swear by Love, a wrong impression he was giving,
O Beloved.
Even though I am reduced to the last extremity by my enemies,
I will still not of my love for You, ever be repenting,
O Beloved.


One who pays court to another person every morning,
will be entertaining some fresh ambition every evening.
Do not rely on the faithfulness of that one's friendship,
for such a person many such as you as friends is having.
That one is cherishing affection and friendship for you,
for as long as you... position and means are possessing.
That one says, 'If I have an intimate companion and a
congenial friend today in all the world, you I'm having'.
But, he will talk to another in the same way and say...
'Without you, this world is a cage my heart is holding'.
Like a bee that one runs about from one door to another,
and wherever there is sugar like a fly to it he is sticking.
That one is full of false professions and without sense.
Truth is, he could be compared to a hollow bell ringing
To that one he criticises, this one... 'He's a stupid ass':
to him he finds fault with him, 'A mean wretch' saying.

When ver you happen to see such a person, do not pay attention to him, for he's a creature not worth knowing.

If a thousand troubles assail me... they would be easy to bear;
my love and devotion are a thousand times greater... this hear!
Journey isn't long to feet of one seeking the Beloved: thorns of
Love's wilderness are like roses and sweet basil, without fear!
If You should ill-treat me it would not be cruelty but kindness.
If You were to brand me it would not be a wound... but a cure.

I am far away from Your side... it is no wonder then that I am
ill at ease, because I'm seared by the brand of separation, here!
The wonder is why are those twisted, ambergris-scented curls
of Yours so disordered, since upon Your breast they lie, there!
People of right judgement are amazed at my lack of wisdom...
handing my heart into Your hands is life threatening they fear.
Not to mention my honour, if You wanted to shed my blood...
I would not say no... I'd do what You wanted, then and there.
That class of human beings not understanding what spiritual
love is... who between a human and a beast do not make clear,
imagine that, in the garden of beauty, Sadi's eyes are directed
to the apple of the chin or pomegranates that chest does bear!
In this matter best I should remain silent, for in the opinion of
those who are truly wise, ignorance being fool's excuse is clear!
Anyway, I don't exonerate myself nor do I declare myself pure;
for whatever can be related to human beings is possible, I hear.

Whatever is said about the beauty of Your face is true,
and what's said about Your eyes lovely sauciness is too!
I have observed closely many a cypress in the garden...
but possessing a figure as alluring as Yours? None do!
You, whom no nightingale can rival in melodious voice,
it can't be said in sweet speech, any parrot equals, You!
You are as indifferent to poor me, as the smiling rose is
to the frantic sound of the passionate nightingale... too!
You said if I should exercise patience I'd win happiness:
patience is help to anyone who can really see it through!
Have you heard of one bearing patience patiently in the
Beloved's absence? No real love in a patient heart grew!
That one worrying himself about ignominy or disgrace...
he never knew, and won't know all his life... Love! True!
One who's accompanied by memories of You isn't alone;
to say I am able to endure loneliness is… sort of untrue.
The eyes of all mankind are directed towards Your face,
but, it cannot be said that everyone has a seeing eye, too.
You've stated that all are hypocritical, deceitful, frauds!
Sadi is not one; but, since You've said it, it must be true!

My Friend is that One whom the Grace of God has befriended;
who has authority over justice and tyranny and power extended.
It's true that the ocean of Love doesn't have a shore, and if it did
it's the breast of such a One according to the spiritually inclined.
In the days of Layla, long ago, all these mad lovers did not exist,
nor was all this trouble arising that in these times has appeared.

There is no longer a mystical lover, who in this season of spring, is not in love with that Rose and who isn't by its thorn wounded. Do you have any knowledge about the dust of which I'm jealous? Listen well, it's the dust lying on that One's path that's blessed! Do not believe it was that One's physical form that took reason away from me... it was that One's Creator that me has deprived. If others turn their gaze upon that One's beautiful face then our attention is to the omnipotence of that One's Protector directed. Even this concession remains quite sufficient for me: that I may die on that One's threshold, so to as a devotee I may be referred. Love is not any concern at all of that One... who so much cruelty and disappointment... poverty and countless deaths has endured. O Sadi always try hard to be seeking the pleasure of that Friend, not your happiness... the slave fulfils what the Master requested.

O cruel Beloved with the silvery chin, please... how long will You keep Yourself away; until when will we be kept mad by You, too? How long must we look longingly at the rose from afar, with our feet pierced with thorns; return from Life's Fountain, thirsting anew? Until when shall our ears become quite mad, by Your sweet voice? How long will our eyes be bewildered by Your charming walk, too? I am always afraid I will let out a cry of distress. How long must patience keep being shown, while my anguish is not shown to You? Every day You are indulging in flirtatiousness: so how long do we have to be sent into distraction through all of this cruelty You do? That colour on Your hands is not from henna, but from our heart's blood: how long will You drink heart's blood by trickery? Ah, You!

One day Sadi will be succumbing to Your power. How long will
he have strength to bear burden of Your cruelty, and separation too?

They, have most certainly been created in pure mercy...
for they are our heart's comfort, light of our eyes to see.
Benevolence is a Divine sign that marks such as them:
while pride fits like a garment on their forms... perfectly.
Their ruby lips exhale milk's smell… it is not only milk
but sugar these sweet-lipped ones have tasted recently.
I think they are the musk-scented deer of Tartary; but...
they have grazed beneath shade of Paradise's Tuba tree.
The Porter of Paradise must surely have opened a room,
so these black-eyed huris might in this world roam free!
Water of life is in their lips... they must have imbibed it
from conduits of Paradise's Kausar fountain... recently!
Beggar's head seldom reaches apples of such company's
chins… as they are like first fruit just matured perfectly!
The roses are picked from rose-bushes day by day… but,
from these rose-trees no rose has yet been picked, surely.
The Hindus, who worship stone idols, may be excused...
those poor creatures haven't seen this Image, all silvery!
See this divine grace, that has been kneaded into clay of
human beings: see this soul breathed into mortal's body!
How well have these mole-spots been arranged and how
charmingly those lines of green down been drawn... see!

You'd say that over the perfect symmetry of their figures
their eyebrows were crescents curved atop a cypress tree!
Cypress and pine are guilty of impertinence in comparing
self with such tall figures like fir-tress swaying gracefully.
Their eyes and hair and ear-lobes keep on working magic!
That such Believers should have followed... secret sorcery!
One's desire is attained at their hands by offering heart's
blood, as that's what they've been fed since being a baby!
What do such heart-alluring beauties whose trains sweep
the ground... care, if crazed lovers tear collars frantically?
Garden of Divine Art contain no fairer trees than these...
birds of lovers hearts flew from their bodies, passionately!
Many are those having fallen victim to alluring beauties,
and heart-entrancing flirtatious ones, so few an escapee!
I've never heard of a group of people to whom my story of
Love was revealed ever listening again to advice seriously!
Beware of looking at that speck of a mole! Do not move...
as the snare of those curls are spread over it, very cleverly!
As such beauties rob us of reason in secular and religious
concerns... that ascetics look for solitude futile has to be!
Seldom has a hand gripped skirt of desire to gain Union,
that it and its owner did not finally only regret it terribly!
Do not wonder at Sadi sitting in the dust of their path...
men would sit in blood, to say nothing of dust, willingly!

It would be impossible for constellations of stars passing
before our sight at night... before the sun to be appearing.

415

As in comparison to You, all beautiful ones are worthless
though them as pretty and lovely others may be regarding.
People deliberately run from a murderer to save their lives;
but, drunken lovers their death at Your hands are courting.
　Never be criticising that wild band of drunken lovers… if
they saw Your beauty into the heavens they'd be shouting.
If one day You came out of a monastery moving gracefully,
the Sufis from every door and terrace would come flocking!
Send dervish's patch-coat and the prayer-mat of reputation
to Winehouse, so Your disciples desire to dance… whirling!
Banish from the hypocritical Sufi's mind Duality's concept,
for it is right to believe in Unity who this Path are entering!
We pay no regard to Hell and we do not yearn for Heaven…
wherever You pitch Your tent… true lovers are congregating.
The sighs of Sadi have wrung with anguish ascetics' hearts.
Day's happy when from cell to Love's desert they're coming!


If You broke off with Your lovers they would still greet You;
cruelty is a custom that one who is a slave has to go through.
Even though a thousand wounds in succession should be felt,
it would be wrong for them to look for any revenge upon You.
If You mercilessly strike them with sword, then turn away…
they'd pay You honour… if one look back at them You threw!
　Don't throw noose around me, I am Your captive of my own
free will; a nose-twitch is only for horses You need to subdue.
Throw stones at me as if I'm a tame fowl… I'll return to You.
That I am not a wild bird a snare should be used upon, is true.

Pay some regard to us a little… out of the corner of Your eye;
it is true that royalty look at common folk… out of the blue!
Who said that it's not permissible to look at a beautiful face?
It is wrong that this be held as unlawful for any lovers to do!
Ask me to pronounce a judgement about the religion of Love:
it's, people should gaze forever on the face belonging to You!
Whenever Your ruby lips are smiling… that the breath of the
eastern breeze shuts tightly the mouth of the rosebud, is true.
It would not be surprising, if strangers from the east and the
west settled down in our city… to become friendly with You!
I'll not turn my face from You, for it's the duty of followers of
Love to seek their desire… and not listen to any criticism too!
O Sadi, don't be begrudging your life for your friends because
it's never real friendship to be doing by half, whatever you do!


It'd be easy for Beloved's lovers a thousand deserts to be crossing,
if they'd the hope some night in Beloved's harem they may be resting.
It's the custom of Love to suffer cruelty and to sacrifice lovers lives…
no resource is left, if they can't a powerful antagonist be resisting.
If the Beloved with the star-like brow should appear on the terrace,
that One would be pointed out as if being Id's New Moon arising.
It is the truth that the door of escape has not yet been closed… but,
where can foot-bound captives, from that One's presence be going?
There is no substance in my body that is more precious than blood…
I offer it to the Beloved; if Beloved, hands with it cares to be soiling.
Perhaps in Your household no attachment is formed with friends…
perhaps in Your city to all Your lovers no pity You are ever showing!

May this life of mine become sacrifice to You! If You should happen
to be requiring it, whatever he is told to do the devoted slave is doing.
A thousand swaying cypresses could not in any way compare with
Your high stature even if their heads arose and sky were touching.
A thousand Laylas and also a thousand Majnuns could never better
the story of Your beauty or the story of my love... I have been telling!
Sadi resembles aloes in that until someone happens to burn it people
will not for one moment the sweetness of its perfume find refreshing.

Darling, all beautiful ones count as nothing when You're present:
that any prince at door of Your Love are dust at Your feet, is evident.
The whole city is consumed in desire's flame through love for You...
a population is drowned in Love's sea in their quest for Your advent!
You shed blood of spiritually advanced: who ever believed that lawful?
They are prey belonging to precincts that the holy frequent!
The idol and cross are worshipped by all of those infidel countries,
but under Islam, Your long hair and face the cross and idol represent!
Please on occasion pass by the ranks of Your heart-sick lovers so
they may sing Your praises, breathe blessings on You for this event.
Every twist of Your unruly curls is a prison for heart of Your lover...
never say captives of Your noose are called 'a few' to any extent.
Those symmetrically arranged lines of down on Your face are, as it
were, characters inscribed with black musk that around a rose went!
In the garden the cypress is waiting and the fir-tree remains silent,
so if You show Your lovely form they will bow down and relent.
One cannot be complaining against such Monarchs of beauty one
sees above the people... they themselves are the judges in any event.

Your slaves can't avoid what You award. They're helpless, whether
You slay or cherish, they're Your servants whatever You implement.
Cruelty of the foe will slay seeker of the Friend; that treasure and
snakes, roses and thorns, joy and sorrow are together... is evident.
I won't divulge to You heart's agony, for You're so joyous of spirit
that to understand Your afflicted lovers suffer pain, is irrelevant!
How can You, lightly burdened and strong, know the weak victims
of Your love, are laden with oppression's burden to such an extent?
O Sadi, the one who is a true lover is never shunning any trouble;
only those disregarding Love's pledge, shrink from Beloved's dissent.

Your two dreamy eyes, on awaking from sleep in the morning,
thousand commotions from each corner are instantly exciting!
Why should not every rational being become attached to You,
when all wild animals aren't from Your bow and noose fleeing?
Just as it is not permissible to be looking at faces of beauties...
it is unlawful for anyone to be abstaining from on You gazing!
I am completely devoted to that One, before whom, on account
of that One's beauty and grace... every head should be bowing!
You don't appreciate Your own worth: ask Your afflicted lovers
about tears in ardent desire for Your beauty they keep shedding.
The stability of our mind has been shaken and the power of our
patience exhausted, for Your form and face are O so charming!
Do not give me advice, for Love and austerity are two states of
the mind that the one with the other can never be harmonising!
O Sadi, choose submission to the decrees that come from Fate;
it's inconsistent with good sense, a powerful Foe to be resisting!

Whoever drank wine with You… caused a commotion;
that one who saw Your face fell deep into Love's ocean!
If You were to pour poison down my throat, it would be
proper to swallow it like it was some sugary concoction.
May blessings of Almighty God rest on the father who
has reared a darling child such as You, that's my notion!
There does not exist a carpet that is fitting to serve You,
face should be laid on the ground, for Your feet's motion.
I was wanting to say… I was the dust lying at Your feet;
but all at once it was Wisdom that counselled me… upon
saying to me this advice… "Do not be dust in the path of
the Beloved, because that One could be upset thereupon!"
My enemies are feverish in their hostility to me… but the
fire I experience doesn't grow cold… but, goes on and on!
If a lover should happen to be flinching from those arrows
of misfortune, then to call such a one a man… is mistaken!
Tell that to one who does not intend to be without a wish
to get away and never again the street of Love walk upon.
O Sadi, if we are not given that pure wine of Union, let's
be drinking draught of pain to the dregs… that are rotten!

Ah… woe is me, if not fulfilled is my heart's desire,
if it's not restored to me from Your bondage, entire!
Distribute this anguish of separation more equally,
so soul alone doesn't bear the brunt of its quagmire!
O cypress-like Beloved, if You pass by the orchard,

cypress would not equal Your shape I most admire!
Let go my imprisoned heart from jail before its sighs
from pain of Your absence rise to the skies or higher!
It's impossible for one like me to be noticed by You:
such may occur at the Resurrection or not transpire!
I pass by Your door so Your glance may fall upon me.
Mote won't reach Pleiades unless by Sun set on fire!
Hand of a dervish like me can at least beg at table of
Your lips, if tray of plunder it cannot reach by desire.
If my blood-raining eyes weep in torrents such as this
I'd be surprised if flood reaching sea doesn't transpire.
I'll endure separation from You if Union isn't possible
for if hand can't reach date-fruit... its spike I'll admire!
Ah Sadi, Union's pinnacle is indeed high... your hand
can't reach it unless you trample on your self... entire!

Whatever you receive from the Beloved's hands is like sugar,
but conserve of roses from another's hand is an axe... to fear.
If the enemy were to scatter a sleeve's full of roses in my face
it's worse than a fast arrow or slung stone I see coming near!
If eyes of the ardent lover, were anointed with dust from feet
Beloved, it'd act like collyrium to his sight... not some smear!
Love prescribes that when the sword is drawn by the Beloved
your precious life should be shield as ransom, standing, near!
God, do not allow my destruction except by Beloved's hands,
so I meet my death in the presence of that One, is that clear?
Whether you give up your life or fall helpless victim at feet of

the Beloved... whatever you do, it would be inadequate I fear.
We bow heads to Your will, its up to You to crown or remove
our heads with Your sword... O moon-face, wield Your spear!
To the ardent lover, that day his life is sacrificed to Beloved's
love is a day of faith and victory, triumph and... being sincere!
We said goodbye to life from the very beginning of this affair...
it's only that one who is fearful who keeps holding his life dear.
That one who is shunning misfortune and is afraid of death is
a reasonable being... the habits of mad lovers is another affair!
Mysteries of Divine Love cannot be revealed to semi-initiates:
the uninitiated knows nothing... of the torments initiated bear.
O my Darling, have some regard for the broken heart of Sadi...
for You know the sighs of those consumed by Love are sincere!

That isn't Love that from the heart on tongue is expressed,
that one isn't a lover who is reduced to despair by Beloved.
Let that one who is giving vent to lamentations on account
of any criticism, look for safety in place where he's secluded.
I have never heard that the boat of anyone who has fallen in
this deadly whirlpool... the shore of safety has ever reached!
Nor is any news heard... nor is any trace discovered, of the
traveller who distraught, in this desert of Love... wandered.
Don't close again the eyes of longing that you once opened
on Beloved's face... even if by spears and arrows confronted.
He's a lover who lost in ecstasy through rapture of dervish's
song, advances dancing... sword of calamity above his head!
God forbid that I should turn away from an arrow if I knew

that it was shot... by that hand and that bow of the Beloved!
People see the victim of Love but they can't identify his killer
for the arrow of the Beloved is shot... without being observed.
My heart is so deeply attached to You, that I feel a loathing
for all of the people in the whole of this great big wide world.
Love's obligation is... against one's Beloved not to complain;
but, by eagerness to tell the tale, upon tongue it is mentioned.
O Sadi, all these lamentations of yours have to be an outcome
of your anguish, for 'No smoke can rise without fire being fed'.

From this foolish love let us see what will happen to me:
what at hands of You who shed heart's blood to my body.
The lover can't overtake dust of that One's horse's hoofs,
so that One's hand he can't kiss: mouth, can he possibly?
Whatever I have to suffer remains all my own fault... so
let us now see just what will befall me at the hands of me!
Come here, for if my hand should reach the collar of my life
I'd not only rip it from passion, life's coat also, completely!
Who's seen orange flower petals with Your cheek's colour,
that puts to shame the rose... but the jasmine more easily?
The guardian's useless: for, into what happens between us
when alone... angel, let alone demon, intruding cannot be!
However beautiful and attractive plants may be they can't
be attaining that delicate-bodied One's graceful symmetry.
Since Khusrau failed to achieve his desire from Shirin's lips
how successful can a mountain-cutter, like Farhad, ever be?

Many are the claimants that ask for alms of Your ruby lips:
among all these suppliants, what can I possibly get for me?
Sadi's lamentations have reached everyone in the Universe:
if aloes isn't burnt how refreshed by its scent can we all be?

Even if a stature like Yours was owned by the cypress,
the charming figure that You had it would not possess.
And if the bright sun was to take a seat in a gathering,
I believe it would not rival You... You'd be the success!
And if the whole cycle of creation were to begin anew...
that a child could be born looking like You is ludicrous!
Who in all the ranks of all of the armies of all the world
has a bow compared to Your eyebrow in such loveliness?
And, if all countries of the Islamic world were plundered,
all of Shiraz would fall to You as booty... none-the-less!
It's not right we should enjoy Union with You to please
us: we'll do without it until it pleases You more, not less!
We banish the Here and Hereafter from our sore hearts...
in the hope they will become home for Your restlessness!
Just one "Today" is in my power for the enjoyment of life.
Can I have patience to wait your "Tomorrow"? Express!
The madness that is in my distracted brain is pleasant...
and especially if out of passion for You is such madness!
If it happens to be the case, that Sadi must lose his head,
it is appropriate for it to be at Your feet, this... I confess!

I'll not take my heart from You as long as heart and soul I'm having:
I'll take Your cruelty as long as capacity and power I'm possessing.
If You cherished me what greater happiness than this could I obtain?
If You slay me without pity, what greater faith could I be enjoying?
Since Your love restrains me from all worldly desires, why should
I about the criticisms of anyone else in the whole world be caring?
If You struck me with Your anger's sword, it'd be my soul's support:
if You gave a cup of poison it would be for my spirit food for drinking.
When I lift my head from the dust of the tomb at the Resurrection,
the fragrance of Your love upon the skirt of my soul they'll be finding.
If You've no love for me, at least send to me a vision of Yourself…
so it for a night confidant of my hidden secrets may be becoming.
Every one cherishes the impossible desire to be fed from Your lips…
but it is true that I've not the good fortune to be a tongue possessing.
I would willingly sacrifice my life if You would call me Your Sadi…
that, is my desire: ah… if only I'd the good fortune to it be achieving!

You cannot talk, without from Your lips scattering sugar;
and not walk without Tuba tree shedding fruit from anger.
Nothing in nature from loving You won't risk life for You;
no bird that is flying after You does not shed every feather.
My heart through its love for You can't stop its lamenting:
my eyes cannot stop shedding for one moment regret's tear!
Because of my love for You I can't save my life, so let me be
slain by You for no one else is better suited to be my slayer!
Sadi's words are pearls picked from spiritual Reality's sea.
What to do with skirt full of pearls, but on Beloved scatter?

That One passed and again burnt granary of peace of mind;
sea of fire dashed waves of blood in my eyes, I'm left behind.
I've for a long time kept concealed Love's pain in my heart…
despair's frenzy has made my tongue to tell it more inclined.
My spirit caused much commotion in the Garden of Angels,
when my sighs a stone at Heaven's azure vault did unwind!
Truly that One's love devastated the environs of my heart…
then with a night attack, my soul's kingdom away did grind.
That heart-alluring face shed Judas-tree flowers at my feet…
that soul-refreshing speech is like music to my ears and mind.
That One likes to bind mad lovers in those chains, and even
if a sane one is there, he some insanity in himself would find!
O God, how did Love's hand pitch tent of passion for You in
a heart where there is no room for thought of the selfish kind?
Sadi, if you're man enough to tread Love's path get rid of self:
only the one who has become selfless that path's end can find.


For God's sake walk that sway so breeze can tear root of pine-tree!
Throw off Your veil, Paradise tearing off jewels from huris will be!
Draw that silken veil from Your heart-entrancing face and mole,
so the sky in presence of Your face it's mole-like stars will set free!
Many like me are confused like Your wild hair from seeing Your
face but only he can be in Your street who giving his head will be!
O my rosy-faced Darling, Love's thorn has entered my soul's foot…
one cares for life so much that he'd extract spike from foot? Unlikely!
Rose no longer possesses either scent or colour because of that face!

Let finger of jealousy gouge out eyes of the narcissus immediately!
Is Your form the moon or an angel… Your lips sugar-candy or salt?
Show face… so sky gives up affection for constellation of Gemini!
If You walk towards desert in flirtatious and heart-ravishing manner,
snow-cock would go mad and peacock pluck out feathers instantly!
Because it's true that Sadi has become  slave of You, O Beloved…
don't let Your fragrance leave him, until Resurrection dawns finally!

Do not criticise the sage who to Love as a victim has fallen:
where is there any hope for Wisdom when Love's the villain?
It's certainly doom of that one who falls in love with the Sun:
a mote in a sunbeam he will stay captive to Love of that One.
Patience is Love's  cure, whether able to or not: to put up with
sweetheart's caprices is like enduring a king's courtly fashion!
One devoted to pretty-faced beauties never fears slanderers…
if you can face that, come; their taunts behind your back go on.
If Karun some night should alight in a household of beauties…
they'd prey on him so that next morning he'd have not a coin!
O breeze of the spring, send us a breath from faith's garden…
its ambergris-scented fragrance is like perfume of… that One!
You're playing… how can You be expected to take pity on me?
Pity should be shown by a sweetheart to lover left to carry on?
Please answer, You can criticise me, as bitterly as You like…
abuse from Your ruby lips would be sugarcane, to chew upon!
I do not know of any other door to which I can turn from You.
Don't deprive my soul of asylum, my pain may go on and on!

The useless criticiser will never understand the pain of Sadi,
until in some street he falls victim to a fair face, then is gone!
If at the corner of each street was seated an idol just like You,
I don't think a soul, except the judge, would keep his religion!
Rukn-ad-din,* ornament of justice's court... Doctor of Divine
Law, by whose judgement religion is like in Mustafa's reign.
The perfection of his excellent policy has so adorned the world
that praise and eulogy will go on during Eternity's revolution!
All the world is invoking blessings on him, and Sadi, the most
humble, prays... "May he be spared for ever in this kingdom!"

*Note: Karun... the richest man in the world at the time of Moses whom
he opposed. Rukn-ad-din... a high official whom Sadi courted.

It is never Your wish to cross the desert for a while in my company...
only care You have is to travel on Your way like the sun... solitarily.
Through pride You keep eyes in front, take no notice of the beggar.
Perhaps it's through Your own loveliness You're not at us glancing!
You are an angel, or a fountain of light? You are a fairy or a huri
who is surpassing in beauty red rose that upon its stalk is growing?
You've a face like a huri, are fair as the moon, fragrant as jasmine,
silver-breasted. Strange if Your face, all over, no furore was creating.
As one can't do without Your face we must put up with Your whims;
for we cannot our heads away from Your street... up, keep holding.
Don't wander here, there, everywhere, in case Your poor lovers are
unaware: no one sees You that suddenly distraught is not becoming.
A world lies distracted at Your feet, weeping blood instead of tears:
I'd be surprised if the desert did not become a sea, from my weeping.

428

Nightly I've a violent desire, hoping for fulfilment tomorrow of Your
promise… maybe there'll be no tomorrow for Sadi's night of passion.
I wept so much on the soil of this place that it has turned into mud…
but, all these sighs are not Your heart of iron, even slightly melting.

Darling, how long must my heart carry the load of loneliness?
I am afraid from all this my affair may end in disgracefulness!
How is it possible to be patient now wisdom has deserted us?
For it needs a wise man to exercise a virtue like that… no less!
My cypress-statured One, if You rose-like come to the garden,
with Your feet's dust its eyes would be washing the narcissus.
Display Your Tajik-like face… so that the Heavens can all the
faces of the Turks of Yagma with the brand of slavery… press!
You pour forth honey when Your lips utter those sweet words;
You excite commotion, when Your hair You delightfully dress.
Your mouth, a pistachio nut, is as yet only a point: but, please
wait until time around it… a circle of blue down does express!
After this… no one's heart would be left to him, even if iron…
it's drawn from him, by Your eyes… their magnetic loveliness!
O Sadi, say nothing if the people are calling You quite mad…
Love, even if it arises in a Sufi's heart, drives him to madness!

If you've not known Love's pain you can't join the Dervishes Dance.
Don't imagine that sighs ever rise from a mere learner, not a chance!
Since everything coming from the hands of the Beloved is welcome,
it makes no difference if it is a sweet drink or it is a poisoned lance.

Breath of eastern breeze is perfumed with fragrance of my Beloved,
after this I'll travel like wind to discover that One's tent's entrance.
Beloved passed, I glanced from my eye's corner so to snatch one look:
but, me... snatched from myself by Beloved was my circumstance.
I wished to conceal my love affair by the exercise of my being patient,
but I could no longer cover up what was obvious... I had no chance!
Who is that rider of Reason, who will not be turning his back in that
place where the Monarch of Love has given him even... one glance?
Who will convey my message to the Beloved to say that our pleasure
is submit to Beloved's will, whether wounding or making us dance?
Every night that passed, Sadi said... in consequence of Love's pain,
"Another night's come: how will day come without You, perchance?"


You have a head that will not bend down for us...
I've a heart that is incapable anymore of pleasure.
Is there one whose eyes saw Your face all his life,
and not had tears like dew on cheeks... in surplus.
One cannot point to any defect in Your beauty...
except, being kind is absent from You towards us.
What cruelty's not inflicted on Your poor ball-like
victim... by the curve of bat of Your raven tresses?
If a thousand fortunes hit his wounded heart from
Your hand, he'd be no lover who denies it a success.
If I cut short my hope's tongue from talking of You,
saying no advantage comes from what we discuss...
people would think that the fire of Spiritual Reality
had died in my chest's censer, as no perfume left us.

Who's that lover whose cries aren't full of any pain?
What circle's that where cries of joy don't rise, thus?
Surely Sadi must have drunk deeply of Love's frenzy
with his mother's milk: but he's now old, an old cuss!

What can a slave do, but endure cruelty with patience?
Although heart may be sad, his love stays in abeyance!
Heart and religion are lost in this affair, they're nothing.
Demand my life and soul... the mad have no reluctance!
It's said magic's unlawful now, but Your eyes have done
what Harut in Babylon could not, with magical science!
Immersed in the ocean of Your love I am uneasy because
in the course of time upon shore I may see my emergence!
I'll not go to rose-garden as long as You're in my embrace;
if nightingale saw You, to seek rose wouldn't make sense.
No one will again appear before his mind's eye... who like
Sadi... for a happy moment with Beloved, has an audience!

What cypress is this that displays such a graceful figure,
and snatches away reins of control from hearts so secure?
Who can have produced this form... such a beautiful face?
I have no idea at all what effect such a form will procure!
If I should see that One, resembling the sun's bright disc,
a hundred times my eyes would flow with tears, I am sure.
There's not a one like that beautiful One in this, our age...
but... I am afraid that One will not a pact with us ensure.
On Your side there is indifference as much as You please,

while on my side Love continues to become more and more.
Tale of the Beloved's love cannot be expressed, and if you
try to tell it, you must a sympathetic ear to hear it insure.
Enquire from the sleepless ones of the length of the night...
for it appears too short to those who are sleepy, immature.
I've no power to escape whether I'm bound or I'm set free:
measuring strength with the powerful will fall the insecure.
It is not proper to be shedding the blood of Sadi unjustly...
but, since it is the Beloved's will, it is permissible for sure!

Your beauty won't remain like this forever; one intoxicated
will not always suffer from the effects of his drunken head.
You smiling rose, who has of late come to bloom... think of
nightingale's feeling, for spring isn't forever... let it be said.
Your heart-ravishing beauty is like a henna-stained hand...
the dye will not remain on it until the whole world is dead!
In the end nothing is remaining of us except for some dust;
so, you take care that not a heart because of you feels dread.
Your experience of joy and sorrow last year has now gone...
this year will also pass, like the last leaf of autumn is shed.
The revolution of Time may grant you your heart's desire...
and if not, does it matter... if Time's cycle has already fled?
O Sadi... why have you become so distracted and perturbed
in your search for something with no stability, not a thread!
Those of discernment can cultivate the habit of Love, or not,
as they please: when Fate intervenes 'no option' can be read.

That one who fears for his own life, no love for the Beloved is having:
if he is gaining Union at price of his life, cheap is price he is paying.
What are mimosa thorns that they'd turn pilgrim from the Kaaba?
Star thistles are like a silken carpet that on path the lover is treading.
No one has anything to do with You except the madman whose love
for You is planted in his soul… and his lips he cannot be opening.
O fairy faced One, why are You hidden from the pupils of my eyes?
But it's habit of fairies to themselves from mankind be concealing.
I don't wish to leave the world except at foot of Your wall, so that
when I come to give up life, my head at Your threshold I'll be laying.
If I were to do something to stop any of Your pleasure I'd be so mean:
ask of me to have my soul and what You command I'll be obeying.
I'm immersed in the ocean of Your Love and shunning all mankind,
just like a man flees from an enemy who arrow in his bow is holding.
People are bewildered by You, and it is indeed a surprise they see
the moon on the earth, for the moon's place in the sky one is seeing.
If You measured Your waist and hair in a hundred ways, Your waist
would be thinner than a hair, Your hair Your waist… be reaching.
Even the sword could not make me turn away my heart from You,
and if You make me blind, desire for You would never be changing!
Sadi, like Farhad, will be leaving this world with many bitter regrets,
but his sweet moans for as long as the world endures will be lasting.

My sweet sleep, dear boy, has become a trick of the imagination:
the ready cash of my life's hope has been in quest of Unification.
If love for that One had not overcome my patience and wisdom…
why is the latter overpowered… former trampled by exhaustion?

It would not be very strange if Your Union was forbidden to me...
it is strange if to shed my blood You found plenty of justification.
 If the sun's rays turn a crescent to a full moon... then why is the
full moon of my body now a crescent from seeing You... a vision?
It's right You, with a thousand Josephs as slaves to Your dignity
and wealth, demand in heart of Egypt's empire, royal succession!
Don't think it strange I now emit a cry of rapture from my heart,
for when the fire of heart flares, it can't be letting patience go on.
 If Sadi should take a look at You don't be suspecting him of lust;
he is not in love with hair and moles as are folk who are common.

My heart will not renounce its passion for the Beloved,
it can't pursue the way of those who only use the head.
O God, release our souls from the calamity of Love, for
we'll not abandon this business, even after we are dead!
I keep burning and try to make the best of the situation:
patience prevents revealing secrets, I keep them instead.
My sick body, crushed by weight of Heaven's tyranny...
cannot support additional load of cruelty of the Beloved.
It's up to Beloved not to pretend to be close to the lover,
if the Beloved does not lift grief from his heart and head.
If that One to fulfil promise allows at least one embrace,
what purpose would it fulfil unless my 'self' is left dead?
Sadi's consumed in the fire of Hell by Beloved's absence;
but still he doesn't lose hope of the joy of seeing Beloved!

A cypress like You is needed to the garden adorn...
it'd be right if no other cypress was there... forlorn!
Reason cannot conceive, nor imagination imagine,
that, from human seed, such a child could be born!
Your ruby lips stole so many hearts that in the city
for them to plunder is no one: the city's been shorn.
Everyone has some craze or desire: I'm an obedient
slave. Let's see what the Beloved orders this pawn.
If head one day fell at Your lovely feet it'd be easy;
I am afraid You'd not defile hands... me just scorn.
It is true I do not want this world without Beloved,
for what use is it if my heart was to elsewhere torn?
Many heads strike door like a knocker out of desire:
see whom Fate opening Beloved's door to is drawn.
I fear Layla will perhaps treat her Majnun unkindly
'til the blood of his heart out from his eyes is drawn.
That hard-hearted One, feels no pity for wounded...
perhaps when he's dead compassion will then dawn!
Winebringer, give... and take from this world all joy
it can give: life doesn't last and this age is its spawn.
People say, "Sadi, why don't you refrain from Love?"
I'm drunk! One is sober... for such an idea to dawn.

The moment through my door that walking cypress returned;
the spirit, to this body of mine, you could express... 'returned':
and auspicious Fortune, that used to be friendly towards me...
to my door in the morning in a spirit of real kindness returned.

435

The Friend came back and enemy collapsed due to misfortune.
The breeze of spring in spite of autumn's harshness, returned.
I'd aged because of the tyranny of fate and time's revolution...
but now to my aging head... a new kind of freshness returned.
O my soul, congratulate me... all of this distress is now gone:
O my body, don't be downcast... for a new liveliness returned.
I can't believe my good Fortune that the cruel, harsh Beloved...
through door with a mind thinking only of kindness... returned.
O soul's solace... when You returned through invisible world's
gateway... to renounce desires, to each consciousness returned.
The love of Your face is forbidden to all but Sadi... for he, from
his love for You, has... to give up all this worldliness, returned.
O friends, do not be finding fault with me or be criticising me...
this is a story I cannot help tell... my need to confess returned!

Look at the sweet mouth of that mischievous Darling:
    pearls between those lips, ruby-red, sugar-scattering!
See the garden of those cheeks full of jonquils, violets
    and pomegranates, heart's garden that is so pleasing!
That One carries off a thousand hearts by one glance;
    see lustre of that face, its splendour of beauty shining!
Though trouble is rare in our just king's reign, see the
    drunken eyes of Beloved whose glances are murdering.
Today Beloved's face is more lovely than yesterday...
    worse this year than the last my love affair's becoming.
See how hyacinths are arranged over a deep red rose...
    see how ambergris around a jasmine bed is scattering!

The moment Beloved lets down curls of that wild hair,
you'll see a hundred hearts beneath that hair, thieving!
Listen carefully to the sweet speech of that Beloved...
and watch more carefully Beloved, gracefully walking.
That pearl casket enclosed within the Beloved's twin
cornelian lips is a treasure but see snake over it coiling.
Those eyes, with sword of their murderous, relentless
glances... conquered a city; their power be considering!
Yesterday that One's glance said, "Sadi, I am yours!"
But, see once again, a flattering lie that One is telling!

What scheme can I devise to make an impression on You...
and where to be ridding my heart of You, can I be going to?
I have lost any social position in the eyes of all of mankind,
but... it's impossible for my brazen eyes to avoid loving too!
This weak heart has not the power to be making any shield
against the arrows of Your love... and, it does not want to!
When You hear about my life's bitterness break into smiles;
for if You do, the world would become sweeter through You.
If You should pass by Your wounded lover, he'd be restored
to health; if You looked on the dead they'd come to life too!
The pen has shed many tears from my heart-rending words;
for a blazing fire quickly kindles a reed that is dried through.
Your two dreamy, luscious eyes subdue a city with a glance:
a world's captivated by one loving, flirtatious look from You.
If I should sit in a corner of my house because of Your cruelty,
Your image would ruthlessly drive me from my door, roof too!

Don't act as You're doing, for day of Your beauty will end if
some night Sadi grips shirt of dawn, with a prayer's hand too.

Does one desert his Beloved... except for that one
whose heart's harder than a stone weighing a ton?
Who can say he knows anything of Love's reality?
He is a liar... if consciousness of self isn't undone.
God forbid he who sees Beloved with a pure heart,
cares more for the Here and Hereafter than none!
We shall perish in the desert of Love; so, where is
one, who desires to journey in our company... one?
Though arrow menace him in front, sword behind,
he isn't a lover whose concern of danger isn't none.
And even if Paradise was decorated for the lover...
it'd not be right to look at any one... but that One!
Among presents scattered at Beloved's feet, I've a
head to offer, but don't know Beloved's idea of fun!
It'd be a shame for Beloved to put feet on the dust.
Why doesn't Beloved our head and eyes walk upon?
The herd reproach me for being a lover all my life…
what fault is it of Sadi's, to such a virtue not shun?
May it be forbidden to one to glance at Your face...
having another besides You in the world, isn't done!

Does a person abandon his friends and country?
He has to, if Fate against him turns, completely.
I don't blame the faint-hearted, who can't stand

pain the rose inflicts, if he shuns thorn so prickly!
If he fighting foe fails in stratagem, he must take
to heels like one who is helplessness, completely.
My heart's blood's thirsty for the sword of doom:
how long half dead in blood must it keep sinking?
What remains for one under stone of misfortune,
except to like a wounded snake be madly rolling?
I've no heart left from the quantity of blood from
it that gushed... then into my ruby eyes is raining!
Although Sadi's wearied of his country because of
loneliness, don't think from friend he'll be turning!

That saucy silver-bodied Sweetheart will be the death of me...
snuff me out some day like a burnt out candle in the assembly.
If that One gracefully walks a thousand hearts are stolen; and
a thousand bodies will be slain... if that One fights vengefully.
Although the Water of Life is in that One's mouth and lips...
it wouldn't surprise if that mouth and lips are the death of me!
If one stood against that One, he'd be captured by that One's
Love; if fled, that One's absence would hunt... kill mercilessly!
How will the calamity of Love, slayer of that mountain-cutter
Farhad, spare one who hasn't even the strength of a straw, me?
People criticise me and advise me to give up love... if love does
not kill me on the spot then these words I write will eventually.
If, according to the Divine Law, an idol worshipper must die...
what is the need to execute me, for that Idol will be slaying me.
I complained to a friend about that One's saucy eyes and reply

was if a drunken One with sword killed me how strange it'd be. Jealousy will soon be putting an end to my existence... because that Friend for just a moment with some strangers was friendly. Beloved said with a smile, "O Sadi, I'm the light of this party... do I care if a moth should commit suicide, it doesn't bother me!"

Let down Your long curls so they may fall in such disorder the confusion Your face excites will tear the world asunder. If You were to flit like a fairy across our minds, it would be causing a turmoil in the bodies of human beings everywhere. My heart has fallen victim to You... lend it a helping hand, Beloved! Don't throw it down, such a heart... none is rarer! That wretch who's drawn sword of his glance at Your face, will be shot down like me by cruelty of Your arrow O archer! Don't break this heart... a casket holding Your secrets; that they may fall into the hands of one untrustworthy is my fear. Time has come for You to approach me... place lips on mine. How long must I... in this quest for You, be made to suffer? O Sadi, endure wounds inflicted by Beloved's cruelty... until the chance of securing a balm for them your way, comes near.

Do not fall asleep; for if You happened to see a vision of You in a dream, it would deprive Your eyes of sleeping like me too. Power of endurance, extent of patience have reached all limits. Delay no longer... such waiting I can't for eternity go through. What traveller's souvenir is more acceptable than the sight of one's friends? Come to me Yourself... for nothing else will do!

Although there are many beautiful ones in this world to see…
it's true that after the sun has risen, stars disappear from view.
The servant woman has given up all making up of Your face…
as she realised to adorn the sun was an impossible thing to do.
You'll never see in the world a sweetheart endowed with grace
of my Beloved, who practises hostility… and yet loves one too!
It is not only the living who feel love and affection for You; for
even the spirit of one dead will be revived by the breath of You.
I do not begrudge in searching for You spending all I possess…
for of what value's my heart and of what worth is my soul too?
The why and the wherefore do not come within the thoughts of
the afflicted lover… only obedience to Beloved's orders will do.
If sighs from Sadi's breast reached the Friend, to say nothing of
affecting that One, they'd even move the enemy to pity me too!

Surely the morning breeze brings the fragrance of my Beloved,
because it gives solace to my heart, that the Beloved expected.
The tulip and also the rose are lying at the feet of the cypress…
perhaps it is possessing the characteristics of form of Beloved!
Do not ask me about the track to the way of safety… for Love
is holding the reins of my will that power of control has lacked.
O rose, O fresh orange flower, your cheeks the freshness of my
rose and fragrance of my orange flower… have never possessed!
It is not possible for my head to again lie peacefully on a pillow
because this poor brain of mine is with this desire… consumed.
All of my life I have spent in vain, thinking only of that One…
while that One hasn't a thought for me or what for me is fated.

Surely the sighs of my heart have reduced me to the last gasp…
O God, from whose favour will this distress be at last relieved?
Beneath Your load Sadi's reduced to despair like an ass in mud:
by the thought he bears Your burden… is Your heart untouched?

What can I throw at Your feet worthy of Your acceptance?
My life would not be a fit offering to lay there for instance.
That face is a happy face that is facing You for all eternity;
this only happens if it pleases You… no other circumstance!
There's not an atom in this poor body, this mote suspended
in Your ether, not devoted to Your Love, if given the chance.
Since You, graceful cypress, have been planted in my heart…
I want no one to occupy Your place, under any circumstance.
I swear by Your love, that if they made bricks from my clay,
love for You in my heart would stay, though I be in absence.
Our aspiration is to die while pursuing this affair with You:
we don't fear death, for Your life has an eternal permanence!
O lamp of Chigal,* if I were burnt up like a moth before You,
it would not be my fault, and not the fault of Your presence.
It'd be strange if he, who had seen You and heard You speak
didn't desire for all his life to be with You for every instance.
Cries of heartsick lovers, that are the outcome of their pain,
are pleasant, when Your hands of the cure offer some chance.
Sadi's ambition would not be realised by the world's empire.
The sovereignty to satisfy him is… beggar in Your presence!
For many ages the worship point of mystics will be upon that
ground, due to treading of soles of Your feet, You experience!

This isn't a night when between us room could be found by anything.
I swear by Your feet's dust... a bit of ether between us isn't fitting.
Take off Your crown of arrogance and pride, loosen Your girdle: for
I've not seen cypress like You that any tunic could be containing!
Don't ask me for an account of our separation on the night of Union.
Whose criticism can on privacy of our coming together be intruding.
Don't offer me sugar, and don't scatter roses at our meeting-palace;
because that anything should interfere between us isn't really fitting.
The happiness of Wisa* and of Ramin* was not in need of any roses:
what need was between Khusrau* and Shirin* for sugar-scattering?
When the commotion of Love is supervening... Reason is dethroned.
Is it possible... that in one empire two kings find room to be ruling?
There is no longer any scope in the mind of Sadi for music and song.
Is there a chance for a pious man's advice to again get... a footing?

*Note: All famous Persian lovers.*

For a man of wisdom to avoid Love is the wisest thing to do indeed:
but, my nature is such... wisdom seems repugnant to what I need.
That one who has a heart adorned with spiritual Reality would cast
the Here and Hereafter at the feet of the Beloved, with Godspeed.
If a flood of criticism overtakes him the mad has no fear, and if the
arrows of misfortune rain down on him to avoid them he has no need.
I'm not alone in the desert of desire, because the love of that One's
sweet lips excite many in the population into a frenzy, many indeed!

With Fortune up in arms against me, what am I able to do to enjoy
the fruits of Your Union? A beggar is helpless… no  matter his deed!
It would be kind of You to call me and  be just if You drove me away.
One not taking Your criticism is really an unworthy one! Agreed?
Since I've attached my heart to You I have closed road to all else.
Wherever You sit down many tumults arise… from Your good deed.
Sadi will never be taking his eyes off Your face… and if You should
turn Your face from him, he would still cling to You… out of need!

It's the time weakness  overcomes strength that is departing…
and the power of the poet to utter sweet poetry is now waning.
All of a sudden the blast of autumn comes, then away all this
brilliance and beauty from the rosebush you see… is sweeping!
My feet will soon be losing their power of motion. Happy is he
who's extremely cautious and the path of goodness is treading.
God knows… if I weep, a stream would run from my eyes, until
day when the water, that flows away… to riverbed is returning.
How can I hope to go to Paradise with such stock to my credit?
Who would ever be allowing the devil… to Heaven be entering?
All Sadi's stock in trade consists in his sweet poetry… and this
will survive him. I know not what with him will be finally going.
What use is this poetry and eloquence to me who has burned all
my life like aloes… so their scent the world might be pervading?

O charming Beloved, O heart-ravishing moon, one can do
with everyone else, but one cannot be dispensing with You.

Since Your image has been imprinted on my sincere heart...
that there's no room left for another idea in my mind is true.
People ask... "How long will you run after beautiful ones?"
Why should anyone taken captive, not be their slaves too?
One bound in chains of Your curls doesn't quickly get free.
Time and effort for one sunk in pitch, is all that one can do!
If one sweet of heart with a graceful figure and silvery limbs
like Yours passes, he not looking must be with life through.
If I don't mention Beloved's name no matter, for who is like
that One: it goes without saying, One perfect is proud too!
The beautiful figure of the cypress, on which so much praise
is lavished, though tall is in reality low, compared with You!
Everyone searching for You will not shrink from the sword...
one in love with You is not put off by darts Your eyes threw!
Let me imprint some kisses, like a slave, upon Your feet, and
if life is lost due to this desire, do not blame helpless me too.
O Sadi, if your life and property is spent looking for Union...
the price will be paltry for such a high honour coming to you.
Although You are independent of us and are in need of none,
nevertheless we seek support from You, what else can we do?

O patience, be firm, for the promise is broken by the Beloved,
I am finished... and to be winning my Sweetheart I've failed.
Sighs have risen from my heart and blood wells up in my eyes.
My God, what have I done that my companionship's refused?
In my love for the Beloved I don't begrudge silver or even gold,
but it is only my tears and anguish that me have accompanied.

The Beloved had no pity upon my poor form, bent like a bow…
for Beloved away from my side like some arrow, quickly darted.
On Beloved's threshold for a lifetime I placed my adoring face;
I thought that One might open door for me… but it was closed.
Does any enemy act as You have been doing towards a friend?
In short, is that One a friend who with foe is friendly, instead?
O Sadi, since the treachery of your Beloved established now is;
break off all hope in Your heart for broken is promise of Beloved.

Each night I plan fresh schemes and designs that are new
to escape in the morning to another place, away from You.
But, at morning when I place one foot outside Your house,
my loyalty does not permit me to put down the other shoe!
Every one's longing for something… yearning for some one:
we are desiring nothing else in the world, except You. You,
because… no other face or figure is ever pictured with such
clarity as Yours in mirror of the imagination, I see through!
There lived a Wamiq who was madly in love with an Azra:
in this present time, You and I are a Wamiq and Azra too!
It's the season when rose and hyacinth bloom are blooming:
people venture out… to a different pleasure-grounds to view.
So come out in the morning, enjoy a promenade in a garden,
as we can't in anything else dispense with company of You.
Each dawn a new grief hits me through Time's revolutions…
and I say to myself, "Must I add this, all other sorrows to?"
Again I say, "Lay it here," for… all revolutions of this sphere
come to nil. O Sadi, be patient today, and a tomorrow… too!

One is highly favoured by Fortune through whose door You appear.
Come, please come, for You'd be welcome. Where are You? Where?
Why did You show Your face… away from which, peace of mind
is unimaginable: and why don't You show it once again? Be fair!
What have I done, that You do not open again that double-lidded
door of Your saucy heart-entrancing eyes, to my face… over here?
Whether You are caring for us or are unsympathetic towards us,
I shall never be unfaithful towards You and for You I'll always care.
Wine of Your Union has been in the throat of my soul from Eternity
even now I am still intoxicated with the cup of Love, this… I swear!
That one, who has lost his wretched, wounded heart in Your street,
will most certainly find it again by the light of Your face, elsewhere.
It is certainly the right thing for You to be moving to another city,
for there is no heart still left in this city for You to ravish, anywhere.
The common herd are reproaching this ardent lover by saying this…
"Why not refrain from this desire and control your nature, you hear?"
I answer, "O sober ones, if you tasted the sweetness of intoxication,
you would never again think of being sober… this, I truly do swear!
And, if like Sadi, you were given a morsel from this door, you would
never from then on relinquish the habit of begging, so go elsewhere!"


Before form of that One, cypress of the garden is embarrassed:
always capturing prey, are the curls like nooses of the Beloved.
The breeze became angry when it saw tree of that One's form,
so it tore up by the roots each cypress that grew in the orchard.
It was from vanity sun boasted of comparison with that One…
how dare new moon aspire to be horseshoe of that One's steed!

447

My weak body is so helpless that it has become quite incapable
of helpful cure by any counsel, or restraining hand outstretched.
If I had firmness of purpose to take my heart from the Friend...
I shouldn't hear criticism from behind my back... inside my head.
The sweet words of Sadi produce no effect whatsoever on You...
many the parrots like him... who before Your candy have waited.

Pleasant is the pain for which there is no hope of a remedy;
a wilderness that has an end doesn't seem long to anybody.
If you are in love with the bow of the Beloved's eyebrows...
to make your life a shield against arrows' rain, is your duty.
The lover who is yearning for the rose garden has to put up
with the gardener, and no matter how great is the difficulty.
May winning of Union with Soul of the world be forbidden
if paying any regard to this world or even his own soul is he.
One should not be turning away in despair from the Kaaba.
It's only a small sacrifice to perish in its wilderness, you see?
Even though I'm stupid and foolish, this much I know... that
my glass is no match for that One's anvil, and never will be!
But, in spite of Beloved's faults one bears with the Beloved...
so how can separation from that One not be endured bravely?
If a thousand arrows should assail me at Your hands, then it
would be wrong to flick even an eyelash at their points by me!
The rival who fears for his own life only is indulging in empty
boasting about his love for the Friend: that, is so easy to see!
Don't expect prudence and understanding from a philosopher:
he who lost his heart and is helpless in spite of his philosophy.

If it was at all possible to see a rose like Your face in the world
then don't ever be hoping to discover a nightingale... like Sadi!

O friend, your life is precious, so make the best of it...
carry from its polo-field any ball of good deeds; it, get!
How long will dominion last? For the upshot is this...
Heaven in spite of its power eventually makes an exit.
It is only God Almighty... the Eternal Lord of Power,
Whose Kingdom is the only one never changing a bit!
This life of ours is a subject for tears, for like rosebud,
its smiling lips last only a short time, not eternal is it!
Mother nature doesn't give its child a mouthful of milk
without sucking its lifeblood, taking it when it sees fit!
You possess knowledge and a stock of earthly goods...
what's better than eternal faith, give them up... take It!
That one's fortunate who today heals wounded heart's
pain; for after death he will not be able to cure it one bit.
One not scattering grain on the earth during the winter
can't expect to reap harvest when summer heat does hit.
Clutch hem of the coat of Perfect Men and don't worry;
whoever associates with Noah fears Deluge not one bit!
May you be fortunate and to tell the truth that one's life
is fortunate who's praiseworthy when coming to end of it.
If you erect a building to live in, well and good; if it's only
to use as a temporary lodging... don't trouble to furnish it.
The occupation of Sadi is to give advice. How can he help
but give it? He has musk and must reveal it like the civet!

What a miracle is the Beloved's form that one is embracing.
Wine of Paradise's Salsabil, from fountain of life is flowing.
Who does that Beloved favour, that Sweetheart who's made
us all that One's servants and slaves, devoted and waiting?
That One's a fairy-faced Darling through the spell of whose
eyes these eyes of mine last night of all sleep were depriving!
That One does not keep on coming back into my memory…
because it's only too true, that One I am not ever forgetting.
And if that One's shedding my blood don't let it be allowed.
It's better my head roll at those feet than on neck be staying.
That one who keeps on criticising us, he has no sense at all:
go to him… that he should mind his own business be telling.
A drum under a blanket can't be hidden from people forever,
and… neither can a fire under a hair-net of muslin be hiding.
O Friend, come to me, and if the enemy should be seeing us,
what can he do? Let him look… with rage let him be boiling!
You're indifferent to us even though we're Your companions.
We keep on crying out but You, You're still silent remaining!
Ask for the description of Your beauty from somebody else…
Sadi's too dazed… bewildered by You, to You be describing!

Whether You accept me, or drive me from You… far away,
even if I had to sacrifice my life, with You I'd want to stay.
You know best whether You should cherish me or hurt me:
do what seems right, what Your enlightened mind may say.
I don't derive any benefit from advice of strangers, for I am

content to endure ill-treatment from Your hands... any way.
It is very true that to look in our direction would be a favour
and a good deed because You'd be loving this slave that day.
And even if You should prohibit my seeing You face to face,
I will never permit Your face's image in my mind not to stay.
Story of my patience in absence of Your face, is best shown
by a suckling baby that from mother's breast... is kept away.
You'd be quite justified in driving away all of mankind from
Your sight: You'll never see one as beautiful as You anyway.
I thought I would sacrifice my life for the love of Your face...
then I saw again the paltry offering at Your feet I had to lay.
It's out of the question You'd ever entertain the idea of being
with Sadi. How could such a stupid idea ever come my way?
Do you know what this overpowering feeling is doing to me?
It's just like what the ant suffers with his heavy load all day!

If I'm not to enjoy the world, do I care for this heap of rubbish?
I am the eagle of generosity, crow's nest as home I don't relish!
If all of my wishes were granted half of a loaf would satisfy me,
and if the course of my life is run, being half-dead isn't my wish.
I am lying like the dog of the companions of cave at door of the
Perfect Ones. I don't wander from door to door, bones to nourish.
The pearls of spiritual Reality are strung on the throat of form...
I'm not narrow-eyed like needle, let thread go, or it can diminish.
When sleep overtakes you... lay head at base of poverty's wall...
no matter if you climb wealth's terrace, if world you impoverish.
When I have put greed aside I don't require assistance of anyone.

Since I've ceased to speak, for any interpreter why should I wish?
How wonderful it is that my great passion's set the world on fire!
But as I've fallen in the fire I don't care if the world should vanish.
If I am to burn in Hell... then let my vile body be consumed by it.
If I fail to enter Heaven, I don't care if it exists, or it They abolish!
If I'm nothing in Paradise's garden, I care if even a leaf's growing?
If I am nothing in ruler's kingdom, does watchman cause anguish?
O Sadi... what is the use of your obeisance, at the gate of Glory?
Do not let dust of the defiled, the Holy threshold try to diminish!

To the heavens, because of my good fortune, I am exalted:
because I'm one, who with You, along desert has travelled.
I've spent ages in searching for You, seeking a way to You:
to devise a way to escape Your cruelty, years I've wandered.
Today I've attained my aspiration... today my wishes have
been fulfilled, in accordance with desire of heart so afflicted.
How'd I win You... Ocean reflecting drop? How'd You fall
to my lot, O You droplet beyond my capacity, let it be said.
A royal crown is on my head that is soiled with such dust...
and a royal pavilion upon the beggar's crown's also pitched!
I'll not place another's balm on sword-wound of Your love...
I am a golden bowl, and with glue I cannot ever be mended!
If Sadi gains honey of Your Union it wouldn't be surprising,
as he's been stung for years, by the bee of what You've said!

That one still possesses patience and the power of endurance,
who is still able to be going to sleep in the Beloved's absence.

452

But, that one, cannot be expecting sleep from both those eyes
that in flood of tears have been thrown hence, as subsequence.
The victim of love is unable to move of his own volition, for...
by hand of One he's dragged like fish on hook as consequence!
What can a man do who's in bondage to love of a *Sweetheart*,
to be avoiding cruelty... that One's attendants may dispense?
That one who wants to approach the court of any king has to
be putting up with the doorkeeper, or get away, this instance!
And, that one has to be accepting whatever is offered his way:
bitter, sweet; date, thorn; poison, rose-sherbet; each experience.
This saying is quite fitting at this time, namely... to know the
Tigris will not quench patient with dropsy takes no brilliance.
The night of separation from the Beloved is as black as pitch:
this is so, no matter how moonlight is now, or may be... hence!
The spirit of the afflicted lover may be leaving his body... but
the seal of Love is never effaced from his soul as consequence!
*Sadi*, tell me to whom can the sheep sacrificed be complaining?
That butcher about to take his life, can he hear of recompense?

Don't let that man who for his own life has a care
go boasting about his love for Beloved, anywhere!
It's the physician who is the cause of my suffering:
from whom can I seek any cure? It's... O so unfair!
Who ever has his head in the noose of that One...
cannot move, unless that One gives one the order!
What can the contemptible slave be doing... but to
obey orders of One who owns him, then and there!

It is quite inevitable that a passionate lover, must
with all of the criticisms of his friend… try to bear.
But, what difference does a shower of rain make…
to anyone who in the Red Sea's again going under?
The rose has finally reached perfection in its body,
so, now be letting the nightingale's cries fill the air!
Although Reason may have a thousand arguments,
Love puts forward a claim… that drives it to despair.
To that one whose lot this arrow is happening to fall,
its sharp point will rankle in heart's wound: in there!
That one is crying out like a child who is weeping…
whose pain that's hidden, isn't understood anywhere.
So, you take care, and do not go discoursing on Love,
or, if you do… offer proof that you are a sincere lover.
The wise man will never just enter any water he sees,
without first discovering if that water is deep or clear!
O Sadi… if you are offered the Here and Hereafter in
exchange for a moment with Beloved… accept neither!

That Sweetheart, in whose absence peace of mind is an impossibility
has passed by and dipped those ten fingers in my blood, deliberately!
That One asked, "In your grief at Fate's cruelty how do you fare?"
I replied, "I am not a one who can be asked that… can't You see?"
From the time that Your face became the worship-place of my eyes,
I'm bearing like a pillar of endurance the weight of slander, patiently.
Do not believe that I, who have become like some broken-down wall,
except in Your street have suffered from any others any such cruelty.

When I write down the particulars of the pain I bear loving You...
there's a danger pen will catch fire from my heart-burning so fiercely.
Please, tell to those ones who are thinking that I am sane and sober,
to note this down as evidence... that no person is as mad as me.
Lift up Your sword and say that Sadi's life is what You are after...
and, if I fail to lay head at Your feet, I'd be a lover who is unworthy!

There is not a night on which the lover's eyes can be sleeping:
blessed inhabitants of Paradise's garden to sleep aren't going.
The kindly influence of the breeze of spring revives the earth...
that one must be stone whose heart the breeze isn't refreshing.
I smell the scent of the lost Joseph, but if I should say so all of
the world would shout out, "It's the old delusion... obviously!"
The lover is not one to listen to any advice and my pain is not
that type that any treatment of any physician can be a remedy.
People keep on advising me to repent of caring for the Beloved:
that wouldn't be repentance at all... it'd be a sin that's deadly.
O fellow travellers, keep your hands far away from me because
I wish to remain sitting at the Beloved's door... for an eternity!
Brother, try to understand Love's agony as the fire of Nimrod,
because this pain feels like it did to Abraham... to poor old me!
If You were to pass over any old bones when they were rotten,
the dead from the dust of the grave would rise dancing joyfully.
I'm longing to gain Your Union... I dread separation from You:
I've not hope nor fear for what the world gives, I fear this only!
A victim lying slain at door of Beloved's tent doesn't surprise:
the wonder is over he who survives... how he escaped to safety!

O Sadi, it is true that Love and lust do not go together, ever…
that Devil can't approach Angelic choirs praising God joyfully.


The load of separation from Beloved on my heart heavily is weighing.
I am ready to go on, but the camel under my litter will not be moving.
The camel flings down her load when she reaches the halting stage…
heart's load is the same, still a hundred stages it I must be carrying.
O You who pull the nose-ring, exercise patience and go gently, for
while on one side You draw me, chains on the other me are holding.
Weighed down under the load of cruelty… my love secrets exposed,
journey ahead and heart left behind, difficult my position's becoming.
How can distance prove to be hindrance to our friendship? Although
absent in body… present in spirit before me: You, I'm remembering.
You are my ultimate objective, goal of my endeavour and my desire.
Until I reach You, hand of hope from Your skirt I will not be taking.
How can tongue cease praising You, or mind cease thinking about
You since You every vein and joint of my body are now penetrating.
I am so occupied with thoughts of You I can think of nothing else…
I am so absorbed in You that of any other person I am never thinking.
If You'd only cast a glance at me, fruit of my patience would flourish;
if this isn't possible, from root of vain hopes a fruit can be growing?
O Sadi, will you never be abandoning the path of Love? Please tell
how can a habit, that was kneaded with my clay, mind be leaving?
In spite of my learning, I'm unable to supply a cure for desire's pain;
even with all my wisdom, no resource in affairs of love I am knowing.

While we shed heart's blood, You are hidden behind a curtain.
If only the veil were thrown off we'd raise a tumult, for certain.
Others are only concerned about their own lives... while we, if
you ask, are so overcome we'd surrender ours again and again!
People avoid a commotion: they fail to understand how we, in
our yearning for You, desire the Resurrection, no matter when!
It is evident we, who have jeopardised our mad hearts, exposed
our hearts to danger... won't flee from calamity's arrows again.
Don't paint in rosy colours Paradise's garden... for we mystics
have no desire to cling to Paradise's virgins skirts now or then.
If You drive us away a flood of tears, we will shed tears on the
fires of Hell hoping for You, not through fear of Hellfire's rain.
As it's really You who has blended the colour of good and evil
in that invisible world, can we be deceiving You... ever again?
O Sadi, a claim that is devoid of truth, cannot be established.
We are slow to act but O how swift to speak... now and then.


Ever since I began thinking of You, in my heart is no other.
Who in the world is like You that I'd stop loving You, ever?
When I pass to that other world, killed by the pain of Love,
everything growing from my dust will cure Love for a lover.
I'm passing away, Your name is still passing on my tongue;
I crumble to dust... Your love in my very fibre, lives forever!
I have spent the harvest of my life in quest of Your Union...
if, in spite of all my trying You stop me... what did I gather?
All my yearning in quest of my heart's desire will be in vain
if favouring Fortune's cycle does not come and be my helper.

I'm not worthy of Your service as I lack in merit and worth...
if You accept me I'd be a paragon of virtue although a sinner.
If You were to slay me without a cause no one would put out
a claim for blood-right against You as I'm slave of the slayer.
My boat was wrecked in the Ocean and sank: if the morning
breeze carries anything ashore, of my bones it'll be the carrier.
Cypress and garden have totally faded from my mind's eye...
fir-tree never leaves it as it has taken root in my heart forever!
How can I think about the quest for Union with You, for I'm
always remembering You... but still of You I am the forgetter!
O Sadi, that army of Love has been plundering your reason...
so you may never again imagine yourself as a one who is wiser.


As long as I think of that One, of myself I'm unconscious:
because of that One's existence... to say I exist is facetious.
I tear my garment each moment through intensity of desire,
that One's my whole body, of being garment I'm conscious.
O guardian, don't get in a rage, nor seek to argue with me...
I'd rather tear out my eyes, than look at that One even less.
I choose that I would say nothing about this love affair... so
neither friend nor foe might from my words this state guess.
There is not one meeting assembled in any place in the city
where gossip is not about my love for that One's loveliness.
That One deserted me... was indifferent to my heart's pain;
I couldn't break off relations with that One, that is obvious!
If the same anguish should be my companion in the grave...
you'd see my shroud burnt up, if to my body you had access.

If You're still thirsting for my blood, look... here is my head!
It's better on Your saddle-strap as my body's a bloody mess.
Let all men and women get up and criticise me: I'd be not a
man but a woman... if I then my love for You didn't express.
It would not be unreasonable for men not to avoid an arrow;
if Your hand shot it I'd not flicker an eyelash, or be anxious!
The fear is... as soon as Your sweet mouth opened to speak,
because of it I would throw the world into mad feverishness!
How far removed are Sadi's lips from Your mouth! Let this
suffice me... let praise of Your lips, my tongue forever bless!

In midst of the anchorite's cell, I'm only a pretentious hypocrite:
clad in dervish's patch-coat, eaten by false pride, I'm without It!
I'm idolater of the physical form in the house of deceit and fraud,
and a worshipper of Manat, Sawa, Lat and Uzza*... I'm so unfit!
And... I keep on shamefully boasting about my being a real man,
but I've really gone and prostituted my soul like a dancing harlot!
Under this old patch-coat I am, from hypocrisy, Phararoh of this
Age, yet claim... Moses on Sanai of that One's Love, me does fit!
I entered idol temple and saw its inmates; but... I was an idolater
among a congregation and still professed to be faithful to all of it.
"O Sadi, become like me through wine that is pure... it's through
such wine... that I'm loved by His Holiness, the Master of IT!"

* Note: Names of idols worshipped by the ancient Arabians.

It is a long time since I have been in love with Your face...
except the dust of Your street, to sleep I don't have a place.
I swear by Your long hair that's more upset than my fate...
that than Your hair, I've been more disturbed by Your face.
Coin of understanding I had in purse of my imagination...
in Your scales were worth less than nothing, not one trace.
I've no intimate friend who'd repeat a word of Yours to me:
I have no confidant who'd convey news of me to Your place.
A lover doesn't turn aside his face from the arrow of doom...
I'm afraid it may pierce my eye, make me blind to Your face!
All mankind are followers of my poetry for this reason, that
I worship at prayer niche of eyebrows... Your face's grace!
The hand of death will uproot the peg of my life's pavilion...
if good Fortune doesn't pitch my tent near Your resting place.
Don't imagine that I'll leave Your door due to criticism; for...
if You hit me with the sword, I'll Your arm wait to me efface.
How sweetly does Sadi sing to 'the tune of all of the lovers'!
Sweetheart, throw off veil, I am devoted slave of Your face.

Everyone is longing for a companion who is loving,
and is an intimate friend: I am one who is so doing.
To look at beautiful ones is an established custom:
it's not an innovation to the world I'm introducing!
If you're claiming to be abstinent... I'll believe you,
and if it happens to be true, then... God's knowing!
But, if you are saying that you have no inclination,
such an assertion as that I would not be admitting.

460

And... if you are saying that it is a sin to talk about
Love, well, Adam and Eve were first to be sinning!
That one held captive in the snare of beautiful ones
about either being praised or blamed is never caring.
I don't know of any other remedy in the whole world
like a sweetheart's hand on a wounded breast laying.
O Winebringer, keep on circulating that brimful cup:
from the sky, lesson of perpetual motion, be learning.
If you realise that the world is not worth any worry,
in presence of friends be happy and keep on rejoicing.
If you understand that each day that passes is a day
less remaining in your life... it as a gain be counting!
O Sadi, do not set your heart on life's permanence...
for its foundation is unstable... this be remembering!
O heart depressing friend, go your way… be happy.
You'll finally turn to dust, so... give up this grieving.


My heart-ravishing Sweetheart's broken the pact of affection:
my unfaithful Beloved's severed the bond of love and has gone.
I swear by the precious dust of Your feet that through my love
for You I've given up desire for this world and the one later on.
The tyranny that You have practised against me in friendship,
I wouldn't against my blood-thirsty foe give any consideration.
Although You have severed Love's bond and broken Your pact,
I'm still faithful to my promise and to my oath I gave earlier on.
Intoxicated Winebringer, bring here the goblet of Love's wine...
give it to me... despite all those who advise, full of admonition.

I am not one who is prone to listen to the criticisms of the wise:
I do not care if even my father should call me his shameless son!
I swear this… by the dust of Your feet and by all of the souls of
those whose hearts are truly alive, at You feet I long to pass on!
Come, ah… come to me, my Idol; on account of my madness…
the only chains holding me are Your curls: that is my condition.
Beloved laughed… said to me, "O Sadi, flee from such danger!"
I replied, "Where can I go… for I am confined in Love's prison!"

If I had a thousand lives, still to live,
them all at Your blessed feet I'd give.
Beloved, please pass over me, see me
as dust of Your threshold, submissive.
All Your orders against me are easy…
me, from Yourself don't be dismissive!
You don't have a desire for our Union;
I am fully aware my Fate is oppressive.
How impossible… a Royal falcon like
You, should my nest come in… to live!
If Your name's uttered in my presence,
from my soul an anguished cry I'll give.
No night passes, that cries to Heaven
from being far away from You… I give.
If my heart's too dark and mean for You
on my two bright eyes I'll make You live.
Please, were not we pledged to our love,
You and I? But, Your pact is not active!

I will not scatter the dice of Your Love,
until my dead bones make it prohibitive.
It'd only be from soul's separation from
body that Your Union becomes elusive.
I'd be mad if I accepted the kingdom of
Arabia and Persia: price, Layla to give!
You are indeed the Shirin of the time…
as a slave of Khusrau of the Age, I live.
You are a king who has the right to say,
"I'm lord of the great, most impressive!"
His lofty palace says to the heavens…
"You are the earth, it's in the sky I live!"
You know he does not allow oppression:
any complaint I make don't to him give.
Each prophet has lived in his own epoch:
but… I am Sadi… in the final Age I live.

How I wish that unfaithful Beloved, whose victim I am, had passed
by me again… so that by that One's fragrance, I may be revived.
That One's deserted me but I can't forsake that One. What to do?
I don't have heart like that One's that of iron and brass is composed.
As long as I possess these feet I'll stumble in my quest for that One.
As long as I breathe I'll ask way and towards that One be hastened.
What imagination and desire of mine it is to hope those lips will be
pressed on mine, except when a potter, cup from my clay has potted.
Monarch of Beauties, why inflict separation's wound only upon me?
I am not the only one like ball who in curve of Your bat has landed.

Wherever there's a beauty possessor I've been praising, eulogising:
but, You're so lovely, when I go to talk I'm completely flabbergasted!
Last night You said, "O Sadi, such hopeless love for me give away."
You don't realise, even if life's forfeited I'd not leave You Beloved.

I became a free man on the day I became enslaved to You…
I'm a king while in Your chains, them I don't want to undo!
All of the sorrows of the whole world have no effect on me,
because that I became happy on seeing Your face is so true!
And happy will that day be when I die in my quest for You:
my friends will come, congratulate me… and be happy too!
And I, who hadn't really pitched anywhere the tent of Love,
have settled down near You and I've fixed my heart on You.
You know what hope I have from my belief in Your Union?
Thoughts of You may obliterate from me… selfishness too!
I swear by Your love: from the day You captivated me, that
I have not given my heart, or opened door to anyone, is true.
As long as image of You form is before my eyes… I am like
a free-growing cypress… even if all men were cypresses too!
Words fail me in expressing the sweetness of Your mouth…
and the wonder is this, that the Shirin of this Farhad is You!
I have not any wealth that I can throw like dust at Your feet:
in short, I am like an empty drum in which only hot air grew!
It looks as if the tyranny of Fate will never let go of my coat;
until it in the end becomes the complete ruination of me too!
What can I do if I don't patiently endure Time's oppression?
There is no judge who to get redress that I can go running to.

I am becoming quite tired of this society of Shiraz, so now is
the time when you'd best ask me... what in Baghdad they do!
I have not the least doubt that my cry for aid will reach there,
and I would be surprised if the chancellor didn't want me too.*
O Sadi, although 'love of home' is a tradition that's authentic,
still you cannot die of want, because there you were born into.

* *Note: In this ghazal, when Sadi was an old man, he seems to have
fallen on hard times and he thought to remove himself from Shiraz and go
to Baghdad.*

I can't bring myself to turn myself away from the Beloved…
leave me to my fate, good sir, because my strength has failed.
My body is wasted, my mind has gone, but my love remains…
I would give up my life: I'm no lover but an imposter instead!
O lovely Winebringer, bring… I'll not say how many goblets:
if You poured me out the ocean, You'd not make me satisfied!
Your face is my worship point in the country of the Believers:
even if I faced a Tartar spear, from worship I'd not be turned.
My desire from Here and Hereafter is this and nothing else,
before I pass from the world to pass a moment with Beloved.
O friend… close my door against everyone in the whole world;
I can't bear others as my heart only with Beloved is absorbed.
From helplessness I thought I'd wander as mad in the world…
then faithfulness to my promise with friends, my feet fettered.
Didn't You say, O faithless Beloved… You'd help our hearts?
If You're going to help, come: water over my head has passed.

It's winter, the leafless season... come to me, breeze of spring!
The desert and it's dark, so, come out, O moon well-rounded!
It's the beginning life for Sadi to die on the dust of Your door:
I know no other door, from this one, do not let me be excluded!

O You, looking at You my universe-understanding eyes are opening;
please, will You not to my sad heart... a little pity to me be showing?
I have dropped like a moth and I am now on the ground at Your feet;
but, Your heart, like candle at my bed-head, I can never see burning.
Soon as I saw You enveloping the sun with constellation of Virgo,
the sky, dazzled by my tears resembling the Pleiades, was becoming.
If the orange flower, the tulip, wild rose, cease to grow... I don't care:
but, my orange flower, tulip, wild rose: for me Your veil be removing!
If You appeared in all Your beauty... alas for my patience and mind!
If You strut flirtatiously my wisdom, religion, are... disappearing!
How long will I suffer the thorn? Plant a tulip in my garden of hope.
How long to endure wound? Apply salve to my spirit that's aching!
I've not cherished a hope from my friends, nor felt fear from enemies
since role of being Kalandar in street of Love I have been adopting.
Neither the sour face of the enemy, nor most bitter words of friend,
the exuberance of my sweet-talking genius are able to be lessening.
People were often moved to great pity because of my lamentations,
but You don't ask, "How much is my poor Sadi still lamenting?"

When the hand cannot reach the neck of the lovely cypress,
there's no alternative but to look and to some regret express.

The one who seeks but lacks in strength to succeed, he must
exercise patience… whether or not he that virtue possesses.
What can one bound by feet do… but be exercising patience?
The duty of a lover is to suffer calamity… not show distress!
You must rub your face upon the dust of the Beloved's door,
if you can't take it near to Beloved's face to with kiss caress.
What good is half a life, if a lover fails to offer it to Beloved?
One can't risk upsetting that One, even for a hundred lives.
The harsh words that beautiful ones utter are easy to take…
cruelty of sweet-lipped ones, is not hard… even under stress.
I've no doubt at all Your musky down and gazelle-like neck,
even Tartary's famous musk deer would totally embarrass.
Someday I will sacrifice this precious life of mine for You…
after all, I will have to die in Your exalted presence, no less!
O Sadi, to refrain from looking at a beautiful face is not like
you surrendering your heart and helping your soul, I confess.

Yesterday, my sweet speaking cypress out to the garden, was going
in case rose happened of its colour and its fragrance was boasting.
Petals of the red rose is the one of the beauties of spring's festival;
the rosy-face of my Beauty even lustre of the rose garden is dimming!
Shield from Wisdom's hand slipped when Beloved, clothed in armour
of long hair, cruelty's sword from ambush of rebuke out was drawing.
Since fore-arm of my heart lacked strength of patience's upper-arm,
the hand of that One's love that powerful grip of mine was crushing.
I was advancing towards that One many times in the street of Love;
but… that One never a kind of glance in my direction, was casting.

Like a slave I endure that One's cruelty: if I'm slain it's that Ones
business 'to slay innocent blood', and to endure such fun is my doing.
O sweet-scented rose of mine, You will remember me later, and say
"Ah yes, I remember poor Sadi, my nightingale… sweetly singing!"
Love has plundered all of the chattels of the patience of this heart…
it's true, away from where I am, ill-fortune its tent won't be pitching.

Separation from lovers and friends be the lot of that one
who has caused our separation from our most loved One.
My body has worn out from the bondage of loneliness…
like nightingale in a cage when the spring season's begun.
This destruction of me was considered about as lightly as
the death of an ant under hoofs of a horseman on the run!
Among attendants of all who I approached for protection,
all promising to defend me were liars, faithful were none.
I did not realise that after our long friendships, those who
had 'obligations to discharge' remained faithful to no one.
I'd found a very valuable treasure but I hadn't understood
treasure has a snake as guard that can bring one undone.
O my heart, if you possess a single friend, then you must
inevitably put up with the tyranny a thousand have done.
O Sadi, it is against the duty of Love to turn away upon
the day when the shower of arrows is raining upon one!
How happy is the head which is yielding up its life with
sincerity and devotion at the feet of that most loved One!

Upon my pale face the tears that quickly flow
are a witness to my pain that in me does grow.
Pity the complaining of Your nightingales...
O tenderly natured rose of spring, pity show!
Because, if our separation continues like this,
the wind my dust to Your presence will blow!
Who has ever seen such a fire as this fire from
which arise my cold sighs of... "O no! O no!"
My complaints are not against Your cruelty,
but against my fate that keeps dogging me so!
I'm not worthy to be Your slave, while You are
infinitely worthy to be my Owner, isn't it so?
What the object is the foolish ill-wisher hopes
to gain by Your rejection of me... I don't know.
If I am deserving this punishment, forgive me
and don't ask me to explain... generosity show.
Do this then, in Your bounty hold me excused
if through any deed of mine, any sin I did sow!
It is true that You are feeling no pain at all...
so You know nothing about what pains me so.

It is wrong to wander without You in the garden; and for me to
pull a thorn with You is better than to pick a rose without You.
And, if at a party where You weren't present I reached for a cup
to drink wine without You being there... it would be wrong too!
The curls of Your long hair, falling coil over coil on both sides of
Your tulip-flower face, would teach even hard flint to love You.

If the people of far off China were to see that fair face of Yours
O my Idol, that they'd give up idol-worshipping for You is true!
The depreciation in the value of sugar would be apparent in the
world if You would only smile just once again, the way You do.
All the cypresses of the garden would be withering on the spot...
if they saw Your form out gracefully walking... a moving statue.
How can any poor beggar like me ever aspire to attain Your lips?
That enormous luck it would be to kiss dust of Your feet, is true!
I take pleasure in making love, in being intoxicated... in disgrace;
but, the ascetic does not relish the taste of love like us lovers do!
The ascetic delights in practising forms of piety and of devotion:
the joy of a lover is in looking at what beautiful eyebrows imbue.
If Your favour is promised to Sadi's soul... then why be he afraid:
why worry about the Final Day's Judgement... when he has You?

What is making love? It's to lose one's head at Beloved's feet:
one must be headless to practise love in the Sweetheart's street.
My soul is on fire, from burning incense in secret communion:
of nourishing a secret desire... repentance of mine is complete.
I half-turn my steed manfully on evil reputation's polo-ground:
one can't play bat and ball at home... impossible to be discreet.
Asceticism is useless, unless one gives up wealth and position:
Love is a losing game, unless faith and unbelief one does delete.
If you play on Love's backgammon board then wager all goods,
your religion and life: every child plays with no stake to defeat.
In one hand is the glass of the religious law and in the other is
Love's anvil: not every lover can carefully make the both meet.

O Sadi, mystical lovers play the chess game the Perfect Way.
Go and watch their game, such players are beyond your street.

It is true that Your image never leaves my mind, so let us see
what my state of mind in my desire for You will ultimately be.
My wailing pitched in a plaintive key, gets sadder and sadder
each moment Your love, playing separation, plucks at poor me.
Your face, like the sun, robs the stars of their brilliance, while
my body, thin as a new moon, people point at when they see!
My eyes with silent eloquence disclose to You my condition;
so be merciful, as no impression my tongue makes, obviously.
The rays of light coming from Your face continually reach all
others... when it is my turn for Union it does not come to me.
If You are so determined to be shedding my blood, then even
those who wish me ill, will attaining their desire certainly be.
You passed, not looking at me: look back, for my poverty and
Your wealth will pass too, and my patience and Your cruelty.
The sky heard my sighs and it said this to me, "Wail no more
O Sadi, for your sighs are dimming the mirror of my beauty!"

It would be flying in face of truth to oppose the opinion
of Dervishes:
if you've the right spirit bow at feet without hesitation,
of Dervishes.
If you are requiring a mirror in which to see the light of the Truth...
you'll look at nothing but the faces, without exception,
of Dervishes.

Any robes that are on the bodies of any kings are not so beautiful as
this dust-soiled, thread-bare cloak that a body is on...
of Dervishes.
Will any Dervishes be condescending to be abiding in a mansion?
God forbid! And if there's a Paradise, it is the location
of Dervishes.
Can anyone ever attempt to injure the Dervishes? No... no by God!
For if you offered them poison it'd be sweet confection
of Dervishes.
You possess gold and silver and property, life, interest and capital:
how can one interested in all this, interest look upon
of Dervishes?
Because, they see  Truth, speak Truth, seek Truth and every spiritual
idea that's crossing their minds is Truthful Revelation
of Dervishes.
The Here and the Hereafter... do they have any value in their eyes?
No idea of separation is in Oneness of the Religion
of Dervishes.
O Sadi, be ready to lose house, silver, gold, wisdom, life and heart:
they're your foes if you're into business from now on,
of Dervishes.

*Note: Hafiz composed a ghazal very like this one and was obviously
influenced by it... as he was by many of Sadi's ghazals. See my version of
the 'Divan of Hafiz', New Humanity Books 1986, New Humanity
Books 2012. ghazal no. 36.

What kind of face and hair, earlobe, down and mole is one seeing?
What sort of figure and shape, walk and symmetry is one beholding?
That one who, throughout his life, has contemplated these qualities,
isn't able to contemplate any other and at himself can't be looking.
Everyone that I was asking about the perfection of Your physical
beauty quickly replied it was something none could be surpassing.
If anyone was witnessing Your two eyebrows on the terrace at
evening-prayer he'd say, "This must be the new moon I am seeing!"
Your lips are dyed red with all Your lover's blood that You drink…
You admit it's blood You drink, but isn't it unlawful to be drinking?
I'm so happy in thinking of You, that because of this love of mine…
whether it is separation or Union I can't possibly be discriminating.
One night I thought I'd see a vision of You while asleep: how stupid
was that idea… that while obsessed with You, I could be sleeping.
O friend, ask the eyes of those who are afflicted about the length of
the night: whether it's only a night, or a thousand years is becoming.
The pen… through memories of You, drops pearls from my hand,
and it's not ink but pure water that from it continues to be flowing.
Some people keep prattling on about the crazy state of Sadi's mind
due to Love's pain: but what this condition is, they are not realising.

You, whose face has surpassed in its fresh beauty highest Paradise,
Your face is unique in all of the world's picture galleries I'd surmise.
And though Mani's* fingers could never paint a picture like You…
Your face points out that in his pictures perfection he didn't realise.
You're more fair than a rose, the moon or a fairy! Is it a rose or moon
or fairy robbing me of my heart? No, it's Your face: no compromise!

Beauty's market would become dull for Egypt's daughters, if…
like Joseph Your face was unveiled, a great loss they would realise.

The moon and the Pleiades would hide their faces through shame,
if Your face shone out like a sun at night and their fame jeopardise.

My weeping eyes are like Farhad's and Your lips like Shirin's.
My crazy mind's like Majnun's. Your face is like Layla's to my eyes.

The blind man from desire, would tear off the film covering his
eyes pupils, if Your face in the field of his vision suddenly lies.

You've become the undisputed sovereign in the kingdom of Beauty,
since Your face was embellished by its down's writing… so precise.

It is wrong to describe each beauty's face as being like the moon…
if one must call a face the moon, then it should be Yours I'd advise.

All those hermits, from antagonism, were strongly criticising me…
until Your face appeared in the market of piety for them to idolise.

Since we are bound to be dying through some cause or the other…
one should seek the best occasion and Your face the best supplies.

My judgement keeps prescribing the usage of piety in love making…
Your face keeps beating plunder's drum in piety's realm, I surmise.

O Beloved, don't criticise Sadi, for it's no small matter to burn
in Love, then put up with separation from You, don't You realise?

*Note: Mani was the celebrated, magical painter who lived in the third
century A.D. He founded the sect of the Manichaeans and was put to
death by Shahpur, the king of Persia. None of his paintings have
survived.

I said to Wisdom from that One's shackles I'd withdraw my feet,
but no effort lets me escape that One's noose that me did defeat.

O heart of mine, you are deserving to be criticised because Wisdom
often was warning you, but such advice as wise you did not treat.
That One is a garden of sweet fruits, whose lofty tree the hand of
my endeavour... with only a great deal of difficulty, we can meet.
I thought I would seize the reins of that One's Arab steed... but,
in trying to reach that One's charger's dust, I was suffering defeat!
That One completely blinded my eyes to the whole wide world...
so that One's afflicted lover sees nothing but that One... replete!
To escape that One's power I'd have wandered through the world:
but, how can one caught in such charms ever flee that One's street?
If that One was to smite with a sword instead of a fan... where
could the poor fly be flying away from such a One, who is so sweet?
I don't despair about that One giving me a medicinal draught for
without it there is no cure for this lover... who is too sick to eat.
Perhaps out of kindness that One might become our Owner... or
else... what act of slavery can we perform, that approval will meet?
O Sadi, since you cannot be resigned to the absence of that One,
it's best for you to endure patiently pain that One to you does treat!

It is impossible for me to move away in any direction
from hand of that One's eyebrows archers perfection.
These two eyes of mine are dazzled by such brilliance,
I do not know if it's the sun or Your face's emanation.
It is really Paradise that I see, it is not really a face...
a noose that One has, not curls: there's no confusion!
Ruby lips of that One resemble the blood of pigeons...
raven black of hair is like swallows wings in profusion.

And that strong grip that the saucy deceiver possesses
isn't one that's overcome by a grip any arm can put on.
That One demands the whole soul from ardent lovers;
has no small weight on scales, under any examination.
Only that One's breath is possessing such fragrance...
perhaps musk-pod is in tongue's pocket for exhalation.
Is it not true, that pearls are to be found in salt water?
But, truly in sweet water is that One's pearls location.
A very popular stranger suddenly made an appearance:
in Turkistan of that face, a black mole finds habitation.
It would indeed be strange if when that One stands in
the garden... cypress does not kneel down in adoration.
One shouldn't call such sweetly smiling, sweet-talking
lips by a name other than Zahhak, that enchanting one.
If that One was to walk gracefully in a public assembly,
from all sides would arise a dumbfounded exclamation!
All through the night I feel a thorn in my side from the
memories of that rose-scented face and rosy figuration.
O Sadi... bear patiently the Beloved's cruelty, because
such ill-treatment is an excusable fault... of such a One.


Is that henna with which Your lovely finger-nails You've dyed,
or blood of Your heart-sick lovers You've slain as You worked?
Nowhere else have I seen a human being with grace like You...
surely You're a Virgin of Paradise, not by Adam's clay formed!
And this is more strange: ever since my heart has been by You
afflicted, it's never been with me while You never disappeared.

There is no circle in which there is not any mention about You:
there's no place in which the seed of Love You have not sowed.
We have inscribed a scroll with the story of our love for You...
while You, O cruel One, have gone... and, up it You've rolled.
There's a limit to human beauty, to ways of decorating oneself!
The figure and attributes You have to an Angel once belonged!
Those musk-scented long curls You have let down to Your feet,
have in fragrance ambergris and the freshest violets surpassed.
I'm much too bewildered to be describing Your beauty, because
there are limits to beauty... and all of them You have exceeded!
All of the Masters of Persia fall prostrate before Your mandate.
Surely in it a couplet from Sadi's poetry You must have quoted!
O You, whose face is the treasury of gems of spiritual Reality,
we've in our hearts Your Love's brand, a treasure none can see.
You know that the sighs of those consumed by love have effect:
so don't let any cries of anguish arise from our breast suddenly.
Your only ornament is consisting of two rows of perfect pearls
and a rich display of long hair covering Your breast luxuriously.
I would not be bowing down in homage to any ruler of this Age
if only I could be numbered among Your slaves, however lowly.
It would be wrong if I were to look at anything but Your face...
and any moment I pass without You is another loss, obviously.
We have no resource left to us but to throw down our shields...
our antagonist has a stone in hand... like a glass goblet are we.
It'd be permissible for that one to boast of love for the Beloved
who drives from his heart both his love and hate... completely.

It's not only in this town but in every city in this country that there is no one in the arts of gallantry who is surpassing Sadi.

> O You, You whose face like a mirror's shining,
> beware of these sighs of mine that are burning.
> Jealousy, proper to Your regal beauty… blind-
> folds my eyes to others, like a falcon's binding.
> Old Reason keeps bearing such a cruel burden:
> from young Love it always a lesson is learning.
> It is a shame that whatever wisdom I amassed
> during a lifetime… in a moment I was wasting.
> I purchased sorrow in exchange for Your Love…
> for desire for You my soul I have been bartering.
> The lamp of Your Love is in the heart of Sadi…
> it is a torch… and for all of eternity it is blazing!

O You, who have drawn over our heads the sword of cruelty, You have failed to distinguish between the friend and enemy. Darling, I'm not at all occupied with myself, heedless of You. To whom have You attached Your heart… instead of me? Many a night I've passed longing for Your face, but You have never once inquired of my welfare nor did You treat me kindly. I've thought of withdrawing my heart from out of Your control, but then I found that in Your powerful grip You've seized me. You've made bows and arrows of Your eyebrows and eyelids… so that no prey from Your hair's snare will become an escapee. Of course there is no heart left as a prey in the universe…You

have not hunted down with Your bows and arrows mercilessly.
Sun and moon, fairies and human beings… all feel embarrassed
in Your presence, for You are exalted above them all, obviously.
In spite of peacock's splendid display, partridge's graceful gait,
You have one fault, that of ringdove You feel even more lightly.
Everyone who sees me cries, "O Sadi, what sorrow is weighing
down on you on account of your love that you grieve so sorely?"
I am fearful of being checkmated in this game that is so foolish:
but… what can I do, because You have won by playing unfairly.


One night I passed Winehouse, dervish patch-coat I was wearing,
cell of the wine drinker such a spiritual intercourse was illuminating!
There exists a chamber for spiritual communion in heart's mansion,
so that brain's palace may become secure from strangers speaking.
Winebringer began serving wine among the crowd, saying, "Drink,
until full!" Some, "The old philosopher first," were foolishly replying.
The old Vintner sharply said, " I've already drunk wine of a crowd
around whose candle moon could not be moth… around it circling!
How can the subtle ear of heart that has heard Truth's mystical
song from World of Unity, to poetry and fiction again be  listening?"
I thought that they were beginners… and so I spoke to them about
spiritual mastership. And this the old Vintner was to me saying…
"Light of the Highest Heaven keeps on shining forever and ever…
you can see it in hermit's cell and in Winehouse's corner it's shining.
Whoever enters this sanctuary with spirit of sincerity, if he's devotee
or ascetic, priest or a mad-drunken debauchee… it matters nothing."

A door into the Spiritual Truth was opened within the soul of Sadi…
when key of dawn the locks of Heaven's doors were finally turning.

If you were to offer a thousand lives as a present to Beloved,
it would be a paltry gift and it should not even be mentioned.
To talk of one's life in the presence of the Beloved is just like
bringing gold to the mine or even roses to the garden instead.
Sun-faced Darling, hasn't it yet crossed Your mind to throw
the cool shade of Your favour, on Your afflicted lover's head?
What do You care if I can't sleep because of my love for You?
How can You… a sovereign, even the watchman have called?
I fear for the religion of the people, for through the beauty of
Your face, You could introduce a heresy that's never existed!
No one takes a sideways glance at Your face, who in the end
by You, into Your society, due to Your face's beauty, isn't led.
It's incumbent on the sober to guard themselves against Your
drunken eyes; but, You make secret inroads into them instead.
Don't hesitate to say whatever bitter answer You have for me,
as it would seem pure honey if from Your mouth it was uttered.
And if You should smile… let alone it as a salve for my wound,
You could easily revive all the bodies of anyone who was dead!
Listen to this saying from me: one might travel throughout the
world, bringing back curios from ocean or what has been mined,
but if you've not this book, the *Badayi* of Sadi, in your baggage,
what other useful traveller's gift… can be to a seeker presented?

Even if a hundred times You should send me away,
I'd still be hopeful of Your favour... some other day.
The oppression Your love uses against my mind I'd
liken to the tax Muslim warriors make infidels pay.
When Fate's unfavourable you can't quarrel with it;
it is best that you put up with it... and nothing say.
Alas for the strong arm of piety, when Your silvery
hand makes a play with its fingers to me... to slay!
We've often contemplated the pictures of the world;
all we did see You surpassed in beauty in every way.
What does it matter to You who're lapped in luxury,
if a thousand like me are suffering hardships all day!
I would not have divulged to the herd my love's tale,
if shedding of these tears hadn't about me had a say.
What a horseman! You carry off a hundred hearts by
a loving look... run down a hundred quarries in a day!
If You'd a slave like Sadi, could it harm You to have
this Shirazi hold onto Your stirrup as You ride away?
If You drove him off in anger, he'd return gracefully...
for gold remains the same even if melted another way.
Persian language runs off his tongue like water due to
his genius: it is not a steed that any Arab can outstay.


Like a ball in curve of Your bat I'm so sick at heart;
in Your eyes I'm useless, a foolish, babbling upstart!
The thirst of my bold eyes doesn't lessen in spite of
pouring out a stream from where my eyelashes start.

Your love's hurtful arrow killed the wounded victim
from where it hit him... double-pointed is Your dart.
Autumn's hand wouldn't spoil the feast of flowers if
breeze to garden, a scent from Your hair did impart.
We're of one heart, while You're not ashamed to be
unfaithful each moment... daily new games to start.
Still, it'd not be strange if You cared again, because
'good from the good' wouldn't surprise this 'upstart'!
O Sadi, keep that One's love even if your wishes are
not granted... where can one get such a Sweetheart?

O breeze of morning, bring news of my heart-ravisher to me:
give me some description of that unkind Sweetheart's beauty.
Leave musk alone... bring me the perfume of that One's hair:
don't mention sugar, just words of a mouth that talks sweetly.
Like the ant I put heart and soul into loving that One's waist:
bring up this subject with that One if you get the opportunity.
Tell the wing-singed nightingales of my heart, words of those
two sugar-scattering parrots... those lips speaking eloquently.
I understand that you'll be passing over that One's long hair,
if that One will listen to You, whisper to that One my story,
saying, "O You, who robbed heart from breast... it is Yours to
command, even if, for example, You say 'give up life'... to me!"
The secrets of my heart spring every moment onto my tongue:
my heart worries... "Your life's passed, tell it all now, freely!"
The secrets of my heart will never be disclosed by my tongue,
unless my heart consents with, "O tongue, speak out, clearly!"

Sadi's been ruined because of the schemes that Fate performs.
So... the only thing one can do is to tell to his friends his story.

If there was a rose anything like Your cheek in the garden...
the earth by its perfect beauty would be exalted to Heaven.
Your beauty adorning the gathering could be compared to a
cypress if a garden-cypress talked and moved now and then.
How sweet if I had the power to embrace such a lovely face,
fragrant hair, sweet nature, silvery body… again and again.
You could then say... that in all my life this good fortune, to
win from life my desire, if only for a while… had been given.
I know of no fault in You except this… You're an unfaithful
Sweetheart, charming from being so beautiful, unkind even.
Sugar in my throat without Your sweet face tastes so bitter,
even if it is like sweetmeat surely poison is in it when eaten.
A moment with that angel-natured and fairy-faced Beloved
would be like Paradise… if it could hopefully again happen!
I'll be faithful to You, not only while life is in my body, but
while my body's in the grave, even if my bones were rotten.
People say to Sadi that his pain is a secret one, but news of
it would not be circulated in east and west, if it was hidden.
Every single heart that is possessing a spiritual companion
in secret is resembling a mystical speech spoken in a garden.

Your figure is so fine, like I've never seen in a straight cypress,
if You do anything hurtful to me I'd prefer it to friend's caress.

Be hard on me as You want to, for masters ill-treat their slaves.
The lion that is bound by the feet yields up to the fox's success.
Where to go from Your sight: he goes, You're forever with him:
he departs, You don't free him: he returns, You allow no access.
Knowing my pain, it'd be right to glance once at me, and if You
don't, dawn sighs wrung from my hurt heart may be auspicious.
You pay no regard at all to anyone... be that one Sadi or Umar*
or a Zaid; while I keep on boasting like drum full of hollowness!

*Note: Sadi means any Tom, Dick or Harry.*

O bewildered Sufi, you're in bondage to a good reputation,
no relief from your pain, until you drain cup of intoxication.
What gain or loss can be added to the kingdom of Eternity
whether you're a Hafiz* of Koran or of an idolater's religion.
Of what use is asceticism to you, if you end up being out of
His Court? What harm's in infidelity if your end is Union?
Both the good and wicked are hopeless of His Divine grace:
the mystic and ignorant are helpless against Predestination.
O you prey that are caught in the snare... no effort of yours
will free you! O bird in this cage, your flight is imagination!
How can the glass goblet remain safe in the path of a stone?
You're a glass goblet, good sir; stone is the sky's revolution!
This power of yours must fail even if you're Rum's Emperor;
if you are Syria's ruler this day of yours meets night, later on.
Count as nothing, O Sadi, all desire for this world, for we've
to leave it for another... our hopes not coming to realisation!

If you are wise and prudent and understand your heart, then
I'll call you a human, or you're not even a beast in evolution.

*Note: A 'hafiz' of the Koran is one who knows it off by heart as did the
famous Perfect Master Poet Hafiz of Shiraz... and hence his takhallas or
pen-name.

O how I long to see You one night in these arms of mine,
dead drunk and heavy with sleep, made happy with wine!
Bright day would appear in the murky night of separation,
when as day dawns I did see Your face, like the sun shine.
If Your love has slain me because of such harsh treatment,
it is easy; if only I'd see a little softness, in note You sign!
The pen would drop pearls over my pitiful letter if I should
see once a hope of reconciliation in Your reply, even a line!
The truth is it's right for You to shun me, if I were to look
at You with sinful eyes, like those of the squint-eyed sign!
I wish I could see You some time like a rose in the garden,
or a lotus in the water, or on the flower walls, the jasmine.
If I cannot see You like the sun, if only I could once like a
new moon, a little open to view, the rest unable to define.
There's no barrier between us except fear of the guardian.
You without guardian, behind a screen… is wish of mine.
But can this desire of mine be attained while I'm awake?
If only I could sleep, so in a dream I'd see You sometime.

I haven't the good fortune of the mirror that is seen by You...
I am less than the dust of the market, that You walk through.

I'm so in love with Your face… I've lost consciousness of me:
You're so charmed with You, with us You have nothing to do.
To what shall I compare You to in the whole of the Universe,
You are much more lovely than any dream I've been through.
Such a face as Yours shouldn't be unveiled… You'd steal the
hearts of all mankind by each sideways glance that You'd do!
Blindness is the only disease that can be ascribed to that eye
that is not completely in love with that face that adorns You!
I thought I'd wander the world due to pain Your Love causes:
how can I, for wherever I roam, only seeing You is all I can do.
The morning sighs from my breast are reaching up to Heaven,
yet You don't even open an eye from sleep at morning, do You?
Sleepers know nothing of the distress endured by the sleepless.
One can't sympathise with others, until that grief is yours too.
Whatever's said in praise of Your beauty is quite true, however,
Your fault… Your temperament changes every day, is also true!
If You should happen to unveil and be revealing Your fair face…
the secrets of all of those in seclusion would be revealed by You!
One who doesn't know You won't excuse Sadi: who hasn't seen
such a fairy doesn't understand one who has… this madness too!

That one who's a novice, to become an adept must travel widely:
until he drinks dregs of cup, Sufi doesn't become one with purity.
Whether you are a religious leader, devoted to prayer or an imbiber
of the Winehouse, each one's end is predestined… by the Divinity.
Tomorrow when the court of retribution will be held for mortals,
everyone will show good works… we will hope for Infinite Mercy!

486

O nightingale, if you complain in song, I will be your song-mate:
you're in love with the rose and I'm in love with my Rose's body.
Those who have not seen our cypress on the edges of the terrace,
exclaim, "How beautiful is the cypress on stream's bank to see!"
Some day you will see my life offered as a sacrifice in that One's
street: this will be a festival that'll be observed each day by me.
You, whose Love is fixed in my stricken heart like soul in the body:
at least mention, even in abusive terms, one blessing You sincerely!
Perhaps some day You will Yourself inquire about our welfare,
or else, who, alas, will take a message from us, to where You be?
Even though the night of ardent lovers seems so dark… still, they
should never despair that the morning's dawn they will not see!
O Sadi, how can you ever obtain pearls while on ocean's shore?
Enter even a crocodile's throat if desire you attaining want to be!


If You would return to me, I'd give up my life at Your feet,
for a sacrifice of anything else there… would be incomplete.
I hope Fortune gives me such a lease of life that a shower of
rain from clouds of Your bounty may my thirsty dust meet.
Even if a desert intervened between the lover and Beloved…
instead of a Mimosa bush, a Judas-tree* would grow replete.
Surely my Layla does not realise that without her beautiful
face the wide world to this Majnun would seem incomplete!
Alas that I didn't realise the value of the time of happiness…
you know Union's worth, when separation you does deplete.
It is not only I who is caught in the snare of that long hair…
each dishevelled curl of that One's hair, a heart does secrete.

487

What charm is in Your eyes, that steals the hearts of lovers?
There lives no charmer in Shiraz who with You can compete!
It isn't right to shed Sadi's blood unjustly: but come, it's easy,
if You hold a mandate that being the Master's… is complete.
The season that has passed away will return… but patience is
needed, for spring won't bloom again until winter is in retreat.

*Note: A Mimosa-tree has sharp thorns where a Judas-tree or arghavan
has beautiful red blossoms.

O fairy-faced One, today You are so lovely
that You surpass even the moon in beauty!
When You appear, all of Your upset lovers
run after You… in every direction I can see!
See me, caught in those black infidel curls…
see You, with eyes pupils working magically.
You have put magical glances in those eyes,
and twisted those black curls mischievously.
To hunt down hearts, You have fixed arrow
of those eyes in eyebrow bow… dangerously!
Value of roses and rose-jam… are depreciated
by such lovely face and lips entrancing openly.
The king of all the constellations is Your slave
and Leo's become dog of Your street… happily.
And Saturn has become Your black watchman
upon the terrace of the palace… of Your beauty.
Your cheek, symbolically… an eglantine's petal!
Your figure's description's a wild cypress to me.

488

What comb do You use to be combing that hair?
What water do You use to wash that face daily?
For You lend colour to the tulip from Your face,
and fragrance to musk from hair... flowing freely.
A hundred thousand nightingales just like Sadi
sing praises to rose-garden of Your face, joyfully.


The spring season has come, every hour for the garden one is longing,
every bird like the nightingale into an ecstasy of songs... is bursting!
You might imagine the New Year's morning breeze to be Jesus'
breath that 'rest and fragrance' to the dust that is dead is restoring.
Garden cypress assumes a swaying pose and moves with grace.
O spiritual cypress, are You at last Your graceful action displaying?
In every lane one finds a fairy-faced beauty playing ball and bat;
You also surely have a chin for a ball so a bat of Your hair be making!
In spite of the skill and artifice with which I've surpassed all others,
still it's so... such a ball as Your chin into my bat is not yet falling!
O gardener, if you can, bring a cypress with a form to ease heart,
because in any garden such a rare rose I have never been seeing.
O my deer-eyed One, You'll not release me from Your power until,
like a deer, in the desert... because of Your cruelty, I am wandering.
It is impossible for me to describe the perfect beauty of Your face:
I'm bewildered by it, and what can one who is distracted be saying?
If there's any rest or peace for my heart it will be from Your Union:
if there is any end or limit to my grief, upon Your breast it is coming.
The physician was at his wit's end about me... "O Sadi, cut short
your story... no remedy for your pain but patience can I be giving."

O fire of passion, how long will you be rising to my head?
O bitter wailing, how long from my heart will you be fed?
O you fountain of quicksilver that's there in my two eyes:
how long to pour on my gold cheeks, from loving Beloved?
 O image of Beloved, if some night you had left my path,
my eyes just for a while might have then in sleep indulged.
O bird of dawn, by what science can you announce day…
isn't it my early morning sighs by which you've wakened?
O sorrow, you constant companion making my heart sick,
 doesn't it occur to you, for God's sake, to leave my head?
Why are You so stubborn and are showing such cruelty…
in spite of being charming, with a nature that is so kindly?
I fixed my heart on You entirely, in preference to the world:
I didn't know that You so false to Your promise would be!
I have been so tormented by the black night of separation…
O bright light, enter like a candle through my door, quickly!
I am holding this life of mine in readiness to be surrendered
so as to sacrifice it at Your feet when You enter it suddenly.
It would be the wrong thing on my part to discuss with You
all of those beautiful ones, inhabiting the whole of Tartary!
You are a sweetheart and One who is much loved and very
acceptable…. but, You are also so cold and faithless to me!
 O heart of mine… if you are in love, be always prepared to
experience hardship, and bear up under the trials of cruelty.
And if you lack the power to bear the cruelty of the Master,
then be off, O Sadi, because unfit to serve that One you be!

O fairy-born One, where You've come from I don't know,
for You can't be born of human, as such beauty You show.
Truly, it is not right for everyone to see a face like Yours...
nor is it right You shouldn't let such a beautiful face show!
The cypress cannot claim equality in its stature with Your
beautiful form in Court of the garden, this I truly do know.
I'm charging You by God, not to shed the blood of poor me:
I am not worthy that You should be soiling Your hands so!
Without Your face I've no eyes to see: I demand Your eyes
never leave mine, You through whom my vision does grow!
However great is the cruelty that I suffer at Your hands...
still, more sweet and more beautiful in my eyes You grow!
There is no one else whom we can love, anything like You.
No alternative... loneliness if You leave, we'll only know.
And if You did drive us away in disgrace from Your door...
we would thank You just the same because we love You so!
I will not turn away from this door because of Your cruelty,
whether You shut the door in our face or to open it You go.
What can the faithful slave do who's become unacceptable?
We are eager to serve... but no orders from You to us flow!
O Sadi, this poetical genius of yours will steal many hearts,
for your adornment with spiritual reality's jewels does show.
The breeze of the New Year that has the perfume of the rose
and hyacinth doesn't fragrance that You give off, ever know!

You have not fallen into the snare and so may be held excused.
Are you proud of the strength with which your arm is imbued?

If that One who burned our granary becomes attached to you,
making love with restraint... could not any longer be combined.
My heavenly-faced One is that Darling of a fairy cheek whose
beauty is such... no huri of Paradise could ever have surpassed!
Fearfully I said to that One, "O cypress-statured, silver bodied,
Beloved... no cypress can exist, that by such a rose is crowned?
Such harshness and infidelity are unacceptable at Your hands...
because You're such an attractive and such a beautiful Beloved.
In the eyes of all the people with an enlightened mind You shine
among us mortals like in a dark night... a light that has flashed!
If the Universe contained a physician as beautiful as You are...
none any cure for whatever his disease, would ever have desired.
Your eyes are so playful from Your arrogance and flirtatiousness
that I could imagine that without any wine You are intoxicated!
I will not ever forsake You on account of Your unfaithfulness...
You'll be forgiven, no matter the sin You may have committed."
Conversation was engaged in on several topics and the subjects
of making love, poverty, separation... between us was broached.
Then that One said to me with a smile, "O Sadi, stop talking...
for an empty chatter-box is like an instrument, already plucked;
and he who like a shadow has no substance is a mere nobody...
if you are as conspicuous as the sun, then should I have cared?"

Why, O why, are You obstinately turning away from me?
Don't... You will make me go round the world, willy-nilly!
Someday, because of Your cruelty I'll change my religion!
What harm could it do to change Your heart full of cruelty?

Would it matter if You didn't try to come near us... if only
You took the trouble to do just a little remembering of me?
Don't think we will take our hands from Your saddle-strap,
no matter how often You tell us to... "Leave immediately!"
My body is bowed like a pen in submission to Your orders:
I'd not turn away even if like a pen's head You twisted me.
If You were to leave an impatient one like I've become... or
if You turned eyes from such a helpless creature, suddenly,
I do not know where You could get a shield with which to
avert all of the arrows of my sighs rising to the Almighty.
Whether You utterly destroy my peace of mind or if You
even reduce me to despair, by Your criticism and cruelty,
do not think that You could be ever diverting Sadi's love
from Your threshold 'til the Judgement Day in Eternity!

What is that You keep in Your mouth, words or sugar?
I think none in the world equals the taste that You are!
The lover is not to be held guilty for his pursuit of You:
guilt is Yours... for having a face that's such a charmer!
O You, endowed with such curls, earlobes, cheeks, form,
do not enter the garden, You have one at home to enter.
You've beauty of the sun's face and form of the cypress:
if You need proof to make a claim... these You can offer.
O belt, I do not know how you are worthy of such glory
that around such a Beauty's waist you remain a holder!
It is a long time since I sought that lost heart of mine...
Your eyebrows gave a clue that You were its possessor.

As You've such attributes my heart's not a fit place for
Your presence; come near, for path into my soul is here!
From Your swaying walk like the peacock, it's not only
my dove-cote that's Your nest, the Universe and more!
If You step outside Your house put Your foot carefully:
on threshold lies from Sadi, many a blood-stained tear!

I want to be distraught and I'm longing to be restless,
for patience and depression can't gain me any success.
I'll lower my head to enter the wine-cellar of criticism,
so the patched-coat I wear stays one of uncleanliness.
Each moment You fling a thirsty one in the whirlpool;
number of victims tied on Your saddle-strap's endless.
You quench thirst by thirsty hearts surrounding You!
You're happy but about You how many are in distress?
O God, this must be the water of life… so sweet it is!
O Lord, so agile that is... must be the graceful cypress!
That cloth's too wide for workshop of contingent Being:
that morsel is too big... to be able to know or to express.
Ah no, for this heart that in coils of Your hair, is prey of
two snakes from that Zuhhak-like* cruelty You possess.
Will the breeze ever carry my sighs to the ears of Yours?
No, we are on earth… You are in the Heavens, no less!
I cry for help from You who are my pain and its remedy!
Protect me, O You my poison, and… antidote, I stress!
Sadi, there is enough water to quench your desire's fire:
O handful of dust, don't engage in something profitless.

494

O God, what sort of face is that which one could call the sun…
and, if the moon had a sense of modesty… it'd be a shameful one!
And if the rose had eyes like the narcissus so it could see the world,
it'd plunge in water like a lotus, ashamed before cheek of that One.
At night I can't sleep and by day I've neither peace nor rest from
those dreamy, wine-coloured eyes that look like sleep had overcome.
If that Sweetheart that I know was to show such a face to all others,
theologian would dance ecstatically, preacher drunk would become!
I'm so drunk you might imagine there's no hope to be sober again:
Majnun would've become sane again if he'd only wine to overcome!
If hero, Rustom,* had as powerful an arm as that One does possess,
even within an hour's time over Afrasyab* he would've victory won.
O You beautiful Winebringer, bring us wine whether bitter or sweet,
for from Your hands it would taste like sugar even if it is pure poison.
Nothing mars Your face's perfect beauty except a capricious nature.
Ah, if only from those sweet lips a sweet answer would also come!
If You found as long as I've lived my eyes were on anyone but You,
then it would be right on Your part to treat cruelly this poor one.
If there was as much water in the clouds as in the tears in my eyes,
the thirsty earth wouldn't need any more rain now or even later on!
I feel jealous of the ground on which You tread, because how would
Sadi be if he was even the dust that You happen to be treading upon?

*Notes: Rustom and Afrasyab were two warrior-heroes in Persian
History. See the 'Shahnama' by Firdausi.

A window from Paradise for that one You surely open
to whom You reveal Your face at the coming of dawn.
Mother Nature will never produce a child better than
You for You are far the most beautiful since she began.
It is dark as night to that one whom You are leaving…
it's like the dawn of a lucky day when You return again.
Not a one who has enjoyed Union with You for a while,
afterwards can experience patience again, now or then.
Because of the excessive delicacy of Your lovely body…
You appear inside clothes like water in glass, unbroken.
I'm unable to say anything more that is in praise of You,
for one becomes tongue-tied by such beauty's perfection.
I have now shunned the babble of all of the vulgar herd,
and from now on I'll be quickly returning into seclusion:
but faithfulness to friendship with Beloved whispered in
soul's ear, "You're not a real lover if you disgrace shun!"
Whatever suffering I have endured Your love has caused:
I'm still waiting to hear Your orders to keep acting upon.
These few days left of my life be sacrificed for Your soul,
if You took them from mine and to Yours added them on.
If that One does not look at you Sadi with a kindly eye…
your efforts to win favour would be fruitless: why go on?

I saw a full moon that on the earth was slowly travelling
with the graceful walk of a cypress on a highway moving.
And it was as if a door had been suddenly opened for me
from the Paradise of God Almighty during that morning.

It's true that I've never seen in all this life I've lived a full moon on top of a cypress! Have you ever this been seeing? And also, have you ever heard of a sun that any father or any mother upon this earth have together been producing? I thought to shut that One from my sight... so that then I mightn't any danger because of my two eyes, be incurring. That One walked with a graceful sway... in a quiet voice, "The mystic… is on guard against temptation," is saying, and, "Since one look isn't sufficient, your only way's to be patient and resigned to such separation," is emphasising… then says, "O Sadi, against the arrows of these glances of ours, you, a much better shield than piety will be needing!"

You're still present in my thoughts though You have departed: it is exactly like that… that before my eyes You were pictured. The extent of Your beauty is far beyond my power of thought... You're more beautiful than anything that can ever be imagined. The moon's never walked on the earth, a fairy's never raised her veil, so that Your face to be a moon or a fairy's I'd have believed. It is true that You must be an angel and not moulded from clay. You're musk, ambergris; if mortals of clay and water are formed. If we've a complaint against You it must be laid with Yourself... because, before anyone else one is not able to have You accused. In Beloved's company a poor corner's like a garden in Paradise... in absence of Beloved, wealth and riches as poverty are counted. It's impossible for you to enjoy any pleasure as long as Beloved is not in your embrace... in fulfilment of what Your heart desired.

If I was to lose my eyes through weeping from my love for You...
it wouldn't matter: You're dearer to me than the eyes in my head!
We have been hurrying in our quest by putting in all of our effort;
but what's the use of all this effort when us Fate hasn't favoured?
O Sadi, as you cannot be attaining Unity with the beloved One,
pass at least a little while thinking of that One... your Beloved.

That one who sleeps at home without a beloved is living
but is really like a corpse that body as shroud is wearing!
Pleasure can't be called pleasure when You are absent...
what would the body be, if the spirit was never existing?
Breeze hasn't found a cypress like You in the flowerbeds,
ever since it all across the garden has been softly blowing.
It seems to me to be an impossibility for a sun from collar
of a blouse... to like Your face, towards me be... shining!
And, those curls that coil, curl upon curl, in such a mass,
surely there's some calamity in each one of them lurking?
There is a market that is happening in the street of Love,
in which a thousand lives no price would be commanding.
If You want to show Your bounty this is the opportunity
for one who is more poor than me You will not be finding.
The world's seven regions will not convene an assembly
today without at first to the sayings of Sadi be listening!
One has the choice of these alternatives, that either Your
heart is a stone... or my words Your ears are not reaching.

That cypress-statured One in the midst of the assembly,
is more lovely than seventy cypresses in an orchard to me.
It would be foolish to abandon the society of the Beloved,
in exchange for pleasure tulip and jasmine give vicariously.
You who hasn't seen Your equal in beauty but in a mirror,
when looking at Your equal of course then You forget me!
Your form in a tunic is like a soul that a body's containing:
to say nought of Your mouth, too small for any word it be!
One seeing Your bare form imagines it a tunic full of roses!
Being with You, why look to Khata or Khutan, for beauty?
If the wind was to blow over me, it would blow me away...
for under these clothes there's remaining no more of a body.
O Sadi, it's true, your only resource is your lack of resource,
for there is no way that remains... and certainly no remedy!

You are moving all at once with surpassing grace
that the eyes are dazzled by You, at such a pace!
It'd be right for You to show Yourself to a fairy...
so that one might learn what is such a fairy's face.
The pack-animal of that one who slips before You,
that it would not be able to rise again, is the case!
Your drowsy eyes are drunk like me all year long...
without drinking that wine, that is commonplace.
Patience isn't possible for those You've wounded,
so either cure them or them now completely efface!
For as long as You want it the Friend's kind to us,
and all who are envious remain a confounded race.

O Sadi, you be submissive to orders of that One,
for that the lover has only helplessness is the case.


The cypress had better stay standing, when You are moving:
and the parrot had better remain silent when You are talking.
Not a one is voluntarily surrendering his heart to Your love...
it's You who is setting the snare for it a heart to be capturing.
Ah, what a plague You are to steal the reason of sober people:
with those lovely, drunken, drowsy eyes... You are plundering!
Because of the love I have for You and the jealousy that I feel,
I am so angry that You at strangers glances should be casting.
You said it is wrong to look at You, but... You steal my heart:
You do a wrong, but that others are guilty You are pretending!
Will You never forget those times that You were so angry with
your friends, so that with them You continue to go on arguing?
Your hands are dyed with fresh blood of Your helpless victims:
O treacherous One, does anyone else act, like You are acting?
You're friendly to our enemies, yet You show anger to friends:
this is not really love which to Your lover You keep on making.
For as long as I hear the mystical song I'll not listen to advice.
O pretender to love... only useless advice to me you are giving!
If You're drawing Your sword then here's my body for a shield!
There remains peace upon this side that You keep on opposing.
Never turn away Your face from the Beloved to look at the sun
because you would from the sun to look at that face be turning!
O Sadi, you be careful of that cruel, stony heart of that One...
what does an infidel care if for compensation you're appealing?

It is like that this night does not wish the sun to ever rise:
my mind cannot stop thinking, no sleep comes to my eyes.
O morning, why wait so long that I'm reduced to despair?
One can't do duties, muezzins can't make prayerful cries!
Has the cock choked so that it doesn't crow out the dawn?
Are all nightingales dead… do only ravens await sunrise?
Do you know why I'm loving the fragrant breeze of dawn?
It's like the Beloved's face after the veil on the ground lies!
My head is wishing to God it may fall at that One's feet:
it's better to be drowned in water than it from longing dies.
Heart's unfit to triumph in struggling with Beloved's love.
Can a fly possibly overcome an eagle that up so high flies?
I am not so guilty You should hand me over to my enemy.
If You've to punish me, let it be that at Your hand it lies!
O Beloved, it would be strange if Your stony heart wasn't
moved by Sadi's tears… a mill would turn due to my eyes!
Get away you poor beggar, find another door… for you've
asked a thousand times… without any reply for your cries!

The time… night: a candle and a minstrel and One of beauty!
I have no other desire in all of the world but all of these for me!
An angel would be jealous at such a splendid, loving, meeting;
if by One as beautiful as You such a meeting graced would be.
Another Wamiq like me, caught up in the work of love will not
be found in the whole world, nor an Azra like You… obviously!
To induce affliction and to suffer cruel treatment at the hands
of One, who is perfection in beauty, is… much more than likely.

501

It is the Day of the Resurrection that has appeared in our time.
It's the truth that One is not just a fine form, but a... calamity!
If you turned your face from that one what else can you look at?
For in all of the world than that One there's no greater beauty!
There is no heart in that One's time not given to those charms
and not one head that does not desire that One... passionately.
If you look at that One, then be doing it from a long way off...
because if you come too near then losing your life you might be!
So openly that One robs me of my heart one could think that a
feast of table-plunder is proclaimed by the Emperor of Turkey!
That One is not afraid to cause distress to the hearts of Sufis,
even if they should raise a furore before Tabriz's Chancellery!*
Even if all do that today in all the world any goal of aspiration
or place of refuge, except for his Court... reliable will never be!
He is the most excellent minister upon the face of the globe...
Heaven waits to serve him like a slave before his high mastery.
O philosopher, do you understand the objective of my remark?
It's as the saying goes, 'If one gives a greeting expectant is he'.
O guardian of this age, to God are due thanks for the favours
and gifts given to the people of the world during your ministry.
Thanks to God that I've this merit... that in spite of all of my
faults, this high spirit of mine doesn't ask from just anybody.
People take their ships to sea and gain a profit by doing this...
but, there's no vessel of poetry like Sadi's, nor like you, a sea!

* Note: In his old age Sadi was said to have visited in Tabriz Ala-ud-din
Juvaini, the celebrated minister of Hulaku.

502

O if only there never existed in the world love for a sweetheart:
or if it did, then I wish to God that it had been less in my heart.
I have experienced the brand of Love at least a thousand times.
O if only the Beloved had felt just once... how it tore me apart.
I don't sleep for I don't see that One as a vision in my dreams.
O God, if my weeping eyes shut one night then sleep can start!
Why doesn't that heart-alluring One show face? I'm willing to
barter my life! I wish the Beloved a vision of face would impart!
I always say, that One, by Love's brand and grief of separation,
robbed my heart. O... if only with my life that One did depart!
It could be that all of the people do not hear these pitiful cries...
O if only Beloved might listen at night as my bitter cries start!
Sadi swears in all sincerity, and to his heart he is saying this...
"O, if only faith in promise was shown by such a Sweetheart!"

Is that a rose, or an idol, or a moon, or can it be a face?
Is that night, or jet, or is it musk, or is it hair like lace?
I know Your lips are rubies and Your body's like silver,
I do not know if Your heart is stone... or brass at base!
I don't think there's a cypress that's as stately as You
in Paradise's garden, or on stream's bank has a place!
How sweet are those two eloquent lips that are Yours:
trying to describe them baffling to the poet is the case.
We are crying out in wonder at the fragrance, saying...
"O breeze, such fragrance came from... which place?"
Hey, listen, O You lovely, rosy-faced Winebringer...
wash off my mind, with water of wine wash my face!

O perverse charmer, what a disturber of city's peace!
O rose-petal of natural beauty… the feast You grace!
O my heart, since you have fallen on Love's polo-field,
you must of necessity become like a ball hit any place.
O my heart, if you're in love, burn and keep enduring:
O my body, if you seek ask your way, move on apace!
Beloved: "In this path, give your life and abandon me:
lay your head at this door or go look at another's face."
Ill-wishers criticise me, saying… "How long will you
put up with an ill-natured Sweetheart, it's a disgrace!"
But, it's impossible for Sadi to ever give up Beloved…
O foe, give up that One, if you don't desire the chase!

No one will gain access to my heart as long as of You I am thinking:
You, tent outside my inmost heart for a moment are not pitching.
You may tear up the tree of Love by the roots but the love-plant
of the faith I planted for You will become more fresh and flourishing.
If You drive me from Your door no one will count me of any worth;
but, I would be acceptable to both worlds if me You were receiving.
It would be a pity if a person of surpassing beauty like You, without
cause for resentment, faith's pledge to Your lovers were breaking.
It is impossible for my patience to bear Your love's burden anymore:
how can a grain and a hundred tons of weight level ever be keeping?
I was avoiding everything else until I could gain peace with You:
whatever You have split apart… no one can never again be joining.
O heart, if separation from that One and passion that One inspires
make no impression, not a heart but a piece of iron you are becoming!

Your door I approached for some redress against Yourself... You're
defendant and judge and there's no resource for slave but submitting.
O Sadi, what does it matter whether You are complaining or not...
for what does an expert archer care if armour's thin, one's wearing?

Even if I lose my head with each step on my way to see You,
that I am not able to leave Your door for anyone else is true!
So that my love for You may undergo no change in my heart,
I do not turn my eyes upon myself... not on anyone else too!
There's now no Azur*in existence and if there was he would
not be able 'til Doomsday, to make an idol as lovely as You!
Except You, I've not seen in any country a moving cypress...
I have never heard of a moon being born to any parents, too!
And if a star like You were to be approaching on the horizon,
that all stars would hide faces with veils, out of sight, is true!
Your ears and neck need neither gold, nor silver, nor jewels...
nor antimony, indigo, perfumes of *abir*... nor ambergris too!
The strength of a rank-breaking warrior would be powerless,
if with Your great beauty his army would be broken through.
You've closed the door of my grief-stricken heart to people...
so I might not take a sideways glance or look at anyone too!
Although You are the best and I'm of the least of mankind,
still it's unseemly for a noble to glance at a peasant or two.
O Sadi, don't fear if your life is a sacrifice to the Beloved...
for whoever's attaining to greatness will give up trifles too!

*Note: Azur was the father of Abraham, and a skilled carver of idols.

Who will be helping the thirsty soul with some water?
O kind-hearted folk, please come… and be my helper!
I am still hoping for a reply from those lips of Yours…
whether the answer is sweet… or whether it is bitter!
Even though it is true that You do not come near me,
if You did You would resemble in a ruin… a treasure!
By Your eyes I swear… if You should send me poison
I would quaff it… just as if it the sweetest wine were.
If there's a cypress with Your figure that's so graceful,
it would have a sun to be crowning it? Ah no… never!
That fairy-faced One would not be hidden from sight,
even if that One to put on a veil a hundred times were.
I long for just a short while to sleep both day and night
so that for a short time of Your face I'd be the beholder.
I am hoping that the thirsty wretch is not going to die:
water that flowed away, to its old channel will go later.
O ant, you are only courting the destruction of yourself
by measuring strength against an eagle, O you boaster!
I know that one night before the breaking of the dawn…
a voice reached me in separation's prison… "Listen here,
O Sadi, as you have endured being separated from us…
you will not the terrible torment of Hell have to suffer!"

Whether You are tormenting me or You comfort me…
You are still increasing the love in my heart terrifically.
I will not turn away from You due to Your sword as a
stranger may; for our friendship dates from pre-eternity.

I do not desire any escape from being captured by You,
even though all birds desire to be released from captivity.
Patience helps me to be enduring the severest torment...
except for separation from You... that's an impossibility!
And if strangers should be bestowing dresses of honour,
let them do so; I still prefer to beg from friends, hopefully.
O my life, I'm one who is at the last gasp through desire.
Give me one kiss as the price for it, if You've one for me.
Some people find fault with us and they say that we can't
between the spiritual and material discriminate properly.
Let all ascetics know that Sadi's repented of asceticism...
I dread not wine, harp, flute, gong, as much as false piety.

Lay aside all arrogance, if of the Sufis You are the Beloved:
preferable to a frowning huri is a devil who is good-natured.
I long for a moment's companionship with You in a garden,
but, because You're a garden, then in a nook that's secluded.
Be pleasantly with me for a moment, a victim of separation,
so by that spiritual breath of Yours perhaps I can be revived.
If You were to wander through the Universe, You would see
no face except for in Your mirror no face that You resembled.
It is said that no cycle passes without a calamity... perhaps
You are this Age's bane... Your beauty makes all distracted!
If You drive me from You and I'll not go, please forgive me...
it's due to my helplessness and not my disobedience, Beloved.
I have a granary of charming phrases expounding Your love...
I am afraid You'd regard them as not worth a grain to be said.

O You, whose heart hasn't been worried for even a single day,
how could You know the plight of those with hearts perturbed?
I can't do without You, nor is it possible to escape Your doings.
My resource is patience, O You, my pain and remedy preferred!
Show kindness to Your servants and be with us even for a while.
The fire in me is not one that by any breath can be extinguished.
You may not be returning through the door that is Sadi's again,
but that You can't leave his thoughts have I already mentioned?
Listen to the speech of the enlightened Sufis from Your victim…
"How can my heart fail to be alive when it You've enlightened?"

If one heart-sick should pass a moment in Your company
how would he differ from a fly in a sugar basin? Tell me!
O You who don't deal justly with hearts of afflicted ones
surely it's not right to show everyone Your face so lovely?
Someday, I shall fall at Your feet and be losing my life…
many better than I have died out of desire for Your Unity.
One can't for all the world take hand from Beloved's skirt:
to barter a skirt of jewels for a straw would be a great pity.
Until today my poetry was lacking in this note of pathos,
because I was not caught in the snare of longing so deeply.
It was like the singing of a nightingale that is sounding so
sweet in the garden, but lacks appeal it has in cage… pity!
O Sadi, if your pen was not catching fire from your heart…
why is the smoke continuing to rise from its head? Tell me!

Sweetheart, no one anything of the grace You have, is possessing:
but, the wounded hearts of Your lovers You're grievously torturing!
It is not I alone who has fallen victim to the noose of Your love…
everyone is in love with You, but… for whom are You really caring?
O You angel and moon! You effigy and idol! You image and statue!
I am bewildered… I don't know what name it is that You're having!
Cast only one glance at an army… for it is a thousand times more
effective for fighting than the Indian blade Your scabbard is holding!
Your soft, delicate body is possessing all of the attributes of marble:
You have a heart in it… and it no less than of hard stone is being.
All eyes turn in Your direction, to see the beauty of Your face…
while I'm that poor bird of Yours that in Your trap You're keeping.
What repugnance did You feel that You severed all communication?
Unless it was that You're of nobility, while we are beggars begging!
I am guilty of no fault but this one… that I am in love with You:
for what other offence revenge against me are You now proposing?
I'll not raise my eyes from You during all of my life until I'm dead,
for my heart is Your abiding place and there You are always staying!
God forbid that anyone should make any complaint against You…
but, there's only this one: Your promise to me You aren't keeping!
The elegant language of Sadi isn't language, it's Egyptian candy;
though it feels ashamed before sweetness… when You're speaking.

I am passionately in love with You in spite of Your cruel harshness:
You're my Beloved, even with all my shortcomings and brashness.
And so, what am I truly worth, that Your love I should try cultivate?
And who'd dare to mention a name in Your Royal Presence, no less?

Mystics do not approve of people boasting of their love and then
throw down shield on account of arrows of misfortune, nevertheless.
And that one who is embarking upon the quest of Union with You,
must not be regarding his life to be of any value... but so much less!
Your cruelty is really kindness and Your tyranny is really justice:
Your curses: more pleasing than blessings of strangers... I confess!
Every promise that I have made is the outcome of lust and longing,
but for promise of my love for You which remains one of faithfulness!
And, if I should be fortunate enough to lay my head at the feet of
Your steed, in payment for exemption from plunder... then I guess
it'd be fitting if this inscription were to be written in blood on my
tombstone, "Here lies one, who to end to Beloved kept faithfulness!"
How long can anguish be concealed in heart of the afflicted lover?
There is no doubt this secret pain finds outlet somewhere, I stress!
O Sadi, good breeding demands you should put up with your pain,
and not solicit a cure for it at all doors of other people, nevertheless.


Totally captivated by the love of a Sweetheart, is my heart...
One jasmine-breasted, rosy-cheeked, such a cruel Sweetheart!
That One's a mischievous tyrant, a heart-disturbing source of
trouble: a wonderful trickster who does many heart tears apart!
With raven-dark long curling hair, with bosom like a wild rose,
with fragrance of jasmine and beauty that makes moon depart.
That One has dignity of the Phoenix, beauty of the peacock...
parrot's eloquence, dawn's glory, pheasants walk does impart!
That One robbed my heart with a glance and then departed...
I now feel like a picture on a wall... without that Sweetheart!

Since I couldn't hope for an embrace from that One's Unity...
I stood aside and was content to be looking and remain apart!
One can do without everything... but Beloved's indispensable.
What resource has the captive of that One's snare, the heart?
I am lamenting out of desire for the great beauty of that One,
just like the nightingale that in the rose-garden plays its part.
And since the words of Sadi in praise of that One are in vain,
he's kept silent, for he can't find any suitable words to impart!


I do not know what You require of me... one who is broken-hearted:
You've stolen my heart with Your loving looks, what else is wanted?
If You were to take some pity upon Your lovers with broken hearts,
what more miserable lot than what mine is could ever be discovered?
My life has been spent in vain thinking about the love You have...
Your cruelty's passed all bounds. What is it of me You've required?
I have heard that You desire a poem from Your slave... but You've
a mine of honey, sweetmeats, so why of me sugar have You asked?
In all my life I stole only one glance at that beautiful face of Yours.
What penalty do You now wish for that glance to be on me inflicted?
My head and eyes are at Your disposal to do whatever You want...
my eyes, do what You want, with my head, whatever You've desired!
Sadi begrudges You nothing of anything that could ever even exist.
He does whatever You may say. What else have You ever wanted?


I never heard that the moon a cap upon its head was placing.
or a cypress on the road with young companion was walking.

And the moon doesn't rise every day through the collar of the
tall cypress of the garden even in spite of its graceful bearing.
I am not testifying upon the beauty of Your beautiful figure,
Your figure testifies to it more truthfully than my testifying!
I wish that someday You would sit like kings are sitting…
to listen to complaints and appeals from whoever is asking.
What need for You to go with an army, against any enemy?
Your eyes and eyebrows soldiers into confusion are throwing!
A host of suppliants are standing in Your path waiting to see
if You would mercifully a glance at Your victims be casting!
Do not be so sure that Your face is a bright mirror. For how
long with sigh from every quarter will it bright be remaining?
O moon with the stature of a cypress, inquire now and then
about the welfare of Your underlings, as a thank-you offering.
What fault have You seen in me, that You've treated me as
an enemy? But for my love, I do not admit any shortcoming!
A lion in this affair of the heart is of less worth than an ant.
Mountain in these scales, less than grass' blade is weighing!
I fear I'll have perished before You return, and that through
thirst You not even a blade of grass on my tomb are seeing!
O Sadi, submit to whatever comes, for that's right to do so.
Against such a Monarch, to whom can you ever be appealing?

In expectation of meeting someone I'm heaving many a sigh,
one who for years has never given a thought to one such as I!
That One is never looking on my face with eyes full of pity…
and punishes me with cruelty's hand and I do not know why.

That One robbed me of my heart and gave my life no quarter.
Does anyone in your city treat a person like this, or even try?
In everything that I look at I see nothing but that One's face.
"Who has ever found in all the world such a passion?"... I cry.
What difference is between a lion and ant under love's power?
How does a swift falcon in separation's cage differ from a fly?
Do not be surprised at my pale face and bitter lamentations...
a hill becomes a straw if to endure torment of weeds it did try.
Sadi's laid his head upon the threshold of Your perfect image:
the sleeve of Your Union is beyond reach of hand of such as I!


I will never be able to get over the effects of my drunkenness:
I was as yet in existence when You my heart did first possess.
You can't be likened to the sun... limited to rising and setting.
Others may come and go but You stay the same nevertheless.
What complaint didn't I think of making about our separation,
but You unveiled Your face and to the case stopped all access!
Cast one glance at Your lovers... it would be a thousand times
better than to write a greeting or send a present... this, I stress.
O Beloved, place the salve of Union on these anguished hearts
that are Your work: You wounded them by lack of hopefulness.
It's no wonder You break Your enemy's centre on day of battle,
for You broke all lovers hearts, through separation's loneliness.
Be off, O learned jurist! For God's sake spare us! Stick to your
asceticism and abstinence, we will keep love and drunkenness!
Man of commonsense should surrender heart to heart-ravisher:
it's better to worship the Idol than to worship your selfishness!

513

Since the control of Fortune and Faith are not in effort's hands,
what can anyone do but try to be humble, in such helplessness.
O Sadi, don't complain of friends absence or Beloved's cruelty:
be content with your lot however small: you freedom will bless!

I never felt envious of any rank or wealth, but only of that one
who is attaining Union with his Sweetheart... his only One!
Do you know what kind of truth it is that cannot be described?
It's of the eye that each moment on that One's beauty is open.
Happy is that one through whose door the Beloved does enter:
like fortune given to a beggar without begging for even a token.
The lover and Beloved are like two almond kernels in one shell,
being together in close intimacy... each weary of the other one.
Are you aware who the ignorant boor is, laughing at our state?
It's one who can't experience ecstasy for as long as life goes on.
After Beloved left I saw nothing but the image of the Beloved...
and, it left nothing of this poor, shattered body but a phantom.
You might say... a year of being with that One was like a day:
while now during this waiting, a day seems like a year has run!
Time has a new moon once a month, while that heart-ravishing
moon of mine wears a crescent every night... every single one!
The Sufi can only be absorbed in the company of such a friend,
and... Sadi can only sing his *ghazals* in honour of such a One!

# Khawatim...

Many thanks without end and thanks to the Almighty
because that One's creation has created us, originally!
O God, O the Almighty, O that One, O our Creator!
Generous, Beneficent One, Forgiver of sins of you, me!
O You, the King of every king, if only You to us bunch
of the poorest of beggars show us a little more Mercy!
O Great God Almighty, You real faith and conviction
by Your perfect Grace have bestowed upon us, finally!
Because of Your great bounty we're now expecting that
You will never be taking back... Your act of generosity!
With Your Divine Beneficence it is not strange to us if
You are effacing all our guilt and our faults completely.
O God, Almighty... You swear to the glory and grace
that You gave to the prophets and saints most godly,
and be swearing to the men of the praying sphere who
had conquered the inner devil and love of self totally...
and You swear to purest ones who from Your doorway
You don't keep away the most impure one, that is me!
O all you faithful Muslims, with honesty say 'Amen';
because when you say 'Amen' the prayers truer will be!
O God, it's true not any profit whatsoever or any cure
were we ever discovering for Satan or for one's destiny!
Because due to misfortune we kept on drifting far apart
please now make us a close one to Hazrat, O so Holy!*

O Great God, if You are going to be casting out Sadi,
this one will make the soul of Mustafa intercede for me.:
Mustafa, Mohammed... the Prophet of all the prophets
in this world, the light and eye of them all... absolutely!

*Note: Hazrat: Initially, the title was used for the prophets of the Islamic
faith: the twenty-five great Hazrats include Muhammad, Abraham,
Noah, Moses, and Jesus, but is often used as the title of Hazrat 'Ali, the
son in law of the Prophet & first Imam. It is probably used for him here.

O... if I should see that face of my Beloved again...
I'll be grateful always 'til the Last Day does begin.
In caravan they left me, companion who's load fell
those companions who packed own loads back then.
The population hold any different ones in respect...
while our companions, disrespect their companion!
I'm still hoping that after the separation's sickness
some soothing balm will be brought here, but when?
To whoever has been far from home foot in the clay
say: 'After this in a dream... you'll see home again.'
If you want peace don't look at faces of the beauties
and if you do... say adieu to sleep and serenity, then.
Zoroastrians and Christians and Muslims, in their
religions all have a *Kaaba;* us our Beloved, no pagan!
I was longing to become dust at the foot of that One:
I said, 'Careful on skirt's hem I want no dust,' again.
One of nature of a *Huri* I saw last night hidden from
sight of a rival, that with friends, told to companion:

516

'If you're seeking your own interest give up with Me
union... if you want Me then your own way abandon.'
If you hide heartsickness until the liver's full of blood
it is better than showing foe your worried condition!
Careful, that even if stricken with a thousand griefs
don't tell anyone; unless you see your grief surgeon!
O highest of all cypresses, at least grant one glance
to offer to meet my need... to serve my Companion!
Friends ask: 'Sadi, why did you give heart to love by
which in eyes of folk your dignity is brought down?'
Such as us, we see it is the right thing, this misery,
'You see what's right for you,' tell this to everyone.

This free will of ours we have willingly surrendered:
to the dervish free will is what the One has granted.
Say: 'Greed lessen; trouble is more if wanting more,'
to one demanding more than has been foreordained!
Tied are wine of world with hangover, rose to thorn;
if you demand drink, careful, as one must be pricked!
O you who dropped off to sleep, caravan has gone...
so, now you try hard to with companions be united.
I don't see any power in you to break from impiety:
try harder to break from your impure self-adoration!
The ignorant folk wake up from sleep when they die
like the shepherd after the wolf the ewe has mauled!
If you are seeking the good for you, be a well-wisher
for the one who is well in the mind isn't ill-natured.

God's Perfect Masters all did right on saying this:
'O you theologians; first, let your egos be advised!'
Whatever you want for your ego, be unlawful, Sadi,
if for friends and foes alike it's not advised, wanted!


As long as burdened with grief for you is heart, crazy,
of mine...
fire of loving you won't stop from boiling liver, bloody,
of mine!
The thought of the rose and hyacinth won't cross my mind
until I've that hair and earlobe in mind, permanently,
of mine!
Than separation from you, a drink more bitter is needed to
make me erase the joy of union with you from memory
of mine.
With grief for you every night I lay my head on the pillow
if arms around you in an embrace is not the destiny...
of mine.
If not from your mouth I am given a hundred fine wines...
if I take poison from your mouth it is the fine ability
of mine.
Sadi, captive in the hands of grief's executioner of yours is
saying, 'I'm a slave, kill but don't sell off this slavery
of mine!'

For us, vice the virtue, for each friend and companion
is...
and what enemies may say not acceptable to this one
is!
From heart the mark of kindness has never been removed
O brother... because it etched upon the hardest stone
is.
What could one ever say about the Friend's tenderness?
Because... whatever I may say it a more tender one
is!
And, that one, who is there in this eye and this heart...
makes one wonder if really other sun or other moon
is.
Be telling everyone, to go on feeling exactly the same...
O brother; because our feeling quite a different one
is!
O you, the one who has been asleep every single night,
what from the morning's nightingale your real gain
is?
And that being who does not know heart of the truth,
a tree without fruit truthfully that one's condition
is.
We two have always been disunited in unity together,
because our Friend both absent and present, anon,
is.

As time is passing, the wet leaf will be turning dry...
and the leaf of our eye always wet as time going on
is.
The sweet soul be sacrificed for union with Beloved...
but, I'm really ashamed because it a worthless one
is!
This amount is beneath the dignity of the Beloved...
but, all we have this amount that isn't common,
is!
The veil not a one can never be wearing around you
O brother... for love tearing veil once and again
is!
And, now... Sadi, from that Court of Acceptance,
when being informed the really uninformed one
is.
Now, that we have wished to be one who obeys...
let us see what the wish of the Almighty One
is!


You came to me late, O intoxicated Beloved...
we won't let go Your garment, not by a shred!
No matter how much on fire of Your love we
poured the water of tact, it was not quenched.
One cannot be disobedient to what You order:
from Your face a glance away can't be turned!
I cannot go anywhere from being by Your side:
I am like a fish, that by You has been hooked!

The desire for that lip of that mouth of sugar
of right-doers, broke what had been repented!
O that highest of all cypresses in the garden
is low when to stature of Yours is compared.
Anyone who disunited with You is miserable:
contented is any being who with You united!
My blood was spilled by grace of Your eye...
should a drunk repent of murder unintended?
Sadi, from the noose of the thread of beauties
as you are still alive no way to have escaped.
If you do not lay your head on that threshold
what else to do; there's another for your head?


One like me had better not try to attain the union
of the Friend...
as I shouldn't bring imperfection to the perfection,
of the Friend!
I'm feeling so much jealousy for the pupil of the eye...
for this impertinent eye will face keep looking on,
of the Friend.
Who is this moth, to be attaining union with candle?
For, anyway, it will be burnt by the light, divine...
of the Friend!
Companion, in dissipation days, practice abstinence:
in Night of Power hope is attained with Union...
of the Friend!

Not avoiding incitement of the self in presence of evil
it is not possible to be granted one's perfect vision
of the Friend.
If the Friend demands heart and head we welcome it...
for with this fate the faithful, presence may attain,
of the Friend!
One is happy who sacrifices soul for faith in Beloved:
a head's fortunate that lies where foot falls upon...
of the Friend.
If we've complaint against You we can it tell to You:
to our enemies we can't talk about the going's-on,
of the Friend.
Sadi keeps taking eyes off all of the world all the time
if the whole world looks like to one, the epitome...
of the Friend!


Friend, greatly intoxicated by me was passing,
that one was like a rose in bud, openly smiling.
When I saw that fine, beautiful down on face,
is this that one, myself I was wrongly asking!
Has the angel Rizwan opened paradise's gate?
For the sense of scent of the soul I'm smelling!
And then, I was quickly running to that one...
and on arriving I knelt down and was saying:
"Friend, You suddenly thought of leaving us,
and if You do... it is not right to this be doing

to me as my heart can be likened to a candle,
whose garment of grief is a candle, burning!"
The eye of that one gracefully talked to me...
"My gazelle-eyed narcissus is what holding?"
I answered: "Nothing but beauty I see, but...
that is why it can be unfaithful and hurting!"
For just one breath, listen to Sadi's prayer...
even though to You all the world is praying!


If due to You heart is patient, or patient being
is not...
patience is due, proper; another choice having
is not.
O Kind Sir, into the street of the stealers of hearts...
careful not to go there, for a way to be leaving
is not!
This old world is knowing, that in the ways of love,
reason that the mind believes in, truly working
is not.
This is what they're saying: 'Choose another way!'
Another way than that One's, a sweeter thing
is not!
In every garden I went on looking and looking for it,
but... on all the trees I found, this fruit growing
is not!

Have you an idea who is aware of what real love is?
All who are aware of the whole world, knowing
is not!
O Sadi, while there is still some hope for true union
any of the loss of the head and heart, fearing...
is not.
At one time the moth was fearful of candle's flame:
now, it has been burnt, any fear of its burning...
is not.


Do what You want, for ability to disagree with You
is not...
to engage in a fight with the powerful sensible, too,
is not.
Who can I give the heart to, that from You, I take away?
In world is none like You; that it isn't small, untrue
is not!
Not every eye can see our Sweetheart in a clear fashion:
reflection of creation needs the mirror which askew
is not!
O... to that one giving me advice, 'Put it off until later!'
For now ear only hears harp and heart in hand anew
is not!
If you're given union the Beloved's union sooner or later,
if after you're remembered for disgrace, this to be true
is not.

Promise breaker, against all tact and intellect why make
    peace with enemies if with friends such a peace too
                        is not?
If You, have no inclination for union with us, no matter!
    For us companions any inclination but to see You...
                        is not!
And, if You should so coldly be driving this one away...
    in the end heart will pity me as it as a stone will do
                        is not.
Sadi, you became famous in the world for drunkenness:
    why be afraid anymore because black any other hue
                        is not!

Printed in Great Britain
by Amazon